MW01361751

BOOKS BY DEWITT S. COPP

FICTION

A Matter of Concealment
A Different Kind of Rain
The Far Side
The Man They Called Mistai
The Notebooks
Shadow of a Man
Dead Man Running
The Pursuit of M
Radius Of Action

NONFICTION

Forged in Fire
A Few Great Captains
Famous Soviet Spies
Overview (with Brigadier General George W. Goddard, USAF [Ret.])
Incident at Boris Gleb
The Hidden War
The Odd Day (with Marshall H. Peck, Jr.)
Betrayal at the U.N. (with Marshall H. Peck, Jr.)

A MATTER OF CONCEALMENT

A Novel

DeWitt S. Copp

W · W · NORTON & COMPANY · *NEW YORK · LONDON*

This is a work of fiction. Except for known historical figures included, any similarity to persons living or dead is without intent and purely coincidental.

FIRST EDITION

The text of this book is composed in Times Roman, with display type set in Caslon. Composition and manufacturing by the Haddon Craftsmen. Book design by Marjorie J. Flock.

ISBN 0-393-02626-4

W. W. Norton & Company, Inc., 500 Fifth Avenue, New York, N. Y. 10110
W. W. Norton & Company Ltd., 37 Great Russell Street, London WC1B 3NU

1 2 3 4 5 6 7 8 9 0

For JOHN C. WARREN, FNP

Contents

Rome, February 1940—Partenza

Assistant Passport Control Officer Anthony Hansell sat in the darkened office, waiting. There were two vehicles, one at each end of the block. It had been raining all day, and the sedan at the lower end of the Via Rasella was in water up to its hubcaps. Hansell felt it would be changing its location soon. It didn't really matter. The surveillance was routine; Bocchini's OVRA knew Passport Control was cover for MI 6, so it kept the *edificio* under observation. What the chief of police and his Organization for Vigilance and Repression of Antifascism didn't know was that Hansell would make his exit beneath the back alley. That was if the passageway under the cobblestones hadn't become a millrace.

"You may have to swim," Claire said.

"Possible. I'm practicing deep breathing." They were sitting in the dark, and he held his arm up the better to read his watch in the pale light coming in from the window where the curtains had not been fully closed. "I'll come to your place later."

"Shall I leave a lamp in the window?"

"Do."

"It might be considered a signal," she said teasingly. The insouciance of her soft, throaty voice disturbed his concentration. They had been in Rome since August, a month before Hitler had sent his Wehrmacht into Poland, and for most of that time they had been lovers. She was officially his secretarial assistant, and together they ran the overburdened, understaffed office, the legitimate concerns of passport and visa traffic interfering with the pressing needs of His Majesty's Secret Service. Cables sent to headquarters at Broadway, describing the problem, asking for an increase in personnel, had not brought any response, and Hansell was too old a hand to push the point. The fact that no one had been sent out as a senior PCO meant that in spite of his rank, they were for now leaving the show to him. He arose, patted the top of her head, and said, "It's time."

She was wearing raincoat and broad-brimmed hat and had umbrella in hand. "Don't be late, Tony." What she meant was, Be careful. It was obvious that Mussolini's OVRA was out to entrap them in what could be termed a hostile act and so declare them *persona non grata,* but he knew she feared Bocchini's thugs had something more lethal in mind. He accepted the former intention but argued that as long as Italy remained neutral, the Duce would not want to jeopardize relations with Whitehall, particularly now that Italian ships were preparing to bring much needed coal from North German ports in the face of the British blockade. Further, he felt that Ambassador Percy Loraine's relations with Count Ciano were such that Mussolini's shrewd son-in-law and foreign minister would not permit Bocchini to issue any nasty orders. Claire's perception was that while his reasoning was correct, he overrated their importance in the scheme of things. Whatever happened to them, they were not worth the Chamberlain government's breaking relations with the Duce, who might still play a key role in the flagging hopes to restore peace. In fact, that was the single overriding question facing MI 6, Rome: What were the Italian dictator's plans for the new year?

Hansell stood to one side of the window and watched her go down the steps in the rain, her umbrella canted against it. He saw her safely reach her Balilla in the parking area. In a moment the headlights shone, and she swung the car around and drove out the gate. He had bet himself that it would be the black Fiat at the piazza end of the street that would follow her even though she was headed in the opposite direction. He was only half right. Both vehicles moved out. There was something circuslike about the Fascisti. He supposed had there been five cars waiting, they all would have joined the parade to her flat, then stopped for a cappuccino before coming back to see if he was bedded down or going out for the evening.

As it was, he found she hadn't been far off in her swimming prediction. The tunnel that so conveniently allowed a back-door departure had been discovered long ago by some Passport Control johnny. Thinking the crumbling walls that served as a cellar might be propped up and converted to a file room, he had unearthed a portion of an ancient Roman drainage duct. For some time afterward it became a standing joke at Broadway that anyone posted to Rome PCO must first pass a course in bricklaying and masonry restoration. And what Rome had once wrought, MI 6 types, over time, had restored to former glory, if not to original use. So if nothing else came from the Rome station, everyone knew it had an escape route second to none. Yet when Hansell slid away the tunnel hatch and shone his flashlight downward, it appeared to him as though the duct had reverted to what its ancient builders had in mind. He went down the ladder with care, relieved to find that the flooding was only knee-deep. The water dripping from the ceiling, accompanied by bits of masonry, made him wonder, however, how soon it would be before the earth above caved in and MI 6's Roman artifact was exposed to the light of the Duce's wrath. "Not tonight, anyway," he mumbled as he began wadding.

The exit was into a storage shed of stone and timber, one of a group strung along in the alley next to a government building attached to the Ministry of Transport. The sheds were jammed with a jumble of automotive parts, mostly rusted, old, no longer usable, and, like the sheds, molding away. The tunnel's back door was through a large oil drum securely anchored to the floor and with a lid that could be rotated from within. Hansell emerged like a submariner coming up out of a conning tower, spewing seawater.

Silvio had been alerted to be at the alley's entrance at exactly 1930 hours, giving Hansell all of three minutes to wring himself out and reach the point of contact. He did so just as the heavily dented vintage Chevrolet swung in and muttered to a halt. He entered it quickly, and they were away, Silvio accelerating evenly, departure in keeping with arrival.

"Nicely done," Hansell said, twisting water from his pants leg.

"Maybe you've been in the Tevere," Silvio said. He spoke Roman Italian, and *Tevere* was the Tiber.

"Maybe under it. Take the Via del Tritone to the Piazza Colonna. Then circle a bit, and we'll cross the river at the Ponte Garibaldi."

Silvio grunted and suited action to the word. As a mechanic, with the hard, square hands of a stone carver and the patience of a true artisan, he was able to keep his vehicle running when others would have long ago consigned it to the junk heap. Cigarette stub fixed between heavy lips, unshaven jaw, cap brim a shield to swift black eyes, he drove with one hand fixed on the wheel, the other fastened over the knob of the gearshift.

"Anyone interested in your activities?" Hansell looked over his shoulder at the rain-blurred rear window.

"*Phaa!*" Silvio glanced at him. "Those bastards don't even know I'm alive."

"Yes, but they know I am, old chap."

The fact was that both the *carabinieri* and Bocchini's *polizia* did think Silvio Mira was dead. And that was a big plus in his use. The other was that he possessed an implacable hatred for the Fascisti. He'd never said why, had told Hansell it was something personal that had nothing to do with politics. "All politics are shit," he had declared at their first meeting. "I am an anarchist. To hell with them all, that scrawny little king and that fat clown who has an asshole where his mouth ought to be." He had been serving the station for nearly five years—driver, courier, spotter, informant, a very ill-paid asset of great support value who drove a truck by day and kept his feelings buttoned up, his true identity buried in an unmarked grave, covered by false papers.

They drove a circuitous course through the higgledy-piggledy of the city's rain-slick streets, not hurrying. The traffic was thin, beneficial for spotting surveillance but making Hansell feel exposed. When the war began, Mussolini had ordered the city blacked out, but he had quickly remanded the order both to reassure the restive population and to emphasize Italy's neutrality. The eleven o'clock curfew, however, remained in force.

When they crossed the bridge into the district of Trastevere, Hansell directed Silvio along the twisting Via Montefiora to the Via de Luce. He had not been over the course himself, but Claire had made a complete reconnaissance of the entire area from the statue of Giuseppe Belli at the district entrance to the Manifattura Tabacchi halfway up the Viale del Re.

On any assignment it was routine for Silvio to leave him at a point some distance from where the contact was to be made. The precaution was basic so that if Silvio were picked up by OVRA, even under torture he would not know where Hansell had gone.

"You can drop me at the Palazzo Mastai, if you please."

"You like this getting wet, maybe." It was said as a joke, Silvio always couching his undercurrent of mocking with *forse,* "maybe."

Hansell knew that while his driver served the station at real risk, he did so not out of any real belief in His Majesty's cause. "I'll be at the Ponte Cestio at twenty-two thirty," he said.

Silvio grunted and stopped by the curb. "Stay dry," he rasped in farewell.

The rain was slacking off, and by the time Hansell reached the Via Santa Cecilia, it had become a drizzle. Marco's, he saw, was at the edge of the *palazzo.* According to Claire, *Marotta* had selected it because he knew its proprietor, Antonio, and it was in a neighborhood that served not only the tobacco workers but also many low-level civil servants who were not all that admiring of the regime. "*Niente capi. Niente dottori,*" Claire had said. "Just Romans."

Since August he had met with Dino Marotta three times, the first at the Stadio della Farnesina during the races. It was a delicate business, and it had worked well because of Claire's planning. He had been cautiously impressed with the young correspondent for the *Roma Corriere della Sera.* The journalist had a wry manner, a sharp, incisive mind, and a politically observant eye. If there was anything about his anti-Fascist fervor that disturbed Hansell, it was that he did too little to hide it, treated their sensitive relationship too lightly. Nevertheless, Marotta's information, gleaned from contacts within the Fascist hierarchy—he played golf with Pavolini's secretary—had been appreciated at Queen Anne's Gate, and Hansell was encouraged to develop the contact. This became particularly true after Marotta had delivered hard intelligence that Italy had only ten poorly equipped divisions and was in no military shape whatever to involve itself in war.

At their last meeting at the Giardino Zoologico, Marotta had reinforced this position by passing him a copy of a letter from Marshal Emilio de Bono to Piero Parini, both high in the Supreme Council. The letter quoted Air Marshal Italo Balbo as having told Marshal Pietro Badoglio that at all cost Italy must remain neutral and that if Mussolini convinced the king otherwise, they must be prepared to act. It was a dangerous piece of correspondence for the sender, the receiver, and those quoted, and Hansell suspected it might be a forgery put out by Roatta's SIM. London, in usual fashion, had not responded one way or the other. But true or false, the key question remained as to Mussolini's intentions, and Hansell was hopeful that he was about to receive something significant on that score, perhaps some pertinent information on the visit of the American diplomat Sumner Welles. Welles had met with both Ciano and the Duce. The very fact that Marotta signaled a need to rendezvous fewer than ten days since their last pas de deux indicated something more than rain was in the wind.

Hansell had thought that with the weather, the café would be largely empty. Instead, the *trattoria* was full of chatter, clatter, and smoke, a mixture of tobacco and cooking, the smell laced with garlic and Parmesan. Despite the dimness of the lighting, he spotted a waving arm. "Ricardo!" a bright voice called.

He responded with a return salute, going forward.

A large man who he knew must be Antonio interceded, small, puffy eyes sizing him up. "Signore?"

"Yes. Good evening. I see my friend." He gestured toward Marotta.

"But, of course." The jowled, perspiring face managed a grin of acceptance. Hansell, with his dark coloring and brown eyes, his rumpled clothing, worn raincoat, and broad-brimmed black fedora, did not have the look of an Englishman, and his Italian, although more Tuscan than Roman, was without accent and sounded perfectly at home.

He strode past the proprietor, going toward the corner table, observing as best he could the other customers, all of whom seemed to have their eyes on him. He was a stranger, and strangers in Trastevere or anywhere in Rome these days did not escape notice. Those who watched and listened would have taken the pair for relatives, cousins who had not seen each other in a long time. They spoke without fear of being overheard. They revealed the health and condition of respective parents, children, uncles, aunts. Marotta produced a photograph of Pia and the new bambino, and by the time they'd drunk a glass of Frascati and ordered pasta, passing interest by other diners was gone. They played their roles well, and it was obvious to Hansell that the journalist enjoyed the game, perhaps too much so. He must caution him not to overdo it.

Dino Marotta had aristocratic features, Roman nose, firm chin, smooth-planed face, black pelt, magnetic brown eyes, luminous. He spoke swiftly, colorfully, with gestures. But Hansell knew the young journalist was treading a very thin line. Claire, through an admirer in Bocchini's office, had gotten hold of a list of citizens who had become candidates for *domicilio coatto,* "compulsory residence," which meant at best house arrest but most probably imprisonment. Marotta's name was on the list with a question mark. It was information Hansell had had to weigh in keeping the *Treff,* as Marotta liked to call their contacts. He used the word mockingly, saying that since the Communist comrades and the Nazis had become one in spirit and in blood, Hitler in Poland and Stalin in Finland, they should get in the habit of using such terms as well. Hansell tolerated his whimsy, his predilection for intoning Latin phrases in an attempt to inject humor into the deadly serious. *Dominus dedit, Dominus abstulit* was a favorite. Hansell saw the journalist's playacting as just that, and while "The Lord giveth and the Lord taketh away" might encompass everything, including their dining at Marco's, he accepted that Marotta would not have signaled the need to meet unless he had had something vital to impart. Additionally, there was that quality in Hansell, silently appreciated by superiors in MI 6 as long as he was successful, of being willing to accept odds with finesse. Recently the *polizia* as well as the *carabinieri* had been instituting unannounced roadblocks and searches, indicative of the nervousness that gripped the regime.

Thus Hansell had passed the word through Claire that at the café everything must be verbal, no documents. And so, as they were mopping up the last of their meal and Marotta set down his glass and said clearly, "I brought you a paper," Hansell was jarred and fiercely annoyed.

He focused his attention on feeding the last of his spaghetti into his mouth, and as he chewed and then blotted his lips, he grunted, "Your name is on the compulsory list, and I can understand why."

Marotta smiled wickedly and toasted Hansell. "I mean my newspaper." He reached around and extracted it from his coat. "I thought you might like to read my article on chances for peace now that Roosevelt's man is here."

Hansell took the rolled-up newspaper and spread it out on the table and calmed himself by pretending to read. They had been here too long. Marotta's cuteness, intended or not, had startled him. It had been a foolish thing to do. It was time to leave, to get out. He looked at his watch. "I must think of getting back. Angie will start to worry. Your article is good, but it doesn't answer the principal question."

"I know, I know." Marotta laughed.

They drank up and left the café, and Hansell sensed that eyes noting their departure were not all that casual. He was pleased that the rain had slacked off to a drizzle, mist rising. They skirted the *palazzo* in the chill night.

"I heard about the list." Marotta broke the silence. "It seemed to me that possibly the three across the room from us were OVRA." He sounded assured.

Hansell's annoyance had not had time to settle, and this new revelation forced it higher. "If you suspected you were under surveillance, why the bloody hell did you expose me? Why didn't you leave?"

"They were there when I arrived. They couldn't have known I was coming. I don't think they recognized me, and they may not be OVRA at all."

"That's a poor excuse." They had reached the end of the *palazzo,* and he could see they were not being followed on foot and there were no cars in sight. "You think this is some kind of joke!"

"No, no, of course not. I apologize. Sincerely, I do. But I felt—I feel the information I have been given must be passed to you immediately even at risk." *Arrischiare* came forth on a puff of smoke, for he had lit a cigarette.

Marotta contriteness did nothing to alleviate the danger. All they needed was for someone to step out of the dark and ask for identity papers. They turned into della Fratte, where the lighting was poorer, and it seemed to Hansell that their footsteps were too loud. Or was he hearing the footsteps of others? He stopped, his hand on Marotta's arm. They listened. Nothing but a cat complaining of an empty stomach. His own was settling down. He was now annoyed at himself as much as he was at the Italian for having misjudged how Marotta would behave under the circumstances. Something was gnawing at his guts, a presentiment. Nonsense! Wet pants on a cold, dark night. He realized all his previous meetings with Marotta had been in daylight with crowds around, and he wished this one were, too.

He nodded at the newsman, and they began to walk again.

"What is it, what is the information? And please do not raise your voice."

"*Morbido,*" Marotta said, not joking now but in agreement, cautioning himself. "I have this from three friends at the Palazzo Chigi. Three." He held up his fingers. "One is assistant to Ciano's deputy Fucello. You understand? Very top secret cables are being received from our embassy in London. They are coming in the pouch. They are not our cables. They are from the U.S. Embassy. Stolen. Some are exchanges between Roosevelt and your first lord of the admiralty, Churchill. They are evidently very compromising, very sensitive, indicating the American president's support in spite of his public claims of neutrality. It—"

"Have you seen any of them?" The question was automatic while his mind scrambled to assimilate the swift-flowing words.

"No, but I'm hoping to soon. I'm told Churchill's responses reveal that he is plotting to get rid of Chamberlain so as to be named prime minister."

Hansell snorted. "That's all right for what goes on at the Palazzo Venezia, but not Whitehall. It sounds like one of Colonel Roatta's fairy tales."

"No. I assure you this is not SIM's work. The Servizio Informazione Militare is not that clever. One of my friends—he's a translator—has actually seen some of the cables."

"But I haven't."

"I know, I know, and I said I will hope to do something about that." Marotta's voice rose impatiently. "But if this is all false, a fake, why would Ciano be turning the documents over to Mackensen, who is sending them straight to Berlin?"

"How do you know that, Dino?" Hansell's ingrained skepticism was dented.

"I said my friend was Fucello's assistant. He personally delivered a packet of the cables to the German ambassador."

The information was totally different from what Hansell had anticipated. And if the last part was correct, not some Italian opera manufactured by Ciano, the implications were serious. They could have staggering political consequences. "Let's go over this again, old chap," he said softly.

As Marotta repeated his information, Hansell, between questions, considered the ramifications. Apparently the president of the United States was dealing secretly, not with the PM but with that dogsbody

Churchill. God knew His Majesty's government needed America's support, but let this sub rosa relationship become known, and while it would probably get the first lord sacked, the outcry in Washington could finish Roosevelt. If, indeed, the information was being forwarded to Herr Hitler, who could say how he would use it? Of course, since Hansell did not know what was actually in the cables, it was impossible to assess what the damage might be or how far it might reach. Thank God, that was not his wicket. It was not his responsibility to make judgments. It was just to pass the word to Broadway, and that, alas, meant Claire's lamp would be left burning. It was going to take the best part of the night to encode the information. He had no radio operator, having to depend on the embassy code clerk to handle his traffic. Mostly he favored sending his reports in the diplomatic pouch. It was old-fashioned, but there was something about codes he did not trust. The pouch went by plane, took longer, and, of course ran the risk of getting shot down. So far that hadn't happened. As to the security of cable traffic, if Marotta's tale was only half correct, it proved his point. Not only that, but going to the embassy meant he would have to fill in Sir Percy, and that, if nothing else, spelled delay.

He quickened his pace, and as they came to the corner with its clotting of pines, he looked back at the mist-draped street but detected no movement.

"You don't think much of what I've given you." It was more a question than a statement, a touch of disappointment in the tone.

"Not at all, Dino. It could be extremely important, invaluable."

"But you want more proof."

"Look, old boy, we're meeting too often, particularly now that your name is on the list. You may enjoy the risk of it, but I can't afford to be sent packing, not and do my job."

"And if I get the proof you want, is that worth the risk?"

"Possibly that won't be necessary. And London will send its thanks." He wanted to let the Italian know that he valued their relationship. "You are my *primo* contact, you know."

"Listen!" Marotta refused to be mollified, a newsman after a story. "If I can actually lay hands on one of those cables, I'll write a column using the word *departure* in the lead, *partenza.* Maybe I'll use the word as the title."

They were approaching the arched tram car stop, and with its single overhead light, Hansell was relieved to see there were no other passengers.

"I'm going to leave you here."

"You keep your eye open for my signal."

"Of course." He did not wish to debate the issue, but signal or not, he had decided he would not be meeting the journalist again for some time. If, indeed, Marotta got hold of tangible evidence, he would work out other arrangements for picking it up. He extended his hand, anxious to terminate the meeting. "Watch yourself, Dino."

"You, too, Tony . . . *ciao.*"

In the light Hansell saw Marotta's puzzled frown, and he turned away, knowing that the Italian's zestful nature was such that he couldn't really grasp the basic need for caution. It seemed to be an Italian quality. Even in peril, reality was some kind of illusion, Pirandello's *Six Characters in Search of an Author.* It was all a play without the ability to accept or see the difference between taking a well-planned chance and flaunting danger. The meeting at Marco's never should have taken place. It was his fault. He had refused to equate what he had already noted in the man. The old force driving him had overridden good judgment. It had begun to rain again. He turned up his collar and cocked his head against its slant. He came to the Piazza de Luna, the splash of the water fountain in the pool seeming unnaturally loud, the water in the pool black, black as the mood that now gripped him. On the other side of the fountain he saw movement and tensed . . . a couple, close together under an umbrella, circling the piazza, hurrying to get in out of the wet.

He, too, walked faster momentarily and then, glancing at his watch, slowed. Despite the weather, he did not want to arrive early for his pickup by Silvio. Claire had walked the route, and he must gear his timing to hers. He had to admit that some part of his displeasure had to do with not being able to pay her an expected visit. Dear, sweet Claire, so young, so wise. He sneezed, and in the empty, darkened street the sound seemed huge. He was half hoping to hear someone say, *"Salute!"*

Although time and weather had worn the street sign off the corner wall, he knew from Claire's instructions that he had reached the Via Anicia, and he turned onto it with a sense of relief. It was almost a straight shot now to d'Anguillara, where he'd find Silvio. He felt himself relaxing a bit. He knew what lay at the root of his mood was not only Dino's carefree attitude, but the question of his information: the president of the United States in secret communication with the first lord of the admiralty even while his roving ambassador was proclaiming America's neutrality in a search for peace. If true, certainly it was a devilishly important piece of intelligence, more important than any he had yet received. And now he did pick up his pace. He had often observed that Rome and its hills were totally deceptive. You did not feel the hills were really there until you stood, say, on the Monte Gianicolo and looked out over the city's rooftops. Then you knew, and he was reminded of the fact now as the gradual incline of the Via Anicia curved into the steepened Tolomei, the rainwater in the gutters flowing swiftly. At its bottom the street expanded in a spadelike approach to the bridge entrance with clusters of pines at each side. He could make them out because there were lights, and it was there to the right that Silvio would come, and he was anxious now that there be no delay. He could not afford to be left standing like a beacon light. Traffic on the Cestio seemed practically nonexistent. If Silvio was not on time, he would find the horse carriage stand Claire had described and at least get clear of the district.

Hansell was not looking back; he was not thinking back. He neither heard nor saw the black Lancia with headlights off swing onto the Via Anicia. Its engine idling, it came coasting down the street, its speed accelerating rapidly. Instead, he spotted the lights of a vehicle moving across the bridge from the Isola Tiberina and knew it was Silvio. It was then he heard!

Pivoted! Saw!

The hurtling black mass mounted the curb, and in the final instant Anthony Hansell desperately sought to avoid it by flinging himself outward into the street.

Silvio, coming off the bridge, spotted the swerving object, knew its intent, shouted a futile warning, saw the impact and Hansell's body careening through the air like a rag doll. He did not stop but turned onto the Lungo Tevere road and sped away, howling obscenities, knowing there was nothing he could do and that as a witness to the crime he could assure his own safety only by immediate escape from the scene.

Because months past Hansell had instructed her to read everything Dino Marotta wrote for the *Roma Corriere della Sera,* making note of agreed-on code words and phrases, she continued to do so by rote. When a week later she noted the journalist's by-line, she didn't know what code words she was supposed to be looking for because Tony had not told her before— She knew she was in a dreadful state of shock, sleepwalking, waiting for Broadway to make up its bloody mind on her recall.

Marotta's article was an analysis of the Welles peace mission. The headline was a single word: PARTENZA.

PART I **LONDON**

I N The Navy wryly referred to the ferry that shuttled between Bolling Field and Gravelly Point on the Potomac River as the Air Corps's navy. The scowlike craft's purpose was to save time for the top army brass flying into Bolling with urgent business at the War Department in Washington. Crossing the river and catching a staff car or army bus at the Gulf Oil dock were supposed to cut in half the time it took to make the land journey via Anacostia.

Never having taken the voyage, Second Lieutenant Peter Burke had no way of knowing whether the service was a time-saver or a brief introduction to water travel for the high and mighty. He only knew he'd received totally unexpected orders to board the ferry, catch the bus, and report to Major General H. H. Arnold's office on the double. It had been obvious from the look on Captain Hood's face in giving the orders that he, too, had no idea of the cause for the stunning summons.

"You're to find a Major Cutter," he said, staring at the paper in his hand as though it would explain. "In Plans, I think, or maybe Personnel."

Burke knew the same thought was in both their minds: Why was Hood's newly appointed operations officer for the yet-to-be activated 41st Pursuit Squadron being summarily ordered not to headquarters at Bolling, which was heady enough stuff for any lowly shavetail, but to the seat of the Almighty?

Hell, everything at Bolling was in a state of turmoil with the sudden increase of green personnel. "Controlled chaos" Hood had termed it, but the officer cadre of the 41st Pursuit-to-be, which numbered exactly three, was, according to GHQ Air Force at Langley, to remain fixed! Untouched! Now it seemed someone up there wanted to touch. He refused to let his thoughts fasten on where that touch might have come from; it just couldn't be.

The CO's farewell suggestion was that were he in Burke's shoes, he'd put a polish on them and report to Air Corps Headquarters in Class A uniform. In the rush to do so, Burke forgot his overcoat, and once on board the ferry, a shabbily converted barge, he stationed himself in the lee of the pilothouse with his back to a chill wind, gusting up the river, curling whitecaps.

Irrespective of the weather, there was a more primal reason he wished to remain inconspicuous . . . out of harm's way. His fellow voyagers, all of whom were in uniform, were very senior passengers. They were grouped together in the ferry's makeshift cabin, a shed whose aft end was open, and from quick glances cast in his direction, he knew that some among them were curious about sharing accommodations with an officer of such lowly rank. As the privileges of rank bestowed, he knew they would like to inquire into the reasons permitting his rite of passage.

It was not really their presence but what their presence reminded him of that intimidated him. They were Old Army, not Air Corps, and he had grown up amidst Old Army. He knew how its officers thought, how they viewed the scene, which right now with wind and wave was preventing any of them from making a direct approach. In his own view nothing in their outlook but rank and age had ever changed. Their line of march was straight enough. It ran directly to his father, the "Iron Duke," as Rod had dubbed him so long ago. And that was where his suspicions, his concern, yes, his fear lay, and the real reason, aside from the unspringlike cold of March, that he had chosen to keep himself apart. He knew if he gave them the chance to question him, there would be recognition and more questions, and he wanted neither. What he wanted was for this bobbing, grubby brass hat yacht to make its landing before he froze and before the upper echelons of the Army disgraced themselves, proving what kind of landlubbers they really were by puking all over the deck.

The War Department, along with the Navy, was quartered in an unprepossessing complex of temporary three-story buildings, extending for half a mile along the south side of Constitution Avenue. The buildings were comb-shaped, and in Burke's mind they formed a kind of labyrinth. From the barlike entrance desk in the main foyer he was passed through a maze of narrow corridors into crowded offices of plasterboard, wooden desks, and ringing telephones, up several flights of stairs to the newly erected fourth floor, housing Army Air Corps Headquarters. He was unfazed by the clutter; it was Bolling Field on a larger scale. What did trouble him was that Captain Hood's advice did not seem all that sage. He appeared to be one of the very few inhabitants in uniform. He had long known because of the attitude of church and pacifist groups that men in uniform were not welcome on the city streets. Even with war in Europe and the talk of a draft, he knew this to be so; it was SOP. But even though civvies were the unwritten order of the day because the administration and the War Department were anxious not to arouse the isolationists and pacifists, he had not thought the rule would apply in the labyrinth. Obviously it did, and he wondered how his apparel was going to go down with Major Cutter—that is, if he ever located him.

He found the answer in a windowless box-shaped office, housing the major and three other officers, each wearing civilian clothes, each at his desk, and each with a name, rank and designation plaque on it. Major Cutter was Lawrence A., "Asst. Chief Plans."

As Lieutenant Burke saluted and announced himself, he observed the major had a lean and saturnine look. Cool brown eyes measured him.

"I see you came dressed for the occasion, Lieutenant." The voice was spare, noncommittal.

"Yes, sir."

Cutter glanced at his watch. "What did you do, walk?"

"Took the ferry, sir, to Gravelly Point."

"That must have been bracing. In any case, you're late, very late."

Burke said nothing. The cliché of mild intimidation by rank was a built-in routine as old a tradition as the West Point ring on Cutter's finger, a way of sizing up, a reflex action.

Cutter's colleagues, occupied with their own endeavors, had paid no attention.

"See if you can find a chair somewhere," Cutter said. "I don't suppose you brought your two-oh-one file?"

"No, sir. No one said anything about that."

The officer at the adjacent desk indicated he was free to take the extra chair stacked with official file folders.

The major rubbed his brows and said to no one in particular, "Nobody knows what the hell is going on around here anyway." He got a cigarette lit while Burke cleared off the chair and placed it and himself in front of Cutter's desk. A faint hope was rising that whatever the reason for his summons, it was going to get strangled in a paper chase.

"Well, since Personnel hasn't been able to supply me with a copy of your two-oh-one, I don't really know who you are, Lieutenant, what you are, or why an assistant secretary of state wants to see you. Maybe you can enlighten me. How do you come to know Ambassador Jay Bertram Stark?"

The question actually caught the breath in Burke's throat. The suspicion he had sought to reject surfaced, and the air went out in a long exhale. He saw his father's angry face, and his own anger flared to match it. The major was studying him, cigarette poised in hand. "Well?"

"I knew Secretary Stark when he was an ambassador to Austria and my father was military attaché in Vienna. I had also known the Starks earlier at other embassy posts where my father served." His response was flat, rapid and definitely caught the major's interest.

"Lieutenant, by any chance would your father happen to be Brigadier General Alfred Burke?"

"He would."

"Are you Regular Army?" He saw Cutter's eyes probing for a Military Academy class ring.

"No, sir. Reserve. Called back two months ago. I'm operations officer with the Forty-first Pursuit. We're in the process of activation."

A faint smile flickered across the major's lips. "Yes, I'm sure you are," he said. "Everything is. Well, I hate to spoil your fun, but General Arnold's office received a call this morning that you be requested to put aside your helmet and goggles and make yourself available to the secretary at eleven-thirty." He nodded at the wall clock. "That gives you about seventeen minutes to keep your appointment. Report back here, Lieutenant, when it's over. I'm sure General Arnold will be interested in knowing what the State Department has in mind for the ops officer of the Forty-first Pursuit Squadron in the process of activation."

Peter Burke fumed his way up Seventeenth Street, his thoughts a swirl of angry conclusions. Behind Stark's request he believed lay his father's handiwork. Hell, he hadn't seen or had contact with the ambassador in years, not since Austria. And now, suddenly, like this. For what? Some military-minded scheme to show that the Iron Duke was still in command even though their final break had been seven years ago. Final, but never final because somehow Alfred Burke managed to take cover in his son's thoughts and, like a ghost, unbidden, rise to haunt him. Hood's announcement had given root to the process, Cutter's had brought it forth from the bottle, and now Assistant Secretary—Ambassador—old Uncle Bertie Stark was going to flesh it all out. *Peter, I'd like you for my military aide.*

He had always considered the massive gray eminence of the old State, War, and Navy Building the ugliest, most commanding structure in the entire city. With its pillared tiers, its projecting buttresses, and its French-style mansard dormers, it rose ponderously in bleak contrast with the pristine elegance and Grecian lines of the nearby White House. *A kind of Sumerian, Babylonian, French Empire ziggurat,* he recited to himself as he crossed the entrance infield of slate slabs and mounted the granite steps with their decorative green-dyed cannons squatting impotently on guard. Despite the building's bizarre edifice, its interior was something else, something special. With its lofty ceilings, the black-and-white-checkered floor patterns of its marble corridors, the rich patina of pine and mahogany office doors, the sweeping circular stairways rising to ornate rotundas, a sense of the regal, culminating in the carpeted appointments of spacious office suites.

As he hurried along the east corridor toward the stairwell, he supposed his liking for the interior had something to do with his eye for the architectural simplicity of line, whether it was the curve of an airfoil challenging the blue or the harmony of geometric configurations.

The assistant secretary's office was at the northeast corner of the second floor, and in reaching it, he tried to force his thoughts away from the encounter ahead by absorbing the grandeur he remembered from an earlier time. Now it was this time, and Major Cutter, as an afterthought, had called to him as he'd gone out the door, "Hey, you're to ask for George Wheeler." He entered the reception room, prepared to do so.

There were two women at desks behind a counter, the light in back of them coming in through long, curtained windows. The usual file cabinets, wall paintings, and a large photograph of President Roosevelt dominated the secretarial area. On the entrance side of the counter were grouped chairs, a settee, and tables with reading material.

"I'm Second Lieutenant Burke," he said to the elder of the pair, who had stopped typing to observe him. "I'm here to see—"

"Yes. Good morning, Lieutenant," she said with just the right degree of acceptance. "If you'll make yourself comfortable, I'll notify Mr. Wheeler you're here." She picked up the phone receiver.

He made himself comfortable and scanned the headline of the *Washington Times-Herald.* FDR SAYS NAZI WHITE BOOK TO BE TAKEN WITH THREE GRAINS OF SALT. The subhead read: AMBASSADOR BULLITT DENIES ALL. The White Book, he discovered, was a compilation of sixteen documents the Germans had just released, said to contain cables from the captured archives of the Polish Foreign Office in Warsaw. They supposedly consisted of prewar reports by Polish envoys in Paris, London, and Washington, quoting conversations with U.S. diplomats that revealed U.S. support for Allied action against the Third Reich even before war began.

The president had made light of the Nazi propaganda at his press conference. Secretary of State Hull had declared that he was unaware of any such purported statements. Ambassador Bullitt denied having ever made any of the statements attributed to him, and Senator Key Pittman, chairman of the Senate Foreign Relations Committee, had stated the purpose of the propaganda release was "to stir up opposition to the President and create fear in people's minds." The *Times-Herald* added that the White Book's real purpose was to undermine talk of Roosevelt running for a third term.

"Lieutenant Burke?" It was a soft voice, sounding almost reluctant to intrude.

Burke snapped to his feet, depositing the newspaper back on the table. "Yes, sir."

George Wheeler had emerged from the hallway leading from the office area. He was a slight man in a three-piece navy blue suit, white shirt, black tie, wearing thin-rimmed glasses, his dark, straight hair neatly parted in the middle. There was nothing distinctive about his looks, a pale, bland face, broad forehead, pointed chin. *Fastidious* was the single word that came to Burke's mind as he moved to shake hands.

Wheeler did not give him the opportunity, turning, instead, and leading the way. The way was past several modest offices, a pause at a closed door at the hall's end, a single warning rap. Then Wheeler opened the door and stood aside so Burke could enter.

He did so, to be greeted across the commodious room by Jay Bertram Stark, who came around his desk, long arms outstretched, grinning hugely. "Peter, my dear boy!" His voice had lost none of its Brahmin lilt or the specialty of an Ivy League accent.

It had been a long time, and in the brief hug of greeting, firm handclasp, and mutual inspection, Burke saw that the older man did not seem to have aged all that much: close-cropped hair a bit grayer; stains beneath the alert blue eyes a bit muddier; the lines creasing the high forehead and lean face more firmly etched. But his lanky length was still supple and quick-moving. "Not a fighter," the Iron Duke had once commented, "but an accomplished negotiator, a gifted compromiser." In short, a diplomat and, beneath the neatly tailored double-breasted gray flannel, a dedicated public servant born to the purple; not stuffy but certainly aware of position, prerogatives, place. He felt an Edwardian responsibility to serve his country, his party, the two probably interchangeable in his thinking, yet silently he shared daily with his wife of some thirty years the burden of Myron, an only son, who was mentally retarded. As they shook hands, Burke suddenly thought of Myron, the memory stimulated by an almost tearful glint in Stark's welcoming.

Myron, exploring, climbing onto the rim of the well. Disappearing! He, running, shouting. A body floundering in the water so far below. He'd gone down the rope like a monkey in the dark. And the cold, cold water. Trying to hold on to the rope with one hand, grasping for Myron with the other, getting him by the hair, and Myron thrashing and beating, struggling to pull him down. Shouting for help, losing his grip on the rope, going under, fighting! Fighting for air and to get free of Myron's incredibly strong hold. He was ten, Myron five, and rescue had come for them both through the strong, sure hands of a gardener whose face he could no longer remember but whose hands he would never forget.

Myron's father would never forget either. Peter was a young hero in his mind, always would be. "I'm your uncle Bertie from now on, no matter what. You remember that, Peter."

And looking into his eyes now and remembering, he realized that whatever the assistant secretary had in mind concerning him must stem from that long-ago incident in Austria.

"Let me look at you. You look splendid, simply splendid. You must be proud of those wings. Sit down, sit down. Tell me about yourself. Would you like coffee?" Stark had an attractive baritone voice; its tone added a subtle touch of virility to his willowy frame.

Burke declined the coffee and quickly filled in his background, anxious to establish the importance of his new assignment at Bolling. As he spoke, the thought came to him that if indeed, Uncle Bertie felt beholden to him, the favor he would ask would be a quick return to his squadron.

"How long have you been on active duty?"

"When I graduated from the advanced flying school at Kelly in early '38, I expected to be kept on active duty for at least three years, maybe longer. But in less than a year some budgetary cut put me on nonflying reserve status."

"Was that before or after Munich?"

"About the same time, I think." He smiled at the obvious connection as Stark shook his head.

"Europe's wars are Europe's wars." The secretary sighed.

"Well, I figured it was going to be temporary, particularly after Hitler went into Poland. I had a teaching job at the University of Vermont, German and French. Recall came in December. We've been promised P-40s—"

"Tell me about your education," Stark interrupted. "You didn't go to the Point, did you?"

"No," Burke said flatly, wanting to get by it, wanting to skirt that, wanting to get back to the main point. "I went to UVM, took ROTC. When I graduated, General Anderson—Paul Anderson—helped me get into Randolph. Now I'm helping to organize a new squadron. I can't tell you how puffed up I am about it. I'm not sure where we'll be assigned."

He watched Stark move toward the handsome mahogany desk, the American flag in its stand behind it, a photograph of Roosevelt beaming from above the marble mantel. If Uncle Bertie hadn't gotten the message, he never would. Stark was looking for his cigarette case. "You are wondering why I was so anxious to talk to you." He turned, case in hand. "I spoke to your dad, and he asked me to make sure that I made it clear to you that I called him, not that he called me. Would you care for one?"

"No, thank you."

Stark used a gold-plated cigarette lighter, moving back to his chair, his eyes on the mosaic pattern of the Persian rug. "I know it's none of my business, Peter, but I wish there were some way in which you and your dad could make up. Families, military families in particular, well—" He waved away the smoke as though waving away the line he was following. "Is there any way I can help?"

The question made Burke feel uncomfortable, aroused his suspicions again. "I—I, ah, appreciate your interest, sir. Did my father know I was at Bolling?"

"No, I don't think so. He put us in touch with Colonel Spaatz, Tooey Spaatz, in General Arnold's office. They found you for me." He smiled. "You know, I first met Tooey Spaatz during the war when he came home from France a hero. He'd shot down two or three German planes, and he was mad as hell at being sent home by Billy Mitchell to set up a training program. President Wilson wanted to pin a medal on him." He smiled in memory. "Speaking of old times, Peter, do you recall Scott Reardon?"

Scott Reardon? A name from out of the blue. No, not so much from out of the blue as from out of more years past than he wanted to recall. Later he perceived that the secretary's dip into memory lane had been not an exercise in patrician vagueness but a game of staging, that the inquiry had been purposeful. For now the name Scott Reardon, the unexpected throwback in time and place, was not unlike flying wingman and having your flight leader bank left and, without any warning, snap his plane into a vertical reverse to the right. You were either with him or alone in the sky.

"He played some kind of strange instrument, didn't he?" He was grasping at the long ago. "Blond hair that stuck up like spikes."

"Yes! The bassoon." Stark smacked his leg, excited. "You remember him."

"Only very vaguely. Why? Is he here?" He looked toward the door.

"No, no." Stark chortled. "It's just that I came across his name, and I immediately thought of you. You must be about the same age. I believe his father was consular head in Berlin when your father was assistant M.A. there. Must have been '27, '28, part of '29. Do you remember if you were chums, did things together?"

"No, I don't think we did. He wasn't much of a mixer if I remember correctly. I think there was a fight one time. I wasn't in it. Some bigger kid, a kraut, made fun of his playing that weird instrument. He put the bigger kid in the hospital. I remember that." And he did. There was a fragment in his memory. A circle of shouting children, he one of them, and the blond boy straddling his adversary, pounding his head on the curb and the blood running. "What about Scott Reardon?" he said.

Stark was up again, letting out a great sigh of smoke, looking off beyond. "You may be seeing him again. But that can wait," he said, turning back to face his puzzled guest. He'd become all business and no more old memories. "I realize from what you've said that you're pleased with your present assignment, and I don't suppose you think there's any other duty that would suit you as well." He smiled knowingly, a hint of just-you-wait-and-see in his tone. "Peter, how would you like to be posted to the RAF, the Royal Air Force?"

Vertical reverse, hell!

Stark had a breezy laugh at the expression on his face. "I'm sure the question is a bit like getting hit in the breadbasket by a medicine ball. Right? Well, bear with me, my boy. A request has come through from our embassy in London. Colonel Marlow, our principal air attaché, passed it along with the blessing of the RAF. The Air Ministry wants to establish a program which would permit our sending Air Corps personnel on temporary duty to study the RAF's Fighter Command system of air defense. Only in England, of course. Marlow particularly wants pursuit pilots like yourself, one at a time for a three-month tour." He grinned widely, tapping away more cigarette ash. "I thought you might like the opportunity to be number one on the list."

"God almighty, sir! You sure do toss quite a medicine ball." And they both laughed.

"Sound interesting?"

"Overwhelming. But I'm afraid I don't follow it—I mean, hell, sir, my orders come from the Air Corps, don't they? Major Cutter at headquarters didn't know anything about this."

"No, he doesn't. Very few people do. The president is very anxious that the offer be kept absolutely secret. I must impress that on you, Peter, and in fact, nothing we say here can be repeated to anyone. If it got out that we were cooperating with the British in this fashion, there would be political hell to pay. The neutrality issue is extremely sensitive. I'm sure you know that. You'll be going over, assigned to the embassy as an aide to the assistant military attaché for air. Your observer status with the RAF will be handled sub rosa through Major Dunn. The details will be worked out when you get there. How does it appeal to you?" He was smiling again.

"Well, the thought, the idea, the whole thing takes a little getting used to, but I think it's something I could get used to very quickly, provided I get to fly some of their stuff." And Now he was grinning as well, the impact of what was being offered catching hold. "But—but won't the Air Corps or someone in it be mad as hell that they didn't get to make the selection? I'm certainly not anybody's favorite pilot."

"Oh, yes, you are, son. You're mine."

"But, sir, I—I don't take my orders from the State Department."

"No, in this case you take them from the commander in chief, the president."

"Well—well, I can hardly argue with that, can I?" He shook his head as though clearing it.

"Hardly. Peter, you let me worry about handling the backup. Those who need to know will know."

"It's sure terrific of you to pick me out of a hat, but—"

"But nothing, Peter, my boy. There's no hat in this. There's a method to my madness, and the president likes the idea, so . . ." He stubbed out his cigarette and rose.

"I'm afraid it's still called favoritism, Uncle Bertie."

Stark, pleased that Peter still remembered the relationship bestowed so long ago, beamed down at him and then grew serious. "It's not favoritism, my boy. It's something quite different. I could be disingenuous and let you believe that selecting you was simply repayment for an old debt of gratitude, and I wouldn't really mind if that were the case; but I must be honest with you, for this entire matter is one of trust. It's because you once knew Scott Reardon, not because you're a pursuit pilot, that you've been chosen for the RAF post. Naturally I had forgotten that you ever knew him, but a recent FBI investigation noted the boyhood association."

Burke was not inclined to reflect on his capability to adapt to sudden changes in direction, whether flying inverted or trying to follow the line of thought of an assistant secretary of state. Partly the capability was inherited, but it was also the result of his having grown up in half a dozen countries in a sophisticated milieu in which an impressionable youngster observed the cosmopolitan world of European diplomacy, a *haut monde* where good manners, if not intentions, prevailed and where change of locale or school or language was taken in stride because that was the only way to take it. Now he said nothing, waiting, watching Stark, remotely recalling a remark his father had once made about the secretary's tennis-playing abilities: "He's so good because he doesn't know how to stand still, physically or mentally."

"The Reardon family has had a distinguished record in government, going back several generations, like yours in the military, I suppose." He glanced at Peter and then went on recounting, reflecting, a hummingbird. "Scott's father, Dwight, was a gifted Foreign Service officer with a brilliant career and an assured future. Possibly you can recall him in Berlin. Unfortunately he took to drink, got into a messy marital scandal, ruined his chances for an ambassadorship, and finally killed himself in a car accident. Terribly sad. Terribly.

"The son, Scott, was an equally gifted scholar. But apparently, when it came time for him to take the diplomatic service entrance examination, he was blocked. The details are unimportant now. It's enough to say the action was vindictive, unprincipled, vicious. It had to do with personal animosities toward his father, who had made some powerful enemies. Had the action been exposed at the time, it would have been corrected, but it didn't come out until this most recent FBI investigation. Nonetheless, young Reardon entered the service as a clerk, which required no examination. Certainly he had reason to be bitter, doubly so because it appears his turndown affected his mother's health, and she died while he was serving in Moscow. Through some oversight, perhaps more vindictiveness, we don't know for sure, his request for emergency leave at the time was rejected when under the circumstances approval should be automatic. There is an unsavory set of circumstances from which no accurate conclusion can be drawn. But apparently it was the embassy's second secretary who was responsible for preventing Reardon's return. He was found murdered in the Lenin Hills. He'd been beaten to death. The Soviet police were unable to solve the crime. The best guess was that he'd been set on by a roving gang of thugs. That was in '38 during the purge trials, and there was considerable lawbreaking going on in Moscow. The only other possible connection is what the FBI learned. The second secretary had been one of those involved in Washington in blocking Reardon from taking the diplomatic service examination. I'm not inclined to think young Reardon murdered the man, but there it is." He shrugged.

Indeed, it is, Burke thought, *but what is it?* Again the memory flashed of the boy with the spiked blond hair pounding his taunter's head on the pavement.

"Reardon was assigned to our embassy in Moscow in 1934, about a year after diplomatic relations were established with the Soviet government. He went out as an interpreter under Ambassador Bullitt. Following the death of Forbes, the second secretary, he was posted to Warsaw in the same slot under Ambassador Biddle. He served there during the attack on Poland and the Nazi-Soviet partition. Evidently he conducted himself very coolly under fire. His being shifted to London at the end of the year to work in the embassy's consular section made good sense. He's aiding in the processing of the large increase of refugees seeking to emigrate here. With his language skills and particularly his Polish experience, I'm sure he's of value."

Burke waited while Stark busied himself lighting another cigarette and then spun away, going toward his desk. "Have you read today's paper?" he said, lifting the *New York Times* from his in basket. "The release of the German white book?" He shook the newspaper and set it down again.

"Yes, I think I saw something about it while I was waiting, but—"

"Then you know the contents," Stark announced. "Documents supposedly taken from Polish files, compromising some of our ambassadors."

Again Burke found himself struggling to hang on to the wing during the assistant secretary of state's mental acrobatics. Scott Reardon had suddenly disappeared in a cloud bank.

"Of course, the president and Secretary Hull have issued statements saying there's not the slightest credence to any of it. So have Kennedy and Bill Bullitt and Tony Biddle. Unfortunately, in spite of our denials, there are some very disturbing aspects to this Nazi propaganda that has nothing to do with its obvious political implications. There are certain quotes in the body of the material which are accurate and of far more recent date than the white book portends. They add up to prove something we have suspected for some time." He paused, contemplating the end of his cigarette as though making up his mind whether to reveal what was suspected or, Burke surmised, perhaps again to change the subject altogether.

"We can only conclude," the secretary said, looking directly at him, "that some of our most secret information is getting into Nazi hands, is somehow being obtained by them. Very disturbing." He shook his head and sat down again, exhaling smoke, stubbing his newly lit Chesterfield in the ashtray.

"How long this has been going on we're not sure, and why someone in the Wilhelmstrasse would tip us off in this manner, we can only guess. Possibly an anti-Nazi agent. But from the British, who are also very concerned, we have come to suspect that our embassy in London may well be the point of the leak. All our cable traffic dispatches, telegrams from Europe clear through our London post, which, of course, makes it a prime target for Nazi espionage. But how it's being done, if it's being done there at all, we do not yet know."

Again he shook his head, glanced down at the handsome sheen of his cordovans, and looked up to stare at Peter, a wry smile curling away the seriousness from his eyes. "And you, no doubt, are wondering what this all has to do with learning how the RAF Fighter Command expects to best the Luftwaffe when and if the time comes, and I believe it's coming very soon. But that's another story."

Burke couldn't resist, "Yes, I suppose it is." He, too, smiled, and then they both were laughing.

"Well, bear with me, son. Bear with me," Stark said. "It all fits together, believe me. As for what I've just told you, I don't think I need elaborate on its seriousness. We are working with the British in seeking a swift resolution. We don't believe the information getting into German hands has anything to do with our cipher system's being compromised. What we do suspect is that someone is passing on the verbatim text of the deciphered cables."

Stark now stood with his back to the decorative marble-framed fireplace. On either side taffeta-draped windows looked down on the west lawn of the White House. From where he was sitting, Burke had the vague impression that the spacious room, with its formal furnishings, the overlarge oil paintings of Jefferson and Chief Justice Marshall, was not an office but a stage setting, in which he wasn't sure whether he was a spear carrier in the cast or was one of the audience.

The secretary sighed heavily, moving to sit down behind his handsome, somewhat ornate desk. "It's a nasty business." He picked up a folder and gave it a shake as though its contents would prove his point. "I regret to admit that we pay our clerks poorly. They have very little hope of real promotion. We choose them as single men because their salaries would not permit supporting a wife, much less a family, abroad." He put down the folder. "Peter, I'm telling you all this, which is terribly confidential, for a special reason."

"Sir, do I gather you figure it's Reardon who's swiping the stuff and passing it on to the Nazis?"

"Why, yes, yes. That is our suspicion." Stark's slightly adenoidal voice rose with a touch of surprise that the obvious conclusion could be so easily drawn.

"From all you've told me, sir, it seemed logical." It came out almost as an apology.

"Yes, yes, of course, you could easily surmise that." Stark came around the desk to join him once more. "The thing is, we don't really know." He could be as patriotic an American as you or I. But"—Stark gestured—"the suspicion is there."

"Well, sir, if he's suspect, why not bring him home and see if that plugs the leak?" He supposed his manner bordered on the impertinent, but without knowing exactly what Uncle Bertie was leading up to, he realized it had to involve himself as well as Reardon, and there was something about the possibility—whatever it was—that he didn't like.

"That was our first thought, Peter," Stark said patiently. "The British pointed out that if Reardon is the guilty party, he cannot be acting alone. There may be others in the embassy—Ambassador Kennedy has a staff of two hundred—and certainly others outside it, and it's extremely important to get them all.

"Now I've said we have no direct evidence that he's guilty of anything, no more than we have evidence of espionage by any of his colleagues. The British have had him and others under watch for some time, searched their quarters, and found nothing. However, there has been a recent development, and it puts a somewhat different light on the matter. John Keith, one of our code clerks, acting as courier, was killed last week in a plane crash. Examination of his effects disclosed a number of decoded secret cables, some very sensitive. All were in an envelope with an unmailed note to Reardon, the words possibly a code.

Reardon and Keith served together in Moscow before Reardon was transferred to Warsaw and Keith to the Hague."

"What does this all add up to?"

"The British suggest Reardon may be a Comintern agent, working for Soviet military intelligence."

"How does that fit, sir—Nazi spy and Soviet agent?" Burke blurted in disbelief.

"May I remind you, Peter, that Hitler and Stalin are now allies, and we must assume their cooperation entails intelligence exchanges." Stark's tone had a slight edge of coolness in his classroom manner. "I repeat, however, there is no hard evidence that Reardon is so engaged. These are simply threads, lines of suspicion, to be considered and pursued in an effort to find out. You understand, Peter?"

He understood, but not how these lines of suspicion were supposed to entangle him.

"Toward that end," Stark continued, frowning now, approaching a point to be made, "I met Monday with several senior people in the department. We decided on a course of action that both Secretary Hull and the president have now approved. We recognize that overall our security, particularly abroad, has been very lax. With the aid of Mr. Hoover of the Federal Bureau, the problem will be corrected. Meantime, as you can imagine, there is no more important task than to get to the bottom of this leak. And finally, Peter"—he sat down and leaned forward, facing Burke—"that is why I have brought you into it and why you are here hearing things, learning things, being told things that no more than a half dozen people in the department are privy to."

He paused, and Burke could feel the sudden weight of his words and see a new hardness in his expression, almost an angry look, come swirling in as though he'd just kicked the plane into a spin.

"We believe that if Reardon is the guilty party, the way to find out, the way to get him, is through personal contact, through someone he knows, someone he has no reason to suspect, someone who can observe him, listen to him, sympathize with him, penetrate his thoughts." Stark spoke rapidly, moving about again, waltzing, conducting, selling himself as well as his audience. "Not an easy job, not by half. We recognize how difficult it will be. If he's working for the Nazis, the Soviets, or whoever, he's certainly on guard. Very clever. Very cool. Quick to react." He stopped his peroration and looked at Burke. "Peter, we want you to be that person. Now wait!" He raised his hand. "Let me explain what we have in mind, and believe me, my boy, a great deal of discussion and thought have gone into this. A great deal." He paused and gripped his elbows, head down, reciting. "First, you have perfect cover. Your assignment is legitimate. You will be operating out of the embassy, just as he is. As an observer of RAF bases you will come and go, and in the course of your business you will run into him. It's only natural for you to do so, not obviously but casually, by happenstance."

He stopped talking, and Burke, who had been studying the convolutions of the rug pattern, looked up. "Reardon and I were never really friends as kids" was the best he could say, knowing he'd already made the point, wanting to say that the whole thing sounded half assed.

"All the better, really. You will still have the past in common."

"I doubt if he'll remember me at all, sir."

"Yes, but you'll remember him."

"Even so, he may have no desire to. Since he's a loner, why would he?"

"As I said, Peter, we know this is difficult, a chancy mission, but we believe it's worth a try. You'll have the cooperation of the British, their counterintelligence, MI 5."

"I'm not sure, sir, how that will help me to get to know Reardon. Wouldn't someone at the embassy, already there, be a more likely choice?" He asked the question, not because he thought the answer would be of any benefit but because he was playing for time, the tone of his voice showing a decided lack of enthusiasm.

Stark's expression had become pained. He shook his head, not in negation but in disappointment. He ignored the question.

"Our counselor at the embassy, Henry Sutterby, is in liaison with the British. He is the only one who knows of your assignment. Not even Ambassador Kennedy will be acquainted with your dual role. But you will have no need to approach Sutterby. Someone from the British will make contact. For the most part, you'll be—what's the phrase you pilots use?—flying solo."

"You know, sir, you're piling this on me pretty fast." He said it ruefully, with a smile, wanting to soften Stark's pique. He knew he was hooked. He'd fly with the RAF, and the hell with Scott Reardon.

"Yes, yes, I'm sure I am." The secretary managed a smile in return. "But I must tell you, Peter, I consider it in the nature of a miracle to have made the discovery that you and Reardon were in Germany as boys. We had been looking vainly to find someone who could approach him without arousing suspicion. Remember, I do have some knowledge of your capabilities."

"And how's it supposed to work, sir? I mean, with me being Air Corps. From pilot to counterspy. Major Cutter ordered me to report back to him."

"Well, Peter, I don't think you need concern yourself with such details. We'll handle everything from here. The proper orders will be cut by G-2 and approved by General Arnold's office, assigning you to Colonel Marlow's staff. The Pan Am Clipper leaves for Lisbon from Miami Wednesday night. It lands at Charleston, and you'll board it there. You'll be taking the sleeper to Charleston tonight."

Stark's rapid but firm recitation left no room for debate. Burke realized his assignment was not open for discussion, never had been. These were orders.

"You'll be met in Lisbon and passed on. Colonel Apple is military attaché there, although mostly he's at our embassy in Madrid. Once in London, you'll take up your duties with the RAF through Major Dunn and work out a meeting with Reardon. Although the official staff is not inclined to associate socially with embassy clerks, there are functions in which the barriers are down, and in any case, you won't lack opportunity, I'm sure."

"And just how long is this supposed to take, sir?" He was damned if he was going to lie down and acquiesce without making a point or two.

"Realize, young man, that other efforts in other directions are going forward right now, and it's possible the answer we are seeking will come anytime, but assuming not, we hope you can manage some determination within your allotted time with the RAF."

"And if I do discover that Reardon's a bad guy, what do I do about it?"

"You inform your British contact."

"I'm afraid I don't understand something," Burke said, easing the edge out of his tone. "It's our embassy, supposedly our guy. Why do the British come into it before we do?"

"You might say it's their war, son. Further, they have reason to believe some of the information reaching Berlin concerns very secret information from their Foreign Office." Stark was eyeing him intently, still a bit unsettled.

"Boy, sir, you sure know how to hand out a hell of a mouthful before lunch."

That restored the ambience. Stark let out a laugh, clapping his hands, reassured. "I'm sure I have, Peter, I'm sure I have; but I thought I knew my man, and I do. And speaking of lunch, let's have some. We can iron out the rest over it." He was washing his hands with enthusiasm as he turned and looked beyond Burke. "George," he said, "could you see about getting us some lunch? We'll have it right here."

2

It was raining as the Boeing Clipper let down through the overcast, making landfall at Cape Roca. As the plane banked, he could see the broad mouth of the river and Mount Sintra crowned in gray scud.

"That is the Tagus," said his seat partner, Dr. de Loos, his accent more British than Dutch.

In the twenty-three hours since takeoff, Burke had found his seventeen fellow passengers a very mixed but high-level lot. He was by far the youngest and would, therefore, as Stark had advised, arouse curiosity. "Your cover, Peter, is that you're an aeronautical representative of Lockheed. We'll supply you with technical manuals and the necessary data. I'm sure you'll be able to answer any questions. And of course, you can always fall back on the need for security."

There had been questions, but since everyone on board, aside from the crew, was engaged in some aspect of the war effort, his answers satisfied normal curiosity. Talk was of the war and where it was headed. All seemed to agree that Hitler was preparing to strike. The only question was where? Romania, Norway, the Low Countries, England? What would Mussolini do? And Stalin, now that his weight of numbers had crushed the gallant Finns? Would he and his Nazi ally divide Europe the way they had divided Poland?

Mostly he listened. The four French passengers neither listened nor joined in and spoke only in their own language. He did not let on that he understood their conversation, which seemed to center on the French economy almost as though the war were an afterthought. After all, wherever M. Hitler went, it would not be against the Maginot Line. *D'accord!*

There was only one less than placid outburst, and it came from the Dutchman de Loos. It was after midnight, Azores time, and some of the passengers were already in their bunks. De Loos had been sharing and drinking copiously from his personal supply of Bokma gin. "You tell me," he suddenly burst forth during a discussion of air power versus sea power, "you tell me what has happened so far and what is happening now. Air power, sea power—it is meaningless! It is what we are doing, and we are doing nothing but debating where he will strike. You British"—he glowered at the UK purchasing agents—"what are you dropping from the air? Not bombs but leaflets. My God, is that how to fight? Finland. Little Finland, like my country. For four months it devastated the Bolshevik army, the Red Army, Stalin's army. And what help did it get from us in the West? Nothing but promises. Words, because Sweden and Norway said, 'No, you can't cross here. We're busy sending iron ore to Hitler from the Gallivare mines.' And our French friends, they are sitting on their asses, hoping Hitler will go east. Well, I'll tell you where he will go. Right through the Netherlands and Belgium and anywhere else he wants to go because we refuse to admit that we are in a war. There is no leadership amongst us. Not in England, not in France, not anywhere. The will gone!" He banged his glass on the table, poured more gin into it, and none of those gathered around him had a word to say, somewhat embarrassed by the outburst, as though de Loose had broken some unwritten protocol.

Now he sat next to Burke, clean-shaven and contained, none the worse for the Bokma, pointing out recognizable landmarks.

"It's been a pleasure to meet you, Dr. de Loos," Burke said.

"Mine as well, young man. Should you come to The Hague, I would enjoy showing you something of my country. Not as large as yours, perhaps"—he smiled thinly—"or as safe, but worth seeing all the same. Let me give you my card." In his voice was a faint touch of regret for his show of emotion all wrapped up in Dutch pride, but in his yellowish eyes was a glint of anguish.

The landing on the Tagus was smooth and graceful. Yet the sudden transformation from majestic bird of flight to heavy boat with wings, checked and settling in its bow wave, was a shock. It was accentuated by the sure knowledge that the transient world in which they had come together as strangers was now ended, and as strangers again they all would go their separate ways into a far more unfriendly and unsafe world.

Stark had told him that someone from the legation would be waiting to pick him up at customs, and the plan then would be to get him aboard the next courier flight to Poole, which was outside London. If, however, by some mischance, no one was on hand, he should go to the Aviz Hotel and wait there. "Lisbon is a city full of spies," the secretary had advised, "from all sides and from everywhere. Anything you carry and leave in your hotel room will be opened. Anything you say will be overheard. Do not pack your uniform or anything that will indicate you are military. We'll send that sort of clothing by pouch."

"Sir, I don't even have a passport."

"Oh, you will have, my boy, you will have."

And he did have one, which was examined with care by the customs inspector, uniformed and looking severe. The setting was picturesque at any rate. Customs, adjoining the Pan Am passenger lounge, was an old chapel attached to a mill tower emplaced long ago beside the riverbank.

There was no one on hand to say, *"Bem-vindo ao cidade dos espiãos."* So he bade farewell to the last of his fellow travelers, who all had been fetched by someone, all offering to give him a lift. A good soldier stands by and waits—at least for a little while. He did so under the overhang of the arched entrance, out of the rain and somewhat out of sorts. Too much had happened all at once. He was feeling its effects, a letdown. Everything had moved so swiftly, and now everything had been brought to a sudden halt. The pattering rain suited his mood. They'd had breakfast at six. It was now seven-thirty, and for some reason he was ravenously hungry. He had been instructed by Uncle Bertie's little man Wheeler not to make any phone calls while at the hotel; but no one had said anything about his not calling the legation from pierside, and he was debating how long he would wait before making the attempt when he saw a car turn into the muddy entrance road and come slopping toward him.

He gave a sigh of relief and stubbed out his cigarette. Somehow the vehicle did not have the look of officialdom. It was a dented, rust-patched Nash sedan with a taxi sign on its roof. Its driver was a burly, mustachioed pirate, wearing a beret and a brass-toothed grin. "Senhor, you are Mistair Burke, *sim?*"

"Sim." It took no more than a nod for the driver to exit the cab,

grab up the suitcase—Burke held on to his musette bag—deposit it in the front seat, and announce, "We go."

And they went, Burke feeling a bit off-balance, surprised, a bit annoyed that the driver knew his name. "I am Piro," the driver announced, looking back at his passenger. "I take you to Hotel Aviz, *sim?*" The grin had not faded. In doing so, he drove much too fast, jabbering questions about the flight on the *grande avião,* apologizing for being late and relating the latest war rumor. "Have you heard, senhor? Soon Franco will attack Gibraltar? It is known everywhere, *sim.* Hitler will supply all that is *preciso.*" In spite of a heavy accent, Piro's English seemed surprisingly good, and Burke decided he would not attempt his very limited Portuguese.

He had never been in Lisbon, and the impression he got as they sped along a very straight, treelined *esplanada* was of spaciousness and majestic cathedrals contrasted with a closely packed jumble of white, pink, and blue structures marching in tiers up the hills. He recalled having read somewhere that Lisbon had been built on seven hills. Piro, swinging into a cross street, was suddenly heading up one, shifting down into a shrieking first gear, bouncing on the cobbles. Between the man's rapid exposition and his flare for speed, Burke had had no chance for serious reflection. Something at the root of his thoughts was tugging at him. It was probably the fact that whoever at the legation was handling his passage to England hadn't bothered to show up. Too damned early in the morning for him, so he'd sent this vaudeville comedian from the Grand Prix who seemed intent on burning out his clutch while scattering cylinder heads all over the street, preparing to rob him blind.

The street narrowed sharply so there was barely room for the car, and fortunately, with the rain, no one was on it. The incline was steep and appeared to terminate in a dead end. Before reaching it, Piro banked hard off the upgrade into a paralleling side alley and brought his chariot to a shuddering halt, Burke finding it necessary to dig in heels and brace outstretched hands against the back of the front seat.

The grin was wider, the stubble blacker, the brown eyes shining. "I bring you safe, *sim?*"

"Thanks to a merciful God. Where's the hotel?"

"*Aqui!* Here, Senhor Burke. This, the Aviz." He reversed his position, pointing to the building they were parked beside. It was one of a tightly packed cluster of cement blocks, white-faced with a trim of blue *azulejos,* four stories high with a nineteenth-century made-over look, possibly a *pensão,* not what he had expected.

"How much do I owe you?"

The grin remained fixed, but the response was surprising, not the price of a new car. "Only two hundred and fifty escudos. You see, Piro no rob you, no *engano,* no cheat. You give me a good tip, *sim?* I take you anywhere you want to go. You call me. I give number. Gambling, *lindas raparigas, sim.*"

Burke was not listening. Not one but two porters had come out of the iron-grille front door. They approached the cab, and he got out, fishing in his pocket for money.

"*Boa-tarde,* senhor." The smaller of the two greeted him. "I'll see to your fare, and you can repay me." His English did not have the flavor of Estremadura, more Irish, Burke thought as he nodded his thanks and left the man to do battle with Piro, who was no longer grinning. The larger porter—who, Burke saw, was very large—was in the process of getting the bag out of the front seat, so instead of standing in the rain, Burke entered the hotel, thinking it a bit strange that the establishment had no name designation on its front and was in a hell of a location for a hostelry. The dim foyer was simply an entrance. There was no front desk, no entry to the usual hotel lounge, no elevator, just stairs going up. He'd sure as hell been booked into a triple A nothing. The place was obviously a *pensão* and apparently without food accommodations. Somebody out there was getting even for upsetting the routine. Either his stay was to be extremely brief, and that was fine, or some assistant secretary at the legation was having fun. He heard Piro drive off in an unmuffled roar of displeasure.

The pair came in. "Would you care for breakfast?" the leader asked.

"That sounds good."

"A nice surprise."

"How much do I owe you?"

"Oh, we can take care of that with the bill. Let me show you your room, and then we'll see about something to eat." He led the way up two long flights and then down a darkened hallway to a rear room. "Unfortunately, senhor, we are very crowded," he said, unlocking a solid-looking door, "but we hope this will serve for the time being. How long do you expect to stay with us? Your legation did not say."

The porter's information startled him. This all was supposed to be so damned hush-hush, and some ass had already blabbed he was government-connected. Security, hell. Uncle Bertie didn't know the half of it. "I'm not sure. I'll let you know."

The room was sparsely furnished, the bed little more than a cot. There was a single back window, a sink, several chairs, a table, an overhead light hanging from a cord, no rugs on the dusty floor. It had the atmosphere of a cell, and he knew as soon as he found a phone, he was going to make connection with the colonel or one of his staff to get him the hell out of here. The muscular porter had set down his bag; the other was testing the light.

"May I have your passport, please?" The request was as polite as all the rest, but the question brought him up short. From experience he knew it was customary in some countries to show your passport to the concierge as a matter of form so it could be checked against a police list.

"I took care of all that at customs," he said.

"Yes, but you see with the war we are required to notify the police of all new arrivals and give the passport information. I'll return it to you presently. Just a matter of a telephone call."

"What about a phone? This room has no phone." He looked around.

"Apologies, senhor, There is one below you are free to use."

"Fine. Now how about that breakfast? Can I get some coffee, eggs, rolls?"

"Yes, by all means." He turned and spoke in Portuguese to his companion, who nodded and left. "It will be convenient to serve you here?"

"Yes, fine. Then I'd like to use your phone."

"And the passport, senhor?" His tone was one of wry apology; he was smiling.

The guy was awfully smooth. Except for the odd accent, his English was perfect. What was he doing playing bellhop in this fleabag? "I'll bring it down after breakfast, and we can check it against your list."

"Of course, as you wish." He jerked his head in acquiescence, not at all pleased. Burke handed him a tip, and again there was the head jerk of a bow, and he left the room, closing the door behind him.

Burke stood in the center of the room, hearing the rain dripping but not listening to it. He was listening instead to thoughts that came rushing in on a rising tide of doubt. He now realized what had been bothering him. Here he was on a mission so damned secret that a cabdriver knew his name. That jarring note triggered the memory of Uncle Bertie's saying, "If you have to wait for the courier flight, the legation will put you up at the Aviz. It was once a palace. I think you'll like it."

This was no palace. What the hell was going on? What had he flown into? "You make that call right now," he said aloud.

He strode to the door and felt an electric shock run up his arm as his hand twisted the knob. The door was locked, and the porter had left no key. Twisting the knob, pulling and pushing, didn't change a thing. Stupid as he'd been, it didn't take much to realize he'd been picked up, nabbed, kidnapped.

He quickly discovered there was nothing in the room that he could use to force the door. The window was his only exit. It was wedged shut. With the nearest chair he smashed out the glass and the wooden frame. He acted by reflex, not wasting time wondering why he had been trapped, only knowing he was determined to escape. He was more angry than frightened, furious at himself for being so easily gulled and at some stupid jerk at the legation.

The window gone, he leaned out and saw that without a rope there was no way down the side of the building into a narrow alleyway. The only chance to get out was to make a leap for the roof ledge of the adjacent building. It meant somehow being able to balance on the window ledge and take flight with an almighty jump across too wide a gulf and then to hold on long enough to get a leg up. He had no time to debate angle, distance, or the impossibility of what he was going to attempt.

There was also no telling how soon his captors would be coming back. His luggage would have to stay. He could sling the musette bag onto the roof before he tried to follow it. Sneakers were a must. He swapped them for his shoes, which he managed to stuff into the musette. He would sling it by its strap through the window frame onto the back roof. The frame was narrow, and getting a proper swing was difficult. He stood back, took aim, and with an underhand pitch let fly. The canvas bag lurched upward into the rain and came down with room to spare. He hoped he could do half as well. If he missed, the drop into the alley would be convenient for them. They could bury him where he lay. The window ledge had stone trim, which, in spite of the rain, should give a solid purchase. Getting properly placed on it was the trick. Some trick.

He thought he heard footsteps, and he went out the window in a crouch, hands gripping the frame. Straightening and keeping his balance against the pull of gravity, he rose partially, legs flexed. He did not look down. He looked at where he had to go.

"Enough of this crap," he muttered, carefully crouching lower, every muscle tensed. The trigger was his thought that he heard the door being unlocked behind him. He leaped, arms outstretched, reaching, reaching! His fingers made contact with the roof ledge as his body slammed against the siding. If there had not been a molding around which his fingers could desperately clasp, the weight of his body would have pulled him loose. As it was, for a frantic moment his feet scrabbled for purchase, his hands sliding on the wet molding. Then his foot found a toehold, and using all his strength, he got his other leg up over the rim.

He lay flat, sucking in air, eyes shut, the rain pecking at his face. Playing Icarus, even without the sun, was for the birds. He snorted at his pun and, rising, saw that he'd torn his pants and that his knee was scraped and bleeding. Small enough damage compared with what it might have been. He recovered his bag and glanced back at his takeoff point. It seemed very far away and notably empty.

At first there did not appear to be a way off the roof, not even a trapdoor. Then he saw the stone stairs on the building side. They curved down into a courtyard which was at a much higher elevation than the abyss he'd flown across. He took the crumbling steps with care, knowing they were very old, realizing that the stairs and the courtyard had been retained when a later structure had been built.

Again he was in luck, for the courtyard had a gate and a passageway that led to more steps, newer and steeper. He went down them in a rush, feeling they would eventually lead to the street. He was pleased at not having met anyone. He was only anxious to get clear of the area and locate a phone, a policeman, a taxi *sans* Piro—in whatever order.

His first discovery was the phone, but not right away, for the steps led him into a cobblestoned alley too narrow for automotive traffic. It took him to a similar alley which turned and twisted between shuttered shops and came out into an empty square where the rain beat on the worn flagstones.

Although he had no idea where he was going, there were two things he did know. Wherever he was, with every step he was farther from where he'd been, and every step was one of descent. With the rain there were few pedestrians, and only when he passed a timeworn church did he see a grouping of mostly women flocking in to mass. Everything about him, even the indefinable smell arising from the wet stones, had a medieval quality. He was passing through a time warp, a maze of tan and dirty white facades, wrought-iron balconies, low dwellings, their masonry fused by the passage of uncountable yesterdays. And then, suddenly, he was no longer descending. He stepped out of the narrow street into the flat, into the present, into a broad square with palms and shrubs and a fine avenue with traffic amid modern shops and a hotel. Not the Aviz but the Casa Belfont . . . with a telephone.

He called the legation and got the duty officer.

"This is Lieutenant Burke. I wish to speak to Colonel Apple."

"He's not here, sir."

"Well, suppose you connect me with someone who is there. It's urgent." He hoped the snap in his voice sounded businesslike.

"Yes, sir!"

He waited, soaking wet, making a puddle on the rug.

"Burke?" The voice was high-pitched, full of wonder. "Where are you?"

"I've been informed that I'm at Largo do Chafariz de Dentro, at the Casa Belfont."

"In Alfama? How in the world did you get there?"

"It's a long story, chum. Who am I speaking to?" He could not keep the annoyance out of his reply.

"This is Peck. I'll come fetch you right away."

"Good. But before you do, would you please tell me why someone official didn't pick me up at the Pan Am dock?"

"Hibbard was stopped by the police on the way. By the time he got rid of them and arrived at the pier you were gone. Why did you leave?"

"Who sent the cabdriver who knew my name?"

There was a ringing moment of silence and then an exhaled "Jeezuz!"

"That wasn't his name, but He could have been there." He hoped the sarcasm indicated the underlying anger he felt.

"Don't move till I get there. I'm driving a black '36 Ford coupe. I've got red hair."

"Are you an MA?"

"No, third secretary. I'll be there in fifteen minutes."

It was less than that, but in the interval Burke located the hotel café and had his coffee and rolls. Sitting down helped conceal his wounded knee and the wetness of his clothing. He was pouring his third cup when Peck arrived, small and Scottish-looking with high cheekbones and freckled complexion to go with his neatly parted red hair.

"I think we'd better be going," he said, quick blue eyes taking in the wreckage of Burke. "I have some good news," he added. Burke nodded, not replying, rose, and followed him.

Peck did not notice the blood until they were in the car. "What the devil happened, Lieutenant? Are you hurt?"

"More in need of dry clothes or any clothes," he said, tying his handkerchief around his knee. "Do you have a dry cigarette?"

As they drove, Burke related his Lisbon reception, Peck, muttering, shaking his head, concentrating more on Burke than on the Avenida da Liberdade, which, fortunately, ran perfectly straight.

"Suppose you tell me what the hell goes on," Burke concluded. "Nobody knew I was headed here until two days ago."

The third secretary shook his head. "No, that's not exactly correct. Colonel Apple knew you were coming at least two weeks ago."

Now it was Burke's turn to be nonplussed. "Two weeks ago! How could he have known when—"

"We didn't know who you were, just that an assistant MA was coming through, London-bound."

"Well, somebody sure as hell knew it was me unless Portuguese cabdrivers are on your staff."

"Let me give you an idea of how I think this could have happened. Salazar, you understand, is very close to Franco, and Franco, of course, owes a great deal to Hitler and Mussolini for his victory over the Loyalists. Salazar's secret police, PIDE, work hand in glove with Nazi agents, and the city is crawling with them. I told you Hibbard was stopped and questioned by the police for no particular reason. That was probably PIDE's work, and the cabdriver was one of their people. He took you to one of their safe houses in the Alfama district."

"But what the hell for?"

"Obviously they wanted to question you."

"And then what?"

"I don't know. I don't know what your mission is. They might have let you go. They might not. Nobody thinks there's a war going on in Europe. There's a nasty gutter-type war going on here. People disappear." As he spoke, he now had his eyes on his rearview mirror.

"Who at the legation knew I was coming? Who could have told these PIDE people?"

"Colonel Apple, who's in Madrid. Captain Stone, who's with him, and myself. Hibbard simply knew he was to pick you up. But that's where the good news comes in. You're getting out of here right away. We're not going to the legation." He turned off the avenue onto a rising esplanade. "We're going to the airport. Directly after we spoke, word came that our courier plane from the UK had finally made it. They don't like to stay any longer than necessary. They're loading right now, and they'll squeeze you on board. Under the circumstances I think you'd better clear out of here."

"That's fine with me." The news was good. It lifted some of the load, but not the main part. "Look, I suppose you learned my name by cable."

"Colonel Apple got word from G-2, signed by Miles. That's General Sherman Miles, the new head."

"It doesn't matter who signed it. If no one in the legation talked, then the only way this PIDE bunch could have known my name was by having gotten a copy of the cable, too."

Even as he spoke the words, the answer was coming through to him. He didn't even hear Peck's response—*"That's impossible!"*—and the explanation of why it was impossible because he thought he knew how the word of his arrival had been passed. Undoubtedly the same cable from Miles had been sent to London. Had Scott Reardon somehow got hold of it and passed it on? "Holy shit!" He sighed and saw that the third secretary was looking at him askance.

"You can be sure we'll raise some hell about this," Peck said, "although everything will be denied."

"No! No, I don't think you'd better say anything outside the legation. Not by cable anyway. My duty is to be kept absolutely secret."

"Well, aren't you already compromised? Someone apparently knows what your duty is."

"Not necessarily. I didn't hang around to be questioned, did I? I'll handle it from London. I have someone to report to there, and I'm getting out of here right now even if it is without my clothes. Let word come back from London."

"Well, I'll have to take it up with the charge. He—"

"Look, Peck," Burke snapped, "it's my ass we're talking about. It damn near got busted because somebody somewhere talked. Please hold any more talk until you get the word from London or Washington."

3

There was the flame. Always the flame, its coloration and intensity hidden behind the secret door where the spectrum was a bow of many hues, stroking across the strings of his mind. He smiled at his alliteration.

The hour was late as he came down the stairs into the dimly illuminated lobby of the chancellery. Actually the theme of the Vivaldi concerto where the bassoons come forth *da da dadada da dum* was occupying that part of his thought process he permitted to wander about in the fields of Elysium. But . . . the flame was ever there, and he could glimpse its present shade, a moderate yellow, burning low and even, all under control.

In his jacket pocket he was carrying a copy of the Kennedy cable to Roosevelt, reporting on the Supreme Allied War Council's decision to begin mining Norwegian waters on April 7. Churchill, as first lord of the admiralty, had been pushing the idea for months, wanting to seize Norwegian ports as well, and Kennedy thought the undertaking ill advised and was so advising the president. On the other hand, those who received this most secret gift would see its color as yellow also. Pure gold. Not that they didn't know of the plan already. It was the decision to act and the date that mattered.

With the Kennedy cable he had included the Chamberlain War Cabinet report on the yet unresolved decision to go to war against Stalin, bombing Baku from the air while launching a submarine attack on Soviet oil ships in the Black Sea bound for German ports.

As a dividend, folded in his back pocket, was an equally delicious cable from Marlow to Marshall on Royal Marine, another British March Hare scheme—he liked his pun—involving the dropping of aerial mines up the Rhine. Who had passed the information to Marlow he didn't know, but the idea was that the mines would float down the river and raise hell with German shipping. The French high command was opposed because of the fear of Hitler's reprisals, yet it was demanding a more vigorous approach to the war, believing that the British blockade was not enough. He knew that if he were caught in possession of any one of the three documents, his bassoon-playing days would be over, perhaps permanently.

He'd begun the game a month after his posting from Warsaw. Oh, the gold he'd panned. The real nuggets were the exchanges between that phony bastard in the White House, POTUS he called himself, and that puffed-up Churchill, Naval Person. Those asses in Berlin. All they had to do was publish the exchanges, and Roosevelt would be finished. Instead, they put out some crappy white paper. Here he was, risking his neck to put an end to it, to expose the cabal bent on dragging the United States into war, aiming to get his knife in the balls of that wheelchair Svengali, and what—and what did it bring?

It brought the question, Have the hounds picked up the scent? There had been no baying, no growling, just a faint shifting somewhere. He had felt it but could not lay his hands on the scruff of a neck. There was only a sense of something ajar.

In the cafeteria, raising his eyes from the *Times* and across the room, he had caught the swiftly averted gaze of Counselor Henry Sutterby. Sutterby barely knew he existed; diplomats do not mingle with clerks. Why stare? His fly was not unbuttoned . . . a warning? Nothing? . . . A mote in the counselor's watchful eye? Find out.

In the beginning he had moved with great care. He had learned the technique in Moscow, had practiced it under General Surov's tutelage, and there had been no problem in picking it up again here. Not that he gave a damn for the stupid Bolsheviks or Surov and his Fourth Bureau. His purpose was his own. Ever that. But what he did care about was making sure the Concerto for Bassoon and File Room—as he blithely dubbed his after-hours activities—was composed without chance of exposure.

For some time he had maintained the practice of going to the men's room and using the tube, as he had been taught in Moscow. But as his selections mounted, and he saw there was no real security, he had dispensed with caution, becoming cute and daring, waving his gems directly under the noses of those around him. Often he packaged his gas mask container, the inside of his bowler, even his folded umbrella. It was he who chose, he who determined what was to go. He! He, who sat in the dark and quietly sifted the gold, reading the secret minds of little men. The question remained, however, Was he not being just a little too cute?

To him the duty officer, Vice-Consul Geoffrey Amidon Crabtree III, was an elegant, dim-witted buffoon, serving his first tour abroad, full of his own sense of grandeur. He knew Crabtree had seen him coming down the stairs but was now deeply engrossed in a copy of *Life* magazine.

"Good evening, m'lord," Reardon said, setting down his Burberry and gas mask on a chair. He did not take off his hat. "I'm getting out while the getting is good."

"Good for what?" Crabtree took the bait without looking up.

"I just saw a dispatch for the ambassador that said the entire Luftwaffe is headed this way, and Grosvenor Square is the target. Do you have a pen?" He had pocketed the pen beside the duty roster, wanting to agitate the moon-faced jerk.

"That's not really very funny, Reardon. Don't you have one?" Crabtree began looking around as though one might materialize out of the air.

He turned his back on him. "I'll use my forefinger," he said, retrieving the pen from his pocket, signing the roster on its pedestal and including the time.

"You can also sign this," Crabtree said, his accent having taken on an insufferable *haut Britannia* intonation. "It's a *nota bene* issued by the ambassador." He plucked a single sheet of paper from the desk drawer, his rather empty eyes leaking with anticipation.

Reardon took the paper and saw that J. P. Kennedy's latest instruction to his staff dealt with security. Immediately the orchestra within stilled. The ambassador had become aware there was not enough security, and in these times security was not just a precaution but a top priority as well. Henceforth all personnel should be prepared to have inspections made of personal property when going off duty and leaving the embassy.

And there it was. Not just an insulting implication the staff would resent, but the screaming virginity of the page beneath the order. It did not contain a single signature; it was aimed directly at him. And although he was pleased that his antennae had been tuned sharply enough to sense the wind's sudden *volta,* he was furious with himself for allowing his conceit to override good judgment and put the entire orchestration in hazard. *"Durak!"* "Stupid fool." Surov's voice rasped in discord. *"Your arrogance will kill you one day."* "Goodness," he said, "who's been swiping the cardinal's cigarettes?"

"It's not a joking matter, Reardon."

"What? The *nota bene* or the cigarettes?" He let his voice rise, pretending to be offended. "Here, start with the gas mask." He plunked it down on the desk and piled the coat on top of it. "Or maybe you'd like to examine my coat first. That's where I hide the scotch. Do I strip here or do we go to the men's room? How about my hat?" He flipped it onto the coat and began unbuttoning his jacket, outrage in his voice and look.

"Now wait a minute." Crabtree rose from behind the desk. "There's no reason to get on your high-and-mighty horse. There's a war going on."

"I hadn't noticed."

"And the ambassador is perfectly within his rights to make sure that—"

"We're not robbing the place blind because rations are in short supply. I understand perfectly. I'm late. I'm off duty, and I want to get the hell out of here. What do you want me to take off?"

Crabtree, thrown off-balance by the vehement and swift reaction, was not sure which tack to follow. "I—I don't want you to take off anything. I just—I just want your sig-signature on the instruction so that you understand, to alert you."

Reardon scrawled his name on the paper and said, "Consider me alerted." He plunked his hat on his head, "And you're alerted, too." He swung into his coat. "The Luftwaffe is coming. Ta-ta, old chap. Think what life will be like for you when you start searching the ladies of the house."

He went out into the night, embracing the blackout as a protective cloak, alerted. Alerted! He was alerted to hell and gone, and if Crabtree was a bloody jerk, so was he. There would be no more damnfool intermezzos. He crossed the street into the park, cutting across it, heading toward South Audley. The breeze was raw, the air damp, acrid with the smell of coal smoke. He turned up his collar. He liked walking in the blackout with the close feel of heavy buildings all about, their irregular tops blackly silhouetted, lumped against the paler darkness of the sky, where the sound of a plane's engine droned and a thin pencil of useless light probed.

The blackout was a little like hiding one's thoughts. Of course, there was no flame. A flame would bring the fire warden running. When Hitler finally sent his bombers, there would be lots of flames and lots of running, just like Warsaw. Now the stillness was like the dark. Protective. Concealing because his own stillness permitted him to hear all about. The orchestra remained silent, no tuning, no theme. Still.

He reached the center of the park, where the walks crossed, and sat down on a bench, waiting. He wanted a cigarette. *"Défense de fumer."* He sighed. He listened, and all that came to him were muted traffic sounds. Driving in the blackout was for cabbies and females looking snappy in their ARP uniforms. He unbuttoned his coat and extracted the folded documents. Their whiteness seemed very bright in the dark. Quickly and adroitly he rolled them to form a short cylinder. He secured it with a rubber band from his pocket and deposited it in the depths of his coat.

Five minutes later, having left Grosvenor Square, he was moving at a good pace toward Aldford Street. Time was important, but when he turned the corner, he slowed. It was a short way to the dead drop, but between it and himself there could be a bobby or a warden on patrol or both.

He walked a few paces along Aldford, moving away from the towering silhouette of Grosvenor Chapel, and stopped. And in the sudden halt he heard what he believed was the faint scuff of a heel on pavement. Tensed, eyes vainly searching, nose raised, seeking in the air what he could not see, he waited. He'd waited before. The flame within flared in the dark breeze of memory. Not here. Not here. Not now. Wait! He waited, hunched in his coat, and there was no further sound of warning until he heard the tinkle of a woman's laughter and then a man's voice joining in.

They were coming toward him from Park Lane, and he walked toward them, making no effort to conceal his approach. He had placed the overheard footstep behind him. They could be working together. He began to whistle "I've Got You Under My Skin." There would be no drop. He might not have really heard the footstep, and the approaching couple could be exactly what they seemed to be; but he prided himself on quick perception. He was not in the mood to risk anything more this night. He quickened his stride, continuing to whistle, and then sang out, "Good evening."

"And to you, too," came the hearty response. He could see the dark glow of her cigarette as they passed him.

Now he was faced with a choice. Did he go home to his flat or did he stop in at Fanny's before closing time? Surov made the choice for him, reciting in his ear, "*Never try to improvise on a broken plan. You can always make a new plan. You can never take back getting caught.*" When he reached Park Lane, he strolled to the Dorchester and hailed a cab, asking the driver to take him to Sloane Square.

On the way he began making a new plan, wondering what Surov might have to say about improvising had he known that Royal Navy subs might soon be torpedoing Soviet ships and that RAF bombers might be hitting the Caspian oil center. Maybe once Adolf got the word, he'd pass it on to his bloody buddy Joe. But swiftness was essential if anyone was to get it. As he looked out the rear window, it was difficult to tell if he was being followed, but when the cabby turned off Knightsbridge onto Sloane, he detected at least one vehicle behind him. In the darkness he was able to distinguish the long length of Cadogan Park, and when they reached its end, he asked the cabby to pull over and stop. As he paid his fare, he saw what looked like another cab ease on by. He waited on the curb until the thoroughfare was clear. Then he walked the short block to Wilbraham and turned down it to the hotel. He went up the steps and rang the night bell. It was Masters who opened the door a crack, the blackout curtain concealing his identity but not his sonorous voice. "Sorry, we're fully occupied and closed for the night."

"Masters, it's Mr. Reardon. I hate to disturb you, but I wonder if I could have the use of your telephone. Ours is not working."

"Oh, my, yes, Mr. Reardon. Excuse me for not recognizing you. Come in, and watch your step on the lintel."

He had used the Wilbraham not infrequently for tea, and its drawing room on occasion for an after-theater drink, before escorting his date down the block and around the corner to his flat. Masters, and the small hotel staff, were used to him, and he perceived that they found his manners as a Yank acceptable.

"A pity your service went out, sir." Masters led the way around the narrow foyer's front desk to the booth under the stairs.

"We'll chalk it up to wartime inconvenience," Reardon said lightly. "I appreciate your help."

"Not at all, Mr. Reardon. Let me have the number, and I'll ring it up for you."

"It's the embassy, and I've got to use not one but two special numbers, so if you'll just give me an open line to the operator, I can make it a bit easier for her, but thanks all the same."

He smiled his thanks, and although Masters didn't know what he was talking about, he accepted the explanation with the tip. "Very good, sir. I'll ring when I have the operator."

It worked smoothly enough. He heard the click of Masters's disconnecting his jack plug as the operator made her inquiry.

As soon as he heard the receiver lifted, he began speaking, using a British accent. "I say, I'm sorry I couldn't make it this evening. An unexpected caller, you know. I was wondering if you might have any time tomorrow in the forenoon, or perhaps an early lunch. There are several paintings in the collection you really must see."

"What a shame, old chap." The voice was full of bonhomie; it had a garrulous quality. "I do have to go out of town tomorrow. Say, I'm leaving from Waterloo at ten. We could meet at the station by the clock, say, around nine. How would that suit?"

"Grand idea. I'll see you there."

"Good, good. Until then."

He sat at the desk with the table lamp's illumination bathing the desktop, the rest of his single room with its bed alcove submerged, the kind of soft interior darkness he liked. The flame fitted into it nicely; only it was the glow of his cigarette, not the flame, he was contemplating. The cigarette tasted good. The brandy supplied a fitting warmth against the chill. But he was not pleased.

It was he who had set up the telephone code for the count, and although Asardi with his fruity Cambridge accent was letter-perfect, he was not enthusiastic about the Italian's selection of the new time and place. Waterloo was O'Leary's Bull and Bear, and nine in the morning meant noon.

Now, as he was looking at the desktop photograph of his father—but not really seeing the aristocratic features, the fine, high forehead, the curving mane of hair, the classically formed nose and mouth, young

Byron in apogee framed in gilt—sudden recognition hit him. It was not his father's face but the memory of a face triggered by it. Coming up from the underground at Charing Cross, again a glimpse in passing on the Flower Walk in Kensington Gardens. And at the Bull and Bear, by God! Yes, by God, he'd been there at the bar, back to him, but there! And now he knew what had stirred the flame in the first place, had made it flicker in the dark.

"He didn't look like you, couldn't look like you." He spoke to the photograph. "But somehow you've warned me. Hamlet had his father's ghost, and you're mine." He raised his glass. "*Salud,* Father. We'll bring them down together." The last was a whisper.

What had begun like a whiff of smoke, as a faint suspicion, was now burning bright. Attention was being paid him not only from within the embassy but also from without, meaning the British. That shoe on the pavement had been the scuff of Scotland Yard. If nothing else, his acuity pleased him.

System and routine. He heard Surov preaching the watchwords. *The system is put in place. It is the same in every embassy. The routine of operation follows accordingly. To penetrate, you study the system. You learn the routine. You act.*

Indeed, he had. The code rooms in Moscow, Warsaw, London—all were constructed along the same pattern, all joined to an index file room in which the traffic was stored: secret and classified in a separate section; unclassified in a larger one. To gain entry, you needed keys. You got them by laying hands on a set long enough to make a soap-bar impression. That was not difficult if you got a code clerk drunk enough to borrow them for a moment. Fanny had seen to that and the duplication. The rest was timing, slipping between the gates of routine: when best to enter; how best to select; when best to depart. Here, too, system and routine were the guides.

Thank God that blue-eyed, bald Bullitt wasn't ambassador here. He'd sure shot routine to hell in Spaso House. He'd brought in a whole detachment of Marines in civvies to keep the Russian help out of everybody's desk. And that had been that. His system and routine trumped Surov's until elegant Bill went off to Paris to play ambassador there, and that consummate ass Davies came to replace him. The Marines were sent home, system and routine were restored with a vengeance, and the gates were flung wide.

But it wasn't Bullitt, or Davies, or Biddle, or Kennedy he had to think about. It was Scotland Yard and MI 5. They, too, had a system and routine, not like the embassy certainly, but he would adapt to it. Oh, yes, he would. In his mind he picked up the powerful theme of the allegro from Brahms's First, humming the bassoon support.

The military attaché's suite of offices was on the fourth floor. He came to the section with no appointment, but since he knew he was going to be picking up papers on the families of missing Polish Army officers from Sergeant Rosen, reportedly down with the flu, he had decided to stop by and see Colonel Marlow or one of the other officers. He wanted to find out how much of a load was going to be dumped on him.

The MA's offices were fronted by an anteroom, a secretarial square-shaped bull pen, defended on three sides by what looked like a picket fence. Behind it Miss Robins, Miss Baker, and Miss Hobbs held the fort against all infiltrators. He had privately dubbed them, spinsters three, faithful army warhorses, the Macbeth Sisters.

"Good morning, Miss Robins," he said, nodding deferentially to her two cohorts. "I stopped by on the off chance that Colonel Marlow might have a moment to spare."

"If he does, Mr. Reardon," she replied, not looking up from her desk, busy with a folder, "he won't be able to spare it for you. Colonel Marlow won't be with us today."

"And Major Dunn, is he out for that spare moment, too?" He smiled at Misses Baker and Hobbs, giving them the benefit of his wit, noting they were faintly amused.

"Major Dunn is with Colonel Marlow." Miss Robins continued her desk work with the folder, putting neatly organized papers into it. He did not wish to make a game of it, naming the other attachés so that she could nippily inform him one by one that they all had died of their wounds. "Well, perhaps you can spare me a moment, Miss Robins? Sergeant Rosen—"

"Is ill with flu," she interjected, "and you have been assigned his duties." She closed the folder and lifted it with both hands toward him. "Here are the files that will need attending to. We hadn't expected you so soon."

"Goodness," he said, pretending the weight of the folder was pulling his arms down. "Thank you."

She was looking up at him now. There was nothing faded in the sharpness of her gaze. He felt its impact like a soft blow to the solar plexus, no loss of breath but a tightening of the muscles.

"I hope the sergeant will be back on his feet soon." He tried to make the double meaning comic, meeting the coolness of her stare, smiling.

"We hope so, too. Until then, if you'll plan to stop by before going on duty, we'll have the package ready for you." She was no longer looking at him. He sensed she had seen all of him she wanted to see and was now occupied putting a pencil in her desk stand; that, or she was afraid that by staring at him, she'd give away feelings she could not hide.

"Thank you, Miss Robins." He nodded his farewell to her colleagues and turned to leave.

"Excuse me, but aren't you Scott Reardon?"

He was automatically on guard, with a sensation of being hit from behind. He had been remotely aware of someone sitting in the reception area. The stranger's grin was lopsided because his mouth was slightly canted. What struck home wasn't the diffidence of the smile but the deep-set eyes meeting his.

"You don't remember me, and frankly, I don't remember you very well." The laugh was self-mocking. "But your name I remember. I think we were embassy brats in Berlin long ago. My name is Peter Burke." He thrust out his hand.

Reardon took the hand and matched the grip. " 'Fraid you have me there. What did you say? Burke? Burke." He tasted the name as his memory scrambled. "Maybe I did know someone of that name."

"My brother, probably. Rod."

"Possibly. What brings you here? Are you military?"

"Yes. Air Corps. Just arrived yesterday."

"Hope you're not trying to get a moment of Colonel Marlow's time, too."

They both laughed.

"No, not right now. Mostly filling out forms."

"I see you've got your gas mask. Good place to tuck your laundry."

"All kinds of IDs to be collected, ration cards, permits to—"

"I know, I know." He raised his hand, not wanting to be bothered with familiar litany, but suddenly he did know. He saw clearly what he would do. It was perfect. "Look here, I don't imagine you know your way around this town very well. Why don't you join me for lunch if you have nothing better to do?"

"Why—heck, that's very kind of you." The military was obviously surprised at the offer.

"I'll introduce you to the neighborhood pub. Food is terrible. You go ahead and fill out your forms, and I'll drop this off and pick you up here in fifteen minutes."

"That's great. Hey, do you still play that funny-looking kazoo?"

"How in the hell could you remember something like that?" He was truly startled.

Burke was grinning again. "How could I forget it? Actually I just remembered it."

Reardon went away, playing the sight, sound, and impression of Peter Burke up and down the scales. He did not remember him at all. The name he faintly recalled but in a different context; perhaps the brother. Air Corps, a new yes, sir boy for Marlow. Was he as guileless as he seemed? He'd find out soon enough. He wondered if Asardi would appreciate the irony; he knew Surov would have.

At the noon hour O'Leary's Bull and Bear was full of sound, if not fury. Snookered in off the corner of Gees Court, the pub was convenient to a host of underpaid government, business, and embassy staffers. There was nothing gourmet about it, outside or in. Its worn wood facade needed paint, as did its name sign. Its scarred interior with wooden tables and benches and kitty-corner cubicles was extensive, as was its bar, which gave a false impression of accommodation and rooms for all. With rationing, its menu was meager, its waitresses were too few, its food was wretched, but through habit and association it had long been a popular gathering place, a place of noise and smoke and overcrowded noontime camaraderie over a half-pint or two of bitters.

They had gotten their drinks at the bar and settled into a corner slot that looked over the chattering scene. Reardon had to raise his voice. "At some point we may get service. If Gertie comes by, grab her. I mean literally. Best to order soup, fish and chips. It's all garbage anyway. Cheers." He lifted his glass, and Burke, who appeared to be taking in the scene calmly, returned the salute.

The walk from the embassy had given Reardon a chance to size up Marlow's new recruit.

As for the Burke and Berlin relationship out of the long ago, he recognized that it was genuine. His prodded memories did include a vague impression of Burke's brother and even a fragment of recollection reading of his death. Since the connection was doubtlessly real, it was not important. All that was really important was the use to which he was going to put this lean, quick-striding Army boy. He had no interest in him whatsoever beyond that.

He had observed that Burke had the black hair, high cheekbones, stubborn chin, and coloring of the Highland Celt. There was a quickness about him difficult to place because it was more than physical, an alertness that did not appear limited to the cockpit of a pursuit plane, fast on the uptake but a bit heavy on the stroke. He judged the intellectual difference between them as that of the claymore and the rapier. As they walked and talked, he played the role of the gracious extrovert, pointing out landmarks, suggesting shortcuts through the red tape of getting properly vetted, and when Burke asked about shopping for clothes, he pointed out Toby's. He did not ask questions about Burke's assignment, not wanting to bore in and not really giving a damn what it was. Coincidentally he noted that Burke did not query him about his own job apparently because it had nothing to do with air power and the RAF. By the time they reached the pub, he had decided that if nothing else, the lieutenant was going to make the drop possible even if the Bull and Bear was swarming with Scotland Yard shoe scuffers.

Above the sound Burke said, "Where's all the Italian coming from? This place sounds more like Mama Rosa's than O'Leary's. You sure we're not in Rome?"

"Should have pointed it out to you," Reardon said. "That fine Georgian manse next door to our own is the Italian Embassy. For some reason the Fascisti like this place better than their own spaghetti parlor. You may see some Japs in here, too. Their embassy is also in Grosvenor Square."

"All pals together, hey?"

"Something like that."

Over the clatter and jumble of voices a determined statement blared forth: "I say they bombed hell out of the place, and it's long past time to give it another go!" Cries of ragged approval were topped by a supporting admonition: "Maybe they think one bloody raid is going to stop the bloody Hun." The chorus sang a mixed refrain.

"What's that about? Did the RAF drop something other than pamphlets?" Burke was all ears.

"Yes. Week or so ago, they bombed a German seaplane base at Sylt off the Danish coast. Evidently very successful. It was in response to the Luftwaffe hit on Scapa Flow."

"Tit for tat, hey? Does that mean the phony war is coming to an end?"

"You'll have to ask Colonel Marlow. He's in very close with the Brits, practically one himself."

"I guess there isn't much of a war going on here. At least I don't get that impression." Burke sounded sorrowful.

"Be patient. The daffodils are starting to bloom. You know what happens to armies in the springtime." He saw the count, who had been standing at the bar, turn and start moving across the room toward them. He couldn't believe the dumb bastard would openly make contact. He lowered his gaze, examining his glass.

"Gertie!" He was surprised and pleased that Burke had acted. "Can we order?"

"What'll it be, dearie?" She obviously liked his smile.

By the time they had told her what it would be, Asardi had gone past, heading for the loo. In the beginning they had used the loo as a drop; but the facilities were too small, and the traffic in and out was too heavy, making it unnecessarily risky. He didn't like using the Bull and Bear for a drop in any case; but when it was necessary, the coat trick replaced the earlier method, and he hoped now that the Italian idiot hadn't forgotten. The coat trick was a matter of swapping Burberrys, same size, same shade. The pub had no coat room and too few stands to accommodate the noon load, so customers used the shelflike wainscoting along the wall to lay them on.

The method of exchange had worked so far, both showing up at the pub three days later to complete the swap. He had to assume the drop worked or they wouldn't be free to try it again. But he didn't like their being at the same place at the same time ever. It was a point Surov had often stressed, and it made sense, and although he did not believe he and Burke had been trailed, there was nothing to rule out an agent amid the throng particularly now because of the remembered face. On whatever that chance might be he must base his actions. Attention, if it was there, would certainly be fixed on Burke, the newcomer, at least until someone had a chance to check on his identity. Meantime, Burke's trench coat would be put to good use, and Asardi had better have his signals straight. As the Italian passed by them again, heading toward the bar, Reardon raised his voice. "Aren't you awfully hot in that?" He pulled his own coat wide and, then half standing, shrugged out of it. "Here, let me have yours." He held out his hand. "I'll put them over there."

Burke stood and followed Reardon's lead, handing him his coat. As Reardon carried the apparel across his arms toward the window ledge, he removed the cardboard tube from his Burberry pocket and slipped it into the sleeve of Burke's trench coat. When he set them down, Burke's coat was on an open space by itself. He saw that the lieutenant was watching him as he returned and that the count, again at the bar, back to him, had the mirror to help him figure it out.

"You think our coats will be safe there?" Obviously Burke had counted on their being hung up.

"Haven't lost one yet." He didn't sit down. "Before Gertie comes with the swill, you want a refill? I grant you it's a poor grade of lion's piss, but it helps."

"I'm game, thanks." Burke handed him both glasses.

Reardon edged in several bodies down from the count, at the bar, where the argument for and against bombing the bloody hell out of Hitler continued in earthy debate. He did not plan to speak directly to Asardi, who, thanks to his English mother, looked like a Londoner, pale skin, long nose, jowly, pipe-smoking, definitely British with the given name of Clarence—in full, Count Clarence Giovanni della Ponte Asardi, counselor at the Italian Embassy, secret agent not by choice but by circumstance. A joke. So far a good one.

"Where is this Sylt place they bombed anyway?" a hoarse voice queried.

He responded instantly. "At Hörnum. It's said to be hidden like a fair-size teat inside a sleeve of islands off the Danish coast."

Over the laughter he ordered the refills and rejoined Peter Burke, pleased with himself. If he were being watched, the attention would be focused on Burke, not on the count. That was a point he took pride in. Not since their meeting at Fanny's, when he had put the arrangement into operation, had he publicly exchanged a word with Asardi. "Ha. The more the merrier," he said aloud, handing Burke his glass. "And lorluvaduck, here comes Gertie. She's fallen for you."

He knew the count would not make a move until they were engrossed in the meal. He had placed the coats far enough out of eye range so that Burke would not see anyone picking up his unless he turned sharply to the right. He'd prevent that by keeping his attention. "Something I meant to ask, have you found digs, a place to live?"

"I'm staying at the Army Club temporarily. Major Edwards says he has a flat with an extra bunk, so I may move in there for the present."

Customers were starting to drift away, and he saw Asardi drink up and start his move.

"That can't be very satisfactory. You'll want something a bit better, I should think. Have you checked with King Cole at the embassy?"

Asardi ambled across the room, wending his way between the tables, and in spite of his pride in staying cool, Reardon felt a tightening in his stomach. Something was wrong!

"Who is King Cole?"

"Oh, he's a fixture. Been here forever. Actual name is Ben Cole." He knew he was speaking too fast. He picked up his glass, eyes sweeping the room, looking for interest in the count. Nothing he could spot.

"What has he got to do with finding a place to stay?"

"What? Oh, well, he knows everyone in London." Facing Burke, he could see past the edge of the stall, could see Asardi's bulk as he bent to the coats.

It should have been all right, would have been all right if the damn fool had simply picked up the coat, slid his arm up the sleeve, seen he'd made an error, and set the coat down, tube in hand, which could have gone into his pocket easily enough. No one was paying him the least attention. He could have located his own coat and departed. Instead, the idiot slung Burke's coat over his arm and headed for the door.

Because he forcefully pulled his eyes away and addressed the chips on his plate, he did not see how Burke had caught sight of the count and recognized that it was his coat about to be filched.

"Hey!" It was an explosive sound that froze everyone in the place except Burke, who was halfway across the room before Reardon could get free of the table and follow. "Where the hell do you think you're going with my coat!"

The flush of color in the count's hound doggish face was a fine-textured pink, his luminous brown eyes fixed in shock, bulging, hands gripping the coat.

"Oh! I—I s-say!" He held out the garment in supplication. "I—I must have—"

"Made a mistake!" Burke angrily yanked the coat out of Asardi's hands. The eaters and drinkers had become intensely interested in the drama. It looked as if a blow in anger were about to be struck.

"Yes, yes, I did, sir! You—you see, sir, without my glasses—m-my glasses—" He patted his chest as though searching for them, struggling to pacify this inflamed savage.

In Reardon, desperation was close to the surface. If Asardi had not removed the tube—and it did not seem that he had—Burke was bound to discover it when he put on his coat.

"Easy does it, Burke," he said, laying his hand on his shoulder. "This gentleman obviously made an error." It seemed his own voice shook.

"Yes, yes, I do hope you'll accept my apology." The count was regaining control, showing a mouthful of teeth, the color fading down. "Perhaps I could buy you both a drink."

Reardon felt the muscle in Burke's shoulder relax.

"Hell, I just lost all my clothes in Lisbon," Burke said wryly. "I bought this coat this morning to cover my nakedness." The anger had gone out of him.

"Oh, hard lines, hard lines, sir. What about a stirrup cup of brandy to soften the blow?"

"That's awfully nice of you," Reardon chirped, wanting to buy time. "What do you say, Peter?"

The clientele of the Bull and Bear, realizing violence was not on the menu, raggedly resumed its full-throated lunch hour.

"Perhaps we can get an extra chair at our table." Reardon was anxious to get seated, and as he turned, he heard the object hit the floor. So did Burke, for it struck his foot first and rolled between him and the count. At that instant there was no flame, no Vivaldi theme, no bassoon foolery. There was only a gibbering silence in which he prepared to leap. But Burke had seen the object, acted, and rose with the cardboard tube in hand, wondering what he had found.

Asardi supplied the answer. "Oh, I say, I believe I dropped my cigar container." He held out his hand. "Antonia will allow me only one a day."

Burke handed it to him.

"Fair swap, I guess," he said. "Seems to be that kind of a day."

He had told Fanny to contact him by phone only in case of real emergency, otherwise to contact him with a card he had given her, which was a rental advertisement with his name and address typed on it. Finding the card, along with a note from Burke, in his embassy mailbox had given him a momentary jolt. The flame had flickered, then quickly steadied, for the warning was but added confirmation of what he felt he already knew.

Windley, the embassy doorman, in frock coat, asked if a cab would be required, and he declined, saying the weather was fine for walking even if the dark was moving in. He walked briskly in the fading April eventide, planning his route.

At Bond Street he took the underground, got off at the Piccadilly interchange, caught the tube at Charing Cross just as it was leaving, and debarked at St. Giles Circus an instant before the doors closed. He moved quickly along the platform and exited up the escalator to Oxford Street in a rush.

The bus stops were crowded with homegoers, anxious for the twilight to hold ere the darkness came and the blackout shut off quick surface travel. He had thought to take a bus, but under the circumstances he realized it would be difficult to determine if he was being followed. So far he had not been aware of it, but aboveground or below, he knew this was a bad time to make contact because the whole city was on the move, and anyone following him could be easily concealed in the swarm.

The side entrance to Fanny's club, for which he had a key, was down a narrow sideway, and turning into it, he stood still and waited. No one approached, but he did hear activity at the front entrance, someone arriving. He did not like the timing. If, in fact, the customer was a tail, it meant the hunters already knew of his connection with Fanny. It could be a trap, but he felt he must chance it.

The side entrance led into an unlit hallway and a flight of stairs to her living quarters. His entering he knew would activate a jingle bell which would register in the kitchen and her flat. He entered and could hear the muffled sound of voices from the clubroom. He needed no light to guide him up the stairs and into her dwelling. He sat down on her old-world divan, lit a cigarette, and waited.

It had begun with Fanny O'Rourke, not by direction but through curiosity. Soon after his arrival in London he had heard of Fanny's Tara, a club not like others. It catered to a moneyed West End crowd, show people, and odd sorts. In spite of rationing, Fanny knew where the eggs were laid, and she brewed an Irish coffee and served an Irish mulligan that was all the talk. But mostly Fanny herself was the attraction. She was no Queen Maeve, more like something out of Joyce or Synge. Big-boned, squarely built, large-breasted, she strode about her court with its paneled eatery, its clubroom bar, its tublike stage, from which the singing and the playing came, like Cormac's daughter. Ugliness had given her a flick of its paw, but she had knocked it away. Eyes and voice and boldness had won. Eyes that were not round and luminous but small with fanlike lids and a downward cast. Hidden was the word, not out of any shyness but to conceal what lay behind the pale jade of her glance. There was nothing hidden about her voice, lusty and Gaelic. Her singing had a throaty, sad quality, reminding him of Tatiana. Instead of a balalaika, she accompanied herself with a zither, and when she came past his table, he greeted her with the only Gaelic toast he knew. " 'Tis a high health to Ormonde, dear lady, and a low death to Cromwell." He raised his glass to her.

"Well, now, darlin' boy, where did you learn to speak your father's tongue so well?"

"At me father's knee." He mimicked her brogue. "His name was Strongbow."

"I knew it all along. Tell me more."

And before the evening was over, he had told her enough, and she, in turn, had been the one who had told him more. Attraction had flowed between them, she, flattered by a handsome young man's approach, he, perversely amused yet aroused, willing to try anything different. When he spent the night, his amusement had shortly been overwhelmed by genuine appreciation, even awe. At some juncture in their fierce entanglement, he was briefly reminded of Ben Franklin's advice to a young man in choosing a mistress. But only very briefly, for Fanny was wildly demanding in her giving and taking, and there was no room for introspection while locked in such an Irish jig.

From that first encounter all else had followed. Over a breakfast of black coffee and muffins, he asked her about the stack of posters he had noticed on the floor beside her cluttered desk. They bore the message IT'S A JEW'S WAR!

"They're sticky backs, my bucko." In the early-morning light, dressed in a black velvet robe with a silver fox collar, all she needed was a crown and beard to look like King Cuchulain. Her pale blond hair framed her broad face, netting her brow; her lips, bowed at the ends, were puffed like her shuttered eyes. "My girls paste them up all about in the blackout. 'Tis a fine job."

"You think this is really a Jew's war?" His tone was one of inquiry.

"Me darlin' boy, you poor Americans are so run about by the Jews, you can not see the stones for the brook. To be sure, this whole silly business is a Jew's war—that and the damned high-and-mighty bloody British Tories, God, spit in their tea." She spit in the sink.

He did not argue the point, wanting to draw her out.

She helped him. "Have another muffin or you won't grow strong where strong you should be. I'll lay odds you never tasted the like when you were duckin' the bombs in Poland."

"Never anywhere." He had mentioned Warsaw but not Moscow. "Never anywhere," he repeated. "You are a lady of many talents, all of them impressive." He patted her rear.

She let out a yelp of rough laughter and patted him on the top of the head in return, going to the stove to fetch more coffee. "Would you be knowin' your Roosevelt's a Jew and will be bringin' your country into this bloody war if he can?"

Her statement, not the raving anti-Semitism but her conclusion, caught him. "And you think putting up those—what do you call them?—sticky backs will stop him?"

"You're a nice young bucko, darlin' boy. One day they'll be makin' you a fine ambassador. I like the look of you and the way of you, and I'm not thinkin' you're a silly fool." There was a faint tinge of ridicule in her reply. "But you don't know the real story of what's goin' on here."

"Why don't you tell me? I'd like to know"

"Have you heard of Lord Wilmot and the Association of Peace for All? Wilmot's a fine leader with a seat in the House of Lords, you know." She drew herself up as though she sat next to him. "We members know that behind all the blarney this is a Jew's war. It's not Hitler who's the villain; it's them that's out to spread the war, like they did the last one. Have some more coffee, me darlin' boy."

Over the course of the next month, which included several all-night and morning breakfast sessions with her, he had put the operation together. It was when she told him of her close relationship with Count Asardi that he realized the plan might become workable, and unlike his arrangement with Surov, the results could have the kind of effect he had long been seeking. That Fanny and her titled playmates were a pack of silly anti-Semitic fools was all to the good. Their cocktail meetings at Lord Wilmot's manse and their volunteer sticky back forays he had been able to learn were of no real official concern. What concerned the Chamberlain government was to make sure assiduously that freedom of expression was given full rein—no matter what the expression was.

Recently the matter had been raised in the House of Commons with respect to the pronouncements of all extreme political groups—from the orators in Hyde Park to the more private meetings of the peace advocates. Racial prejudice was frowned upon, of course, but the law granting the widest latitude of public opinion was reiterated.

As for Fanny, he knew almost at once that she wanted something more, something more daring to command her flaming political beliefs. Her father had been killed by the Black and Tans, her mother dead soon after. She had been reared by her aunt in London. At heart she was a militant IRA Sinn Feiner, fiercely hating British authority, wanting to get even, but smart enough to make her way while keeping her bitter prejudices from public view. When she confided to him, almost casually, that her uncle Liam in Dublin was an IRA officer with a way of getting word to friends in Berlin, his plan took firmer shape. It required a single meeting with the count to put it into action.

The Italian-Englishman had had no experience in espionage, but because of his years spent in the United Kingdom and his vast array of contacts, Ciano's Foreign Ministry was anxious to keep him in London. For his part, the count was threatening to retire if he was not recalled soon. Fanny had told Reardon this, and his major concern was to ascertain how closely Asardi was being watched by Scotland Yard.

"My dear fellow, they became tired of watching me long ago. They know I'm aboveboard, a fixture in the diplomatic corps, phaa! Why do you ask?"

He did not explain right away, not until he laid it out for Fanny. The plan thrilled her. "Oh, me fine bucko, I knew you were one of us from the start. Let's be makin' love in celebration!"

"Fanny, wait a moment, hold on! This is not for anyone but us." He took her by the wrists and held them tightly, staring into her eyes. "The three of us. Any more than that, and you could have a rope around your neck."

"Never you fear I'll be speakin' of this to anyone. Never, me darlin' boy. Never." She put a finger to her lips and to his own.

"The question is, Will the count come in?"

He would indeed. Impress Rome, and Ciano would have to give in to his wish to be recalled. They could send some smart SIM lad to replace him, and if they refused, well, he might arrange to be caught and be declared *persona non grata.* He did not confess this last to Fanny but assured her instead that his love for the British side of his family was social, not political. All friendships ceased at the embassy doors. His loyalty was to Italy and the king, not to mention the Duce and the party. "Now what is it exactly that this American puppy has in mind?"

Reardon was pleased with the simplicity of his cell. He would pass information of his choosing to the count via dead drops of his own selection given to Fanny verbally at her flat, the cinema, the park, elsewhere. There would be no communication with the count unless emergency demanded. In that case the call would be direct to Asardi's home, and the conversation would deal with art because the count was a known collector. Details of time changes and locations, or a missed drop, were memorized.

At the outset the essential link had to be established. Without it he was not prepared to act. He wanted assurance that Berlin would be receiving what he was arranging for Asardi to send to Rome. It was Fanny's uncle in Dublin who must provide that assurance with a note to his niece that Molly Flannigan had given birth to a boy.

News of the birth of Sean Flannigan arrived from Dublin on the very day that POTUS—president of the United States—sent his third secret message to Naval Person Churchill. At the time Reardon was aware only of the birth, but when he later lifted a copy of the message from the file room and saw the dates were identical, he knew a sense of long-awaited elation. Somehow the dates were an omen, stoking the flame. He would act.

Now, sitting in the dark, waiting, he contemplated what had gone wrong. Could it be something to do with Dublin, Uncle Liam wanting to be kept informed? Absolutely not. Let Ireland take care of Ireland's own.

When she came bursting through the door, she greeted him with her favorite oath: "McCready's balls!" She delivered it as a full-fledged proclamation.

"What is it?" he asked as she plonked herself down and wrapped her arms around him.

" 'Tis too long you'be been away." She kissed his cheek.

"Fanny, I can't stay now. What's wrong?" He kept his tone matter-of-fact because whatever it was, he didn't want to excite her.

"Do you know someone named Burke? One of the lads came by with the question from Uncle Liam. Liam had the question from Berlin."

Now it was his turn to say "McCready's balls!", although he didn't say it aloud.

4

The garden party at Darby Square was held in a stoned-in courtyard. There was no garden, but an array of uniforms and pastel frocks made up for the lack of bluebells and primroses. There, too, was the delicate birdlike chirping over drinks, the female lilt and the male thrum complementing the April blue sky. From where he stood by the arched entrance, Peter Burke could see a single barrage balloon, looking like a tired turd, hanging immobilely above the rooftops. He was out of sorts, his rude metaphor reflecting his mood.

When he found the invitation in his in box, he had thought of sending regrets, hoping to use Saturday to get in some much needed flying time, not only as an excuse to keep up his proficiency and assure flight pay but, more important, to start establishing RAF connections, which so far had been practically nonexistent. But he had made the mistake of mentioning the invitation to Colonel Mike.

"Burke, Burke"—Marlow had the habit of tugging at his British-style sandy-hued mustache as though to assure himself it was really there—"you must go. Absolutely must. Mal Warwick is a wizard. He does all kinds of tricks. Rabbits out of hats. That sort of thing. Splendid show!"

"Are you going, sir?"

"No. Would like to, but Audrey is dragging me down to Cliveden. Lady Astor, you know. But you go. Represent the staff. Be good for you to meet some of their chaps, maybe a charming miss or two." He whinnied at the thought.

At first Burke had taken the colonel's manner of speaking as put on, but he had soon realized that as a result of Marlow's longevity on the scene he'd become a part of it, his mannerisms in keeping with long-developed habit. His great value as a military attaché was that he knew almost everyone of importance in the British military hierarchy and was trusted by those who could be helpful. Or so Major Dunn had informed Burke.

"Who is Mal Warwick, sir? Does he have anything to do with the RAF?"

"In a manner of speaking. Malcolm is with the War Office, very keen on air power, has an ear for it, you might say. Wait till you see." He gave a knowing bark.

Indeed, he did see, for if there was one feature more commanding than the brightly colored jacket Warwick sported, it was the man's ears. They were large and pointed, actually winged. Not ugly but a challenge to Icarus. Beyond that, Burke was not impressed by his host or the courtyard full of his host's guests, none of whom he knew and all of whom ignored him. Marlow had suggested he go in uniform, but he had chosen not to do so because of his lowly rank, and he now realized that had he, curiosity would have at least put him into the swarm.

The fact was, he admitted to himself, he had a very large bug up his arse, and this carnival of jollity was only adding to a sense of frustration that had been building up for the past two weeks. The center point had been his unwanted meeting with Ambassador Joseph P. Kennedy, the freckle-faced fart!

It was Marlow who had insisted on presenting him. After all, he played golf with Cardinal Joe, attended mass with him and his family, drank to Ireland with him. Who could say? Someday Joe might be president. It was good manners, proper protocol. "You'll like him, Burke. He can be very helpful."

Helpful. He had a very strong presentiment against such an introduction. Uncle Bertie had made it clear that Kennedy was not being informed of the mission. He could not confide this to Marlow who was not informed either, and he had been instructed not to contact Henry

Sutterby, the one person who could have headed off the meeting. Instead, insult was added to insult because Marlow, for all his insistence in arranging the introduction, received a last-minute call from Sir Samuel Hoare, the newly appointed air minister, to come running, old boy, old boy, and Second Lieutenant Burke had been left to keep the appointment. The kindly secretary had shown him into an office with brick walls painted a robin's-egg blue. But it was not the incongruous decor or the array of vases decked with spring flowers that roiled his memory; it was the occupant. He sat at a long corner desk, sleeves rolled up, back to his caller. He did not turn, rise, or say anything. The light coming in through the curtained window revealed that his sandy pelt was thinning. Burke had focused his gaze on its center point and waited.

When the ambassador did turn, he had a paper in his hand, and he did not look up from it. "Where's Marlow?" he asked, the voice nasal, high-pitched.

"He was called to the Air Ministry, sir."

"Well, what is he wasting my time for?" The broad brogue of Boston gave an added edge to his obvious annoyance.

"I have no idea, sir." His reply and tone raised the ambassador's gaze to one of inspection. The horn-rimmed glasses did nothing to soften the force of hard blue eyes.

"Who the hell are you? What do you want?"

"Colonel Marlow wished to introduce me, sir. I've been assigned to his staff. I'm Second Lieutenant Peter Burke, sir."

The ambassador swung around in his chair, back to him again.

"Well, you tell Mike the next time he wants to waste my valuable time passing wind, he'd better be on hand. I don't recall receiving any word of your being assigned here, Lieutenant. What are you supposed to be doing?"

"I'm here on TDY, sir, as an observer to study the RAF Fighter Command defenses." He'd wondered as he replied whether it would have been wiser to skirt the inquiry.

He received an instantaneous answer. "You're what!" The ambassador came around and out of his chair as though propelled. "You're what did you say?" His reddish complexion had taken on a deeper hue, the vehemence startling to Burke.

He had tried to explain and got no farther than the plan of assignment when Kennedy began shouting. "The goddamned fools will do anything to get us in this war! Why wasn't I told? Observing, my foot! The War Department will pull any trick to get us involved. I suppose as an observer you'd like to go over to France and fly a few sorties, would you? You bet your ass you would. Or maybe you'd like to go on a bombing raid to Narvik or Oslo!" The man was beside himself, spitting through his teeth with rage, shaking the paper he held in his hand. "Well, I'll tell you something, young man, you're not flying anywhere with the RAF, not so long as I'm here. You tell Marlow I want to see him, and you—you can start packing."

"Sir, I'm only here to observe, to learn ground operations, not to fly missions," he managed to say.

"Don't tell me what you're here to do. I know damn well what's behind this. Now get out of here before I throw you out."

His own anger had risen as the ambassador had spewed his anger in a fine mist through jutting teeth. He was purposely standing in a brace, staring straight ahead, not at the man and his fist-shaking gestures. When the threat was made, he did look at him, a great hollow feeling in his gut as their gazes locked.

"I'll get out of here, sir," he said quietly, "but you won't throw me out of anywhere." For an instant he wondered if a punch was coming his way.

"Get out," Kennedy repeated, his voice now suddenly contained, and turning, he went back to his desk.

Later, when Colonel Mike returned from Kennedy's urgently demanded summons, his color had an ashen tinge, and he was breathing as though he had been running. It required several tries to get his pipe lit, and it was only after he'd taken a series of rapid puffs and stopped waving the match, long extinguished, that he addressed Burke.

" 'Fraid he's in a bit of a tear, Burke. You caught him in a bad moment."

"I hope he doesn't have too many of them, sir."

Marlow glanced up from fiddling with a golf ball on his desk. "I explained that you were not at fault for the situation, and he understands that; but he said you were impertinent, disrespectful, Burke."

"He made a physical threat, sir."

"Just words. He has an Irish temper, and his being upset is not exactly without cause, you know. He believes State and the War Department are trying to block his access to the president, particularly now that things are heating up. On top of that he believes the British are not being forthcoming about their losses in Norway, that Hitler completely outsmarted them. His family is here, and he's begun to worry about their safety. I'm speaking to you in strictest confidence, Burke, you understand. The ambassador is really a very charming and warmhearted man."

"I'm sorry I missed that side of him, sir," he said with a smile, and Marlow had nodded, coughing on a throatful of smoke.

"What about my duty, sir? Has he shot it down?"

"We'll have to work carefully, Burke. Back off a bit. He's willing to let you remain as my aide. Major Dunn is going off on a tour of RAF installations in France. Perhaps when he returns, we can set something up."

"But, sir, it would be perfect if I could go along with him."

"Out of the question, my boy. Things have to calm down. I need you here."

"Damn it all, sir, if I'd only kept my mouth shut."

"Hard lines, as they say, Lieutenant. We'll work something out."

"What about Norway and Denmark, sir? Do you think Hitler's pulling another Poland?"

"Difficult to say. Our friends have buttoned up, gotten very tight-lipped. Paddy Beaumont-Nesbitt, chief of MI, has become a clam. Slessor did indicate to me that Bomber Command is giving a good account of itself, and the Royal Navy—well, you know what the press is saying about victories in the fjords. But there is a devilish question, and it is, I'm afraid, a question that had Kennedy badly upset when you called on him. The timing of the British plan to go into Norway—the plan to make a landing at Narvik, to tighten the blockade and cut off the ore supplies—was terribly top secret. Well, apparently from what we can gather, the date was compromised. Hitler got there first, not by days but by hours. How could he have known? Poor timing on the Admiralty's part, the War Office? The ambassador believes it was bad security, sloppy intelligence. Nazi spies and that sort of thing. He believes that's why they've all clammed up, become standoffish. They won't tell him anything, and he's furious."

"No more than I," Burke had muttered, but his reaction was as much to cover the impact of Marlow's revelation as it was its result.

In his mind there flashed a picture of Scott Reardon, gesturing. Could the bastard have been capable of tipping off the Nazis on the timing of the British move? It hardly seemed likely but—

Since their luncheon at the Bull and Bear he had had no contact with Reardon. It was certainly not for lack of trying: numerous phone calls to the consular section; one personal attempt to find he was not in; notes left in the guy's mailbox. No response to anything. The message was soon plain enough. For some reason Reardon did not wish to continue the association, and what had started out with surprising promise had gone up in cigarette smoke. It sure threw prop wash in his trying to find out if the guy was a Nazi spy. Between Kennedy and Reardon, he was spinning his wheels, getting nowhere.

Marlow had put him to work compiling British aircraft production figures, such as could be obtained. Last week they had driven down to Tangmere in the colonel's Chrysler. It was the RAF's poshest fighter base, and his hopes had soared although Marlow had not been forthcoming on the purpose of their visit. The sight of Spits and Hurricanes parked in the revetments and the sound of aircraft alive and in motion had put a smile on his face. But it was the officers' mess that the colonel had homed in on, and although Wing Commander Pritchard and his squadron COs entertained them royally, they had been guests, enjoying good scotch, not a pair of U.S. air officers who had come for an important briefing.

"My, if you aren't standoffish and fierce." The lilting voice jerked him back into the courtyard.

She had a beguiling look, a slightly rueful expression which he immediately liked. Her eyes chased the goblins from his thoughts.

"I am fierce," he said, "but only standoffish when I'm stood off."

"Well, bless me, you're the Yank."

"Himself. But how did you know?" Her lips, he decided, said, "Kiss me if you can."

"Your colonial accent gives you away. Aren't you a military officer? Mal said he thought it would be jolly to have some of you attaché chaps. Are you Colonel Marlow?"

Her nose had a saucy tilt, and he knew she was playing games, knew that he wasn't Marlow. She was wearing a pale green something and a wide-brimmed spring hat. "My uniform is at the cleaners. I like yours. I'm Lieutenant Burke." He held out his hand.

"Claire Hollier, Lieutenant." She had a small hand and a firm grip. "You have a first name, I'm sure."

"Peter."

"Peter." She tried it out. "I must say that's a nice British-sounding name."

"Not really. More Scotch-Irish."

"Part of the empire. Tell me, why are you standing over here all by yourself? Are you shy?"

"Well, I'll tell you, Claire, the welcome was so overwhelming, typically English, I suppose, that I just had to stand back and adjust my carburetor heat before landing."

"How droll. Your glass is empty. Come along, and we'll see if we can fix your—what is it?—carburetor heat."

He followed her, noting that she curved nicely in all the right places, that he liked the dark tone and style of her hair, but that with all the clever repartee he sensed her manner was forced, put on. Still, she was damned good-looking, sexy, and what more did a lonely aviator in war-torn London need?

She introduced him to Cynthia and Cedric, Pamela and Dudley, Audrey and Oliver, and many others, but the host, Malcolm Warwick, was the only one he'd remember. It wasn't the man's ears or the long, lean length of him, or his quick hands plucking bright ribbons out of the air to the applause of the assembled, or even the mellifluous quality of his far-reaching voice. It was that he exuded a definite sense of command, of authority and dominance behind a prissy manner.

"Well, I'm glad to see that Claire has taken you in tow. Had me worried for a bit. Never knew a remote American, thought you might be ill. You're not ill, are you? Of course not. Tell me, Lieutenant, do you like jazz? I mean, real jazz? Sidney Bechet on the saxophone sort of jazz." He didn't wait for an answer, didn't really care. "Of course you do. I fell in love with jazz in America long ago. The saxophone is my favorite. Do you happen to play the saxophone, Lieutenant? I rather doubt it." He hee-hawed a hearty bellow. "You play airplanes, don't you? Which reminds me, where did my favorite Irish-American flying officer fly off to? France, to visit with the lads?"

"I think it was the ballet, sir. He asked me to convey his regrets, a last-minute invitation from the ambassador he couldn't avoid."

"Ho-ho, I'll bet he couldn't. You know Michael's charming wife,

Audrey, was a ballet dancer, and I understand she's very close to Mrs. Kennedy. Tell Michael I understand fully and extend my sympathies. Oh, my, yes. And what about Major Dunn? Did he go to the ballet, too?"

"No, sir, I believe he's out of the city."

"Well, at least you were free to come, Lieutenant, and we're grateful for that, aren't we, Claire?" He beamed down at her, laying his hand on her shoulder. "Tell me, Lieutenant, have you had a chance to visit any of our flying stations?"

"Not in any detail as yet, sir."

"But you'd like to, I'm sure." The grin revealed that his teeth were large and irregular.

Other guests had moved in to bask in Warwick's aura. His attention turned to them, and Claire took Burke by the hand and led him away. His mood, instead of softening under Claire Hollier's touch, had reverted.

"What are you scowling at now?" She was prying again.

"Besides the ribbon tricks and playing jazz, what does he do?"

He saw momentary annoyance in her expression. Then she laughed, a bright, tinkling sound, like a soft breeze amidst chimes. "Dour, that's what you are, a dour Scot. Mal does something with the War Office. I believe he also does something with the Air Ministry, which could be of benefit to you if you are interested in that sort of thing. Why are you Americans always so quick to judge?"

She was lightly giving him hell, and he grinned. "I'm sorry. It's just that he, you, all of you here give me a feeling of never-never land."

"What does that mean, exactly?" The lightness was gone.

"You see that barrage balloon?" He nodded toward the ugly gray bag. "Well, it's a reminder, like the sandbags piled up and the blackout and the gas masks we're all carrying that—"

"That there's a war on," she finished for him.

"Yes, and all the while we've been here, there hasn't been a word I've heard from anyone, in uniform or out, that such is the case."

"And that disturbs you." He could see the color rising in her cheeks. "You'd feel better if we stood around guessing what's going on in Norway or when Hitler will send his bombers or attack through the Lowlands." Her voice had become very clipped.

"I don't care what you guess just so long as you indicate you know it's there." He gestured toward the balloon. He realized his own frustration was showing, and he was taking it out on the wrong person.

"I could tell you, Lieutenant, that it's our war, and we'll handle it as we choose; but this is Saturday, and we'd just as soon talk of other things in spite of your concern."

"Nothing like a five-day-a-week war to keep the morale up," he cracked.

She took a deep breath, slim body elegant in its rigidity. "You're impossible!"

"You're right." He backed off, realizing he was being foolish. "I apologize. You've been very kind and patient." He held out his hand. "It's time I took off. Maybe you'll give me your phone number so I can try again."

The tenseness and annoyance vanished. She took his hand. "Splendid. But I have a much better idea. Where are you staying? I'll give you a lift."

The offer was totally unexpected. "Well, I don't want to take you away from your friends." But suddenly he knew he'd like to.

She had a teasing smile. "Where are you staying?" she repeated.

"At the Cumberland."

"By Marble Arch. Grand. Just the way I'm going. Come along, and we'll make our obeisance to Mal . . . and friends."

Her car was a snappy little Morris roadster with the top down. She drove it as he'd anticipated, too fast and with quick reflexes. He observed her out of the corner of his eye, liked the fine flexibility of her thigh, her hand moving adroitly from wheel to clutch knob as she shifted up and down. In spite of rationing, the traffic was heavy; it had been a mild day, and the move was to get off the roads by dark. "Everyone a Cinderella," he said.

"What does that mean?" She glanced at him.

"Means your car will turn into a pumpkin if you don't get it under wraps before blackout time."

"Oh, I see." She nodded, eyes on the vehicle cutting in ahead, touching the brake and shifting down. "But Cinderella had until midnight."

"No blackout."

"Oh, I drive very well in the dark of night."

"Then we have until the clock strikes twelve," he said in reply, not really meaning it.

"Why not?" she tossed back at him, looking straight ahead.

Her response both surprised and stimulated him. Was she playing games? Hell, the whole affair had been some kind of put-on cricket match. It had a feeling of being staged. He did not take her up on the offer, waiting to see if she'd add anything. She didn't, swinging around Duke of Wellington Place, concentrating on the pedestrians as well as the vehicular traffic. "You haven't told me what you do," he said.

"Oh, I shall, I shall." She laughed, and he didn't know whether it was the question or the answer that brought her reaction. She seemed to be a creature of quick-changing moods. The delicate, finely molded features combined with the delicate, finely molded manner of speaking, the product of a thousand years of hip and thigh touching, added a vanilla icing to the cake.

"A ha'penny for your thoughts," she said, tossing him a quick, cagey smile as though she knew exactly what he was thinking. She had taken off her hat when they had gotten in the car, and the breeze was doing Medusa-like things to her hair.

"I was wondering," he said, "how your magician friend, Mal keeps from being airborne in a strong wind."

For an instant she stared at him, eyes wide, lips parted, and then she let go with a howl of laughter, and he joined in, relieved that her reaction to his reply indicated a sense of humor.

She parked around the corner from the hotel in a side pocket court, indicating that she was familiar with the area. He had decided he would ask for her phone number and then later determine whether he wished to get to know her better. He knew damned well that he would.

She switched off the engine and swung around to face him.

"I want to thank you," he said, extending his hand, "and I'd like to—"

"Wouldn't you like to invite me in?"

The invitation, the come-hither look on her face startled him but really did not surprise him all that much; the lady was a quick-change artist. God knows, since Eleanor, his connection with the fair sex had been monkish. His recall to active duty had kept him too busy to seek solace in the arms of a new Eleanor. Now suddenly he was faced with a proposition by a desirable and obviously desirous witch. Who was he to refuse, in spite of her quirky British manner? Bed would take care of that.

"Yes, I would like to invite you in," he said. "You really don't mind driving in the blackout?"

"I do it regularly," she said. "It's part of my job."

"Well, then, be my guest." He opened the door with a flourish.

As they walked to the hotel's front entrance, he wondered if Hatton, the porter, would react to his escorting a young lady to his chambers and quickly decided he didn't give a damn how he reacted. He knew that some of the single boarders like himself brought elegant ladies of the night from Piccadilly for a cup of tea or two with not so much as a lifted eyebrow, and this leggy lady was no Piccadilly belle.

Hatton barely gave them a glance as they crossed the lobby to the lift, she busily chatting about how easy it was to drive in the blackout once you got the hang of never driving over twenty. He was not listening to her, wondering if he had anything to offer her to drink and then remembering the bottle of scotch Colonel Mike had presented him as a welcoming gift. He had to laugh at himself, but he didn't because suddenly he was both excited and nervous, like a virgin at a fraternity party, he mused as they ascended.

She had ceased her witty chatter, and as they walked down the corridor, he was hoping that Julian, who went with his quarters for an extra shilling, had cleaned up the mess from his newly arrived trunk. He became aware that he had become singularly silent. He glanced at her, and she was looking straight ahead, expressionless. "You will not find my dwelling anything to write home about, probably in somewhat of a mess, I fear."

"I'm sure it will be fine," she said stiffly.

"I do have some scotch." He said it almost apologetically and was annoyed at himself for saying it at all, callow youth with tightly buttoned fly. She made no reply, and as they reached his door, he turned his back to her, and as he concentrated on getting the correct key in the lock, a warning bell rang. Why the sudden change in temperature? Was she, too, nervous over the obviousness of her picking him up, or was this to be another Lisbon attempt? *Watch your tail, pal.* He swung the door open and stepped aside. She marched past him.

The room was full of twilight, the blackout curtains not yet drawn.

He was pleased to see Julian had removed the trunk. She was standing by the window, fishing in her purse for a lighter, cigarette between her lips, the light from without brushing her features with a hard cast that he had not previously observed. Suddenly she looked older.

He moved across the room, matches in hand, excited, alert, eager for whatever was to come. "Allow me," he said.

She allowed him, exhaled quickly, and waved the smoke away as though it had intruded. "Peter," she said, eyeing him coldly, "this is not what I may have led you to believe." Her voice possessed a remote quality, the seductive role completely iced over.

Even though he was somewhat prepared for it, he had been hoping, and her quick and cold rejection angered him. "And what would that be?"

"Please," she said, stepping around him as though he might be planning to pin her into the corner, "let's not play games."

"Babe"—he snorted—"you've been playing games since you homed in on me at your magic man's tea party. What's the score? What do you want?"

"Your Mr. Scott Reardon is the score." She sat down and began rummaging in her purse again.

For an instant he wondered if she was going to pull a gun. "Who's he?" He was damned if he was going to play to her lead. She didn't answer, still occupied with getting a pad out of her purse, and he crossed to the kitchen alcove, sure he was going to have a scotch whether she had one or not.

"He's the gentleman you had lunch with at the Bull and Bear on Friday, the fifth of April."

"I don't remember seeing you there"—he found the bottle—"and I'm sure I would have remembered. I invited you for a scotch. Are you going to join me?" He turned and looked at her, bottle in hand.

"Yes . . . please. I felt it was better we talk here."

"Of course. . . . Well, go ahead and talk, Claire. Tell me about Scott Reardon."

He found a couple of glasses and began fixing the drinks in the alcove.

"I'll wait if you don't mind. I'd rather not shout."

"No, that would never do. I suppose it was too noisy at the party to talk seriously and too busy in the traffic." He was not enjoying his own sarcasm, but on the one hand, she had pissed him off with her come-hither act, and on the other, he didn't know if she was the British security agent Uncle Bertie had said would make contact or someone from the other side. She didn't look dangerous, but how did he know who or what she really was? He brought the drink in his hands. "Pardon the informality. I'm not used to being unpropositioned so adroitly."

She took the glass. "Thank you. Now, can we stop this, Lieutenant, and talk seriously?"

He stared at her for a moment quizzically, and she met his gaze, her rather large hazel eyes steady, cool, apologies over. "All right, talk seriously," he said, "but stop taking me for a damn fool." He decided to remain standing.

She stubbed out her cigarette and set down her glass. He was thinking she had her notebook in her lap so she wouldn't have to look up at him. "As I said, you were in the pub with Reardon."

"Wait a minute. Who are you anyway? Who is it you represent?"

"If you wish to call Mr. Henry Sutterby, counselor at your embassy, he'll vouch for me. I work for a rather dull department in the War Office."

"You may be sure I will check. Go on."

She went back to her pad. "We believe that unknowingly you assisted Mr. Reardon in passing secret information to an Italian agent, Count Clarence Giovanni della Ponte Asardi. We—"

"I *what?*" He nearly spilled his drink, immediately furious.

Matter-of-factly she recited the encounter over his new raincoat and the cigar cylinder returned to the stricken Asardi.

"Obviously you didn't know what was in the container."

"Did you know, or whoever you had there taking it all in?" He was seething. "If you did, why the hell didn't you put a stop to it right then? And if you didn't know, how do you know it wasn't a cigar?"

"Peter," she said gently, giving him benediction, "do calm yourself. No one is blaming you for anything. Reardon is too smart by half. He apparently was using you, and you happened to catch Count Asardi in the act. A rather stupid act, I might add."

"You're right about that. So why didn't you act?"

"Because until that moment there was no connection between Reardon and the count. Inadvertently, to be sure, you made the connection.

So we have you to thank." She gave him a wan smile. "Why don't you stop pacing and sit down?"

He was on the verge of saying he would pace as long as he pleased. Instead, he said, "You still haven't told me why they weren't picked up then and there."

"It would have been shortsighted. There must be others in the ring, and we would like to get them all at the same time."

He supposed that made good sense. Uncle Bertie had used the same reasoning, but— "How do you propose to do that?"

"Count Asardi has been a fixture at the Italian Embassy for many years. His mother was English, and he's a graduate of Cambridge. More often than not, outside the diplomatic circle, he is taken to be British. Unfortunately security and Scotland Yard have long considered him harmless. He's not military. At any rate it's now believed he's linked to Reardon, and there is some idea by whom." She put down her glass and gave him her best garden party smile. "How would you like to take me to Fanny's Tara?"

He sighed. "Back to the playing field again, hey?"

"Yes, only we're playing on the same team. Fanny's is a charming spot, run by a delightful Sinn Feiner, Fanny O'Rourke. Along with her singing, her music making and happy clientele, her place is a hotbed of antiwar, anti-Semitic, pro-fascist peace lovers. Very well-to-do lot, I might add. Fanny and I have become quite friendly. She believes I'm in sympathy with her cause. Fanny is also Count Asardi's mistress, has been for years."

He saw the connection. "So you're wondering if maybe Reardon and Fanny are also friends?"

"Something like that. There's no evidence they are."

"Then how come you're playing games with Fanny?"

"Part of my job and quite apart from this affair."

"You're a busy girl. How will our going to have a cup of beer with Fanny prove anything one way or the other?"

"It probably won't; but my introducing you, an American who sympathizes with the cause of appeasement, will improve my relationship with her, and it will give you an entrance that may be useful in the future."

"All depends on what you mean by that," he said wryly. "Wouldn't it make more sense to get Reardon to take you there?"

Her reply surprised him. "I have that in mind."

"You know him?"

"He's taken me out several times." She put her pad back in her purse.

"My"—he laughed—"you do get around. What's he like?"

"Smooth, arrogant, dangerous." She rose. "And determined to seduce me."

"Well, bully for him. I can hardly blame him for that." He was still rankled at her for leading him on. "There is one small point we'd better get straight," he said, turning away from her look. "Since that coat trick at the Bull and Bear, Reardon has shunned me like the plague. Won't have anything to do with me." As he spoke, he picked up her glass with his own and carried them to the alcove. "So obviously he knows or suspects I'm here for reasons other than my official job. He must have been informed right after my arrival by someone there or someone here. Do you know what happened to me in Lisbon?" She shook her head, and he told her.

"That does complicate things a bit, doesn't it?" she said. "This could reach all the way to your country, to Washington."

"Hard to figure how. Only a very few people, all of them very high, knew the reason for my being here."

"All it takes is one of a very few. Have you notified anyone there?"

"No. I'm under orders not to notify anyone of anything until I hit pay dirt."

"Well, let's go see if you can—as you say—hit pay dirt with Fanny. You'll love her songs."

"And my name—who am I supposed to be?"

"I'll let you decide that." She moved across the room toward the door. He followed her.

"And to think I invited you here for an evening of delight."

"Better luck next time, old top," she tossed over her shoulder.

"Tell me before I let you out of here, who do you work for?"

"Malcolm Warwick. I polish his crystal ball."

He awoke from a troubled sleep in the hour before dawn, emerging from a ragged-edged swirl of dreams in which he saw his brother Rod's P-26 plummeting out of the sky, the Iron Duke slashing unsuccessfully at saxophone with his riding crop, and Claire and Fanny, arms linked on shoulders, performing a dance to wild music and a cheering throng.

The vestiges of the dream faded as reality took hold, and he lay in the dark with the sour taste of tobacco and too much alcohol stuffing his mouth. It was Claire, or rather what he had not told her, that had taken root in his subconscious and worried him into wakefulness.

Neither the club nor Fanny had been what he had anticipated. She had two fiddlers and a pianist with a shaved head, and as the evening had moved along, progressing from cakes and ale to brandy, the soft, sad melodies of Erin had transposed to stirring rhythms that grew in vibrance and passion. The atmosphere approaching closing time became electric, diners clapping in unison, some calling out in Gaelic, others cheering, led on by Fanny.

It was all Fanny. At first, when she had sat beside him, her thigh pressed up against his, reading his palm, he had thought of her as a green-eyed Gypsy. Later, when she had joined her musicians and belted out a wild lament from County Cork, he decided whatever she was, she wasn't queen of the fairies.

Mostly, he was pleased that Claire had entered the spirit of the evening and had stopped playing mother superior. He was full of fine feeling for her and too much to drink when he excused himself to go hunt for the loo. He was returning from a successful visit when his eye took in a side entrance across the room with its low ceiling, its blocky beams, and its dim lighting. The entrance was thinly screened with a curtain of hanging cords, and what caught his attention was a movement of the cords, followed by the realization that someone was standing behind them. The light was such that he detected the vaguest glimpse of a turning head, caught minutely in profile, then disappearing, the cords shaking lightly as the door behind was closed.

He had stopped in his tracks, trying to refocus on what he had observed, the impact of recognition on eye and mind playing tricks. Had he seen what he'd seen? Scott Reardon standing there, watching? He'd been tempted to cross the room and find out where the door led, but he had had no chance, for Fanny had spotted him, grabbed him by the arm, and said, "Come on, me bucko, you and I will be throwin' a shoe or two."

When they had gone out into the blackout at closing time, he had not told Claire. He supposed it was partly because he had drunk too much and knowing something she didn't know gave him a superior feeling, and then, what the hell, he'd probably been seeing things anyway.

Now, awake and more sober, his head starting to ache, he knew he should have told her for her own protection. If it had been Reardon and he had seen them together, she could be in trouble not just with Reardon but with Fanny as well.

Suddenly he was grinning. She had given him her number in case of emergency. He now had an excellent excuse to call her, to see her again, like today. Maybe Scott Reardon was going to come in handy after all.

5

The printing on the pale yellow jacket for the score read: "Symphony No. 41 in C—The Jupiter, by Wolfgang Amadeus Mozart." Between its covers there were no pages of music. Instead, there were thirty-three documents, some several pages in length, typed single-spaced on flimsies. These were mostly estimates of Allied military strength as gathered by the military attaché's office for the War Department, signed "Marlow for Marshall." The most significant of these was Major Truly's detailed cable, revealing portions of the BEF's order of battle in France, containing evidence that its armor consisted of a single light tank brigade numbering a hundred tanks, twenty-three of which mounted two-pound cannons, the rest .30 caliber machine guns.

Reardon enjoyed the thought that the War Department would not accept any part of the estimates that did not support its own wishful thinking, but certainly there were those in the Oberkommando who would find them of interest, as they would all the rest. Of the rest, three were cables from fat-ass Churchill to Roosevelt, covering the expansion of the U.S. Neutrality Act, doubling the zones U.S. ships could enter around the British Isles and congratulating the president on his freezing of Norwegian and Danish assets, plus his announcement that Greenland was "inside the Monroe Doctrine." The prize was the highly pessimistic cable from Kennedy to Hull on the British lack of preparedness, reporting that British territorials, supported by French Chausseurs Alpine forces, were being roundly defeated in an attempt to take Trondheim and that the Germans had seized, or were about to seize, the key railhead at Stören. In short, the Allied effort to capture Narvik was not succeeding, and Kennedy was predicting that the "bore war" had ended and it would not be long before the British would be suing for peace. Even while the fighting in Norway was going on, RAF bombing efforts over Germany consisted of dropping tons of the *Volkiger Beobachter,* a propaganda newspaper filled with cartoons and jokes. The whole effort was a joke. As soon as Hitler had driven the Allies out of Norway, he'd launch his much awaited spring offensive. Kennedy reported a lengthy talk with Lord Dalkeith, "a realist" who not only believed Hitler was willing to be reasonable but apparently spoke for a growing minority in the Parliament that was determined to find a way to bring peace, possibly with a new government headed by Lord Halifax. It all made for very important reading in the proper hands, and Reardon had held his impatience at bay as he had carefully selected the material and smuggled it out of the embassy in order to get it to the right hands.

The past three weeks had been a time of danger and of frustration. Danger stimulated the flame. Frustration made it dance irregularly. The latter was time-directed—the time it took to repair the damage while events in Norway were rattling the Chamberlain government. Now the frustration was ended, but the danger remained, its stimulus staccato—*tadum-tadum-tadum.*

He reached Trafalgar Square, heading for the National Gallery, the sky a summery blue, the base of Nelson's Column decked with noon-hour lunchers and rude pigeons. He sensed in the air a heightened level of alertness, the press posters black with news of Narvik fighting and new landings, naval sinkings, air attacks. Beneath the flow of traffic and pedestrians ran a pianissimo theme of excitement; it blended with his mood. He paused at the corner, checking the traffic, and an owl-faced little man moved up beside him and piped, "Say, mate, whatcha got there, yer fowlin' piece for the 'un?"

His query brought the attention of others waiting, and Reardon, instead of ignoring the question, replied, "Come to the concert at the gallery and see for yourself."

" 'Tain't me line, thanks all the same, mate." The little man scuttled out into the street, dodging a biker.

"Young man, if you please, what is the program for today?" asked a spinsterish lady in a shy voice, almost a whisper.

"We're doing Mozart's *Jupiter.*"

"Oh, how splendid." She glowed, faded eyes wide with appreciation.

"May I accompany you?" he said, gallantly offering his arm, quick to seize the reed of opportunity no matter how thin. Concealment was all, but it could be stripped away in an instant. Hadn't his own concealment at Fanny's further exposed Burke and also exposed Claire Hollier? So then.

With the somewhat overwhelmed music lover holding on, they traversed the square, he keeping the conversation sprightly. No, his instrument case did not contain an oboe but a bassoon, and yes, it was quite heavy since the wood was maple and the keys were nickel. Indeed, he did think the idea of a daily noon concert by volunteers, originated by Dame Myra Hess, was a grand one, and he only wished he could participate more frequently. Did she prefer Mozart to Haydn or Beethoven to Brahms? He was pleased to think that if some Scotland Yard Special Branch gumshoe were on his trail, he would have quite a time describing this little lady as an enemy of the crown or a bleedin' Nazi spy.

"Isn't it a lovely day?" she exulted as they reached the gallery steps. "If it weren't for those ridiculous-looking balloons, I could almost forget this beastly war."

"Mozart will help, I'm sure."

Ordinarily he would have entered by a side door on Orange Street and gone directly to the dressing room. Instead, he carried his role of escort to the fullest, going up the steps with her, down the corridor to the rotunda and seeing her to her seat, leaving her full of appreciation and a touch of pride as others in the gathering audience took notice.

There were a dozen or so musicians in the greenroom, all making their preparations. Since he had not been able to attend the one rehearsal, the only person he recognized was Anton. He did not look at him. He hung his gas mask kit on the assigned wall hook and busied himself taking the score and the bassoon sections out of the case and fitting the pieces together.

He was excited. As long as Anton played his part as well as he played his violin, the plan must work. He could thank Fanny. She was his good-luck piece. She had wanted to attend the concert, but he had said absolutely not. The impact of his spotting Burke with Claire Hollier was so deeply etched that he could still feel his reaction; smell, taste, and sound fused within the wallop of recognition and its meaning.

Then he had waited for Fanny, knowing the present plan was no longer workable. The contact with Asardi was finished. He must find a new one.

He looked up from fitting the wing joint to the boot of the bassoon and saw Anton staring at him across the body of his violin as he appeared to concentrate on tuning the instrument. Anton was frowning, his eyes narrowed, as though listening to sound as he ran the bow across the strings. The expression was similar to the one he had worn at their first meeting. "Anton Codreanu, at your service." Fanny had arranged it.

She had been consumed by rage when he had identified Claire's American guest. "Oh, my God!" Her face had gone white. "You mean he's the bloody bastard Uncle Liam warned about!"

It had taken some time to calm her. In fact, he himself had to shout. "For Christ's sake, shut up and listen to me!" He swore at her, feigning his own anger. But it had worked, and out of it had come Anton Codreanu, who was now obviously worried. Was it natural worry, or was something wrong?

He looked away, taking in the room, filled now with members of the orchestra, some beginning to drift toward the entrance to the concert stage. Having performed here on two previous occasions, he knew the form, and his quick glance revealed nothing out of order. He looked again at Anton, who had turned away and was facing the wall with its racks for instrument cases and adjoining hooks for jackets, gas masks, whatever. He rose and went past him, heading for the stage, and as he went by, he coughed and through the sound said, "Twenty-four."

"Three," the violinist said without turning.

So that was that. Although they had decided on the number beforehand, Codreanu, he decided, was making doubly sure, and that was all to the good. He took his assigned seat, surprised at the growing size of the audience. Wryly he thought; *Maybe it's the cucumber sandwiches and tea served afterward that's drawing them.* He busied himself placing the score on the music stand and arranging the instrument, using the neck strap to take some of the weight off his arms. The flame was burning low and bright. He felt pride in having reestablished a means of contact that was beautiful in its simplicity and could be executed in such a fashion, all to the sound of great music, although that remained to be heard. The continuing danger was the original one, of getting caught carrying the loot out of the embassy. So far the security checks that Kennedy had instituted were a joke. There wasn't a soul in the place, including Burke the Jerk, who could conceive of his method of removing documents from the index files. All so simple. With keys and timing he could lift anything. The only question was, Did he continue to ignore Burke . . . or should he take direct action?

He watched Anton take his place in the violin section, thinking that on the night of discovery, when Fanny had suggested the Romanian as a replacement for the count, he had not been receptive. Romanians were the most notorious robbers and double-dealers in Europe, he had told her. "Who is he? What does he do at the embassy?"

"Possibly he's a chauffeur or a clerk. I don't ask questions, me darlin'. He does what I ask him. I do know his brother Corneliu was an Iron Guard leader. He was executed by order of King Carol two years ago, and like me, Anton will never forgive or forget."

A week later, in Fanny's flat, he had met the unforgiving Romanian who doubled as a player of gypsy music at the club twice a week.

Short, bushy-haired, round-faced, Anton Codreanu blended in with his fellow violinists. Using the National Gallery daily concert as a point of rendezvous was a masterstroke. The idea had sprung forth with recognition that in the past both men had performed at the noon musicale, although at different concerts. All that was needed was to coordinate, a matter of selecting a date when both could be free and informing Sir Sidney's office accordingly. Clockwork. The rest, the method by which he would put his own composition into Anton's hands, simple enough, but—

"Anton, I know your country is sitting on a spiked fence. How can I be sure that what I pass to you will reach the right hands in Berlin?"

"You can't." He spoke in a soft, mild-mannered tone, the accent attractive. "No more than I can be sure what you pass to me is worth risking my neck in trying. We both have reasons for what we attempt. We do what we can, yes?"

Yes. It was an acceptance of mutual trust without any real basis for trust, an arrangement old Surov would have had him shot for. It was that or having no other option than to quit, to cease, to crawl back in his hole, as he would never do. That, and his finely tuned instincts, his intuition. And now, by God, it was working out!

The handclapping brought him back to center stage. Diminutive and white-maned, Sir Sidney pranced forth to the podium and addressed the audience in his peerless, if shrill, tones: "Jolly good to see you all gathered here. Most heartwarming to know our frail efforts are appreciated while all the world seems to be coming apart. Yes. Today we are being very ambitious in applying our meager talents to Mozart's glorious *Jupiter* symphony. All of us, as you know, are volunteers in the cause, and I believe with you that the cause is just. So we shall get on with it. Yes!"

To the sound of enthusiastic applause he turned to face the orchestra, baton raised, and on the downbeat they were off and playing.

It wasn't too bad, Reardon thought, as the double theme of the allegro was established. The string section injected a nice touch of lightness; he observed Anton hard at it. And so it went along, his confidence secure, the music a delightful umbrella for all else.

Reflectively he began to note audience reaction, seeking out the little lady he had escorted. The impact of whom he spotted, instead, was a shocking blow, jerking his head back. *Claire Hollier!* She was sitting in a middle row, looking chic and smart and totally out of place. She had never impressed him as a noonday classical music lover. His automatic reaction was to look for Burke. He found no Burke.

She appeared to be alone, the callow youth on her right absorbed in a copy of the score, trying to match notes with sound, the austere oldster on her left being pestered by his squirrely frau, distracting him with whispered asides. So what did Hollier's presence mean? No doubt after the concert she would meet him by accident. And then what? More to the point, how could she have known he was performing today? Only Sir Sidney or Dame Myra would have known. And Anton!

He glanced at the Romanian, who appeared to be completely absorbed in helping Mozart survive the grand effort. Suddenly he felt a great cold knot take root in his diaphragm. It impeded his playing, his breathing.

Good Christ!

It came home to him as the strings muted, the basses repeated four bars, and the bassoons established the new melody. He did not know what notes he was playing or if his fellow bassoonist was managing. He knew only that Claire Hollier's striking face had brought the ghastly face of reality into shuddering form. Anton had double-crossed him!

He had grasped at Codreanu all too swiftly . . . *too swiftly* . . . *too swiftly . . . too swiftly!* Should have done *nothing! Nothing! Nothing! Devise a proper plan! No proper plan!*

Move out of here quickly. Never mind tea and Hollier. He was sweating, a cold sweat.

You are one dumb bastard.

He didn't know if the voice was Surov's or his own, nor did it matter. Everything was closing in around him, a low, hissing wind blowing the flame down into itself. His own wind was making the fucking instrument quack like a duck. He had to get out of here!

What stayed him, broke the iron grip of mounting desperation was realization. He grasped at it. There would be no point in her being present if Anton had betrayed him. *No point! No point! No point! Order your thoughts. Sit back. Breathe slowly. Think!* She was here to pick him up, that was for sure. That he could handle. Since Burke wasn't out there, chances were someone else was. But what difference? Either way he had the advantage of knowing where she was coming from, and she didn't know he knew. The real worry was how did she—British security, MI 5, whatever she was—know he and Anton were performing? How had the connection between them been made if it had been made? Was it not a trap whether Anton was innocent or guilty?

Again fear began to work him over, the flame gone cold. *The score seeming endless. Wait a minute! Wait a minute! She wouldn't be here. Wouldn't. Wouldn't, damn it all!* Again he was not sure what notes he was playing, if any, and after a while it didn't seem to matter. The symphony was finally coming to an end, thank God, and he must make his move!

As the music died, Sir Sidney swung around to accept vigorous applause. He took a long, slow bow, then turned, gesturing his performers to rise, and the applause swelled again, the audience rising as well.

Reardon fixed his gaze on Anton, but Codreanu did not return the favor, busy removing his score from its stand. Amidst the babble of sound, the shifting movement of musicians and devotees, Reardon headed for the greenroom. He had no thought but to get clear of the place; there would be no accidental meeting with Claire. He was getting out.

He had reached the entrance to the greenroom when a voice shrilled, "I say there, Reardon!" There was no mistaking Sir Sidney's hail. His instinct was to ignore it and move on; but the call was repeated, and he was compelled to halt and turn.

The maestro, one hand atop his head as though to keep his crown of hair in place, the other waving, was quickstepping toward him, accompanied by a very tall individual whose purposeful stride was in harmony with the thrust of his features, giving a momentary impression to Reardon of a ship under sail.

"Reardon, Reardon . . . *Scott* Reardon, yes!" Sir Sidney was pleased to have suddenly recalled the first name. "Scott, Scott, my boy, permit me to introduce Mr. Malcolm Warwick. Mr. Warwick is one of the sponsors of our programs, a great supporter of our music." He beamed. "And he—he asked—he asked—"

"I particularly enjoyed your playing." Warwick had an ingratiating smile to go with blue eyes that didn't smile at all, and while his tweed jacket looked slept in and his flannels bagged at the knees, his cutting off of Sir Sidney indicated to Reardon a take-charge manner and an unabashed British rudeness typical to some in authority.

"I'll just run along," Sir Sidney said, oblivious of the slight. "Must see to things, yes. Ta-ta." And he slid away.

"Wanted to congratulate you," the admirer repeated. "Your bassoon work is very finished. The instrument reminds me a bit of my old saxophone. That was jazz, of course. Very fond of jazz. Used to play drums, too. Of course, Mozart is something quite apart, although I have the feeling he would have found jazz to his liking, don't you think? But more to the point, the *Jupiter* is special to me, and you played a passage in the andante with which I am not at all familiar." He tried to hum it, and Reardon relaxed a bit, smiling.

"I'm not at all surprised. We didn't have very much time for rehearsal."

"You're being too modest. The notes are all there. You took the solo." He hummed again. "If you'll let me have a peek at your score, I'll show you what I'm talking about."

Forcing a grin, Reardon stared into the large, heavily tufted, discerning eyes and was aware of the oddly shaped ears. "Not really necessary. I'll take your word for it, and thank you for your compliment; but I'm really in a bit of a rush. I'm due elsewhere. A pleasure to meet you."

He turned away and entered the dressing room, feeling light-headed, his fingers tingling, knowing he had not escaped.

"Oh, I say, it will just take a moment if I may have a look."

Reardon focused on the numbered hook where he'd hung his gas mask kit. The kit was gone. So was Anton. He turned again to face his inquisitor, holding out his score.

"Have a look by all means. Excuse me while I pack up."

He retrieved his instrument case and knelt to dissemble the bassoon.

Foxed you, you cute bastard, he thought. There was no doubt that the hounds were close and that this big-eared one was on the scent. But Anton had not betrayed him! He was gone with the kit containing a score that even this bogus Mozartian could understand. As he packed the bell joint next to the long joint, he enjoyed an enormous sense of release; his spirits soared up on the flame. Two or four or six could play this game. And now, by God, he'd play it to the hilt, all the way to the hilt with dear Claire.

He straightened up, smiling at Malcolm Warwick. "Did you find what you were looking for, sir?"

"Oh, yes, quite. Very delicate, very good. This is the passage." He tapped the page. "Will you be able to play with us soon again?" His fulsome manner had not changed.

"Work schedule permitting." He took the score, tempted to say, *"I usually carry this in my gas mask kit."* Instead, he folded the music into his bassoon case, snapped it shut, and, with a farewell smile and nod of his head, retrieved Anton's gas mask pack from hook number three, slung it by its strap over his shoulder, and made his exit in full control once again.

The reception room was packed and full of gobble. He hoped there had been enough so there would be something left to eat. Before he went searching for the fair Claire, he was going to lay hands on a sandwich or two. He succeeded in both endeavors. Only it was she who found him.

"Scott Reardon!"

He turned to her voice, mouth full. "I thought it was you," she gushed. "I didn't know you were a musician."

"My hidden secret. I didn't know you were a music lover."

"Oh, yes. I thought the performance was smashing."

"Mozart would have thought so, too, I'm sure. How have you been?"

"Too busy and getting busier. I've got to rush away and drive out to Guildford to make a delivery or pick something up. I'm not sure I know which." She laughed at her own lack of knowing.

"Lovely day for a drive in the country." He sighed.

"Yes, it's that all right." She was looking at him teasingly.

"If I'm being too pushy, say so. But would you like company? I have the afternoon off."

There was no hesitation. "Why, that sounds jolly good. Driving alone can be such a bore, and Surrey is so lovely at this time of year."

"I'll teach you how to play the bassoon."

"Something I've always wanted to learn." She laughed gayly.

It was all so smooth, so neatly engineered, like parts in a play. Commedia dell'arte.

"I'll have to stop at the War Office first," she said.

"By all means. Then we can go forth and 'all the pleasures prove' with a hey nonny nonny."

Burke threw down his pencil, looked at his watch, and picked up his cigarettes, all in one motion. He had been at it most of the forenoon and felt he was getting nowhere. Part of it was lack of solid information with which to draft the cable. More of it, however, was Marlow and Dunn heading off to the bomber base at Honington and not inviting him to come along, leaving him, instead, to respond to General Arnold's urgent query as to what success the RAF was having over Norway.

Outside of the Air Ministry and RAF Air Staff, who the hell knew? Approval for Marlow's visit to Honington had been finagled only because Colonel Mike and Archie Boyle, of Air Intelligence, were old buddies. Whatever came back from Bomber Command would have to supply the real substance of what he had been able to cull from contradictory reports coming through the Ministry of Information and the latest *Daily Express* tabulation with its headline: GERMAN AIR LOSSES THREE TIMES OURS. According to the *Express,* the official score for the past month was 158 to 49, "with a possible 97 other German aircraft destroyed or put out of action." He couldn't help wondering how, with such a lopsided tally, the British appeared to be taking a pasting in Norway.

As for the lack of hard information, Marlow had informed him that the problem lay with the Air Ministry. Several months past it had turned down a War Department request for detailed statistical figures on all RAF operations. The rationale from Washington had been that since the RAF was in the process of putting into service U.S.-produced aircraft, the Air Corps was anxious to have a performance record. Marlow had shown him General Strong's cabled reaction, in which the chief of the War Plans Division angrily declared the British decision not to comply was "stilted, shortsighted and childish." Both Strong and Arnold were now demanding in even stronger terms what the Air Ministry had refused to give, and it had become his duty to draft the latest turndown from the colonel's notes: "The Air Ministry has informally advised that it is not in the national interest that such detailed information be released." Further, "H.E. Ambassador Kennedy was so advised and is inclined to honor the attitude of the Air Ministry and is reluctant to intervene at this moment." Marlow had seen fit to add that it was "doubtful if the Air Ministry is keeping such statistics on air losses in as detailed a manner in the form desired due to present critical air activities, but the matter will not be considered as closed."

Burke didn't know about General Strong, but from what he'd heard about Hap Arnold's temper, he figured the old man would be spitting cylinder heads over the answer.

In an attempt to soften the anticipated reaction, he had begun the reply, quoting Sir Samuel Hoare, the new air minister: "We are fighting the air war in Norway at great disadvantages. The Germans have the air bases. We haven't. The Germans fly from Norwegian soil. We must fly across 300 miles of open sea to do battle." That meant the Wellingtons, Whitleys, Hampdens, Blenheims had no pursuit protection against the Me's and Fw's. As a pursuit pilot he knew well enough the bomber boys' ironclad doctrine that the bomber would always get through. But the question was, At what cost? He had no specific figures to cite types of aircraft used, bombloads carried, missions flown. Zilch!

Well, that was Marlow's problem, just as the ebullient colonel was his problem. It had been a month since the dogfight with Kennedy. A month of lazy eights, of being put into a holding pattern while Colonel Mike flew off to Paris and weekends spent with good friends, while Major Dunn back from his ten days in France, having sipped scotch with the BEF's "Advanced Air Component," smiled his enigmatic smile and said, "All in good time, Peter, all in good time."

He lit a cigarette and shoved back his chair. The only good thing had been Claire, and the only piece of paper he'd seen all day worth looking at was the one in his pocket, bearing her elegant handwriting. "Peter, can you be at the corner of Adam's Row and Carlos Place at 1:30 P.M.?" Oh, my, could he. He looked at his watch again and began gathering together the mess of papers on his desk, thinking if the bulk represented sought-after intelligence, this pile would be a jackpot. But never mind that now. Claire was real. Claire was earnest, and the grave was not the goal.

"Miss Hobbs," he called, "I've got to go out for a while. You might want to put this stuff back in the file."

Walking from Grosvenor Square to Carlos Place, he thought of where his relationship with Claire appeared to be heading. The excuse for meeting had been business. The question of Reardon acted as a nice cover for mutual attraction, or at least his attraction for her. She was playing hard to get, but he knew she liked him. There wasn't that much they could discuss or do about suspicions surrounding Reardon, so he saw her acceptance of his invitations to dine at Hatchetts and dance at the Berkeley as evidence that she enjoyed being with him. He told her about his flying. She told him about growing up in Cornwall. They discovered a sadness in common which had a mutually sympathetic effect. Her brother had also been killed in a flight-training accident. Beyond that he felt there was something else, a deeper tragedy somewhere, but he did not push it. For the most part they had kept it light and on the surface. He had not made a pass at her, but he knew he was going to, and soon. It was a matter of time, place, and opportunity. Maybe somewhere in the country on this bright spring day they could go apicnicking, he mused, knowing he was dreaming, that her wish to see him at this hour would undoubtedly have something to do with Reardon.

As he approached Adam's Row, he began looking for her car. The traffic was thin, officialdom's ritual two-hour lunch in full swing. From Marlow's daily desk diary and having been invited to accompany him on occasion, he knew all the favorite watering holes of the movers and the shakers—Travellers, Beefsteak, Carlton, Dorchester Grill, Leonie's, Claridge, and, of course, the clubs. Empire made secure over potted shrimp, lemon sole, and langouste. What was happening in Norway should catch someone's attention.

His own was now caught by the absence of Claire's spiffy Morris. Well, being late was a feminine prerogative. Vaguely he was aware of a black sedan that had pulled to the curb of Carlos Place.

"Leftenant Burke?" The man leaning away from the wheel had a long grayish face, heavily bagged eyes, and a spiked crop of sandy hair, all of which registered on Burke as an intrusion, scattering his anticipation. "Miss Hollier asked me to fetch you."

His disappointment was obvious to the fetcher, for he squinted up at Burke with a lopsided grin and said, "Hop right in."

But Burke did not hop right in. The vehicle he saw was a Humber, big and ungainly, paint worn, not exactly official-looking.

"Who are you?" he asked.

"Inspector Goddard, Special Branch." He flashed a card with an identity disk. "I'm from the Yard. Do hop in. We can talk better riding."

Burke complied and asked, "Where's Miss Hollier?"

"Detained, she is, on other business," Goddard said, concentrating on moving into traffic. Burke saw that he was a big man with large, bony hands and black eyebrows that were in sharp contrast with his light hair. His manner of speaking came through as countrified.

"I don't get it. She asked me to meet her here."

"Not exactly, Leftenant. She asked if you could be at the corner here, you know. She didn't allow that she would be. And she sends her apologies that it's me and not herself." His tone was wry, not sarcastic.

"So are you taking me where she's detained or what?"

"More like what, I should say. And if you'll bear with me, I'll talk on some. There are things you should be knowing."

"I couldn't agree more. What's Scotland Yard got to do with my detained lunch date?"

"At Special Branch, Leftenant, we liaise with certain government departments, in one of which your Miss Hollier serves. Our job deals with surveilling, looking things over, in a manner of speaking. As I said, I've got to tongue-wag a bit before you'll get the drift. Our mutual interest, Leftenant, is Mr. Scott Reardon, but it might all go down better over a nice cup of tea and a bun. What do you say?" The lopsided, engaging grin was in place again.

Burke didn't know whether it went down any better, and he had coffee instead of tea; but it went down, and while he was still miffed that Claire had misled him—in typically British fashion—what Special

Branch Inspector George Goddard had to say did catch and hold his attention.

"The situation regarding Mr. Reardon has changed somewhat. His presumed contact, Count Asardi, was recalled to Rome a fortnight ago. Special Branch has not been informed by the Foreign Office of his possible replacement or if, indeed, there is to be one." Burke had the feeling that Goddard was reciting from rote. "But we feel Mr. Reardon's actions point toward a continuing operation on his part."

"I'm not sure I understand. If you know he's doing it, why don't you stop him?"

"Knowing and proving are two different roads, if you follow me. The idea is to make them connect. Would you like another cup?" He signaled to the waitress. "Our job is to know what he's about, where he goes, who he sees."

"What's that got to do with me? I can't follow him around. He's cut me off, won't even go out for a beer."

"It's not a pint of bitters we're after, Leftenant. It's your help we need in an official sort of way. Aside from your Mr. Sutterby at the embassy, you are our American contact in this case." He looked up at the waitress with a smile. "Alice, dear, another spot of coffee for our young friend, if you please."

" 'Ow about another nice bun to go with it?"

"Excellent. Two nice buns, by all means."

Burke half watched him pour tea from the pot as they waited for Alice to be out of hearing range. Goddard continued. "Now Mr. Reardon is here, like you, with diplomatic immunity, which means he has certain privileges of privacy. There is no hard evidence as yet that he has done anything to violate them. And that's where we'd like you to come into it, in a manner of speaking. We want to have a look at Mr. Reardon's digs, his flat. It's his private property, so to speak. We need to make the search with full authority. Your embassy's Mr. Sutterby has granted the authority and asked that you be present as the embassy representative."

He was of a mind to reply that he didn't know the counselor, had never spoken a word to him. Instead, he said, "I suppose you have that in writing?"

Goddard patted his jacket. "You can have a look."

"It was my understanding that you'd already made a search . . . and found nothing." He could feel annoyance building, a counterpart to the coffee's bitter taste.

"Some time ago, yes, but not since Asardi's recall. You understand Special Branch does not initiate investigations. We take our orders from an agency in the War Office, in this case a branch of MI 5."

Burke didn't know whether he was being forthright or apologizing. "Okay, but why the need to search again?"

"It's believed possible that Mr. Reardon, having lost Count Asardi, may be secreting documents in his flat. I can't give you any more than that, Leftenant. As I said, we do the investigating; we don't make the decisions. Ours not to reason why, if you follow me." He finished his tea and downed the cup. "So I'd be pleased to have you come along with me while I have a look, all within the law."

"You mean, if he should catch us in the act, everything will be hunky-dory."

"I beg your pardon?"

"Everything will be on the up-and-up, okay."

"Yes, yes, of course, but you may be sure there will be no interruptions."

Goddard parked on Cadogan Lane, and they walked to Reardon's flat, which was on the second floor of a small three-story gentlemen's boardinghouse on D'Oney Street. To Burke, D'Oney was more an alley than a street. *Hidden* was the word that came to mind. Goddard had keys to a side entrance and to the flat itself, a single room with kitchen and bedroom alcoves. He had cautioned Burke that whatever turned up, conversation should be kept low and to a minimum.

Perversely he hoped that nothing would turn up. If Reardon should walk in, he, not Goddard, would be the patsy. All Scotland Yard was doing was protecting its royal arse with one pissed-off, nonflying pursuit pilot who wished to hell he'd told old Uncle Bertie to shove it!

"You can help if you'd have a look in the closet and perhaps in the dresser by the bed there," Goddard whispered. "Try not to disturb things. If you come on anything, give me a signal." He could have refused to join the search when Goddard raised the question in the car. He had agreed, he told himself, because with two of them the job would get done that much sooner, but there was no denying a heightened sense of anticipation and curiosity.

The closet was commodious, containing few clothes but many books and folders. The floor was stacked knee-high, and the closet shelf above lined with them. It didn't take long to determine that the single suit, tweed jacket, flannel slacks, and Burberry held no documents, in fact, no papers at all, which could indicate caution. He began picking up books, glancing at titles, thumbing pages. He recalled a movie in which a book had been used to contain secret papers by the center of the pages being hollowed out, and he wondered if this meant that all the books would have to be examined. Lord knew, Reardon's reading interest was broad and deep enough, but why the hell didn't he get himself a bookcase? He looked toward Goddard, seated at the desk which faced the bay window with its heavily draped blackout curtain.

The inspector appeared to be reading Reardon's mail. As Burke approached, he saw the framed photograph on the desktop and out of the past recognized Scott's Byronesque father. "The closet is full of books. Do you want me to go through them? There's nothing in his clothes."

Goddard rose, and they went over to the closet. He squatted down and examined the stacks all arranged at the same height. "Neat lad, isn't he? These were gone over last time, but let's have a go behind them." Carefully he eased the books away from the closet wall and felt along it with his free hand, and Burke realized he was looking for a possible place of concealment. He had no luck and straightened up with a sigh. "Bleedin' library." He dusted his hands, glancing up at the shelf. "You might take a look up there. I don't recall its being so crowded last time. Have a squint behind, right?"

With a chair from the kitchen alcove, Burke had a squint. He found the shelf was stacked not so much with books as with music scores, three rows of them one on the other. "Concerto in E Flat Major, Antonio Vivaldi," he read the top title, suddenly remembering Reardon and the bassoon. Looking around from his vantage point, he saw no sign of the instrument. Maybe he kept it under his bed. Behind the books and scores he found no place of concealment, and by the time he'd replaced the chair, his impatience to leave had grown. If he didn't get something drafted for Colonel Mike, it was going to be his ass. Moreover, Reardon's undecorated and sparsely furnished pad did not convey the feel of traitorous acts. Its almost threadbare atmosphere, somehow, was not in keeping with the image conveyed by Scott Reardon. An anachronism, or a guy trying to get along on lousy pay in an expensive town? Certainly, if he were selling secrets, he'd have more to show for it than this.

"The dresser," Goddard whispered, nodding toward the alcove, which, with the drapes drawn back like curtains, the unmade bed center stage, gave the impression of a set in a poorly conceived drama. The dresser held Reardon's clothing but no secrets, unless Scotland Yard would consider a package of rubbers incriminating.

The hell with this.

He saw Goddard still seated at Reardon's desk and experienced his first moment of surprise as he realized the inspector was at work trying to manipulate the lock of a metal file box.

"It was under the bottom drawer," Goddard divulged in a mutter, not looking up. "Any luck at all?"

"Not even his bassoon."

"I shouldn't worry." There was a soft click, and Goddard glanced at him with satisfaction, withdrawing a probe from the file lock. He set it aside with other objects of the trade in a pocket-size leather tool kit and then gingerly opened the file lid as though not sure whether the box might explode or maybe a pigeon would fly out. Burke saw a single file folder within. Goddard opened it to reveal a thin sheaf of paper. "Pull up a chair," he invited.

There were official documents in the folder, but none had been stolen. Instead, they told a sad story with grim overtones, part of which Uncle Bertie had outlined to him and part that he had not.

The first was a letter, carrying a Department of State exemplar with a subhead, "Special Review Board." It was dated July 20, 1933, addressed to The Honorable Dwight T. Reardon, Consul General (ex officio). Its message was one of finality. "The review board wishes to inform you that your appeal for rehearing is rejected. The information submitted, it was unanimously agreed by the board, in no way mitigates against the board's original finding and recommendations. The board finds that the additional circumstances cited are without merit and therefore regretfully informs you that your dismissal from the department is deemed final." The signer for the review board was its chairman, Carlton S. Forbes, Jr., assistant chief of personnel. The five names of the board members were in the upper-left-hand corner of the page, and Burke was amazed to see that beneath the chairman's name was that of Jay Bertram Stark.

The point was hammered home in the handwritten letter that followed. The fury of it came through the age-shaded paper, felt as much in the slash of the writer's pen as in what was written:

Bert—Betrayal is cruel at best. Betrayal of a loyal friendship is unforgivable. Both you and the president could have put a stop to this. I knew the danger but not that it would come from my own side. I knew, too, that Forbes and his cabal would do anything to get me. But you—you I'll never forgive for being a party to it. I am no Christ, but you are my Judas. Not thirty pieces of silver for you, Bert, but an ambassadorship. Was that the price to destroy a life? Ask your mentor in the Oval Office.

There was no signature or date, but at the bottom of the page in a delicate hand were written "not mailed" and the initials HPR.

The shock of the accusation, the power of the words brought a replay of Uncle Bertie pacing about in his office, his lean, aesthetic face hiding what?

Beneath the letter was a brownish *New York Herald Tribune* four-paragraph obituary, datelined November 10, Geneva, Switzerland. It told of the death of former U.S. consular official Dwight T. Reardon, killed when his car hit an abutment, having failed to make a curve. The final paragraph listed all his posts and assignments as a Foreign Service officer. It reported he had recently retired from the department because of illness; no mention was noted of his dismissal. His survivors were also noted: his wife, Hilma Pruck Reardon, daughter, Karen Reardon Stokes, and son, Scott Reardon. Burke had never realized that Scott's mother was German. Goddard was busy, writing down the details in his pad.

Two official letters, addressed to Scott Reardon, followed the obit. The first, dated January 2, 1934, was formal notice that the recipient had failed the entrance examination for the Foreign Service; the second, dated two months later, that he had been accepted into the Department of State in the status of clerk, giving the date he was to report for duty.

Beneath the letters was a page one story from the *New York Times,* bearing the head U.S. EMBASSY OFFICER SLAIN. It was datelined Moscow, October 15, and scrawled across it in red ink was written "October 15, 1938." The story related the known details of the murder of U.S. Second Secretary Carlton D. Forbes, his body found in the Lenin Hills, head smashed in.

The story did not offer much more than Uncle Bertie had related to him at their meeting. The article with all the rest led to the nasty conclusion that the assistant secretary had intimated. The assumption was strengthened by the last item in the file, a piece of paper with two names on it and the letter *R*. The first name was Forbes, and the same red ink that had marked the *Times* news story ran through it. The second name was Stark, and beneath it, after the number 3, was the letter *R*.

Burke carried the chair back to the kitchen alcove. All the elements of dirty poker in high places and possible revenge taken, he thought, but whatever it proved or didn't prove, it sure as hell didn't prove that Scott Reardon was a Nazi spy, and there was nothing here to say otherwise. He decided he'd had enough.

"I've got to get back to work," he said. "Unless you have some other place to search. We could always look under the rug."

Goddard did not respond, carefully returning the file to where he'd found it.

On the return ride he considered giving Goddard the one piece of information missing from the file: Forbes preventing Reardon from being granted leave to attend his mother's funeral. But he decided there was no point; it would only strengthen the unprovable.

"Interesting line there." Goddard broke the silence, teeth gripping his pipe. "Reardon's mother is from a German family, Pruck."

"You must be reading my thoughts. I was thinking about her. She died a couple of years ago when he was stationed in Moscow, I believe. No doubt his mother was a Nazi agent." He did not conceal the sarcasm.

Goddard glanced at him. "You seem to resent all this, Leftenant. We think it's a serious business."

"No doubt it is. It's just not my kind of business. I've been trained to fly airplanes, and it's somewhat different from—from—"

"From muckin' up somebody's private preserve because he might be helping Mr. Hitler win his little war."

"Look, I apologize for being such a pain in the ass."

"It's a hard life," Goddard said laconically, and they rode the rest of the way in silence, Burke having to admit that Special Branch Inspector Goddard had properly put him in his place. He wanted to explain further, but he realized he would just be making puerile excuses.

Goddard eased the Humber over to the curb and let the engine idle, took the pipe from his mouth and extended his hand. "I want to thank you for your trouble, Leftenant."

"And you for yours." Burke grinned, hoping to get back into step with him. "If you should need me again, I'll promise to be in a better mood."

"I'll count on that."

"Good." He opened the door. "One thing I wonder if you'd do for me. When you see Miss Hollier, tell her if she ever makes a date with me again, she'd better show up."

"Righto!" Goddard sang.

The day of blue sky and warmth was softening into velvet eventide as they came into Kingston Hill. He had been taken for a ride both figuratively and literally, and although the desire to strangle her was real enough, though not possible under the circumstances, what occupied him most was the purpose behind her obvious enticement.

It had started off well enough, and it was not she who probed him with questions. Quite the opposite. "So you're an undiscovered music lover. Who's your favorite composer?"

"Who wrote 'Nobody's Sweetheart'?" She smiled winningly.

"Bach, maybe." He joined in.

"No, I rather think he wrote 'Saratoga Spring.' They played it at the Milroy the other night."

"The Milroy, that's pretty special."

"Actually, I prefer the Four Hundred. Their theme song is 'Sand.' Do you know 'Sand'?"

He hummed a few bars.

"Very good. You see how musical I am. Actually," she confessed, "I had to deliver a package, and I recalled Edith Pyle's telling me how good the sandwiches were following the concert, so my tummy said to give it a try."

"You paid for your lunch with Mozart."

"Exactly, and an easy price to pay, I'd say."

It had all gone lightly, subtly seductive with no mention of the war. It was a peerless day as they drove swiftly through the snug, full-leafed countryside; he could almost hear the hum of honeybees over the blended sounds of passage. At her stop at the War Office she had picked up an official-looking package and told him she was to deliver it at the

Albemarle Hotel in Guildford. En route he worked out his plan. It wasn't very complicated, but if he succeeded, he was going to get some answers one way or the other. He observed the graceful line of her neck and pictured his hands around it, his voice whispering in that delicate ear, "*Who is Malcolm Warwick? Tell me about him.*"

"It's such a nifty day," he said, putting his head back and taking in the sky and then looking at her. "Would you be open to a suggestion?"

"You're right about the day, perfectly marvelous."

"Once you've done your duty, what do you say to a stroll in the Surrey hills? I'm sure we could find a shady lane and a babbling brook. We could stop somewhere, and I could find something to keep us from getting thirsty."

"Sounds positively lecherous." She laughed, glancing at him slyly. "I think we have something in the back to sit on and maybe some teacups. Will you need a bottle opener?"

"Not for gin. But if so, I'll use my teeth." He grimaced, showing her his teeth.

"Charming. But you're right, you know. It's such a lovely afternoon. It would be a shame to let it get away without having a fair look at it. Goodness knows what we can expect next."

Like the rest, it was a thinly veiled invitation. Her words and manner certainly aroused him, and he began to wonder if her game was to seduce him into confessing, instead of the other way around. If that was the case, they were in for a grand time. Only she'd lose the game. But she sure as hell didn't, and she knowingly let him go ahead and buy the gin, an expense he could ill afford.

It was obvious that the Albemarle had been taken over by the military, for there were sentries at its gate, and for a startled moment he wondered if he was being taken prisoner. She explained her call, showed her identity card, and they were waved down a long, circling drive to an imposing estate, looking more like a château than a hotel, its pillared front bunkered with sandbags, Union Jack on staff proclaiming ownership.

"I shouldn't be long," she said. "We delivery maids never are." She gave him a "be patient" smile, hefted her package, and approached the front gate, where another sentry waited to check her bona fides. He watched her leggy motion, thinking he was damn well going to check her bona fides. Then he settled down with a cigarette to wait in the pleasant warmth of the afternoon sun.

How near a thing had it been . . . wanting to check his score? Only Fanny and Anton had known the method of concealment. Had Fanny foolishly opened her mouth to someone she trusted, like Wilmot? And he a member of the House of Lords who couldn't keep his mouth shut even if it was wired. If Fanny had said anything to him, the word in some garbled fashion could have gotten back to the British . . . The use of the score but not who was to receive it or how. Fanny would never have mentioned that. He'd wring her neck in any case! If it had been Anton, there wouldn't have been any need for that bullshit artist with his overlarge ears playing peekaboo. Maybe the answer lay with dear, sweet, beautiful Claire, and oh, my, was he going to lay with Claire. As Lenin was known to say, "You commit yourself, and then you see."

He was smoking his third Lucky when she reappeared, but not alone. Coming along behind her and then beside her, matching his step to hers, was a square-set military officer, swagger stick under his arm, row of faded ribbons above his breast pocket, much salt in the pepper of his neatly disciplined mustache. Again, for an instant, Reardon froze.

"Scott, this is Major Treemont." She made the introduction with a look of contrition in her eyes and in the sound of her voice. "We are giving him a lift back to town." The final touch had been that she asked him if he would mind terribly giving up his seat to the major. And so he had made the return ride scrooched in with the gin bottle beside his bassoon case in what could hardly be called a back seat.

With the top down and the breeze, he had not been able to overhear what she and the major chatted about like old school chums. He had been left to smolder and rage at himself for having been so easily traduced, not seduced, goddammit! Equally he had wrestled in the cramped confines of her chariot with the reason why she had gulled him. At one point he even toyed with the idea that her purpose had not been to trick him, that she had really intended to enjoy the afternoon with him. *Rot!*

He knew she'd be dropping Treemont at Whitehall, and as she drove down Regent Street, he called out, "Would you mind letting me off at Piccadilly?"

"I'll run you home if you like," she called back.

"Piccadilly will suit me fine." He figured she knew exactly where he lived, but he was not going to give her the satisfaction of teasing him into thinking that once there, they'd make up for the botched afternoon.

At the end he felt he gained one small victory. First, the major had to get out of the car so he could climb over the seat. "It's been ripping," he said, standing on the curb, looking down at her. "We must try it again sometime when we have a chance to enjoy it." He held up the bottle of gin. "Tallyho, Major."

The light was opaque when he emerged from the tube at Sloane Square, and he walked the short distance to the neighborhood pub, the Bucket, mulling his next move against the day's developments. There would be no more days off until mid-month, when he and Anton were to perform again. He could hear Surov saying, *"Find a new way."*

He appreciated the hubbub and the half-light of the pub; both offered concealment. No one bothered you. You got your half-pint from Harry, the barman, and sat in the cool, smoking a cigarette, easing down.

While the Bucket was somewhat crowded, talk was low, and its rise and fall did not intrude. A single voice behind him intruded but was pitched as low as the rest. "The general sends best wishes."

The voice, smoothly modulated, knifed into him like a stiletto. He could not turn and see the speaker because the speaker was sitting in the next booth and its high backing hid him. He did not reply.

"He reminds you, you are *nash.*"

He considered getting up and having a look. *Nash* was a term Surov liked to use; it was Fourth Bureau parlance. It meant "ours." Instead, he remained silent, taking a drink, pretending to be oblivious of the voice, his eyes sweeping the room to see if anyone was observing him.

"He wants your assistance."

If he got up and left, that would clearly signal he was not going to comply. He debated the move and decided he would wait and see what Surov was after.

"You had visitors this afternoon. Scotland Yard and Air Officer Burke were in your flat. Apparently they found nothing worth taking away."

The unexpected contact had thrown him off-balance. Now the reason and result of Hollier's phony seduction gambit slammed into him.

The information riveted him. He stubbed out his cigarette, almost knocking over his glass.

"You will receive a shopping list. In it—"

"If you can't get rid of Burke, you can forget the list—forget it! He's MID, on my tail. Get rid of him!" He had not raised his voice, difficult as it was, but his final words came out as an order. He got up and walked out of the place.

He went along the street, forcing himself to walk slowly. Several children were sitting on the curb, playing a game of jacks. He was drawn to them. He stopped for a moment and watched. The red ball bounced. The little girl reached adroitly among the scattered metal pieces and picked three up.

The red ball bouncing, that was what the day had been: a game of jacks. To the children's excited chatter—"I did!" "You didn't!"—he moved on. At the gallery he had won the first game free and clear. Claire Hollier was the little girl, and she had beaten him at her game. But in the final toss they had picked up nothing. Nothing! Because the pieces were not there. That was all that mattered for the moment, and Surov's messenger could go play jacks with Burke.

He began to calm down, getting a firmer grip on his thoughts, tasting the irony. It wasn't Surov who had given him the advice that had saved the day but Tony Biddle in Warsaw!

The ambassador was patting his vest, his suit coat pockets, scolding. "You know if you ever have anything important to carry," he lectured, annoyed at himself, "you should always carry it on your person. Never set it aside. Never! Keep it safe. Otherwise, you forget where you put it, and some other fella is bound to pick it up. What the hell did I do with my cigarettes, Reardon?"

He didn't know. It was the point that had stuck until events caused him to risk storing. He knew no mattered what happened, he must never again use his flat to hide the gold. The margin of victory had been so thin. For now he would lie low, take nothing, continue legitimate consular activities in the file section, stay clear of the code index room until the day before the next performance with Anton.

In his flat he drew the blackout curtain, switched on the lamp, and poured himself a generous slug of gin. He sat at the desk and regarded the timeless silence of his father's knowing gaze. "Maybe the comrades can earn their kopecks," he said. "I'll be theirs as long as it suits me."

6

When Miss Baker told him there was a phone call on Major Edwards's line, for a fleeting moment he imagined it might be Claire. A week had passed since his message to her via Goddard, and he was hoping her silence was due to a busyness to match his own. He was relieved to find the major was out of his office, but there was nothing Claire-like in the voice that erupted from the receiver. "Lef-tenantBurke, sah! FlightsergeantQuinnhere, sah! Calling you,sah,at therequest ofSquadronLeaderBoice, Forty-threeSquadron, Ackling-ton,sah!" The blended words boomed forth in a rush combined with an accent that made swift interpretation almost impossible. With much repetition he translated that Flight Sergeant Quinn was informing him that 43 Squadron had shot down an Me-109, which had crash-landed on the North Downs not far from Charing and that Squadron Leader Boice, having learned that Lieutenant Burke was a Yank fighter pilot, was inviting him to come have a look-see. "Strictly hush-hushofcourse, sah!"

Although he'd never heard of Squadron Leader Boice, he was sure Colonel Marlow had and had passed the word on his reluctant aide's qualifications. He saw the invitation as a gift on a platter, a much needed and exciting offer. He'd be able to send back the latest details on the Messerschmitt. It took as long to write down the sergeant's directions as he had needed to translate his speech. "Will Squadron Leader Boice be on hand, Sergeant?"

" 'E'stherenoaw, sah. We'llkeepaclosewatchforye, sah."

"Hope I can get there before dark."

"Comesmartly,sah. Ye'llmakeitsure."

Immediately, on hanging up, he realized that coming along in any fashion was going to be a problem. The colonel was off somewhere in his Chrysler. Major Dunn had the staff car, and Major Edwards had copped the embassy rattler, made available to the MA's office in an emergency. All at once a possible solution came diving out of the sun.

He got the operator and asked for the War Office, and when a female voice announced a successful connection, he said, "This is Lieu-tenant Burke at the U.S. Embassy. May I have the officer in charge of room zero-zero-five?"

The officer in charge listened to his request and the added emphasis, "It's urgent," and asked him to wait.

The wait drew out, and he was beginning to think it wasn't going to work when she came on the line. "Peter, this is not a terribly secure connection. If—"

"That's all right. I need an unsecured favor." He quickly explained.

"A Messerschmitt fighter, you say?"

"Yes, a one-oh-nine, evidently the latest model, and in good shape. I just don't have any way to get to it. It's about eighty kilometers, fifty miles. An hour and a half, I figure."

"More like two hours or more, going down there, I should think."

He could tell she was weighing the idea.

"Evidently they're going to cart it away tomorrow, so this will be my only chance to have a good look. If you're tied up, could you lend me the Morris? I promise not to spin in."

She did not answer, and he knew he was being pushy, but what the hell "Claire?"

"I'll call you back in ten minutes." When she did, it was to tell him she'd pick him up in another ten.

When full of thanks and good humor, he climbed in beside her, her withdrawn manner reminded him of the coolness she had shown in his rooms at their first meeting. After five minutes of monosyllabic responses to his attempt to be ingratiating, he'd had enough. "Look, Claire, why don't you pull over to the corner there and let me out? I apologize for having the nerve to ask for your help. If—"

"Don't be silly, Peter." She gave him a brittle look. "What do you expect me to do? Throw my arms around you and give you a kiss?"

"I certainly wouldn't be offended," he snapped.

"My, you have a short temper."

"It's one of my many failings." He knew he was being foolish.

"Grump, grump, grump." She imitated him. "I hate to disabuse you, old top, but my cheery mood has nothing to do with you at all. I'm really most interested in seeing the Nazi plane, and I'm thinking of the best and quickest way to do it."

He realized his abruptness had pushed aside her reserve.

"I have the directions as best I could get them from Sergeant Quinn." He pulled the pad from his pocket. "What's the cause of your bad mood if it's not me?"

"You've seen the papers, heard the news?"

"About getting kicked out of Norway?"

"There's a debate in the House of Commons going on right now. It may be the end of Chamberlain."

"Would that be bad? From all I can gather, he's made a mess of it. What did he say a couple of weeks ago, that Hitler had missed the bus in Norway? Our information is that Hitler's getting ready to take the bus into Holland and Belgium."

"And who's to lead us? They're talking Lloyd George at the War Office; but he's too old, and Lord Halifax does not impress anyone as being a fighter. We need that badly."

"Churchill?"

"I don't know. He's been defending Chamberlain over Norway. Norway was apparently his idea, like Gallipoli."

"There was nothing wrong with the idea, only with the way it's been so badly carried out."

"Yes, and we believe some of that, at least, was due to German intelligence. Whatever Norway shows, it shows we're ill prepared, and if Hitler does attack—" She shook her head.

"Well, look, fair lady, it's a beautiful day for a drive in the country, so chuck the fate of empire for the afternoon, and I'll explain how to do a slow roll."

"I'd rather you tell me about the German aircraft we're going to see. No one I spoke to at the War Office seemed to know anything about it."

"I imagine they know all about it at your Air Ministry. A great break for our side. I brought a camera." He held it up. "Hope there'll still be enough light when we get there." He put his head back and examined the sky. "Did you get my message from Inspector Goddard?"

"Seems he did say something in passing." She smiled and then laughed, and he joined in, pleased that she had loosened up.

"I suppose he told you what success we had looking through Reardon's spy nest."

"He did say you weren't exactly enthusiastic and—"

"And we came up with nothing."

"That's not exactly so, Peter," she said, shifting down smoothly as a truck in front of them slowed. "It turns out that Reardon's mother was German."

"And she's dead," he said emphatically.

"But Colonel Horst Pruck happens to be the deputy director of the

Abwehr—German military intelligence—and chief of the Geheimer Meldedienst—foreign intelligence. It may be pure coincidence, but there could be a direct relationship."

He shook his head. "It seems that coincidence is most of what you people deal in. I'm afraid I'm too used to what's—well, what's real, like those wheels on that truck you're going to run into if you don't slow down, or like the Me we're going to see. It's there. It's real!" His voice rose.

"Then why don't you read me some directions that are real? I have some Player's in my purse if you care to join me in one."

It took longer than he had thought, following hedgerow roads that wound down valleys and tunneled up hills, all in the full bloom of spring. Charing was a snug Elizabethan-appearing village, every shop and dwelling bent on outflowering the other, a banking of splendid color and fragrance.

They found the road as described by the sergeant. It flanked the square stub of the Gothic church, rising up out of the village onto the Downs. It was a narrow track that after a short distance traded macadam for gravel and then lost the gravel to dirt. He had never been in Downs country, and he was immediately struck by the impression of remoteness. The land was open, sweeping away in low, undulating hills amidst gorse and hedgerowed pastures, splotched with patches of woodland and heath. Farms and their outbuildings had a distant look, and touches of red and gold and pale blue wild flowers scattered through the fields added to the effect. As he took them all in, he saw, too, that the scene was going to change and soon. Behind them the sky was suddenly clouding over. Because there had been so many days of bright sunlight, the immediate change was to magnify the loss of light.

"That stuff is moving in in a hurry," he said, taking the Rolleiflex out of its case, checking the shutter opening. "I don't have a light meter, and I don't know how good this thing is."

"I shouldn't think it would matter very much, old sport, unless we stop and put up the hood."

"How right you are, old dear," he said, mimicking her. "I think that's the fork where we peel off to the left. I'll crank down the gear and you pancake her in."

"I thought you ate pancakes," she said with a laugh.

With the car stopped they felt the stiffening breeze; it pressed at them roughly. Together they manhandled the canvas hood into place and secured it. He could not avoid noticing how the wind molded skirt and blouse to her body.

The rain arrived just as they finished, and they cranked up the windows, laughing at having escaped the deluge so narrowly. With windows shut, the hood a cocoon covering, the rain a thrumming torrent, he felt the physical force of their closeness.

"Would you like an American Chesterfield this time?"

"Yes, thank you." She looked at him, and he saw in her eyes that she was aware of the change.

"I wonder how long this will last," he said, meaning, "Will it last long enough?"

In the flare of the match she closed her eyes and shook her head. "Long enough to turn the road to mud. Thanks." She put her head back and blew out the smoke as though getting rid of something more.

"I haven't thanked you properly for coming out here to get washed away in the flood." He spoke quietly, the rain on the canvas muting his words.

"No need, Peter, really. I wanted to come. A good chance to get a breath of fresh air, and if—"

The blinding flash of lightning topped by a bone-shaking crash of thunder jerked her body, lips parted, eyes gone huge with momentary fright. His own reaction had been no less startled. As the thunder pounded its heavy aftershock down the sky, they looked at each other and burst out laughing. Automatically he laid his hand on her shoulder and drew her to him. She accepted without resistance, her head beside him, her hands on his shoulders. He could tell her hands were there to hold him off, not to embrace him. Much as he wanted to take her, the smell of her hair, her body, her closeness a goad, the loss of pride in being repulsed put a checkrein on his desire. At least he would give her a chance to back out.

"You were saying something about fresh air."

"Yes." She brought her head away from him as though being released. "My being here is really due to my boss. He's interested in Hun aircraft, as he calls them."

"I didn't know you were in the air defense business, too."

"Oh, Mal is a man of many parts, as I told you when you first met him." She completed their disengagement, returning cigarette to lips, the moment ended.

"I suppose magic tricks and Messerschmitts do have something in common." He sat back, annoyed with himself, annoyed with her.

They smoked in silence, and he knew he must try to restore balance, if that's what it was. "You crack your window a little, and I'll crack mine, and even if we get a bit wet, we won't be asphyxiated. And who knows? Maybe I'll get lucky and another bolt of lightning will strike."

He turned his attention to the window and felt her hand on his shoulder.

"Peter." She took him by surprise, leaning forward and kissing his cheek. "Please don't be angry."

"Hell," he said, contrite but even more aroused. "I have no right to be angry, or—or anything."

"Oh, yes, you do." He was astonished at her openness. "Be patient with me." She took his hand and held it between her palms.

"I'll admit that's not easy, my lady. My feelings about—"

The glaring flash and the shredding crack of thunder were not as startling as the first, but her hands clenched his in reaction. Looking at each other, they laughed again. "You see, you got your wish," she said. "And as my grandmother used to say, 'If you're patient, you almost always get your wish.' "

"God bless your grandmother," he said, feeling that indeed, balance had been restored.

She let go of his hand and began rubbing her steamed-over window. "I should imagine your sergeant might be looking for us."

"Not if he's like any sergeant I know. But I think it is letting up. Want to give it a try?" He cranked down his window, impatient to get going. She started the engine and pulled carefully away onto the left branch of the fork.

The rain appeared to be shutting off as rapidly as it had turned on. He could see patches of blue. They drove on slowly in silence, he looking for some sign of their RAF hosts, she concentrating on not getting stuck or sliding into the ditch.

"Look! A rainbow," she announced.

He saw the shimmering span of color arching over the rain-soaked land. "Our lucky day," he said meaningfully.

"Provided the turnoff has not become a millrace," she added.

The turnoff described by Sergeant Quinn was not a millrace, but it was no longer a track the Morris could manage. It was a muddy gulch, leading up a long intervale bordered by hedgerows toward a ridge topped by a ragged grove of ash trees and undergrowth.

"He sure picked a great place to land." Burke stood in the road, surveying the scene. On the far side of the road the land fell away in a gentle wave, and he could see the gambrel roof of a farmhouse.

"Do you suppose we've got the right place?" She addressed the surroundings, hands on hips.

"Look, you'll get all muddy and wet," he said. "I'll go up and borrow their truck. They must have one. You can see the tire tracks there. I'll come back and get you."

"You're a very gallant Sir Walter Raleigh, but you will not. I don't see any lorry tracks. Besides, I wore proper walking shoes." She thrust out her foot to prove the point.

"Nice legs," he cracked, not wanting to waste time debating. Off to the southwest the dark clouds of another squall were piling up. "All right, Queen Bess, follow in my tracks."

"You are a voice crying in the wilderness," she said, coming to stand beside him. "Isn't it a marvelous view? I love the wild flowers."

"What is the saying, 'Kissing is out of season when the gorse is not in bloom'?"

"Wherever did you learn that!" She was truly impressed.

"I learned it from a dame who really appreciated wild flowers," he said. "Come along."

There was a path of sorts, but the going was slippery and the ridge more distant than it first seemed. Halfway to the top he stopped, cupped his hands, and bellowed the sergeant's name several times. The breeze whipped his call away.

At length the path leveled off, and they followed it, skirting the wooded grove. From the sergeant's description he figured the 109 pilot must have cleared the trees and crash-landed in the field beyond. But when they came around the edge of the trees, he saw that there was no field as such but a sharp and sudden depression, the broad lip of a chalk excavation. Roughly bowl-shaped, wide, and deep, it looked like an abandoned pit mine. It was backed by more trees and wild growth, the land to either side sloping and empty, inhabited only by fluttering birds.

"I don't get this," he said quietly, puzzlement growing. She said nothing as they walked to the edge of the pit and took in its ragged, overgrown desolation. "He sure as hell didn't land there," he said, eyes searching out the surrounding land.

"We must have stopped at the wrong place." She shielded her eyes, joining in the search. "What a pity."

"The RAF certainly isn't here, but the directions are right. Look." He showed her what was written on his pad, a feeling of presentiment starting to take hold. "I think we'd better move along."

They turned together, and he saw the man emerge from the trees. He wore a black cap, a leather jacket, dark pants, farm boots.

Surprised, uneasy, Burke called, "Hello! Have you seen any RAF people about?" He began walking toward the newcomer. "We're looking for a downed German plane."

"You can stay right there!" The voice was Sergeant Quinn's, slowed down. "Nice of you both to come." The grin revealed a glimpse of uneven teeth. The jacket was open, and Burke's swift awareness congealed around the glint and shape of a pistol butt extending above the belt.

He could feel the wind pushing, hear its hiss in the gorse, warning, and within knew the all-consuming silence of danger, knew he must act. *Now!* Arm waving, Rolleiflex in hand, looking toward the trees behind the bogus sergeant, he shouted, "We're here, Joe!"

The old trick worked in part. The man's head and upper body started to swing toward the unexpected, hand reaching for gun butt. As he moved, Burke threw the camera in an overhand pitch and followed on the run. Black Cap was quick, managing to duck away from the hurtling object; but his movement put him off-balance, and he was not agile enough to get clear of Burke's diving tackle.

It was not a good tackle. His feet had slipped on the wet turf, his hands making contact too low on the legs. Only the bulk of his weight brought Black Cap down. But not down hard, and Burke knew he was in serious trouble. He glimpsed the hand swinging out, holding the revolver, and he desperately caught at the wrist, oblivious of the arm that had his neck in a choke hold. In the scrambling embrace he tried fiercely to pin the wrist to the ground and to jerk his knee into the gunman's crotch. Black Cap was strong and fast, twisting and heaving, working to break free, and Burke fought savagely yet was unable to get a grip on Black Cap's throat while his own breath was being choked off.

In the fury of the encounter he suddenly was aware of Claire's feet, her legs close beside them, and he wanted to shout at her to get the hell away! Then her foot began kicking. Kicking, kicking, kicking at the gun. Black Cap pulled the trigger, trying to hit her, the sound enormous. Her foot stamped down, kicked and stamped, and struck Burke's hand, nearly breaking his hold. Black Cap pulled the trigger again, and then the revolver was gone from his hand, skidding across the ground. Burke smashed his freed fist into Black Cap's jaw, got his fingers fastened on his throat, and then, in a fierce heave, was bucked off. He rolled over and came upright, knowing he must get his hands on the weapon. It wasn't necessary. Claire stood with the revolver in hand, pointing it at their attacker. Without cap, close-cropped hair streaked with mud, shovel face pale and bloodied, mouth open sucking air, the wolf at bay stood in a crouch, knife in hand.

"Shoot! Shoot!" Burke rasped, running toward her, planning to do just that.

He did not get the chance. Black Cap broke and ran for the pit, scuttling over its edge. Burke followed and then watched as, spiderlike, the assailant moved down the overgrown embankment. He turned to Claire, knowing he would not follow. She was pale and wide-eyed, and the gun in her hand looked huge. He put his arms around her, and wordlessly they stood holding each other, he feeling the pounding not only of his own heart but of hers as well. He kissed the top of her head, and her arms tightened. She lifted her head, looking up at him, defenses down, a yearning in her eyes, and he was kissing her, the softness of her lips wondrous.

"You know," he said, trying to control his breathing, "I think I may be getting you all muddy."

He stepped back and they looked and she said, "Yes, I think so, but I don't mind," and she came back into his arms.

He wanted to stay just as they were while he was getting his wind back, but he said, "We'd better get out of here."

"Yes, before it rains again." She spoke in a daze, in shock. She had dropped the revolver, and he picked it up and pocketed it and with an arm around her shoulder led her back onto the path.

"The camera," she said. "You mustn't forget the camera, Peter."

He retrieved it and saw the double lens was cracked. "The light wasn't right anyway," he said, knowing what his next paycheck was going to be used for.

Halfway back to the road she stopped and said, "Peter, thank you for saving our lives."

Again he held her. Again he comforted her as she clung to him. "We saved each other's lives. That makes us best friends, doesn't it?"

"Oh, jolly good friends," she whispered, kissing his cheek.

"Who the hell do you suppose he was? He certainly picked a sure way to hook me."

"He wasn't something real like a Messerschmitt—was he?—" she said seriously, "so he must have been one of those coincidences you mentioned."

He howled at her sly observation, and she joined in, and he knew his reaction had helped release some of the aftershock.

"We'd better move along double time," he said, taking her arm, "the rain you know," his eyes on their back trail.

The room at Scotland Yard had a single long window through which the morning light streamed, helping dispel the room's cell-like dimensions. Facing it, they sat three at the table, with Special Branch Inspector Goddard in the center, slowly turning the pages of the large leather-bound photographic album, as they sought to match a face with the memory of yesterday's violent encounter. There were no names but identity numbers beneath each photograph. The album was one of four on the table, and as Goddard turned the pages, Burke began to wonder if the black cap was standard wear for British criminals.

His sleep had been infused with black caps, a kaleidoscope of faces, snarling blobs beneath their caps, and he had awakened feeling battered and bruised, his neck stiff and sore to the touch. Mostly, however, he was thinking of Claire.

She had let him drive until it became dark. Then she had guided them from Croyden. Earlier they had stopped in Maidstone "to repair the damage," as she had ruefully put it. She had called the War Office and reported. He had devoutly wished she'd waited, for her orders were to come directly to Branston Court, where Mal Warwick resided. He, in turn, had spoken to Captain Barnes, the duty officer, and informed him there had been no downed Me. The report had been a mistake. He'd explain further in the morning.

He was prejudiced when it came to Warwick because he knew Claire's having to stop to see him was going to interfere with unspoken plans to spend the night with her and repair *all* the damage. Beyond that he did not cotton to the winged-eared autocrat at their second meeting any more than he had at their first. Warwick took over the moment he opened the door, and along with his thinly veiled imperial manner there was an underlying possessiveness toward Claire which she seemed to accept. When Warwick insisted that she spend the night in the guest flat above, and she did not protest, Burke felt anger. Her offer to drive him home was vetoed by Warwick, who said he'd ring up a cab and they all could have a scotch while waiting.

Burke had refused. It was the one option he had to make a decision Warwick could not overrule. Even then the man had insisted upon instructing him how to reach the underground.

Standing before the mirror, preparing to shave, Burke saw that one side of his face was scratched and swollen, raising the question of what explanation he was going to give Marlow and Dunn. What he had told Barnes was going to require embellishment. Misled for reasons unknown, all true. As for his new look, he'd tripped and fallen in the blackout, also true, trying to find that goddamned subway last night.

As he was carefully shaving, the hall porter knocked on the door to say he had a phone call.

"Peter, can you meet me at Scotland Yard at ten?"

"I can meet you anywhere. How are you feeling in the magician's den?"

She laughed softly. "I didn't sleep too well."

"Neither did I. I missed you."

"Until ten. We're going to find out who he was."

And they did, going through the third volume. "There he is! That's him." Claire laid her finger on the photo. Surprisingly he was bareheaded, standing with two others, listening to a fourth, who appeared to be giving instructions. All carried rifles; two wore berets, their clothing nondescript; the speaker sported a bandolier.

"That's a face I could hardly forget," Burke said, studying yesterday's adversary. "Where was this taken, Spain?"

"I'll be back in a jiff," Goddard said, having written down the identity number.

As soon as he was gone, Burke slid over into his chair, took Claire's face between his hands, and gently kissed her. For an instant she sought to draw away and then did not. And when he stopped, she dropped her head and shook it. "Oh, Peter," she said, "this is bad. Not good."

"Bad for what?"

She laid the top of her head against his chest. "For us."

"Why for us? We won the war yesterday." He began to stroke her hair.

She looked up at him. "And tomorrow?"

"This is today. Tonight. What about dinner tonight?"

She shook her head. "I can't."

"Lunch then. A walk in St. James's among the tulips."

He heard Goddard's approach, and he slid back into his chair. Goddard entered, puffing his pipe with satisfaction, carrying a pair of file folders.

"Well, now we know who the blighter is," he said, sitting down and opening the folder to reveal an enlargement of the album photo. "You were right, Leftenant. This is Spain, 1938, and this chap here doing the tongue wagging is Carl Poujout, a bigwig in the Executive Committee of the Comintern. He bossed the International Brigades in Spain, a nasty chap, and these three are his nasties, killers in the name of Stalin. Our man here is Comrade Paul, given name Patrick O'Day, member of the British CP, an agent of the Comintern. He may well be under the direction of the Soviet GRU, which is military intelligence. Even more to the point, he's suspected of dealing in wet affairs, as they choose to call assassination."

"Wait a minute," Burke said. "There's supposed to be a connection between this guy and Scott Reardon, isn't there?"

"It's certainly a possibility we're looking at very closely. Do you have any other thought of who would have been behind luring you into a trap?"

"No. But—"

"Remember, Peter, Reardon served in Moscow," Claire said.

"He also served in Warsaw. I thought that the angle was that Reardon has been playing footsie with the Nazis."

"And as you must know, the Nazis are playing footsie, as you put it, with Stalin." Goddard closed the folder.

"How would this man Paul know where to call you and how to trick you into believing the story about the Messerschmitt?" Claire said.

"I don't know, any more than I know who tricked me in Lisbon. Do you have an answer to that?"

Goddard puffed in silence a moment and then said, "Who, outside your own office, knows why you're in the UK?"

"Obviously an ugly mug named Comrade Paul."

"Let me show you something." Goddard turned the page to another photograph. It was a shot of an audience in a hall, listening to a speaker. The faces of the listeners were small. One in the center had been circled in red. In a following photo the face had been enlarged, and it was possible to recognize O'Day. "This was taken on October third, 1939, at King Street, Covent Gardens, British Communist headquarters. The date is important." Goddard tapped the photo. "Now let's have a look here. This is Reardon's file, and this is a copy of the CP manifesto adopted on that date, found in his possession on the first search of his flat. Read a bit of it."

Burke scanned the page, wondering, as he read, what the point was: "The Central Committee declares that the present war is an imperialist and unjust war for which the bourgeoisie of all the belligerent States bear equal responsibility. In no country can the working class or the Communist party support the war. . . . The first task of the party in this first stage of the war is to operate against the war, to unmask its imperialist character. . . ."

He looked up. "So?"

"You get the gist. Now have a look at this one, which was attached to the manifesto." Goddard put a printed cardboard poster before him:

YOUR NEW YEAR'S RESOLUTION

> We appeal to the workingmen and women of Great Britain to purchase the new Defense Bonds and Savings Certificates, thus keeping the war going as long as possible. Your willing sacrifice and support will enable the war profiteers to make bigger and better profits and at the same time save their wealth from being conscripted. Lend to defend the rights of British manhood to die in a foreign quarrel every twenty-five years. Don't be selfish. Save for shells and slaughter. Forget about the slums, the unemployed, the old-age pensioners, and other social reforms your money could be invested in. Just remember that your savings are much more wisely spent in the noble cause of death and destruction. Come on, the first million pounds.

"I gather this is a sarcastic way of putting the manifesto," he said. "Did Scott write it?"

"Possibly." Goddard held up the poster. "This is called a sticky back. It represents the literary work of either the British Union of Fascists or the Association of Peace for All of which Reardon's friend Fanny O'Rourke is a charter member. Not Communists but Nazi sympathizers. Whatever these two documents show about the similarity of political thought, they clearly show that Reardon is closely acquainted with the thinking of both. Do you follow?"

"And do you recall, Peter, that you thought you saw Reardon at Fanny's club?" Claire leaned forward, looking at him.

"More coincidences, hey?" Burke smiled at her, feeling a warmth that had nothing whatever to do with Nazi-Communist relations and Scott Reardon's involvement with one, the other, or both.

"There's another point," she said, and the look in her eyes made him want to tell Goddard to go fetch some more files. "I remember something that awful man said. He said he was pleased we both were there. So he knew about me, about us. How could he have known that if Reardon hadn't told him?"

"Or one of his mates," Goddard added.

"What about Comrade O'Day? Do you have a hunt on for him?"

"We're looking, Leftenant, but he'll be no easy one to find. He's gone to earth, and he'll likely stay low for a good spell. We're checking the thirty-eight you took from him. It may give us a lead."

"She took from him," Burke corrected, nodding at Claire. "Well, I know a way to settle this whole thing," he said, stretching his arms over his head. "I'll have a talk with Scott, and if he refuses to talk, I'll wring it out of him like he was a wet towel."

"I wouldn't try, lad. Wasn't yesterday hard enough?"

He had been half joking in threatening to take direct action against Reardon. He told himself he was not so blockheaded as to try to beat the truth out of him, even while he could visualize himself doing just that. But after yesterday and this morning's business, the desire, growing in him since the cigar trick at the Bull and Bear, to resove the damn thing once and for all had reached a point where he knew he was going to do something that had nothing to do with closet snooping and looking at mug shots of Commie agents. But he sure as hell didn't know exactly what.

Busy as he was, writing a nonreport for Major Dunn on the Messerschmitt that wasn't there, leaving out the ugly part, substituting an unexplained hoax, and then translating the major's notes on the Bristol Blenheim Mark IV bomber, some part of his thinking was fixed on what he might do to flush Reardon out into the open.

The war situation had everyone occupied, and he knew that Reardon must somehow be sitting in the catbird seat. The British fleet had gone down into the Mediterranean from the North Sea, most of their forces had been pulled out of Norway, and word that Hitler was about to attack Belgium, Holland, and Luxembourg was circulating within the embassy.

At noon he had checked the duty roster and was surprised to note that Reardon had been assigned as officer of the day and would not be going off duty until midnight.

He wrestled with methods of attack, the stiffness of his body matching the stiffness of his mind, unable to formulate an acceptable plan, visions of Claire scattering his thoughts. There was no manifold pressure, the head temperature was in the red, and he could not find the beam frequency. What the hell!

He had hoped to have dinner with Claire and told himself if he had, he would not have ended up sitting on a park bench in Grosvenor Square at midnight. He still had no flight plan, was flying blind. Flying blind with a star-filled sky above, the darkness of the square not all that dark so that he could spot anyone coming out of the chancellery. He couldn't be sure of immediate identity, but he knew few were going off duty at this hour. The night was mild, and except for his wanting a smoke, the waiting was almost restful. There was the quietness, the smell of spring, the silence of the city holding its breath waiting for the bastards to come. And they were going to come. In the cable traffic Marlow had shown him and Dunn had analyzed, there could be no doubt.

His line of thought snapped off as he saw the chancellery door open and a figure emerge. He could see bulk, no detail, but from height and movement he knew instantly it was Reardon. He thought to rise and perhaps to follow. Even this action was not firmly fixed because he knew how difficult it would be in the blackout, and what would it prove, that Reardon went home after work? Instead, he sat still. He watched Reardon cross the street and take the walk that would pass by him. He felt a tightness in his chest and wondered why. This was no dead-stick landing. Besides, in those circumstances, he at least knew what to do.

He sat very still, knew his quarry had not spotted him, was coming along sprightly, humming softly, unaware.

He waited until Reardon had gone one step past before he said quietly, "Hello, Scott."

Reardon pivoted around in half leap, half crouch, the hum going out in hiss.

"It's Pete Burke. I've been waiting for you." He did not rise.

Reardon straightened but still very much on guard. "I'm flattered." The grate in his voice said otherwise. "What do you want?"

"Too late for a gin at the Bull and Bear, but—"

"Too late for lurking in the bushes," Reardon snapped.

"Not exactly lurking, Scott. At least, not like Comrade Paul. You remember Comrade Paul, don't you, Scott?"

"You sound like you've been at the Bull and Bear most of the night."

"You mean with that jolly cigar-smoking Count Asardi? He went back to Rome, didn't he?"

"You do have a snootful." Reardon's tone had lightened, becoming mildly derisive.

"In a manner of speaking, as they say at Special Branch, I've had a snootful of some Commie son of a bitch trying to kill me."

"Well, that's a shame, but you should choose your company more carefully. London can be a hard place . . . particularly in the blackout."

"Yes, you never know who you're going to meet, Nazi spy or Commie assassin."

"*C'est dommage,* as they say in Paree. I've got to run along, Burke. Past my bedtime." He sounded fully relaxed and was standing lean and tall, very much in control of his side of the exchange, and Burke felt there was nothing he could say that would dent him. His own anger started to rise.

"You run along, Scott, and I'll sit here wondering whether I should break your fucking neck or let you do it yourself."

Reardon laughed. "I think you'll be better off if you let nature take its course."

"Or maybe I'll just sit here wondering how a guy like you, with your background, your family, could sell out his country."

Reardon said nothing for a moment, but when he spoke, Burke

knew he had gotten in a solid hook. "I'll chalk up your insults to stupidity and gin. I don't know what you're rambling about, Burke, but whatever it is, stay away from me."

He turned and walked away into the dark, and Burke called after him, "I've got you in my sights, Scott."

7

Peter Burke parted the blackout curtains on the dawn-light, sky crimson tinged, festooned with lumpy barrage balloons, the city still untouched. How much longer?

It had been two weeks since Hitler had struck and Colonel Marlow had noted in his appointment diary, "Germany invaded Holland, Belgium, and Luxembourg." In that short time Burke had seen the world around him change so swiftly and drastically that events crowding in gave the impression of make-believe, each new piece of bad news climaxing on the other. As the appointed aide to the acting U.S. military attaché he had become privy to many press and Ministry of Information releases, for as suddenly as all the rest, Mike Marlow's and Mac Dunn's contacts in the Air Ministry and with the RAF Air Staff had opened up. No doubt it was because of the change of government and, as Dunn had remarked, because of an accelerated need for U.S. aid and support. Whatever the reasons, it had meant his being tied to a desk, drafting cables and reports while Mike and Mac sped from one luncheon meeting to the next, gleaning the latest on the RAF's attempt to block the blitzkrieg. Because of the rapidity of the enormous change in the war's course and the almost unbelievable direction in which it appeared to be heading, he started keeping his own private record. If nothing else, he saw his notes as a guidepost for possible future use.

May 10 Yesterday's British humor: "Blitzkrieg a lightning war that never strikes in the same place once." Not so today. Chamberlain out. Churchill in. Labor party supports govt. of National Unity.

May 13 Liège taken. All major Belgian cities bombed. All major airports taken.

May 14 Luftwaffe bombs Rotterdam. Thousands reported killed. RAF will bomb only military targets. BBC announces: "The Admiralty has made an order, requesting all owners of self-propelled pleasure craft between 30 and 100 feet to send all particulars to the Admiralty within 2 weeks." Preparing for what? Dutch surrender. Queen here.

May 15 Maginot Line hit at Sedan. FDR appeals to Mussolini to stay out. Amb. Kennedy advises U.S. citizens to leave. Ship to pick them up at Galway, Ireland. (Col. M. says K. panicky.) RAF bombing Ruhr targets.

May 16 FDR tells Congress he'd like to see 50,000 planes a year. (Who wouldn't? But I'll settle for one P-40.)

May 18–19 Over weekend observation and machine-gun posts mounted at Whitehall and other important points. Roads and river approaches to London patrolled. Guards now at Broadcast House. French line along the Meuse not holding. Public attitude appears euphoric. Must be the incredible weather. Sunday a workday. Brussels falls. Antwerp smashed.

May 20 War Office announces formation of Local Defense Volunteers. Quarter of a million join in less than 24 hours. Major Truly brings word German armored units have reached French Channel coast at Abbeville. RAF, according to Marlow and Dunn, is superior to Luftwaffe, racking up high score but losses heavy, Reported breakthrough at Sedan. Paris threatened.

May 22 Announcement of Emergency Powers Act. Govt. has power to take control of all persons and property. Morrison, minister of supply, broadcasts everyone will now work at "War speed, full time, 7 days a week, to defeat the deadly menace that has threatened the people of these islands." Bully! Looks like they're beginning to wake up although while everyone is now sporting gas mask and tin helmet, there is an unreal holiday atmosphere. Maybe it's the British way of reacting to peril.

May 23 Police raid hdqtrs. of the British Union of Fascists in Westminster. Arrest Mosley and a pack of his supporters. Also arrest Lord Wilmot. This may mean that Reardon's Irish Gypsy is also in the can. Same goes for Comrade Paul and the Commie peace lovers. If MI 5 and Scotland Yard are really cracking down, Reardon could be next.

He had not seen Reardon since their midnight dogfight. But as the bad news had kept rolling like a tumbleweed, growing in size, he wondered what Reardon could possibly tell Berlin that it didn't already know. As for his own scribbled notes on world-shaking events, they could hardly convey what was felt, the surface atmosphere balanced against the looming reality. Barbed wire going up around the Horse Guards Parade while strollers amble along the lagoon in St. James's Park. The D'Oyly Carte performing *The Mikado,* Sadler's Wells's *Sleeping Beauty,* the whores around Mayfair in high heels and tin helmets, and across the Channel, the BEF continues to fall back, the French fall apart, and the Belgians fall. Claire had known what was coming not because of any secret information but because at heart they'd all known. Now it was almost as though they had wanted it to come, were glad it finally had. No battle counts but the last one. Hell, this could be just that. As for Claire, she'd vanished. No calls returned. No notes answered. Nothing.

He finished dressing, knowing this might well be his last battle, too. Like the Allies, he'd been pushed back for two solid weeks, bombed, strafed, run over, Marlow's and Dunn's private dogsbody. Well, enough. "We may go down in flames," he said to his reflection in the mirror, "but we'll go down with all guns blazing. Switch is on. Spin the prop."

Yesterday Colonel Mike had announced that he and Major Mac were planning an 0600 departure for Watton and a visit to 62 Squadron, not a fighter but a Blenheim base.

At exactly 0545 he knocked on the colonel's open door, Marlow, at his desk, writing, looked up in surprise. "Burke, my goodness, what are you doing here at this hour?"

"Good morning, sir. I'd like to request permission to talk to you, and I thought this might be a good time."

"I've got to be off in a jiff, you know." The implication was clear.

"I'll make it short, sir."

"Sit down, sit down."

"Thank you, sir. It was my understanding when I arrived that I was here at your request to study RAF Fighter Command's defense system, that I had three months to do so. That time is nearly up, and as you know, except for a brief visit to Tangmere, I haven't been near an RAF fighter base."

"And as you also recall, Peter, the ambassador was dead set against the idea, and I can report to you that as recently as this past Sunday when I dined with him, he was even more set against it."

"Sir, do the ambassador's wishes apply to Colonel Brown and Major Ziggler, who I understand have just arrived to carry out a similar assignment?"

"Brown and Ziggler are here under War Department orders." Marlow wrinkled his brow, frowning. "Although you are officially here at my request, I did not originate it. It came through the State Department, which actually went around the ambassador, which only succeeded in getting his Irish up, making him opposed to the whole idea. I'm telling you this in confidence, Burke, because I can understand your frustration."

"So there's no chance of my carrying out my orders, sir?"

"I'm afraid not, under the present circumstances." He shook his head, got cigarette in ivory holder, holder in mouth, and lit up. "That's why I've used you as my aide until something might be worked out. You've been very helpful."

"Well, sir, since I can't do what I was assigned to do, I'd like to ask a favor. You're leaving for Watton. Could I go along? I know something about the Blenheim, having written up the report on it from Major Dunn's notes. It would certainly add to my knowledge, seeing the aircraft up close. And sir," he added wryly, "since it's not a fighter, the ambassador should have no objections."

The colonel passed his hand across his brow, tugged at his mustache, and contemplated the cigarette holder as though it might be used as a sighting piece. He had a worn look. "Major Mac has had to cancel, some meeting with Portal." He directed his gaze at Burke. "It's a longish road to Watton. Best we get started. I'll check you out in the Chrysler."

It was a longish road, heading north, going up through Chelmsford toward Bury St. Edmunds, but from the start it was a fine road as far as he was concerned. The battle he had foreseen and the insubordination he was prepared to dare had been dispelled. Whether the colonel's quick acceptance of his subordinate's request was based more on an overabundance of nightly scotch and too little sleep than on an understanding of his aide's desire made no difference. His aide was where he wanted to be, pointing the Chrysler to where he wanted to go. And on such a fair morning he could not ask for more. Of course, if only the snoozing colonel were Claire—Well, the hell with that for now. Who knew where that magician had sent her? *I'm sorry, sir. We cannot at this time reach Miss Hollier.* Well, by God, she knew where she could reach him. Hell, he'd thought—Well, never mind what he'd thought. He was on course to Watton.

The colonel awoke at Sudbury, stretched, yawned, rubbed his eyes, and said, "How do you like the way she handles?"

"Not quite like a P-40, sir. More like a B-18. Very steady."

"How much time have you had in the Curtiss?"

"Ah, only several hours, sir," he said, caught off base. Actually, he'd had none, and the Curtiss he was referring to was the P-36. Rather than wait for the obvious next question, he quickly added, "When I was taking Advanced at Kelly, I managed to wrangle some observer time in the Douglas."

"Little more closed in than my first observer time," Marlow revealed. "A fellow lieutenant named Hap Arnold invited me to go for a ride in his Wright Flyer. That was back in 1912. Never apt to forget that ride." He stroked his mustache in fond remembrance.

Burke was duly impressed, and Marlow, appreciating recognition, began to reminisce. He had earned his wings in 1916, but unlike most U.S. World War pilots, before going to France, he had been stationed in England. It became obvious that while flying in combat had brought moments of excitement to Marlow, it was his years serving as an assistant military attaché for air in London that had been the meat of his career. And later, on reflection, Burke understood the underlying reason for the colonel's rambling revelations. They were more than a discourse by a hung-over Irish Anglophile recounting the glories of being accepted by and associating with the British *haut monde.* Not only was the colonel's Chrysler proceeding to Watton; but the colonel's thoughts were already there, and en route he was blowing smoke rings to the good and easy life, now possibly gone for good.

"I spent most of last night, Peter, with my old friend Wing Commander Toddy Raymond, a wonderful chap. He's CO of Sixty-two Squadron, or what's left of it, and I'm afraid that's not very much. He's just back from Belgium. The story is very bad, I'm afraid. The RAF is suffering fierce losses. A week ago Ugly Barratt's Advance Striking Force attempted to stop the Hun advance at Sedan. He lost forty out of seventy-one aircraft."

"Forty! My God, what kind of planes, Blenheims?"

"No. Bristol Battles, that two-place, underpowered, underarmed, outmoded excuse for a fighter." He made it sound like swearing. "Lord, I don't know how many times I've told Slessor and Peter Portal the only battle that plane is suited for is attacking barrage balloons."

"But I thought they're using Hurricanes."

"They are, they are. But they don't have enough, and Dowding is trying to conserve defenses here. Toddy doesn't know the figure, but their losses have been high, too."

"And the Luftwaffe, sir?"

"Oh, they've been getting it, but they can afford the losses."

"You said we're going to see what's left of Sixty-two Squadron. How badly has it been shot up?"

Marlow stubbed out his cigarette. "Bit of a different show. Several days past, twelve of Toddy's fifteen Blenheims went off to attack an armored column at Gembloux. They ran into Me's. Only one aircraft got back."

The fighter losses had startled him. This newest tally was stunning. "God almighty, if the Germans are that good, it's all over."

"I wouldn't go that far; but it's damned serious, and we'll have to be very careful what we put into a cable. The information you might say is privileged. It's not official yet. In any case, Toddy is rebuilding his squadron, a mix of the new and crews from other squadrons that have been returned to England."

It was a grim picture, the remoteness of what had been going on in the air across the Channel suddenly brought into appalling statistical focus—forty out of seventy, eleven out of twelve.

The colonel did not give him a chance to assimilate it, tossing a different kind of hand grenade in his lap. "Peter, I know you've been disappointed by duty here. Not what you expected, not what you planned. But I hardly need to remind you, that's Army life, particularly when war looms. I don't know what's coming next, what will happen in France, how soon the Hun will send his bombers in this direction. But I do know we're on the front line, so to speak." He was back to tugging his mustache, and Burke felt something besides "Hun bombers" was in the wind.

"I know your family background, Peter. Knew your father some years back. When I was an assistant MA here in the twenties, he was in Berlin, and we rallied on occasion. . . ."

The unexpected connection jolted him. He hadn't given the Iron

Duke a thought in weeks. Now, full-blown, he was interjected into the picture and just as quickly blown out again by Marlow's next words. "Peter, I'd like you to consider staying on as my aide. Since General Miles's recall, I've been acting MA, and there's good reason to believe I'll soon be appointed as permanent. I'm going to need an aide, an assistant on whom I can depend. Now I jolly well can guess what you're thinking. You're a pursuit pilot, a fighter pilot, and the sky is where you belong. All very well. I know the feeling, but the problem all along, as I recall your father used to point out, is that you need more than happy-go-lucky flying officers to build a proper air force. You need chaps who can think beyond an eight-point slow roll, and I believe you're one who can. I like the way you've behaved under fire, so to speak, the work you've done while Major Mac and I have been gadding about. I can appreciate how frustrating it's been in not being able to carry out your assigned duty, but if you put in for duty as my officially appointed aide, I can fairly well promise you that you'll get the chance, and soon, to study Fighter Command defenses. In any case, my boy, give it some thought. And we'll talk it out on the return."

"I appreciate the offer, sir," he said, not at all flattered by it, feeling that he was being buttered up because Marlow knew that being on the front line meant the barrage of urgent inquiries from the War Department could only grow heavier. Further, somewhere deep down the connection with his father rankled. "I'd like to make two observations about my duty here, sir. The only flying I've been able to do is shooting takeoffs and landings in a Gypsy Moth at Northolt in order to keep my flight pay. And aside from the ambassador, I haven't found the RAF exactly forthcoming."

"That's all changing now. Witness our being here. You turn left at the sign there."

"Bristol Blenheims, sir, are not Spitfires and Hurricanes."

Indeed, they weren't, but Wing Commander Toddy Raymond almost made up for it. He was waiting for them in his sporty Morgan two-seater. Cigarette in mouth, mustache blacker than Marlow's, trimmed so that it resembled a pair of RAF wings, flop-eared spaniel in the seat beside him, he waved and called a bright "Hallo!"

"He left me at three this morning to fly back here, and you'd think he hadn't a care," Marlow said, his tone a combination of admiration and regret that he hadn't fared as well.

After introductions Burke parked the Chrysler, and they crammed themselves into the Morgan, Finian, the spaniel, scrambling all over Marlow's lap. Burke, his legs jammed down behind the seats, sat on what there was of a rear hood. Raymond's ebullience, his eyes bright, quick, full of genuine enthusiasm, quickly dispelled the dark shadows of defeat implanted by Marlow. "Going to show you what we have on the line first off," he called, accelerating to full throttle, speeding past a cluster of low-slung wooden hangars and operation shacks onto a tarmac. Burke counted ten of the twin-engine medium bombers as they sped along the grass. He spotted one in the landing pattern, another just lifting off, and a flight of three moving away. There were ground crews working around several of the planes on the line.

"A new batch of lads just checked in from the OTU," Raymond shouted. "We've got three crews out on escort, guiding a fighter squadron to France, if you can believe. Written orders came down from Group that there was to be no fighting with the bloody Hun along the way!" He let loose a howl of laughter at the asininity, swinging the Morgan in a sharp ninety-degree turn, bringing it to a halt. For a moment Burke thought that he might be continuing alone as he dug in heels and struggled to hold on. Raymond looked around, grinning wickedly. "Bit of turbulence there, Leftenant, what?"

He had stopped just beyond the last Blenheim in the line, the location offering a sweeping view of the entire installation. Taking it all in, Burke jumped to the ground, suddenly caught up in a feeling he had not known since leaving Bolling, the feeling of flight, the sight, the sound, the smell: the long, flat reach of the field, hedged by a low grouping of hangars and support structures; the powerfully imposing line of bombers, noses questing; the confident growl of the plane in the pattern and the throttled back mutter of the one angling neatly to touch down. On the breeze he caught the smell of high octane from the fuel truck attending the last aircraft in the line. The senses brought it all together, and he had the exhilarating sensation of having come home after too long an absence. He was only half listening to Toddy Raymond explaining that Watton was home for 2 Group, and his squadron was but one of seven occupying the base. "That is, of course, when we're not busy elsewhere. Come along, you'll want to meet some of the chaps."

The chaps of a ground crew were loading 250-pound and nine

40-pound bombs in the belly of the Blenheim. The flight crew of three was due to arrive any minute. "They'll be going off straight away in a vic of five to hit a panzer division near Namur," Raymond disclosed. "Should be quite a show," he joked, making it all sound like a game.

Burke, starting to look more closely at the bomber, began to have mixed feelings. From snubbed Plexiglas nose to narrow tail, the Blenheim Mark IV, which he had seen referred to as a fighter-bomber, gave the appearance of something of both but not a substantial version of either. The Douglas B-18 was a far sturdier-looking bird than this one.

Raymond led them in a walk-around, pointing out salient features: the Mercury radial engines, 1,000-pound bombload, 2,000-mile range, top speed of 295, "going straight down, of course. Note her charming color scheme, dark green and brown, conceals her hummingbird nature. How j'you like to lead the element, Michael?"

"You lead, Toddy, I'll follow."

"What about you, Leftenant?"

"Anytime, sir, but I'll need to be checked out first."

"Marvelous. Only difference with a fighter is that we've got two of everything in case you should lose one of something. Much safer, right?" They all laughed.

"Michael, I've got to take you up and introduce you to our AOC, Vincent. Insists on it, you know. Very stuffy sort. Doesn't approve of the way I dress and wants Finian shot. You said something about wanting to stop by and chin with some of the Wellington chaps at Feltwell. Collier said to come for lunch, so after we've paid your respects to Vincent, we'll run on over. Burke, I should imagine you'd like to remain here and learn what you can. Talk with the flight laddies; talk with anyone you like. They've been advised you're here. Get it all so you can make a jolly good report on how well we're all doing." He coated the irony with a smile, not about to let reality intrude on his home turf.

Burke looked for approval to Marlow, who repeated, "Learn what you can, Lieutenant. We'll see you later then."

He was rather pleased to have been left to operate on his own, and after watching the bomb loading and learning how the bombs were released from their cells by the bomb aimer, he headed for the next aircraft up the line, where he'd noticed gathered around its nose a half dozen airmen, three of whom were wearing flight gear.

He knew they were aware of his approach although they remained absorbed in their work. Dressed as he was in khakis, wearing garrison cap and insignia, they had to have taken notice. The tallest of the group, sharp-featured with a mop of sandy hair, dressed in flight gear, helmet in hand, waited until he'd come around the end of the wing, then sang out a greeting. "G'dye, Yank. Come to help us bash the bastards?"

"I'd like to hear how it's done," he responded. "I'm Second Lieutenant Peter Burke."

"Welcome. I'm FO Alec Dunbar." He thrust out his hand. "These sods are my crew." He introduced them by name and rank. Sergeant Roger Ormsby, navigator and bomb aimer, short, bulky, round-faced; Corporal Stan Kulski, gunner and wireless operator, pug-faced, blond, grinning. The names of the three ground crewmen went by too fast to retain.

"What we're about is rigging this bleeding camera up in the nose here, so Roger"—he dropped his hand on Ormsby's shoulder— "can get some pretty photographs for a change, instead of dropping bombs down the kraut's snout. The problem is getting the proper fit. We haven't all day to solve the problem, so while you sods work it out," he addressed the others, "I'll show our guest what makes this clapped-out bird fly." His accent and manner of speaking were not British, more like Australian.

Dunbar led him under the wing to the side of the fuselage. "We go through the roof," he said. "Second-story types." He climbed up onto the wing, using foot slots and then another foot slot to reach the fuselage top. Burke followed and saw an open hatch and behind it another hatch abutting the domed gun turret with its single .30 caliber Lewis gun, looking like a frail reed.

"Is that all the firepower you carry?" he asked, wondering if under present conditions it had been reinforced.

"There's a fixed Browning in the port plane. Fires rearward. Isn't worth a fiddler's fart." Dunbar lowered himself through the hatch, and Burke waited until the pilot called for him to follow. A ladder of sorts brought him down into the cabin. "Sit yourself there." Dunbar, having moved to the right and perched on a jump seat, pointed him toward the pilot's bucket seat.

"You don't have dual controls," Burke said, sizing up the cockpit.

"Some do. Roger packs it here when he's not busy doing other odd jobs. Today he's photographic officer. Kulski doubles as the wireless operator. His station, when he's not in the turret, is behind me." He indicated.

"I thought you carried a camera in the rear somewhere." As he spoke, his attention was on the instrument panel. It blocked out the glassed-in nose, but the canopy above and on both sides of the fuselage offered good visibility, much better than the B-18 or the old B-10.

"It's not much on low-altitude work. Cigarette?" He extended a depleted pack.

"How about a Lucky?"

"Could use some of that, I'd say. Dangerous to smoke in here, you know."

He held the lighter, and Burke was surprised to see that his hand trembled. Up close Dunbar's eyes were bloodshot, lines of wear in his face.

"What kind of airspeed do you get?" He laid his hands on the wing nut-shaped yoke.

"Not what the bloody specs say. Maybe two-twenty on a good day. Not enough against the Me's. Blenheim has a tendency to attract accurate ground fire." His laugh was a cough. "But this little do we're going off on should be a piece a cake."

"A recce mission?"

"Yes, but an easy approach, a quick circuit, and home again." He looked at his watch, cupped his hands, and yelled, "Roger, how much longer?"

"Another five, Alec."

"Make it four! Anything there interest you? Throttles, mixture beside your hand on the left."

"Prop control?"

"On the underside of the pedestal."

"Do you have any protection against attack besides getting the hell out of the way?"

"Steel plating behind the gunner's turret helps. Clouds, weather, darkness." The meaning behind Dunbar's laconic replies was obvious enough, and while from without, the aircraft offered a semblance of strength, from within, the word that crossed Burke's mind was *flimsy.*

"Excuse me, sir." He looked up and saw Roger's round face peering down at him. "Beggin' your pardon, need to slip through."

Dunbar moved back into the wireless station, and Burke moved over while Ormsby swung down into the cockpit and eased himself into the nose section. "Think we have it about ready," he said in passage.

Burke sat again, and Dunbar looked at his cigarette. "Yank, you're here to learn what you can, right?" He looked up. "How would you like to come along for the ride?"

The thing was, he wasn't surprised at the offer, had almost been waiting for it to come. "How long will it take?" he said, smiling.

"Back in no more than an hour. Straight to Dover across the Channel to Calais. A run over the city to get the picture, so to speak, and then straight home. Piece a cake."

"If I get found out, I'll get court-martialed, maybe shot." He was excited, grinning, knowing he was about to risk his ass and possibly wreck his career, but all the frustration of the past two months had run full bore into an opportunity a growing boy couldn't resist. Marlow wouldn't be returning for several hours. No one would know. "What kind of trouble would you be in if it were learned that you'd taken a noncombatant U.S. Army officer on a sortie?"

Dunbar grinned. "They might send me on a dangerous run."

"We've got it, we've got it," Roger called up from the nose compartment.

Somewhere they found him a pair of coveralls to conceal his khakis, life jacket, backpack chute with pack detached, helmet with intercom connections. It was all done so quickly that he suspected it had been planned, that Toddy Raymond had whisked his friend away so that it could happen—a let-a-Yank-pilot-see-for-himself trick. It didn't matter. What mattered was it was happening. And although he knew he was disobeying very strict War Department orders, he was feeling the same exhilaration he'd felt on his first solo.

"Take a look." Dunbar handed him a well-worn chart. "We clear for Dover. Then it's a quick run to Calais, coming in from the north, a loop around the city, and back for tea. The boffins want a clearer picture of what's going on there. Word coming back is a bit mixed. Are the krauts in the city, are our sods holding them off, what are the Frenchies up to? If Roger's camera rig works, we might find out. Buckle up, and we'll go have a look. You can read off the checklist and start earning your keep." His horsy smile was playfully mocking.

As Dunbar taxied the bomber across the grass, he was in brief communication with ground control, double-checking takeoff approval. On the intercom he informed his crew, "We're six to go. Everything working on your machine, Roger?"

"Righto."

"Stan, you remember to bring ammo for that peashooter?"

"Yah, sor. Got plenty."

And Burke, harnessed to the barroom seat beside Dunbar, listened to the exchange, listened to the Mercury engines grumbling, feeling the Blenheim alive, vibrating, smelling the sharp blend of fuel and metal, his eyes on the move from Dunbar's movements to the vista before them: the flat, green earth of departure and, ahead, a Blenheim starting its takeoff run.

"The vic of five going off ahead of us is our protection, so to say," Dunbar explained. "They'll be hitting armor around St.-Omer, east of Calais, and will draw Me's like flies, so they won't be interested in our little arse tweaker."

"And who's going to protect the five?" The plane he was watching seemed to waddle into the air.

"Almighty God and, we hope, a squadron of fighters. You think on my command you can get the undercarriage up and milk those flaps?"

"Let's find out."

He was surprised at how quickly they were off the ground, the field dropping away as Dunbar eased back on the power, turning smoothly. "You can adjust the cowling gills," he said, indicating. "We'll hold two thousand to Dover. Sorry we don't have dual controls. I'd see if you can fly."

"I'll always regret not having the chance, but I'll tell you something, I can't thank you enough for inviting me along."

"We hope others like you will be coming along soon, Yank, and not just for the ride."

He knew the blue above, the green, neatly partitioned land below, ripe in springtime quietude were illusory, that close ahead lay a different kind of springtime. But most of all, he knew he was alive and where he wanted to be.

Dunbar began losing altitude before they reached Dover, ducking around a flock of barrage balloons. "All right, lads," his voice rasped on the intercom, the jocular tone gone. "Let's stay sharp. Check your equipment over the Channel, Roger. I'll come into the harbor from due north, climb to five hundred and make the sweep, then back out over the Channel. Make sure that bloody camera works."

Winging over the sun-sparkled water at wave top gave the impression of great speed. Ahead, along the horizon, the sky, tan and dirtied, swiftly took on an uglier hue, blackened with globs of smoke and flashes of flame. He felt the plane tremble as Kulski tested his Lewis, and Dunbar pressed the button on the yoke to check the rear firing gun. Through the windscreen that gloved the forward section of the fuselage, Burke peered intently, looking upward for anything that might be moving against them.

"Calais." Dunbar pointed, changing course a few degrees, Burke sure he was going to dip a wing tip in the water. Off to his right he caught a glimpse of what he took to be three destroyers, heeled over, the pinprick flashes of their guns firing shoreward. A pall of smoke hung over the long, splayed-out harbor entrance cluttered with shipping, some of it half sunk, some of it with guns firing. Just beyond, like a stage backdrop, lay the emerging barrier of the city's face.

"Steady on, Roger. I'm climbing." Dunbar applied full power, and as they left the harbor and went up over the city, Burke caught sight of troops scurrying along the docks, a destroyer unloading, trucks moving. At five hundred feet Calais was sprawled out beneath them, wreathed in smoke, a mass of rooftops, rubble-strewn streets, a broken church spire. He was sure they were being shot at.

Dunbar angled the Blenheim westerly until they were on the fringe of the city and then turned, looping back toward the Channel. Burke spotted armor on the road below, saw to the east the smudge of a town burning. *St.-Omer,* he thought. Saw the smashed shell of a plane in a field, an ambulance on its side, a defensive perimeter being formed beside it by what looked like toy soldiers. Then ahead, through the smoke, he caught the welcome glint of the Channel.

"Alec"—Roger's voice was choked—"the bloody thing's jammed."

"Have you got it working now?"

"Yes, I think so."

"Can you keep the bugger on track?"

"Try."

"We'll go out the way we came in." He stood the bomber on its wing, and Burke looked down it at a burning tank. There was no doubt now they were a target. Black puffs soiled the air around them, the Blenheim bucking, a thrumming sound on the wing.

"Is it working, Roger?" Dunbar snapped.

"Like a clock."

"Pity it doesn't know how to tell time."

Neither approaching nor leaving Calais had Burke seen other planes in the sky. Nor did he see the Me-110 that pounced on them as they recrossed the harbor. One moment Dunbar was looking at him, no doubt about to say "a piece a cake," and the next the Blenheim was hit by a force so fierce that it seemed to stop flying, staggered, shaking violently, loud popping sounds over the engines' beat, holes disfiguring the windscreen by his head, a whooshing sound beneath, dust rising from the fuselage floor. And Dunbar! Dunbar had reached upward as though stretching, arched his back, and crumpled forward, the upper part of his body covering the yoke.

Burke had no time for anything but reaction. With one hand he flipped his harness catch and with the other grabbed Dunbar's shoulder, trying to pull him off the controls. The plane's nose was dropping and sliding to the left. The angle gave him extra purchase but added to Dunbar's weight. With both hands he hauled him off the yoke and got one hand on it, struggling to lift the plane's nose before it crashed, yelling for Kulski and Ormsby to come. Miraculously the Pole was suddenly there beside him.

"Hold him!" he shouted, getting both hands on the yoke. He saw the water coming at them as the nose began to lift, dropped his head in futile reaction, then looked up to see not water but sky.

"Got to get in his seat." He gestured.

"Ya." Kulski didn't need to be told anything.

While he struggled to maintain a semblance of level flight, the Pole got Dunbar freed from his harness and chute, and together they rolled him out of his seat. Burke slid into it, saw the discolor on his hands, and realized they were sticky with blood. What he knew about flying a Blenheim could be fitted into Major Pete Quesada's axiom: "*If it has wings, a tail, a prop, and controls you push and pull, you can fly it.*" He had no other choice.

But there was a difference. Smoke was pouring out the left engine. There was a ragged hole in the wing next to it. The instrument panel was a mess, the altimeter splintered, the airspeed indicator not registering, the stall hooter hooting on and off, but he needed only the seat of his pants to tell him the score. He shoved both throttles and mixture shafts to the stop, held hard right rudder and with his hand fumbled for the trim tab to try to restore some balance. Instead, he got white smoke and flame shooting out of the crippled engine, its whanging, irregular beat shaking the aircraft.

He had just pulled all power off it when the Messerschmitt hit them again. The pilot must have been green. Instead of dropping down to wave top level before making his strike, he dived at them, angle and speed too great. The attacker streaked past, a twin-engine dalmatian-spotted aircraft with black crosses on wings and tail. He watched it begin its turn, saw it was planning to make a head-on try. He glanced at Kulski, kneeling beside Dunbar, using the first-aid kit, and decided he would attempt to crash-land in the water. It was their only chance. And then he saw the destroyer heeled over, cutting white icing, her pom-poms firing a barrage at the Messerschmitt. The Me continued its turn, sharpening it, climbing, and then fled.

"Thank God for the Navy!" Burke whispered as he made a shallow turn on the good engine, heading for the smudge of the English shore forty miles away. On the intercom he called Sergeant Ormsby and received no response. He laid his hand on Kulski's shoulder and pointed toward the nose compartment. Dunbar, he saw, was still unconscious, his face gone gray with shock, blood on his lips, blood on the bandage the Pole had gotten on his chest. Kulski, having stuck his head into the nose section, looked over his shoulder at Burke, shook his head solemnly, and crawled back to tend to the pilot.

There was no time for impact to register. All his energies were centered on keeping the plane in the air. The engine instruments still functioning indicated head and oil temperatures in the red, oil pressure on the good engine not good. The left engine was dead, continuing to trail white smoke. There would be no problem in trying to feather its windmilling three-bladed prop. It was gone, fallen off. He saw that as a benefit. With full trim, holding right rudder and aileron, he could almost keep the left wing level. The air stank of cod-liver oil, which he realized must be hydraulic fluid, meaning the gear would probably have to be hand-cranked. Worse, the controls were beginning to feel extremely heavy. As the coast took on form, he made a move to gain altitude, at least enough to clear the headland. The Blenheim would not respond. With full throttle, the prop in low pitch, mixture emergency rich, he was fighting to hold the altitude he had. The hooter was telling him he couldn't hold it long.

Over the sound he called to Kulski, "We're going to have to land in the water. Is there a dinghy, a life raft? I'll try to land as close in to shore as possible. Can we get him out the side hatch?"

"We try, sir."

Short-field landing in a wet bed. Ass-first touchdown. The words flashed as he began gauging distances. The secret was to land nose high, dragging the tail wheel at the point of stalling. He'd learned the technique in the cow pastures around Burlington. But this was a different kind of pasture, its motion difficult to measure. The starboard engine was now running very rough, rpm's down to 1900. With the weight of the dead engine, he could not chance a left turn. A turn to the right would put Dunbar and Kulski on the sea side exposed to the current and choppy water. No good.

"I'm landing straight in." He signaled with his hand. To his right, he could see a clutter of dwellings. Help would come from there, he hoped. The shore ahead appeared rock-strewn, and the land backing it high and deadly. He must not overshoot. Judging altitude over water was a bitch, but since he didn't have any altitude anyway . . . Over the damned hooter he shouted, "Hold on!" He eased back firmly on the yoke, trying to lift the plane's nose. Saw the land too close and thought, *Misjudged, too fast, too late,* then felt the tail wheel grab, forward motion checked. He yanked back on the power and got his arms up to cover his face as the weight of the Blenheim smacked down into the water with a huge splash, its thrust braked fiercely, flinging him against the yoke, his arms cushioning the impact of his head against the instrument panel.

Stunned, momentarily disoriented, he knew he must get out, but he wasn't sure of where. *The water, the water . . .* Through a haze he saw Kulski emerging from the nose compartment, crawling, blood running down his face. Dunbar's body lay bent around the base of the navigator's station. Burke could hear water sloshing and feel the plane's belly grinding on the bottom. He could see people on the shore running, saw others wading out toward them, and one hauling himself up onto the wing.

"Jesus!" he said to no one in particular. "I don't want to try that again."

They dined at the Café de Paris in Leicester Square, a farewell dinner with wine and candlelight. She looked lovely and sad, and he knew that he was in love with her, perhaps all the more because this was good-bye. It needn't have been. Shouldn't have been quite so soon, but Kulski, in his wish to express his joy and gratefulness at still being alive, plus the rescue of his badly wounded pilot, had to blabber. And there was no shutting him off, except when they brought the body of Sergeant Roger Ormsby ashore.

"The Yank, he save us! Ya, ya, the Yank, he fly like a damned bird!"

Some bird. And although the Ministry of Information managed to squash the story before it made headlines—U.S. ARMY AIR CORPS PILOT IN COMBAT OVER CALAIS—or something equally appropriate, Ambassador Kennedy got wind of the incident and went up in smoke and flame.

Marlow had come back from Watton that same night and was just beginning to calm down the next day when the call came. Burke could hear the voice cackling out of the phone clear across the room. The colonel's face became very still, his eyes downward, hooded, glued to the pipe in his hand. Several times without success, he tried to interrupt. "Very well" was all he was able to say, and he said it stiffly, angrily, and hung up.

"I'd never seen the old boy really angry, and I suppose part of it was that Kennedy blamed him for my doing the forbidden and unforgivable."

"It's all so stupid, Peter," she said it vehemently, "bloody stupid."

" 'Fraid not from the official point of view. Marlow could have thrown the book at me, preferred charges, sent me home to be court-martialed. Now Kennedy has saved him the trouble, but the War Department will give Colonel Mike hell. It'll probably go on his record. Might even prevent him from becoming the principal military attaché." He shook his head. "I certainly didn't want to get him in trouble," he said, deciding he would not tell her about Marlow's previous offer.

"What about Wing Commander Raymond? Couldn't he put in a good word for you with the ambassador, one Irishman to another?"

He laughed. "Colonel Mike said Raymond's recommending me for a British decoration. I'll wear it when they bust me down to private. Listen, my lady, let's not spend our last evening together going over the wreckage. Kennedy's worried sick that we're going to get in this war, and he sees me as someone leading the charge. The one thing I'm glad about, aside from being alive, is that my performance got me the chance to dig you out of your hiding place." He reached over and took her hand. "You're the only thing that made my duty here worthwhile. Why don't you come to Galway with me?"

"I'd like that." Her eyes, her look said she really would.

"I'm told I'll be traveling there with six or seven hundred of my fellow countrymen who want to go home before the war gets here."

"I think they'd better hurry."

"Hurry to Galway and then stand and wait for weeks for the ship to arrive. Why don't you take some leave? Tell that animal trainer you need a rest."

"You're a dreamer, dear man. Galway is never-never land for me."

"It's all a dream anyway, isn't it? Three days ago I saw a *real* Messerschmitt."

She smiled. "You're quite a fellow, Peter. I'll miss you terribly."

When he had finally reached her and told her the news, remaining restraints in their relationship had seemed to vanish. "Drink your wine," he said, "and I'll take you dancing at the Four Hundred."

He was still holding her hand, and she placed her other hand on top of his. "I didn't wear my dancing pumps, darling." She spoke softly, looking at him. "But I know where there's another bottle of wine."

He awoke in the darkness and did not bother to move his arm to see the time because she was lying on it, and he did not know she was awake also until she lifted her head and kissed his cheek.

"You're awake," he said.

"You, too."

"All but my arm."

She raised herself. "Not a very proper bed, I'm afraid."

"Very proper," he said, withdrawing his arm, thinking it was not as stiff and sore as his bruised ribs.

"What time is it?"

"Time enough, my love. Would you like a cigarette?"

"No, but you have one."

"Never before seven. What are we going to do about us, Claire?" He took her face between his hands and kissed her. "I'll try to find a way to get back to you. If there were time, I'd marry you and take you to Galway with me."

"Oh, Peter, Peter." She sighed sadly, "I always seem to lose what I love. I promised I would not love again, and then you came bouncing along. I tried so hard not to."

"Did he get sent home, too?" he said facetiously.

"No . . . he was killed. In Rome." And she told him about Tony Hansell. "When I came back, I met Mal Warwick. He was a friend of Tony's, and he was able to have me transferred from MI 6 to 5. He gave me the support I needed. That's why he's such a mother hen around me. Protective."

"I'd like to protect you all the rest of our lives," he said, looking down at her in the dark.

She raised her hands to his shoulders and whispered, "Protect me now, Peter."

Through force of habit he awoke again at five o'clock. In spite of the blackout curtain, the darkness was less congealed. He could see the form of her tiny basement apartment, the table with the empty wine bottle, the two glasses. Still life: *Time gone.*

She was awake, looking at him.

"Good morning, my love." He leaned over her. "I'll have to be going away in an hour."

"I know. I was lying here, thinking that perhaps we should write a note of thanks to Scott Reardon."

"Reardon! What the hell for?"

"If it hadn't been for him, you wouldn't be here right now, darling." She ran her finger down his nose coyly.

"My God, what a thought." He began kissing her. "You forget him."

"Would that I could. We did get some information yesterday that means we're on the right track."

"Another coincidence, no doubt."

"No, I don't think so. A packet of documents evidently arrived in Berlin fitted into a music score. We had a lead that—"

"Wait a minute!" He sat up quickly and sucked in his breath at the wrenching pain in his chest. "S-say that again. What kind of music score?"

"One with a cover. You've seen music scores, haven't you?"

"Hell, yes! The shelf in Reardon's closet is stacked with them. All with covers."

Now she sat up. "But Inspector Goddard reported you found nothing."

"It didn't look like anything. Reardon's a musician, plays that damned kazoo."

"You didn't examine the scores?"

"No, not really. Just glanced at a top one."

"Peter, I'll have to get in touch with Mal right away." She sprang out of the bed. In the dim light the silhouette of her body reminded him of a painting. Her nakedness drove away any thought of letting her contact Warwick at the moment. To hell with Scott Reardon! He was out of bed and after her before she could find a stocking.

8

Weary as he was, he had not slept well, his sleep troubled by formless dreams, dark swirlings, washing him back into wakefulness. He lay with arm across his eyes, blotting out the early-morning light that somehow filtered around the blackout curtain.

The sour taste of too many cigarettes was in keeping with his tiredness, his mood. The flame was not burning bright. It was more like flickering. He had not gone near Fanny's since the news of Lord Wilmot's arrest, knowing that if Wilmot had been detained, the chances were that Fanny had been also, or, if not detained, certainly put under close watch. Equally as bad, he had not been able to get free to perform at the scheduled concert. When he had called Sir Sidney to convey his apologies, he'd spoken instead to Dame Myra Hess. The creator of the concerts was no sorrier than he that he couldn't be on hand. What made the lost connection all the more infuriating was her informing him that "Yes, Anton Codreanu will be with us." He asked her to convey his regrets to the violinist, promising to be available to perform with the chamber ensemble on Friday the thirty-first. That was only three days away, and he was determined to be there even if it meant pulling a sick act at the chancellery.

With the Wehrmacht moving so successfully, he wondered if anyone in Berlin would have time to evaluate the information he had been culling. Most of the new material dealt with the U.S. reaction to Allied defeat—Kennedy yowling and Roosevelt and his diplomatic henchmen finagling to get in the war before it was over. Bullitt in Paris sounded like a man peeing in his pants while calling for the Marines. In any case the movement of naval and cargo ships, the gutting of the Neutrality Act, should be of interest to Berlin.

He rolled over, not feeling any better at the thought. There was something underneath, something troubling him, a warning, indefinable, a voice. Whose? In one of his fragmented dreams his mother had appeared. He could see her gentle expression, her blond hair coiffed around her elegant head. Her pale blue eyes had a luminosity from within that seemed to peer beyond. Only Celts and Gypsies were supposed to have second sight. But she had it, a Rhine maiden from the Rhineland. She had known when her husband had died though he had been far away. Other things as well. Moscow. She had known. And that son of a bitch Forbes had blocked him. . . . God, how he had reveled in it, feeling the terror-stricken form, mewling and jerking under him, in a kind of orgasm as he beat his brains out, weeping in fury over her loss. . . . He had not thought of her in some time, and now she had invaded his sleep. Why? To warn him? Or had she passed on to him the power of precognition?

In Warsaw he had awakened like this and had known on that first morning that the bombers were coming. Of course, everybody but the Poles seemed to know that. In April, when Beck had come prancing back from London, proclaiming the Allies would come to Poland's aid if Hitler struck, he had bet on it. Eilert, the second secretary, had preached it to anyone who would listen. Not Smigly-Rydz and the damnfool generals who thought their horses could stop tanks. The quality of smoked salmon from the Vistula and the best brand of vodka were more important topics of discussion among his carefree Polish acquaintances than what Hitler and Stalin had in mind.

He turned restlessly, his thoughts tracking back. That perceptive MA, Colonel Something-or-other, was sure the Poles could hold off the Germans alone, and Biddle, like Bullitt, wanted the Marines to come in right now. The fools, they all were fools.

He supposed if there was any one place his plan had taken root, it was in the basement with the bombs jarring his teeth, someone whimpering, a faint, monotonous theme to the hellish crashing and vibration, all of them taking on a ghostly look in the snowfall of cement dust.

When the sirens had sounded, he had passed through Biddle's office, checking, to see if any of the ladies needed escorting. There were no ladies, just the stack of deciphered secret cables on the ambassador's desk. He'd scooped them up like a vacuum cleaner. Shouldn't leave the secret stuff out in the open. Never knew who'd take a peek.

He'd taken a peek in the toilet before heading for the cellar. It had come together there with the thunderous impact of the bomb that had nearly unseated him. The exchange of cables between Washington,

London, Paris, and Warsaw added up to one conclusion. He could see it clearly, hear it in the shrieking whistle of bombs, read it between the lines like a Moussorgsky theme. Roosevelt was going to lead America into war. The duplicitous bastard had to be stopped, had to be brought down! Huddled and helpless under the mindless crashing impact from above, he had called to his father, *"I'll get him. I'll find a way."*

He'd found the way all right, but what the hell good was it doing? Only the Allies making peace would stop King Franklin.

He rolled onto his back. There was something more. It lay not with his father's ghost but with his mother's look. Was she the figment of a dream, or had she really come to warn him?

He was dozing off in spite of his restlessness when the clang of the telephone in the hall convulsed him; every muscle went rigid. It rang but once, and in the huge aftersilence he was out of bed, in motion. Not his mother's warning but Fanny crying out, sending the emergency signal!

He had on everything but his shoes when through the open window he heard the faint sound of the car docking at the curb. He was out the door, locking it, shoes in hand, hearing the knocking and the bell ringing coming up from below. He could not descend. In the dim light he took the stairs two at a time to the landing above. He heard the gobble of the hunters as they gained entry and came charging upward.

Surov had taught you must always have a way out. Plan for it. But he had not planned for it, not really. He lay by the banister's edge and saw their bulk, three of them.

"Open up! This is Scotland Yard!" The clarion command over the tympanist, pounding the door. The noise was going to bring the attention of other dwellers, doors opening as they kicked in his.

He rose and went down the hall to the attic door. It was not a plan at all, just a place to sit among the cobwebs until the hunters came looking. He had explored it once, briefly, when he stored his trunk. He sat down on the steps and put on his shoes and then felt his way upward. There was more light because there was no need for blackout curtains. He thought of climbing into the trunk, a fitting coffin. The place was a graveyard of packing boxes, dusty furniture, and molding papers.

There was no going out the window. There was no going anywhere. He could only stand and wait to see if his locked door, his unmade bed, his missing clothes would convince them he had already flown.

The flame was still, low, flickering. He sat and waited, listening to the emptiness of the silence, finding no music to fill the void, no bassoon trills. Stillness. Stillness was all.

It was shattered by the door opening. "Is there a flat up there?"

"No, sir. Just the usual storage. Old things."

"I'll have a look."

"Go right ahead, sir. Not much light up there. The wiring needs repair."

A third voice sounding, words indistinct.

The would-be attic explorer shouted in reply, "Going to take a look about in the loft, Inspector!"

Garbled response, followed by a Gloria. "As you say, sir!" And the door slammed shut.

He was covered not with dust but with sweat. With his back against the trunk, he fingered his options. They had concluded he was not on the premises. They would go looking for him. They would leave someone, probably the disappointed attic man, to watch for his return. Where would he watch from? The entranceway, the street, front, back, the flat? The flat most likely, with the door shut to give no warning. System and routine. Timing. By eight o'clock all boarders would be away to their places of work. Mrs. Hodgkins would be in her kitchen, 'avin' a nice cuppa tea. Husband, 'Enery, would be in his front room, reading the news or listening to the BBC or maybe keeping watch for Scotland Yard. 'Enery's bicycle was in the shed, and it was going to be borrowed. The problem was to reach it and ride it down the back lane without notice being taken. If he could get in and out of code files without being seen, he could damn well manage this.

The wait did not seem too long, although the dust got in his nose and he had to fight sneezing. At exactly eight o'clock he took off his shoes again, rose, and went down the narrow steps. Careful as he was, the door did squeak when he opened it. He froze, holding his breath, listening for reaction. There was none. From the landing he could see that the door to his flat was closed. He descended slowly, eyes riveted on it.

A door opened and slammed shut at the end of the hall. He stood immobile as a whistler clumped along the corridor purposefully. He did not look up, going down the stairs in a noisy prance. His high-pitched voice greeted 'Enery, and their voices commingled.

He did not wait or follow but went quickly along the hallway to the loo whence the whistler had emerged. He latched the door and had a look at himself in the mirror and then peered out the half-moon window to check the backyard area. There was no one in sight. *Get out,* he said.

Even though he was in stocking feet, the backstairs creaked under his weight. If the sound carried to Mrs. Hodgkins and she came looking, her screams would be heard in Whitehall.

It was not the stairs creaking that brought her. It was only that the routine broke down. When he eased open the door, she was not in her kitchen across the hall. She was bent over in front of him, doing something with the carpet sweeper. As she straightened, turning at the sound, he reacted fiercely, striking her in the neck with the side of his hand. She made a croaking sound, her body caroming off the wall, her glasses clinking down the hall. He caught her before she could hit the floor, eased her down, stepped over her, and ran for the back door.

Not until he was in the shed did he get his shoes back on. The bicycle in its stall was his Pegasus. He wheeled it to the lane, mounted, and pedaled slowly, his breath churning in his throat, his heart slamming against his ribs.

Poor damnfool Mrs. Hodgkins! Such a nice old mum. Why couldn't she be 'avin her cuppa tea? He put his head down, pumping faster. He had no formulated plan, only a single demand. Escape . . . But where? . . . Hide . . . But where? . . . Get away . . . But where to? There was no one in London to whom he could turn now. Not Fanny. Wait a minute, wait a minute! Ireland! Galway. There was a ship going to Galway to pick up U.S. citizens—the *Roosevelt.* How apt. Catch a train to Liverpool, the ferry to Dublin. Could he finesse it? Could he bluff his way on board with a diplomatic passport? Could he get lost among hundreds of home-scurrying Americans? He could damn well try. It could be a way out. How could he be spotted on a crowded train to Liverpool? By God, it might work. Get out of London. Get to Liverpool!

He swung off Ellis Street onto Sloane, heading toward the square. The morning was still young, the day fair, traffic moving smoothly, and he pedaled in its flow, possessed by a fierce inner resolve. He'd match wits with them. He'd always known that a force came to his aid when he was *in extremis,* that a watchful daimon rose out of the flame nurtured by daring. It had been with him since Fanny's farewell cry. It was with him now, urging him on. In its grip he nearly rode through a bank of bright-colored dahlias. Admiring flower lovers were about to cry out when he swerved. He slowed at once. He must do nothing to draw attention, must remain unnoticed, get rid of the bike soon. Victoria Station would be his first stop. He didn't know whether he could catch a train for Liverpool from Victoria. More likely at Paddington or Euston. But at the exchange window he could get the cash he needed.

It had not been General Surov but his father who, long ago, had given him the word on travel emergencies. He'd been preparing for the class journey down the Rhine.

"Son, did your mother give you enough money?"

"Yes, Father."

"Well, here're one hundred marks. Don't put it with what she gave you. Put it in a secret place. Keep it apart. Never use it for anything but the unexpected. Call it rescue money, to be used when you've spent all the rest." He was grinning, joking, expecting that the boy would spend everything his mother had given him.

"Do you have rescue money?"

"If your mother doesn't spend it all before I can rescue some, particularly when I travel."

He had taken the suggestion seriously and had proudly returned with the one hundred marks. Since then he had never traveled anywhere without rescue money, and the fifty-dollar bill within the lining of his wallet was going to rescue him now.

He parked the bicycle on Hudson's Place and entered the station's wide entrance. Immediately he stopped in his tracks, aware of many police, civilian and military, and a sparse flow of travelers even though the central clock indicated this was still the rush hour. Barclays had a money exchange window on the far side of the waiting room, and it had been his intention to go there first. He saw he could not get there easily, for a double line of military police was being formed to cordon off the center of the station, extending from a track platform to the main entrance. Passengers were being blocked on both sides. He spotted a bobby checking a traveler's identity card and automatically turned away, deciding to get out of the place. It was then he saw the train with its many coaches sliding in and with it heard the commotion at the station front. He turned and watched a group of nurses, joined by ladies of the ARP, Red Cross, and Salvation Army, some trundling a military canteen, make their way between the cordon toward the arriving train. Watching, he realized what all the hubbub was about. The train must be bringing troops who had been evacuated from France. It was.

They poured out of the coaches, a motley noisy ragtag mob of unwashed soldiery, many with faces the color of their grimy brown uniforms, most bareheaded, all weaponless. The ladies mixed amongst them, and the sound that flooded the station and rose into its concave roof was one of homecoming and jollity. No doubt it reflected the joy of being alive, but the surging filthy mass in high spirits seemed to be confusing the shock of defeat with the headiness of victory, or so he mused.

"Brigade!" the stentorian voice of command blared forth over the multitude. "Form up! Form ranks! Fall in!"

The order had an immediate effect. The milling throng stopped milling, stopped its babble, transformed swiftly from a disorganized mass into the geometry of military order. A mixture of different units, shredded by casualties, there on the station platform they formed up and, weaponless though they were, became again soldiers. Under the command of the few officers in their ranks, they faced left and marched smartly through the station to clapping and voices raised in support.

Bloody fools, he thought, not sure whether he was referring to the troops or the admiring crowd. He turned, and a bobby, a very tall and large policeman, coal bucket helmet notwithstanding, was coming toward him. There was no way around him, and he had the sensation that everything was draining into his feet.

"Beg pardon, sir." The bobby leaned forward from his hips, his voice low, confidential. "Would you happen to be with the Eastham Boating Club?"

He had a millisecond to make up his mind. He said yes because he was afraid if he said no, he might be asked to produce identification.

"Right this way, sir." The bobby led him toward a bank of ticket windows, the barrier of military police having dispersed. As he followed, he rejected trying to run for it.

"Right 'ere, sir." The policeman stopped at the chosen ticket window and stepped aside.

He stood looking through the grating at the ticket dispatcher, bald and owl-faced. "You be with the club?"

He nodded, wondering if he had the fare to wherever the club was traveling. The dispatcher pushed a ticket toward him and said, "No charge. Track four to Dover. You'll need to shake a leg. Good luck."

He had no intention of going to Track 4, but by the time his accommodating police escort had guided him to the waiting train, he was beginning to think the unexpected offer might be an opportunity to be taken at the flood. In hunting him, the hounds might trace him to Victoria, but not beyond it because by then, by then he could be beyond their reach! Again he felt he was being guided by a watchful presence more powerful than a helpful bobby.

The train was very short, only three coaches, parked far up the platform. The trainman was checking his watch and waving for him to hurry. "Good luck." The policeman broke off as a guide.

The car was not divided into compartments but was similar to an American coach. The seats were largely occupied by a voluble group of passengers, dressed as though they were going on a hike or, best of all, a sail. They sat facing the front, and little attention was paid to his entrance from the rear. As the train gave a starting lurch, he slid into an empty window seat, breathing as though he had been running. *Easy, easy,* he cautioned himself as the movement began to quicken, and then he was jerked forward when the brakes were suddenly applied and the train came to a jarring halt. Voices within the car were raised in mild disgust. "Throttle forward, you sod" . . . "War's over" . . . "Hitler's missed the bus again." The remarks were a vaguely heard chorus, for without he could hear the shrill sound of a whistle and glimpsed a figure running. How could they have caught up with him so soon!

He stood, ready to try and make a break for it onto the opposite platform. The door at the far end of the car slammed open, framing a large individual wearing a peaked skipper's cap, neck scarf, blue blazer, and flannels, a yachtsman dressed for a club do. "What ho, lads!" he boomed. "Nearly ran aground on a lee shore."

His arrival and announcement were greeted with cheers and calls of welcome. "Rule Britannia, Commodore!" . . . "We wouldn't ha' lifted anchor wi'out ye!" . . . "Onward, Eastham!"

Again the train gave a sudden lurch forward. This one was even more decisive, and Reardon sat down again, his breath going out in a long hiss of release. As they cleared the station shed and the track curved, he saw a sign on a building side, a beer advertisement, the slogan calling to him: TAKE COURAGE.

Twice during the journey they were stopped, each time shuttled off onto a siding, where they watched two very long trains packed with troops being served coffee and food by groups of volunteers. Like those he'd seen in the station, they looked like the filthy remnants of an army, leaning out the windows, calling to the helpers and watchers. The damn fools acted as if they'd won the war, and his fellow travelers seemed sure of it, the dapper commodore leading the cheering section.

Behind the man's deep-throated, hail-fellow-well-met bravado, there was no doubt he was the officer in charge of the thirty or so members of the Eastham Boating Club. And as the train proceeded toward Dover, Reardon watched him pass from seat to seat, checking names on a tote board and chatting with his fellow boatmen.

Sitting alone and wearing a business suit instead of casual dress, he knew he must play the commodore with great care. Beetle-browed, turquoise blue eyes, sturdy-nosed, heavy-lipped with a rock of a jaw, the yachtsman in charge surveyed him with a mild but faintly quizzical expression. "I don't believe I've had the pleasure," he said.

"No, sir. I must confess I'm a stowaway."

"By Jove, you don't say."

"I was planning to go down to Sissinghurst, my uncle Nigel's place, you know, but when I overheard that you boating chaps were off to Dover to lend a hand, I thought I'd like to go, too, if you know what I mean, sir." He spoke with what he hoped was an Oxford accent, his tone faintly apologetic, seeking acceptance.

"*Hmm.*" The commodore gave his jaw a contemplative stroke. "And we had thought our movement was rather hush-hush. Well, no matter. What do you know about boating, and by the by, who are you?" He sat down, and Reardon was aware that his cologne had a sealike whiff to it.

"My name is Peter Scott, and yes, I do know a bit about boating, sailing, I should say. Had an Enterprise sloop a few years back, six meters overall. She was yare," he said in fond memory. Both the expression and the sloop had been his father's, and he could recall as a small boy being taken sailing on the Bodensee. Later there had been the three golden summers on Cape Cod at Chatham where he'd had his no-class clinker-built twelve-footer. Oh, she, too, had been yare. He had named her *Endymion* to impress the girls and because the thought of eternal youth possessed him.

"Where did you berth your vessel if I might ask?"

It was not a question he had considered, and for a moment he was checked.

"Well, ah, we had her at various places, ah, she was really my father's boat, although he had little time for sailing, don't you know?"

"I suppose you've sailed in the Channel, Goodwin Sands, the Deal?"

"Oh, yes, upon occasion." The question stimulated his memory of something he'd read. "Once we kept her at Sheerness and then at Ramsgate, I believe."

"Oh, you don't say. What yacht club?"

Again he was in trouble. "Well, I . . . can't seem to recall the name, or perhaps we had a private mooring."

The commodore's deep-welled eyes seemed to be peeling him. "*Hmm.* Ever sail into any of the French or Belgian Channel ports?"

"Yes, sir. Ostend, Zeebrugge, although not all that much." He forced himself to meet the penetrating stare. "But never to Dunkirk."

"Ah, then you know where we're going. How did you know that, pray tell? There's been no official announcement, nothing in the press or on the BBC."

"That's what I overheard at Victoria, that the Royal Navy was asking for small boats. That's why I decided to stow away, to help if I could."

A grin lit the commodore's broad face. "Good lad, good lad." We're a dozen volunteer crews, all berthed at Ramsgate, all approved for use by the RN. I'll take you on board the *Black Swan,* she's my darling. Incidentally, I'm Commodore Basildon. Come along and get to know the other chaps. I'll introduce you as the Stowaway. Once aboard, we'll find you something more seaworthy to wear."

And so he was "welcomed aboard," as Basildon put it, was immediately tagged with the nickname Stow, and settled down to exchange lies with the club members, a disparate group of weekend boaters who used their small craft for sport and pleasure. "As I gather it," his newly acquired seatmate, Colin, put forth brightly, "we're going to supply our forces with a one-way cross-Channel cab service, don't you know. Really a smashing go, what."

It grew on him that he could not have found a more accommodating or perfectly structured means of concealment. Liverpool and Galway would have offered a tricky way out at best. Scotland Yard would be checking all normal means of transportation, but this was a special means, and he hardly thought they'd be looking for him at Dover or Ramsgate.

What was waiting at Dover was nothing that he, Commodore Basildon, or any of his newly met shipmates could have anticipated. The broad harbor was a mass of shipping, the Admiralty pier and other docks crammed with naval ships and other vessels, ranging from destroyers to patrol boats. Flowing jerkily to the quays was an antlike mass of troops, exhausted, bloodstained, some carrying rifles, most weaponless, others wrapped in blankets for lack of clothing. Ambulances, mobile kitchens, buses, and coaches lined the harbor front and sought to absorb the khaki flow amidst a cacophony of whistles and horns. Unloaded ships edged away from berths, and waiting craft moved in gingerly. It was a convulsive scene, and sitting as spectators on a track siding where their coach had been parked, they saw there was direction and order in the close-packed swarm. Unloaded ships moved to refueling depots, then, amid much blinking and winking of aldis signals, put out into the Channel while other craft made their cautious way inward. There were tugs, taking in tow the badly damaged and the overlarge—hospital ships, merchantmen, minesweepers, and trawlers, the sinking and the blasted with gaping ragged black holes in hull and superstructure. Beyond the breakwater, across the hazy, glittering water, the sky was stained black, and over the whistles and horns came the sound of guns, of artillery and bombs.

There was plenty of time to observe the scene as they waited for Basildon to bring word on how they were to proceed to Ramsgate. *Debacle* was the word Reardon chose to describe the overall meaning of the harbor turmoil, and yet, and yet, he had to admit, it appeared to be a debacle under tight control. However, the British capability of being defeated in good order was not going to impress Hitler, and unless the French were able to stage another Battle of the Marne—and from all the poilus debarking with their British comrades, he thought it highly unlikely—the war should be over shortly. What did this mean to him for now and the future? Should he go ahead with the half-formulated chance this opportunity presented or should he cut and run?

"Wouldn't it be a jolly view if we could watch all this from Shakespeare Head? That's the highest point here, you know," piped Colin. "We could see how things are really getting on over there."

"You can see that well enough right here," someone sitting behind them said with heavy emphasis.

"Look at that one coming in with her bridge blown off," said another.

In the long wait the boatmen began a contest of identifying the types of ships engaged, none familiar to Reardon—corvettes, gunboats, coasters, packets, skoots, lighters, hoopers. They appeared more interested in the ships than in their passengers. *Glassy-eyed, punch-drunk, shattered remnants* were words that came to mind, particularly after Basildon had returned and gave them their orders. "All right, lads, we're to jump ship here. Going to Ramsgate by bus soon as they can find us one, ho-ho. Meanwhile, we'll give the ladies a hand at the mobile kitchens, so let's shake a leg."

And so throughout the day, standing by the town hall tower with its clock, which marked the slow passage of the hours, he served coffee and sandwiches to the bleary-eyed and the unwashed and noticed that woven within the stench was the garlicky tang of gunpowder. He enjoyed every minute of it because he knew there could be no safer place in all England for a hunted man like himself to be.

High overhead the Spitfires and the Hurricanes and the Defiants streaked in hurried passage. Lower down, the fat sausage balloons bobbed in the Channel breeze, looking as silly and impotent as all the rest, and across the Channel the heavy thunder of the guns mocked the swelling tide of the returnees.

They came down into the harbor of Ramsgate in the rain in the last gray glimmer of day and saw that the roadstead, though not as jammed with shipping as Dover, was nonetheless heavily engaged in the same activity.

On the ride from Dover Basildon had held forth, briefing them, stationing himself at the front of the bus with large navigation charts in hand. "Had hoped we would be making our first crossing by daylight, but as you can see, that's not to be. We will be sailing in convoy, towed over by larger ships under RN command, three of us to each ship. We will learn the sorting at Ramsgate. Our route will be roughly fifty-five sea miles. Some of you are familiar with the Ruytingen Light, and the pass there will be our entry point. As you well know, wind and current will be strong factors, and none of us are very used to being towed. Chances are the tide will be running against us at Dunkirk, and all of you who have sailed in those waters know how dicey the current can be close in. Once we are inside, possibly a mile or so out, all depending on conditions, we'll be cast off from our tow and make our individual way into the beaches. I repeat, lads, the beaches, not the Dunkirk moles. There are two of them where the larger ships are loading. We have orders to steer clear of them. We go in as close as we can to the beaches. When you are loaded and come back out, you may or may not locate your tow. If not, come back on your own. Now I'll pass the chart, and you can all have a look."

"Do we come back to Ramsgate or Dover?"

"Dover, of course, is closer, but you saw what it was like. You'll have to make your own choice, and you'll want to refuel before setting out again. Any port in a storm, as the old saying goes, and it could be a bit like that tonight. I should say, anywhere from Ramsgate to Folkestone will do nicely."

He went on, deep-throated, good-natured, slyly making it all sound like a Sunday outing, and listening to him, Reardon realized it was a hit-or-miss operation. Even so, right now crossing the Channel had an immense appeal, not just the risk of what he had in mind but the obvious hazard of getting there. The theme from the Strauss Concertino for Bassoon and Clarinet hummed in his mind. It reminded him that he had parted with an instrument to which he had become highly attuned. Farewell, friend. Not an Aeolian harp but a honey-toned spirit—perverse, subtle, secret.

They off-loaded by a dock shed and took cover from the rain while the commodore went looking for orders. He returned shortly to inform them they had missed their tows and orders had been changed. They could wait until new tows could be arranged, or they could put out in convoy following the motor yacht *Bonny Heather* under RN command. "We'll, of course, be running without lights," Basildon added. "From North Goodwin we'll be cutting across to the Ruytingen Light, as I mentioned earlier. Once inside we'll pick up the inshore channel between Gravelines and Dunkirk. I'm informed our course will be through a mined area that has recently been swept, so try not to hit any and embarrass the Navy, what." The laughter was a conglomerate bark.

"Now again, I repeat, we are to go into the beaches east of Dunkirk, at least as far east as La Panne. I have charts for you with the route and headings marked." He held up a package.

"How long to cross?"

"*Bonny Heather* will maintain twelve knots. All depending on the wind and weather, we should be there within six hours. Now how many of you wish to put out now?"

In the dark the *Black Swan,* her Thornycroft engine muttering, looked longer than thirty-two feet. On the dock Colin held the fore line, and he held the aft. Aboard he could see Basildon's bulk hunched over the binnacle, making final preparations for sea. It had stopped raining, but the smell of rain was strong in the air. They were to be number one behind the leader, the signal to cast off, three toots of its horn. The other Eastham boats in the convoy would follow one after the other, and he could not help wondering how this was all going to be done without lights of any sort. On the wind came the ominous thunder of artillery, ominous yet beckoning.

Bonny Heather sounded, and Basildon called, "Cast off, fore and aft. Lively now."

He jumped down into the stern cockpit, stowed the line, and went forward to the wheelhouse. When they first came aboard, Basildon had found him a heavy turtleneck sweater to wear in place of his suit coat. At the time he had not wanted to chance removing his diplomatic passport. Now in the dark, with the commodore at the helm, he found his jacket and removed the document. It was his ticket to safety.

Once they had cleared the harbor, he was surprised at how well he could see. The sky was heavily clouded, and there were rainsqualls and patches of fog. Even so, he could spot the wake of their leader as Basildon kept to starboard and another Eastham boat held to port, and behind he could make out the silhouette of the craft following.

"Keep a weather eye, lads, and sing out whatever you see" had been their orders, and as he held on to a stay and grew somewhat queasy in the cross chop, the pounding and rolling, and an occasional bucket of spray, he observed the passage of many ships, most appearing larger than theirs. Twice they struck objects, the sudden impact startling, making the *Black Swan* shudder, then lose way as Basildon cut power, swearing furiously into the wind.

"We'll never spot a mine!" Colin called cheerfully.

"Keep a close watch, and don't go overboard" was the advice from the wheelhouse.

It wasn't until they had navigated the pass through the Ruytingen sands that Colin's remark was disproved. The fires burning in Dunkirk, the shells exploding in its environs and the surrounding area provided illumination that lit the sky and revealed the inner channel decked with debris and bodies. Like *Bonny Heather,* Basildon throttled down, and they moved shoreward at slow speed. Under his instructions they used boathooks to fend off large objects. The smell of smoke mixed with cordite became pervasive; the shrill scream and explosion of shells, intense, jarring. They could see in glaring silhouette the Dunkirk moles, the long-fingered jetties where the larger ships docked and the shelling was the most intense. There destroyers maneuvered, and they knew troops were concentrated, waiting to be rescued, while ships and men were being blown to bits. It was a panorama unlike anything he had ever seen or imagined even after Warsaw. He was mesmerized by its unholy violence, and amidst it all, even more so than in the tangle of ships at Dover, there appeared to be order, ships moving off under shelling and others edging in to take their places.

Bonny Heather signaled them to come alongside, and a voice shouted, "Captain Basildon, make for La Panne. You'll find the patrol ship *Caleta* to direct you. Good luck!"

"Colin, Peter, come aft." Basildon summoned them. "Fine way to spend an evening, what." He greeted them, sounding buoyant. "If we miss *Caleta,* we'll move in and see what we can do. Tide is on the ebb. Don't want to run aground. Have to feel our way. Use the boathooks, and when we get in close, we'll try the grapnel."

They did not locate the *Caleta,* but in the area were other ships, some that were large, standing off and sending in lifeboats. Shells were shredding the air, throwing up geysers of water. To their stern a vessel took a direct hit, the blinding flash and roar more violent than all the rest, the air full of the killing *whir-whir-whir* of metal. Instinctively he ducked and covered his head, for once wishing he had a helmet. Lying on the prow, probing with a boathook, in the glare and sound of battle, for it was a battle to save His Majesty's troops from being blown to bits, he wondered how he could possibly make good his escape. Beyond the beaches there was a perimeter attempting to hold back the German attack. He could see the flashes of gunfire to mark where it lay, and it lay as far as he could see to either side. How could he possibly reach it and then cross it?

His pole made contact with the bottom, and he yelled, "Made contact! You've got about four feet!"

He heard Basildon put the screw in reverse, and then a voice out of the dark called, "Mite, over 'ere."

On his belly he saw what looked like a part of a pier and realized it was a pier of men standing in the water. "Ease to port, ease to port!" he shouted. "Passengers off the port bow! Colin, give me a hand." And then, instinctively, thoughts of escape were blacked out as he reached to give a hand to the first of the line.

He did not hear the shell, did not hear the explosion, only knew for an instant that he had lost his position and was hurtling without control into the darkness of the darkest night. Then he knew nothing. Nothing, until he knew he could not breathe and was being choked. He surfaced, struggling wildly, coughing, choking, taking water, sinking. He thrashed to the surface, fighting an unseen and killing force. He sank again. This time his foot found bottom, and he propelled himself upward, coherency beginning to return. Automatically he rolled onto his back, choking, gasping. His hand made contact with a hard object, a piece of wood large enough for him to lie on.

In the cold and wet he would sleep. In the whiteness the whiteness of the fog, a blanket to cover and conceal, he would sleep, for Commodore Basildon had said the tide was on the ebb and he would ebb with it. The rumble of Dunkirk had ebbed as well, but he was not going there. His ticket to safety lay elsewhere. He reached for his back pocket to check the surety of his passport, soaked as it might be, and was struck by an overwhelming realization: He had lost his trousers, and with them he had lost his identity.

PART II **BERLIN**

9 Burke lay on his back, watching the sullen gray mass of cloud rolling in a tumbling wave down off the flank of the Clare Mountains. The morning scene that had brightened Galway and led him on his solitary hike had been rubbed out, and shortly the grayness would suck up the green of the land, bleed the white from the cottages, and the rain would come again. He was not thinking about the weather or the scenery other than that he'd better start heading back soon. He was thinking about Claire and Liverpool, and only vaguely was he aware that the change in light and color of sky and land provided backdrop to his thoughts.

It seemed very long ago that he had left London on a train, accompanying a great gaggle of caterwauling Americans. At the Merseyside Station he had been met by a Scotland Yard officer who guided him to an office and gave him a London number to call. Surprised by the interception, he was even more so when he found himself speaking to U.S. Embassy Counselor Henry Sutterby. Sutterby had informed him that Reardon, about to be apprehended, had somehow managed to disappear. He didn't say "escape." It was Mr. Warwick's belief that Reardon might try to reach Ireland via Liverpool, and since Burke was already there and knew Reardon, he was being assigned to work with Scotland Yard in checking passengers arriving from London.

"And what about my orders?" He had not been at all amused.

"Your orders remain the same, Lieutenant, but your travel plans will be delayed."

"You mean if I miss the ship, they'll send another for me?" He did not try to hide his sarcasm, nor did he use the word *sir.*

"You have your instructions, Lieutenant. You'll be receiving them written in more detail."

He was so pissed off at the unexpected roadblock that he decided he would do as ordered until accommodations had been worked out for the American contingent to cross to Ireland without getting torpedoed. His travel orders had been cut by the military attaché's office, and he'd be damned if he'd disobey them to suit an ambassador who was out to screw him.

It all had changed three days later. It was raining like hell, and he was standing under the station shedding, watching passengers coming along the ramp when he saw Claire. His dumbfounded spirits had shot skyward into sunlight. The rain became a gift, and she was a gift. She had somehow convinced Warwick that the two of them working together would have a much better chance of finding Reardon, his escape having thrown MI 5 into a tizzy and Ambassador Kennedy into a rage. And so for three wondrous days and nights they had met trains, buses, and planes and in between had all the pleasures proved and over drinks wondered where Scott Reardon could be hiding out.

Saying good-bye had been rough, not only for the obvious reasons but also because of Dunkirk, what it meant and what would now follow. "Good-bye thirteen days ago," he said, getting to his feet, and here he was, not high and dry but low and damp in unsunny Ireland.

He began walking down the track toward the city, remembering the joke the barman had made about Galway. It seemed that during the First War a German sub had surfaced in the harbor with the intention of shelling it. The sailor sent on deck to report the city's conditions announced that from the look of the place, it had already been shelled. Well, he might not go so far as that. There was the cathedral and the salmon bridge and the friendly people. He raised his eyes and saw movement on the water beyond the harbor entrance. Large fishing boats? Certainly not the *Roosevelt* coming to fetch him and the trickle of fellow Americans arriving daily. But not a fishing boat either. He shielded his eyes. Whatever she was, she was as gray as all the rest, and then he saw her lines more clearly and said, "A destroyer."

He began to run, not because he thought a British warship had anything to do with him but because it had begun to rain.

It wasn't until evening that he found he had been only half right.

The ship was a destroyer, but she wasn't British. She was the USS *Truxton.* He learned the ship's identity and purpose in Galway, following a knock on his hotel room door. He who knocked was a uniformed, round-faced ensign, wearing peaked cap and yellow slicker.

"Second Lieutenant Burke?" He had an easy smile and sound. "I'm Ensign Walker, *Truxton.* How'dja like to get out of this peat bog?"

"Sounds like a reasonable idea. Come in and drip a minute."

"Can't, thanks. Got to round up the strays. *Truxton* is going to play ocean liner, ho-ho." He rolled his eyes at the thought.

"You're from the destroyer I saw coming in?"

"Aye, aye. Can you get your duffle down to the front? We've got a truck coming in about fifteen minutes. We'll be shipping out *tout de suite,* as the poor French are saying."

"Where for? New York?"

"Ha. Our passengers might not survive the ride. Bordeaux, as of now. As you may have heard, the French surrendered today, so that might change to Lisbon. See you below in fifteen," he said with a wave of his hand.

The *Truxton*'s silhouette in the rain and dark and dimness of the harbor lights gave an impression of bulk and length. As soon as he mounted the gangplank, in line with chattering passengers ahead and behind, the impression vanished, replaced by a feeling of compression, everything being tightly fixed and there not being much room to maneuver. This became immediately apparent when he stepped on the deck, where a petty officer and a pair of sailors were checking in the arrivals, other crewmen patiently guiding them sternward. Ensign Walker stepped out of somewhere and touched his arm, saying quietly, "Follow me, Lieutenant."

The gangway was narrow, and he banged his shin on a projection, sucking in his breath. "Watch your step," Walker cautioned needlessly, guiding him through a hatchway into the ship. They descended a companionway of metal stairs, leading along an equally narrow, dimly lit passage into a cabin which conveyed the same feeling of compactness.

There was a rectangular central table with a green felt cover and chairs, a long settle against the wall, and a shuttered mahogany partition looking like a closed train ticket window. The lighting was no brighter. There were no doors but facing green curtain entrances.

"This is our wardroom." Walker gave a sweeping gesture, his voice indicating the terrain was special. "Make yourself comfortable." And then, with a grin, he was gone.

Somewhat puzzled, Burke dropped his suitcase, looked around, read the engraved, brightly polished brass wall plate, giving the *Truxton*'s date and place of birth. He opened up his raincoat, lit a cigarette, and sat down. From the heavy sounds above he knew they must be preparing to depart. Fair enough, but what was he doing here? Waiting for the captain to give him his sailing orders?

The opposite green curtain was pushed aside, its ringers making a clacking sound. It was not the *Truxton*'s skipper who entered but an Army officer, wearing mufti, including fedora and topcoat. The sight of him left Peter Burke immobilized, momentarily overwhelmed, the impact of recognition stunning!

"Well, Peter . . ." The greeting, the firm voice with its not unpleasant rasp was tentative, noncommittal, as though seven years of silence and animosity could be easily put aside.

He was on his feet. He managed to respond. They did not shake hands. He was aware that his father with his hat off did not appear to have aged. For that matter, from earliest childhood he had looked the same to him. The cropped pelt and closely trimmed mustache were as much pepper as salt. And the eyes, the small, flat eyes with their glitter, were as fixed as they had been seven years ago.

"I know my being here comes as a surprise to you."

His laugh was reaction, its sound more like a cough. "Yes," he said, and they stared at each other.

"You're looking fit." The Iron Duke turned away, setting his briefcase on the table. In the light his skin looked as if it had been glued to the bone, his aquiline features sharply defined.

He had not thought about his father in weeks, had even decided that the Iron Duke had had no part in his being sent to London. Now, as he watched him shed topcoat and plop it down with hat, his original suspicions surfaced forcefully. "I was right, wasn't I? You were behind the whole thing."

"Sit down." His father gestured and sat down at the head of the table, opening his briefcase. "I don't know what whole thing you're referring to," he said equably, "but certainly you can't believe I had anything to do with Ambassador Kennedy's demanding your return and recommending a court-martial." He took a folder from the case and laid it on the table. "And were it not for the fact that the British Air Ministry has recommended you for some air medal or other, and the Foreign Office has given you a highly favorable commendation in the apprehension of Scott Reardon, I wouldn't be here, and you'd be on your way either to dismissal or a severe reduction in grade. Now I suggest you pay close attention. I'm here under War Department orders, and you're here to carry out the orders I'm authorized to give you. Understood?"

The quick, measured monotone, the no "ifs ands or buts" were a goad in his gut. He made no reply, knowing that whatever orders the faceless War Department had issued, it was his parent who had drafted them. He stubbed out his cigarette, letting the motion indicate his feelings.

The Iron Duke contained his, looking down at the folder for a moment and then began to speak matter-of-factly. "With Dunkirk, the fall of France, and the very strong possibility of German invasion of Britain, the situation regarding our communications with affected embassies and legations has reached a critical stage. The disruption of travel, particularly in France and the Lowlands, has made it increasingly difficult for our couriers to operate, to move our pouches. Right now, the State Department has three couriers traveling on British ships at very high risk. A couple more are on the Lisbon Clipper, but with no assurance of getting out of Portugal.

"The most isolated, and right now, as far as the War Department is concerned, the most important, of our embassies is Berlin. I don't think I need explain why. The *Truxton* is carrying the pouches you're being assigned to take there. The State Department has agreed to War Department's request for you to be made the authorized courier. Your official permits, approved by the German Foreign Ministry, through its embassy in Washington, are here." He laid his closed fist on the folder.

It was difficult to assimilate the unexpected words through the shock of surprise and the haze of resentment. The only balancing factor was the nature of the orders. It wasn't enough to still his reaction. "This is the story of the ground-bound career of Army Air Corps Pilot Burke," he snorted, "from spy catcher to postman. Did you think that up to avoid embarrassment should your son get the ax?"

His father blinked, his reply coming in a swift, hot breath, the lines in his forehead more deeply etched. "The word *Army* comes before *Air*

Corps, and while you're in this man's Army, you'll obey any damned order you're given." He paused and flipped open the folder, and without looking up, he added, "Just so we understand each other, I no longer care whether you fly a plane or a kite or get busted to buck private. All I care about is your getting the pouches to and from Berlin. After that do what you want."

The sound of the *Truxton*'s screws beginning to turn filled the silence between them.

"Where am I to be dropped?" he said, beneath it all intrigued.

"Bordeaux. You'll be met by someone from the embassy. You'll have a car, the proper documents, money. It will be a matter of working your way across France, through the German checkpoints. There is an unoccupied zone in France, about a third of the country. There's a map here with a suggested route, but you're free to go as best you can, as quickly as you can. You may wish to come out through Switzerland, Zurich or Bern."

"You say other couriers are moving about. What's the point in drafting me? I've had no experience."

"Actually you've had experience of a different sort. You've lived in Berlin. You know something about Germany. You speak the language; you've taught it." He rose and went to his coat.

Burke considered the proposition and the explanation for his selection, a body who just happened to be on the spot with good enough credentials. His suspicions were not stilled; the unexpected encounter combined with so much past interference. There had to be a catch somewhere.

"I find it hard to believe that you came all the way from Washington just to order me to go to Berlin to deliver the mail. Hell, I was just a kid in Berlin. I haven't taught or spoken the language in more than three years."

His father returned to his chair, pipe and tobacco pouch in hand. "When you're shorthanded," he said, "you take what you can get." While he packed his pipe and got it lit, Burke fired up another cigarette and felt the ship vibrating, getting under way.

Looking at the far bulkhead, puffing slowly, his father spoke directly. "Peter, try to forget your resentment, your bitterness toward me, and I'll try to forget I'm the Iron Duke."

The admittance that he knew the nickname Rod had given him was a surprise, a secret joke, no secret to its bearer.

"The British still don't know where Scott Reardon is, and regardless of their investigation of his activities, neither do we. Nor do they know whether he was a part of some larger network. We do know someone in Washington signaled your arrival in Lisbon, and that in itself could be a connection. We're operating in the belief that it is, and for that reason, as well as others I'll explain, you will not be traveling from Bordeaux under your own name.

"Here is your new diplomatic passport. You give me yours in exchange. Also, you will want to clear your wallet and any papers you have that identify you as Peter Burke, or as a U.S. Army officer. Also your dog tags. I have new ones for you."

He saw his name was now Peter Cannon. The photo was one that had been taken when he had applied for a passport following graduation from UVM. It had been touched up, making him look older. "So I'm a civilian again," he said.

"Yes. You're an official State Department courier, as your permit says. Take notice of all the visa stamps. If you were to travel as a military courier, you might draw attention at this time, arouse suspicion, interest the SS—the Gestapo. Since all State Department couriers are civilians, I'm sure you can follow the reasoning."

It all was coming at him very fast, and he realized the change in identity made sense; but he didn't much like the idea.

"So I lug the mail to Berlin and I lug the mail out. I suppose I bring it back on the Clipper. Then what? Does someone expect me to continue the routine to keep me from being court-martialed?" He did not conceal the hard edge in his thinking.

"I assume once you've completed your assignment, you'll be returned to duty with the Air Corps, and General Arnold can decide what to do with you."

"You assume it, but you can't promise anything."

His father looked at him. "Even though at times it is you who have assumed that I can arrange your career to suit my own wishes, I can promise you nothing. I take orders just like you. Now, shall we get on with it?"

He had no answer.

"You, of course, remember General Paul Anderson. Andy Anderson when he was—"

"General Anderson got me into Randolph, and you know it," he interjected pointedly.

"I'd thank you not to interrupt." The Iron Duke paused, containing his annoyance. "I'm speaking about Koblenz and Weissenthurm in 1923, when Anderson's father-in-law, General Bailey, commanded our occupation forces and Andy ran the air force there."

"And took Rod flying in a DH-4, and you refused to let him take me up and tanned my ass for making such a fuss about it."

His father, pipe in hand, looked at him, a tinge of surprise in his expression. It was obviously not an incident he recalled. "Well, let's see if your memory transcends your personal injury. You may also remember Captain Firman Jones, who was Bailey's political adviser before he went off to Berlin as an assistant military attaché. He used to visit us frequently in both Koblenz and Berlin. Do you recall him at all?"

"Yes. He was very tall. You and he played tennis."

"Good." The Iron Duke nodded his head in approval. "It seems you and Rodney used to watch us."

"After you kicked us off the court, you mean."

He ignored the slight. "Do you remember Jones's friend Paul Sturm, an Austrian? He, too, was a tennis player."

The questions were stoking boyhood fires. "Herr Sturm. I remember him when we were in Berlin later. He carved me a wooden model of Lindbergh's plane. I still have it somewhere."

"Excellent!" The long, thin lips bent in a smile. "Now listen to me, Sturm is presently a lieutenant colonel in the Abwehr—German military intelligence. He is also a gold card member of the Nazi party, having joined it in 1928. Very highly regarded in the Reich hierarchy." He busied himself relighting his pipe and then added matter-of-factly, "He may contact you."

"So I can carry his mail, too?" His sarcasm was automatic as he took in his father's meaning.

"Possibly."

"Jesus." He shook his head. "I must be getting in a rut. Everybody seems to want to use me for something I'm not trained to do."

"The results, no doubt, of your unfortunate upbringing."

"And Paul Sturm is one of ours. He's on our side."

"We played a lot of tennis."

"What about someone in the embassy? How come he doesn't have a contact there?"

"The custodial staff and most of the clerks are German. We assume they report to the SS."

"So how will he learn about my being in town?"

"In his position he'll know about your movements from the time you get off this ship. Also, your new name will be familiar to him. Do you remember his looks?"

"More than he'll remember mine. How long am I supposed to wait around?"

"You're not to remain in Berlin any longer than normal. Two or three days, and you start back."

"Cute." He could feel a churning in his stomach. "Uncle Bertie cons me into going to England, not to learn RAF operations but to play spy catcher, and you want me to make contact with your old tennis buddy, who really plays a different game. I didn't know you were in G-two but God knows, I'm not surprised."

The sarcasm was ignored. "You'll want to look over these papers. They're official documents, everything you need to assure your position, plus money, two thousand dollars." He took the packet from the briefcase. "After you count it, sign for it here, and keep an itemized account of your expenditures. Do you have any question?"

"Yes. What do I do if something goes wrong, like getting caught?"

"You're a bona fide courier. We don't think the Nazis will be anxious to create an incident. Besides, you won't be doing anything irregular."

"I'll remember your words when I face the firing squad."

"Sign your name here, and make it Cannon."

The stirring and stoking of old memories, he and Rod being chased off the tennis court, frequently it seemed, had suddenly brought another recollection into sharp focus. Like the ragged edge of a dream that refuses to congeal on waking, it had been tugging at a thread of his mind since he had read the letters in Scott Reardon's file, and now as he signed the voucher, it came clearly into view. He could even hear the thwack of the ball on racket.

"Wasn't there a fourth tennis player? You need four to play doubles."

His father frowned. "I'm sure there often was. Whom do you have in mind?"

"Scott Reardon's father."

The Iron Duke stared at him, expressionless eyes blinking several times as though pipe and cigarette smoke were irritating their cobalt blue.

"Yes, I suppose he did, once or twice—when we were in Berlin." He puffed thoughtfully. "Dwight Reardon was a brilliant but erratic diplomat. Apparently his son inherited the imbalance."

He had the impression his father did not wish to spend time discussing Reardon the elder, maybe because it had nothing to do with things present, maybe not. But he was damned if he was going to mention the unmailed letter Dwight Reardon had written to Uncle Bertie.

"Pity I have such a good memory," he said.

"Not to disabuse you of your talents too much, you just happen to be available at a time when the War Department is willing to use almost anyone capable of driving a car and carrying pouches."

"Sure, and I just happen to know your old buddy, and you want me to risk my ass so—"

"I believe you took the oath of office to do that on the ground as well as in the air. In the air you've already proved you can violate presidential policy. It is hoped you'll do better behind the wheel of a car." He smacked his hand on the table. "Your orders are to get the pouches to Berlin and return to Washington with whatever you're given. If Firman Jones's tennis partner contacts you, well and good. If not, forget you ever heard his name. Is that understood?"

"Yes, sir," he said exaggeratedly, angrily knowing he was verging on childishness.

"Now please give me your passport and any other identification, your dog tags, whatever."

He said nothing as he did as ordered. The Iron Duke collected the items and put them in an envelope in his briefcase.

"You can pick them up when you come back." He rose. "You'll be bunking with the other passengers in the crew's quarters. I'll be traveling as the guest of the captain. You won't be seeing me on board again, and if you do, you won't know me."

Burke stood and did not reply with the flip remark that came to mind. They looked at each other silently, and for an instant he experienced a tug of remorse that the barrier between them was so high. "Give my love to Mother," he said abruptly.

His father turned away and as he pushed the curtain aside, rasped, "Good luck."

10

For Sturm the day began intriguingly but ended badly. When he arrived at his office, the duty officer was ready with the night's wireless and dispatch traffic. Almost all of it was routine, but one report snagged his attention. It was several weeks old and had passed through a long chain of command, originating with an Abwehrnebenstelle attached to Army Command Brussels. He noted with a flash of annoyance that he was the last in line to receive the report when as head of the North American section he should have been the first. But no. For the better part of a week it had roosted in Bentivegni's counterespionage section, then on to Lahousen and his sabotage operations for another week, and, my God, even to Oster and the central section before landing where it belonged.

The report was brief. An individual claiming to be an American citizen, but with no identification, had been assigned to a work battalion at Namur. He had been picked up near La Panne on 31 May, processed by Abteilung Brugge and assigned to Work Battalion 4, Namur, Belgium, 10 June 1940. He either could not recall or had refused to give his name and insisted that he did not wish to be questioned by the American Embassy consul in Brussels. Instead, he requested to be put in touch with the German military intelligence. "The prisoner is about 30 years of age, suffering from severe concussion. Only routine interrogation has taken place. Request instructions for further action."

One additional point at the end of the report, like a postscript, was actually the most interesting citation of all. Apparently the subject knew the names of the principal officers at the American Embassy in London, including those of the military attaché's office. They were listed, and Sturm shook his head, chuckling at the failure of Lieutenant Ziesel of Abteilung Brugge to recognize the significance.

He considered bringing the report to the attention of Pruck. Maybe he could convince the colonel that he should take a trip to Namur. There was no doubt that Horst Pruck was in high good humor these days and would grant approval. In spite of his anti-Nazism, the colonel could not help being overjoyed by the stunning victories of the past three months, which in some measure reflected favorably on the Abwehr, particularly his own section. The thing was Hitler had won all. There was no denying it, and even those within the General Staff who had been plotting his removal since Munich were now singing his praises. He was sure Pruck had been supportive of Hans Oster's secret determination to remove the Führer.

But the hope, the prayer of so long were lost, and Pruck, military officer that he was, was willing to ride the wave, as, no doubt, was Canaris, their sad-eyed chief, who Sturm was willing to bet had been in on the plotting up to his Iron Cross.

He lit his first cigarette of the day and blew out the smoke as though it would clear his throat. The irony, of course, was on himself. For him as a gold card party member to have given any indication of support to General Oster's plans would have been to risk exposure. By not participating, he had kept his accepted identity as a loyal party member, the *alte Kämpfer* chevron worn with honor on his uniform sleeve, a dedicated follower of the Führer since before '33, a true believer in the thousand-year Reich. Heil Hitler!

He was, of course, an anachronism, a *Oberstleutnant*—a lieutenant colonel—in an organization whose officers prided themselves on being military, not party, men. That he was party and gold card and said to be known by Hitler had given him the twofold benefit of being avoided when possible and of being treated, at least by the underlings, with a degree of deference beneath which lay fear. He knew it had long been whispered in the *Fuchsbau* that he was one of Heydrich's men planted in the Abwehr. Once it had mattered. Now he was reaching the point where nothing mattered.

On that grim, self-pitying thought there was a rap on his door, and Pruck swept in. "Good morning, Paul, old workhorse, everlastingly at it, hey? The admiral would like to have a chat. So put the frown off your furrowed brow and come along."

Tall, fair-haired, vigorously handsome with mild yet nimble blue eyes, the secret service chief exuded an air of aristocratic ease. Sturm rose to follow, stubbing out the cigarette, feeling physically lumpy but immediately alert.

When they entered the admiral's inner office, Canaris was standing on his balcony overlooking the Landwehr Canal, smoking a cigar. On his overlarge desk were two objects that spoke volumes: a model of the light cruiser *Dresden,* on which he had served as a lieutenant with distinction and daring, and from Japan, a trio of bronze monkeys: "See all, hear all, say nothing." White-haired, short and round-shouldered, somber of expression and quiet-spoken, Canaris had on appearance, Sturm knew, that was deceptive. Behind the large, bland features, the expressionless eyes, Wilhelm Canaris was not really the "Little Admiral"; he was the wily old fox.

He came in from the balcony, followed by his two sleek dachshunds, Seppel and Sabine. He nodded in greeting and indicated that his visitors be seated on the black leather couch. Because his desk chair was raised and the couch was low, he had eye-level contact with them.

The dogs, having had their sniff, waddled off to their baskets by the conference table. The admiral's love of animals, particularly dogs and horses, was known to all at the Tirpitz-Ufer. Sturm was pleased the open balcony doors let in a breeze. It helped tone down the ever-present odor, a compost of dog mess and cigar smoke.

Canaris spoke with a slight lisp. "Well, the Führer has returned from Paris." All Germany, if not the world, knew it, and they waited for him to add information, but instead, he puffed his panatela and brushed cigar ash from the front of his uniform. "Well," he said again, waving the smoke away, "I had an excellent ride this morning with Heydrich and Schellenberg. Motte was in fine form. I don't believe there is a more intelligent animal anywhere. She knows so much. Do you ride, Sturm?" The rather mournful heavy-lidded eyes were upon him.

"Yes, Herr Admiral. When time affords."

"One should make time. Is that not so, Horst?"

Pruck laughed. "As much as possible, sir."

The point was not in the riding, Sturm thought, but in the company with whom one rode.

"When Heydrich was a cadet at Kiel many years ago," Canaris reminisced, "I recall he was given the nickname Ziege. He's come far since then, no goat at all. He's become an expert of sorts." He smiled thinly.

Sturm knew there was nothing new in the nickname.

"Not a goat but a hungry wolf with very sharp teeth," Pruck said.

"What does he plan now, Herr Admiral? To take over the Abwehr completely?"

"No, hardly that. What he's looking for is closer cooperation."

"So that when we invade England, he will rush in his *Einsatzgruppen* and end up directing all our intelligence operations?" He gestured broadly.

"No, Horst. You misjudge his intentions. He knows where the line is drawn. Himmler has made sure of that."

They all knew where the line had been drawn. Sturm looked at his shoes. Less than a year ago Himmler, with Hitler's approval, had amalgamated the Gestapo, the criminal police and Heydrich's secret service, the SD, the Sicherheitsdienst of the party, into the central state security bureau, the RSHA. And Reinhard Heydrich, who had been the architect of the joining, became its head. It was true enough that in the early days, when the admiral had taken over from Patzig as Abwehr chief, cooperation with the SD had been fairly close, even up to Case White, because the needs in Poland had been mutual. But everyone in the Tirpitz-Ufer was aware that in spite of the agreement drawn up by the admiral and Heydrich—sarcastically titled "The Ten Commandments"—it was but a piece of paper locked in the admiral's safe. Heydrich's knifelike ambitions, his vaunted arrogance were ever apparent. He was ever seeking to usurp power by whatever means of trickery and duplicity. The line was drawn all right wherever he could extend it.

"Herr Admiral." Pruck, even when serious, managed to inject a tone of good feeling while challenging his superior. "We all know the wonderful cooperative spirit of the Reichssicherheitshauptamt chief." He rolled the title with melodious sarcasm. "He draws the line like a rope around the neck."

"Dr. Werner Best is a man you can trust." The admiral's observation was standard Canaris, seemingly not germane, heading toward some oblique determination.

"As ambassador to Denmark I'm sure he is," Pruck said. "He was also smart enough to get away from Herr Ziege."

"He's here for a few days. We had a drink together last night." Again the admiral went silent, tapping the ash off his cigar while they waited. "You know as Heydrich's legal adviser he did much to smooth relations."

Sturm knew this had been true, at least until Poland, when Heydrich had secretly set up the false Polish attack at Gleiwitz without Abwehr knowledge, giving Hitler his excuse to launch Case White. Aside from that, everyone in both camps recognized that relations between the Tirpitz-Ufer and Prinz-Albrechtstrasse were never going to be based on trust. Aside from Heydrich, the reasons were fundamental, deep-rooted, the military caste against the Nazi loyalists, the NSDAP climbers.

"He can hardly have much effect on Ziege from Copenhagen, I should think," Pruck added.

"No," Canaris agreed, "but all the same, our talk got me to thinking about the future and the need for closer cooperation."

Pruck made no response, and the admiral began to thumb through the pages of a folder on his desk, cigar in ashtray. "Sturm," he said, "your analysis of the American attitude impressed me. Very objective. Very concise. How much of the substance is taken from the diary?"

He had known that the admiral would not have included him in a meeting with his principal deputy unless his services were to be used. As head of the North American section of IH West, the diary was his responsibility, a top secret possession not to be shared. It was passed to him directly through Canaris, and only the admiral knew its source.

"The diary, Herr Admiral, supplies the substance of the political background. I've used it sparingly for obvious reasons. General von Bötticher's most recent appraisal from Washington supplies the military basis."

"Yes, I thought as much." He closed the folder. "The Führer reads your reports with great interest." He looked at Sturm. "So does Heydrich. He raised the question of sharing."

"We do the sharing, sir." Pruck smiled. "What does Reinhard share with us?"

"Sturm is going to find that out."

They both were looking at him. It was like playing a childhood guessing game with clues and tricks along the way. "He asked if we would share some of the diary pages with him."

"Why should we do that, Herr Admiral? The SD gets Paul's analysis like the rest of the OKW. The diary is our prize, is it not?" There was a hard note of resistance overriding the usual good nature in Pruck's voice.

"Sharing," the admiral replied placidly, puffing his cigar. "Sharing, a little test. Sturm, you may select from the diary a half dozen or so excerpts on which you drew for your analysis. Nothing too sensitive, of course. General Heydrich asks that you come to his office tomorrow at ten. He is anxious to talk, says he's heard about you."

Sturm felt the familiar hard knot of pressure in his chest.

"But, Herr Admiral—"

Canaris raised his hand, cutting his deputy's protest. "Hear me, Horst. Heydrich has something to offer us in exchange. He will pass it to Lieutenant Colonel Sturm tomorrow."

"And he couldn't pass it to you, sir?"

"No. Evidently not on a morning ride in the Tiergarten and possibly because Schellenberg was present. But from what he did say, I'm interested to know more, to see what kind of game he is planning. While most attention is focused on the Führer's plans for England, Heydrich is suddenly interested in America. I do not feel that risking a few pages of the diary to find out is all that serious, do you, my dear Horst?"

"Probably not, but you may be risking Paul." Pruck laughed. "Heydrich's bound to try to make him a spy in our section."

"Section Three already thinks that," Sturm said, forcing a smile.

"Oh, Bentivegni and his counterintelligence trolls suspect everyone of being an opposite."

"I'm sure Sturm is too old a campaigner to be taken in by Reinhard's tricks of persuasion." Canaris spoke to Pruck and then addressed Sturm mildly. "Of course, should he make the attempt to suborn you, and you're willing to let him think he's succeeded, the relationship could be valuable to us."

"Ho-ho." Pruck rose and stretched. "A jolly little game."

"Perhaps." The admiral nodded. "But that's entirely up to you, Sturm. In any case, let us see what it is that he is prepared to share."

Alone again in his office, he smoked a cigarette, knowing he had now become a chess piece in the admiral's ongoing match with Heydrich. Diary pages in exchange for what? Did what really matter? Or was it that Canaris had come to suspect him and was offering him up to the SD to get rid of him? . . . Or was his paranoia reaching a still higher stage? The admiral's thinking was like a cloud of smoke. You couldn't lay your hand on it, and you didn't know what lay behind it. Werner Bekker with his round face and large nose came to mind, maybe a good parallel to what Canaris was really after.

Bekker, as chief of the criminal police, loathed Heydrich and his interference into Kripo's investigation of the Bürgerbräukeller bombing attempt on Hitler. Result: He passed on to the admiral everything concerning Heydrich and the SD that was beneficial to the Abwehr. And yes, Bekker had joined the party early, too, '30 or '31. But he was not Werner. He had been a true believer, at least in the beginning. His disillusionment had grown over time. No, unlike Werner, he had had no illusions from the start. He had had passion and Uncle Fronc.

He snorted cynically in the dark mustiness of his office, the smell of polished jackboots and dead causes like wet ashes.

Of course, anyone Heydrich was anxious to meet could automatically expect an investigation, digging into background and antecedents, particularly Jewish antecedents. God knew, he didn't think the ferrets could unearth anything to lay bare the soul of Paul Manfred Sturm; but there was no surety in anything, and he did not need this new threat rising in the ugly face of all else. Sharing be damned.

Well, enough! What was he going to select from the diary for sharing with Ziege? The thought brought into full focus still another disturbing question. Apparently only Canaris knew the diary's author, and only he knew how it was sourced; Pruck thought by way of Spain, where the admiral's contact ran wide and deep. From his own knowledge of top figures in the Roosevelt government, he had, over time, selected the one he thought must be the author. But since the material was coming directly from the admiral, he had never mentioned the possibility of a hoax. He simply took what was offered and used it accordingly and evidently to the approval of everyone from Hitler to Heydrich. Of late he had become more convinced that if some of the pages were counterfeit, were misinformation to mislead, others were not, and in fact, this morning's report from Namur was a piece of proof. But the question was, Why. Why on earth was the admiral willing to trade original pages from this most secret intelligence from the U.S. State Department for an unknown response from a duplicitous bastard who had been working to undermine his position for years . . . and to toss Paul Sturm into the pot for bait? He slammed his hand on the desk in frustration, rose, and went to the safe. The only choice he had was to make the selection, which, of course, could indicate that Canaris didn't think all that much of the material anyway. "Smoke, smoke," he said aloud.

Seated again, he felt a sharp twinge of pain in his stomach, his hand feeling at the bulge overhanging his belt; he was putting on too much weight. He opened the folder and began reading the pages he had used in his most recent analysis.

There were two major themes: concern in the upper echelons of the U.S. Department of State over the president's anti-German public statements, which had been rapidly taking on a more belligerent tone, particularly since his Charlottesville speech attacking Mussolini, and fear that German victories would bring the defeat of Roosevelt in the November elections.

The June 22 entry in the diary did not deal with the French surrender but with the political effect on the American public. The writer declared the Republican party "would have all the Germans, all the Italians, all the Russians, Communists, subversive elements, all the peace societies, the antiwar-at-any-price crowd" on its side. And if it won, it would pursue a policy of rapprochement with Hitler.

There was one entry that dealt with U.S. counterintelligence exposure of Abteilung I operations that he would not share with Heydrich and the SD. To do so would be to indicate that he was willing to cooperate. He was too isolated, too off-balance and depressed to entertain any such involvement.

He turned to the last page, which he read over with great care, absorbing the words like a balm to the pressures within. Here was the answer to the Namur report. Here was intelligence that was his, information he would share with no one. He was not sure how he would use it, not sure he would take the risk of sending it out, at least not now, or until he'd paid a visit to Namur.

The diarist told of the breakup of a spy ring in London, naming its chief as Scott Reardon. The writer had called the revelation a terrible blow, a major catastrophe. But his key fear was that Hitler would wait until the political campaign was under way and then publish another white book, including in it the exchange of messages between Roosevelt and Churchill, exposing their secret dealings and in so doing bring down Roosevelt.

When he first received the excerpt, he had debated taking it to Pruck. It was the answer to why the flow had suddenly ceased. The identity of the source they had know knew through the Irish V man and the admiral's Italian friend and opposite number, General Roatta, and certainly the SD had the same information, coming through Mackensen, but not this, not the background or the political threat to Roosevelt.

He had never raised the question, and Pruck had never mentioned the issue; but he had wondered why the intelligence coming from this unclaimed American had not been put to better use. Except for the few quotes included in the Ribbentrop white paper, nothing had been done with the material except to distribute it to the appropriate commands. Mostly, he believed, it was a matter of Hitler's being totally occupied elsewhere and of two minds in his policy toward the United States, anxious not to intimidate but holding a low opinion of American resolve. No doubt it had been reinforced by Bötticher's dispatches detailing military unpreparedness, supported most recently by the State Department's diarist's two-year estimate to prepare; that, and General von Bötticher's constant anti-Jewish emphasis. The Jews in America, he insisted, influenced everything and would never fight. Since '33, that had been his line from Washington. But the thing was that through this Reardon person Ribbentrop had in hand enough solid intelligence to finish Roosevelt. Still, if Hitler did not raise the question, that fatuous ass never would, nor would anyone else.

His mind had been wandering in circles—circles within circles. *And I caught within, circling.* A fly on a windowpane, seeing out but with no way out.

The work of the day did not temper his mood, the malaise ran too deep, and he left his cell-like office at day's end carrying his depression like a cloak. At the end of the corridor he stepped into the decrepit old elevator with its iron grille, knowing his departing colleagues would use the split marble stairway rather than the ridiculous box that descended from the third floor as though being lowered slowly by a rope. He had no desire to exchange meaningless pleasantries with anyone.

The Abwehr quarters of the Reichswehr Ministry was a five-story labyrinth of dark, Spartan offices. Exiting the dim entrance way into the mellow warm light of eventide offered a modicum of release, however small. He took a moment amidst the departing throng to bid Büller "Good evening." It wasn't necessary, but he did it regularly, for between them lay an unspoken relationship born of service on the Marne and the Somme, wounds taken in the summer of youth and when glory had died in the mud of Flanders. And more to the point, Büller was a mine of information, the best informed doorman in Berlin.

He came out onto the Tirpitz-Ufer, the long stone quay fronting the canal, and instead of heading for the bus stop on the Bendlerstrasse Bridge, as was his custom, he turned and walked to Hildebrandstrasse, heading up the long block toward the Tiergarten, his mood as still and black as the water in the Landwehr. He would seek some peace and quiet in the parkland. The Tiergarten was his oasis, free of the long corridors of granite-faced buildings with their suffocating red and black bunting of Nazi heraldry.

In the streets the atmosphere was somehow unreal. The peace, the quiet, even the hum of traffic seemed muted as though the war had been some remote encounter occurring on another planet. The rumor was that an entire division was to be demobilized, that there was to be a victory parade through the Brandenburger Tor, the first since 1871. Hitler would speak soon, would offer peace to the English and rule supreme. He exhaled the dregs of his cigarette, feeling old and worn.

He chose a bench by a corner of the pond where the swans supplied their own form of ersatz peace. Several laughing children were feeding them, parents clucking their warnings to take care. The smell of summer, of greenery, lay over all. Out of some indeterminate memory, he heard Pruck chortling, "Paul, old workhorse, I like your orderly method of thinking. Your planning is nicely mathematical, careful—the caution of sum and totals. You deal well in the cold neutrality of figures."

Maybe once, but not of late. His thinking had become scattered, diffuse, disorderly, a sure sign that he'd recognized for a long time. He needed to get out. Altogether out. Elsa had noticed a change in him, and if Elsa noticed any difference in his behavior, he thought wryly, others were bound to.

The British were no match for Hitler. The Americans were unprepared physically and mentally, and he was no longer a match for Canaris or Heydrich or any of them. As long as there had been hope, he had been willing to hang on . . . and hope. No longer. Namur. What was the point in meeting an American who had betrayed his country? Because they had something in common? *Ah, but my cause is just.* Just dead! No successes and a thousand failures. An exaggerated total, perhaps. Since Czechoslovakia the idiots in London had been incapable of acting on anything but their own defeat. On their behalf he'd risked all. And what was the good of stewing around in it? *Put your thoughts in order and devise a reason for not meeting Heydrich, for going not to*

Namur but to Switzerland. Go hide yourself in Geneva, and let them hunt for you. Even if he could find a way out, Elsa would never leave, not as long as her mother was alive. He wouldn't mind leaving both of them, but he couldn't face destroying them. The pain of long ago that lay within, the loss of Erik, was a pain for which he could now be grateful; they were childless.

He heard footsteps on the path and out of the corner of his eye saw a pair of black-uniformed SS *Untersturmführers* approaching. He swung around, staring at them, their studied effort to ignore him so obvious. His rising truculence was like bile in his throat. He stood up. The restful Tiergarten had brought him no rest at all. He'd go have a drink, maybe more, even if it burned his aching guts.

It was after dark when he arrived home, the drinks fortifying him against Elsa's anticipated complaints. He was relieved to find her note. She had gone to the canteen to help out. Certainly the young victors returning with their spoils from France were a far more attractive enticement than himself. The note added that he was to call the duty officer. Her absence and the duty officer improved his spirits enormously.

"Herr Oberstleutnant Sturm," the duty officer intoned, "Herr SS Gruppenführer Heydrich has sent word by special messenger that he deeply regrets he must cancel tomorrow's meeting and that he will reschedule at a mutually convenient time."

He flopped down with a great sigh. "Thank God for small favors," he said to the empty room. "Maybe the bastard doesn't care that much about me after all." So or not, thoughts of the man would not trouble his sleep this night.

He went into the kitchen to see if Elsa had left him anything to eat. Bless her wifely heart, she had. Elsa enjoyed eating so much she insisted he enjoy it, too; with his card she knew how to get around rationing. Tonight he'd have a bit of Bokma to wash it down. By habit he had brought home his briefcase filled with a packet of unclassified papers to be run through. And with his mood lifted, he decided he'd get rid of the mess while he ate. But first the schnaps.

He ate mechanically, turning pages quickly, his mind paying only half attention, the Bokma mellowing his fears. And then, suddenly, stunningly, he was looking at a routine report from Abwehrstelle Bordeaux concerning the routing of an American diplomatic courier. And on the report a name. A name! He began to laugh, choking, the sound strangling in his throat. "My God! My God! Would you believe it!" he half shouted. "Somebody wants to know the time in America. Well, I'll tell you the time, it's too late, too goddamned late!"

"What on earth are you shouting about?" Elsa stood in the doorway, looking fat and critical. "Are you drunk so early?"

11

He was going to escape. He had done it once by water. Now he would do it again, not by the Channel but by the Meuse and the Sambre. Standing on the scaffolding, he stirred the cement mixture with a heavy paddle as Philippe poured the sand and Karl the gravel. From his vantage on the high point of the new arch he could look down into the river and judge the swiftness of the current. The storm last night had given the water a chocolate texture, a good omen. For some time he had been practicing deep breathing, a technique his father had taught him when as a boy he competed in underwater events. If you did it carefully, slowly, you got more air into your lungs and could stay down longer. He planned to stay down very long, after he took his backward step and fell the thirty feet, crying out, making it look like an accident.

There were nearly one hundred of them, working on the rebuilding of the two arches that the Belgians had managed to blow up on the Jambes side of the river in an effort to slow the German advance. After all, Namur since ancient times had been the victim of invaders. And now in the late afternoon to him it was a Cibola, the city looking fortresslike and medieval in the summer light. He must reach it, not to find gold but to find food and clothing, to get rid of this scarecrow beard, make himself look presentable, so that when he found a military headquarters, he could make his importance known.

To remain here was to starve or to be worked to death. The NCOs who commanded them were fools, and the guards who carried out their orders brutal bastards. Three amongst the company had already died at their hands. He knew his own strength was failing. Since Brugge, when an attempt at the clearing center to make contact had brought him a Mauser butt across the head, there had been periods of disorientation, his head full of pain, his vision unfocused. Then a week ago he had begun to see clearly again, to understand, and to recall. And now he knew what he was going to do. Once again the flame was in place.

Philippe, the mournful-eyed Walloon, said, "Dummi, keep stirring or it will harden too quickly."

"Yah," Karl agreed, coughing. "Make for fast, Dummi."

They were speaking French, and Karl, who was Flemish, did not speak it well, but both had come to call him Dummi because the guards had dubbed him "Dummi Dummi," which in German means "imbecile."

He liked the meaning; he could hide behind it. When he fell off the scaffolding, he wanted them all to think he had drowned in a stupid accident. Looking downward, he could see his fellow toilers toiling as little as possible, knowing the day was nearly done, looking for an armored car to come with the sergeant, who would give the order to halt, to stack tools, to fall in and march down the valley to the cloister ruins where they had their camp of tents.

"Stir, Dummi, stir," Philippe repeated.

It was not an armored car he saw approaching but a staff car, and he decided now was the time to take his plunge. Attention would be on the car. He inhaled carefully, ready to turn and slip, when out of the corner of his eye he saw the guard they called Têtemerde coming along the plank walk, watching him. "*Schnell! Schnell!*" he ordered, waving his arm at Reardon and then began swearing.

Better still, he thought. *If he hits me, it will make the fall that much easier. Maybe I can take him down with me.* He stopped stirring altogether and stood staring vacantly at the approaching behemoth. Philippe and Karl edged away.

A whistle shrilling from below froze the action, halting Têtemerde in mid-stride. All looked to the sound, which to most meant the long day's work was done. The corporal, standing beside the staff car, cupped his hands and called, "Bring Dummi Dummi down!" It was not the corporal or his order but the officer in dark green standing next to him that caught Reardon. Falling into the river now no longer made sense, not only because everyone was watching but more important because it appeared someone had finally gotten the message.

The guard, instead of belting him, signaled and growled, "*Raus.*" Reardon handed a surprised Philippe the paddle and walked across the plank along the scaffolding to the ladder. He descended, hearing the corporal order everyone back to work. He was trembling from both weakness and anticipation. He stank. His clothes were little better than rags. His matted beard did nothing to reveal the handsomeness of his looks, and yet he knew when he stepped off the ladder, he must be in control.

The officer, a captain in high peaked cap, was wearing boots and uniform jodhpurs. A black belt with an engraved silver buckle encircled his waist. On his right sleeve, below the standard Nazi eagle with swastika, was a diamond-shaped patch bearing the silver letters *SD*. The patch, the jacket lapels, and the white skull above the braid of the cap identified the captain's service branch. Old Surov had done well to insist his apparatchiks learn the identifying markings on all Allied and Axis uniforms.

The pair watched his approach, the captain, a Nazi stereotype, blond and firm-featured; the corporal a peasant with a puzzled glint in his eye.

"You called me?" he said as though they all were equals.

The corporal made a barking sound. "You—you—you! You scum! You come to attention when you address a German officer!" His doubled fist was reaching.

"I'm not in your army," he said agreeably, his eyes holding the captain's.

The corporal lunged forward to take direct action, and the captain ordered sharply, "Obergefreite, enough!" Then, in nicely accented English, he said, "You're the American?"

"Somewhat battered and bruised," he replied in English, "and in need of refurbishing, I fear."

"What's your name?"

He looked at the nonplussed corporal. "Dummi Dummi," he said, smiling.

The captain cocked his head and opened the staff car door. "Get in." He gestured and spoke in German to the corporal. "I'm taking him with me. He won't be back."

Reardon got in, a feeling of exaltation gripping him. The swimming could wait.

He was surprised when the driver did not cross the Sambre bridge into the city but turned southward down the valley. "I know I smell like a barnyard," he said. "Maybe we should open the windows."

"Have a cigarette instead."

"Thanks very much. I certainly will." He saw they were Gauloise.

"I'm Captain Leider. And you?" He held forward the flame of his lighter.

"You're with the SD, the Sicherheitsdienst."

"So you recognize the insignia." Leider smiled faintly.

"I thought my intelligence was going to the Abwehr."

"We share information with MI."

"Where are we headed? Is there someplace I can get something to eat, get cleaned up?"

"We're stopping in Dinant. We have a post there. Your needs will be attended to. Then we're going on."

His spirits continued to soar, rising on the dizzying smoke of the tobacco. "To Berlin?"

"To Luxembourg."

"And what's going on in the old duchy?"

"Some questioning will be going on by a very high-ranking officer."

"I'm flattered. Then what?"

"If you satisfy the general, he'll decide where you go. If you don't, you won't be going anywhere. You'll be shot as a spy."

He began to laugh and choke on the smoke at the same time, a note of glee in the sound. "But—but—I am a spy!" he gasped.

12

It had been twelve years since he had been in Berlin, and the closer he got, the more he felt a rising sense of anticipation. The drive from Bordeaux had been long and somewhat demanding—from the occupied zone through the unoccupied zone and out again to the Rhine crossing at Strasbourg. The Studebaker, supplied by the legation, had held up well enough. His route had been proscribed by the victors. He had checked in at designated command posts and passed through a land benumbed by defeat in which the shock exuded its own stillness, lying like heat haze across the fields of summer. The conquerors had been correct, polite, anxious to help, perhaps too overwhelmed by their incredibly swift conquest to be otherwise for the moment.

At Strasbourg he had gotten a call through to the embassy and knew he would be well received. There had been no pouch in or out since the beginning of May. But by the time he left Beelitz behind and had the environs of the city in sight, his thoughts had been lulled more by memory than by the job at hand. He and Rod had had great times in Berlin. He was recalling the streets and parks through which they had ridden their bikes, naming them in his mind, and he did not see the Volkswagen come darting out of the side road until too late. Automatically he swung hard to the right, braking. Had the Volks's driver sped up, contact could have been avoided, but he, too, braked. Burke swore and held on against the impact as the Studebaker's bumper struck the right wheel of the other car. It spun around on the rain-slick road, went slithering sideways along the ditch, and came to a stop with its front facing where its rear should have been.

Burke had switched off his engine and bailed out fast, trotting toward the dun gray vehicle with its military insignia, appearing for a moment like so many war-damaged cars along the roads of France. Immediately he saw he was in trouble.

The door opened, and an officer climbed out, rubbing his arm and then bending over to rub his knee. "My fault," he said. "All my fault," he repeated.

"Are you all right, sir?" Other cars were stopping, the curious and the helpful.

"Fine, fine, no damage. Just a bump or two." He straightened up, and Burke was looking at a tall, heavyset officer with a melon-shaped face, his uniform indicating plenty of rank, award ribbons embossed by an Iron Cross First Class.

"I'm certainly sorry, sir," he said.

"Yes, I am, too." He took off his cap and passed his hand over his nearly bald head as he marched to the rear of the Volks to inspect the damage. Burke followed, along with a half dozen onlookers. The damaged roadster was going nowhere, its axle broken, its right rear wheel folded inward. "Oh, what bad luck, what bad luck," the officer said, looking at his watch. "I must be at the ministry by three."

"Well, may I take you there, sir? If you don't mind riding in U.S. property." He indicated the Studebaker and saw that though the flagstaff on the bumper was now bent sideways, the flag was still flying.

"Very kind of you, very kind of you, and no, of course not, I don't mind at all. This will have to be reported to the Schutzpolizei." He looked to see if any had arrived. The onlookers were moving back to their cars. There had been no injuries, and it was beginning to rain again. "Well, we can take care of that along the way. There's a station before Potsdam. A moment while I fetch my case."

No one, not even the Iron Duke, had briefed him on whether it was against State Department regulations to give a German military officer a lift in U.S. transportation. Besides, the big bird was certainly friendly enough, not the Junker type. From him he might learn something of value to the embassy. So climb aboard and fasten your seat belt.

Until he had settled into the flow of traffic, they drove in silence, and he was able to get a closer impression of his passenger: broad forehead; heavily bagged eyes; long nose with bulky nostrils; fleshy lips; big, powerful hands with fuzzed blond coating, resting on the attaché case on his lap. The knot of a gold ring centered by an ebony swastika was more in keeping with the Nazi stereotype. What was not were the apologetic manner and the mild tone.

"Permit me to introduce myself. I am Lieutenant Colonel Sturm," he said matter-of-factly while poking in his pocket for something.

The impact of the introduction ran through Burke like an electric shock. The man sitting next to him in no way fitted a blurry memory of the tennis player who had carved a model plane for him. He realized suddenly the accident had been no accident. He found his hands were gripping the wheel. He stared straight ahead, watching the road. "A pleasure, sir," he said. "My name is Cannon. I'm a diplomatic courier."

"Cannon, Cannon, a rather warlike name." He had managed to bring forth a silver cigarette case.

"Not really, sir. I think I was named after a tennis player who had a wicked serve. Do you play tennis, Colonel?"

"Not in some time." He was looking at Burke intently, the softness gone out of his expression.

"He also carved model airplanes for small boys."

"Rodney! You're Rodney." He was holding the cigarette case like a signal flag.

"Rodney had a brother."

"Yes, yes . . . Paul? No, Peter. You're Peter! My God, your father really wanted to make sure this time."

"Something like that, I guess. I'm afraid I didn't recognize you."

"Nor I you. The years have a way of making a difference, don't they?" he said wryly.

"I remember a scar on your arm."

"Appearances may change," he said, pulling up his sleeve, "but old wounds are never forgotten, and I'm glad you can see I am who I am. Now, unfortunately, we have no time for pleasantries and memories." He clapped his hat back on his head, and with it not only his appearance but his entire manner changed. He became decisive, electric, in command. "Our time is short. When we stop at the police station, there will be questions and forms to fill out. I will call my headquarters to report the accident and request that a driver be sent for me. I will make a great deal of your kindness in assisting me.

"Now listen carefully, Within the next four or five days the Führer will be speaking in the Reichstag. He will make a major address, a peace offering to the British, to the world. Your chargé, Mr. Amidon, will be invited to attend, possibly the first secretary, Mr. Donovan, as well, but no one else in your embassy. Following the address, a large reception will be held at the chancellery to which many more foreign representatives, including members of your embassy staff, will be invited. Most will decline the invitation, but you will not, having received a special invitation from me as a token of my appreciation for your most kind assistance. Under the circumstances it will be an offer your embassy diplomatic officer, Mr. Geist, will want to approve, not only to avoid an insult but also for whatever you might pick up over drinks. At the reception copies of the Führer's statement will be made available to the press and to the guests. And I will personally present you with your copy—a historical document—for the memory book of my former tennis partner. One that is to be delivered to him, Peter, and to no one else. Do you understand?" He spoke swiftly, looking at Burke, making no gestures, cigarette case in hand, the gray-green of his eyes still and direct.

"Yes, Colonel. But my friends at the embassy will not let me stay in Berlin any longer than it takes to unload that pouch behind us and to replace it with one for Washington."

"Your embassy will be informed this evening that there will be no courier movement permitted out of Berlin until after Hitler speaks, probably on Friday, the nineteenth. The reason, which will be made clear, is to assure that there will be no outside advance notice on what he plans to say or to offer the British."

"Is the copy of the speech you give me to go in the pouch?"

"Absolutely not. You are to keep it in your possession, a perfectly innocuous memento. It is for Colonel Burke and Colonel Burke alone."

"You'll be pleased to know he's now a brigadier general."

"My congratulations." There was a faint touch of sarcasm in his tone. "It has been some time since we've been in contact."

"I take it you don't want me to report anything said here to anyone at the embassy."

"Not unless you want to have me shot. Your embassy staff, both at the chancellery and the military attaché's offices at Tiergartenstrasse, is served by employees who report to MI—the Abwehr—or the SD Ausland, the party secret service. Precious little goes on in your embassy of which we are not informed."

"And Hitler's speech will simply look like Hitler's speech until translated otherwise."

"Exactly."

"Is there anything you want me to pass on to General Burke verbally?"

"Just this. Unless some better arrangement can be made, I will have to break off contact. Staging automobile accidents is not my forte, and the German Army does not smile on carelessness. Lieutenant Colonel Firman Jones went home last April, and it was my understanding that his place would be taken by Major Albert West, your embassy's present assistant MA for air. There has been no contact, nothing, and I had given up on any further relationship. I'm not inclined to continue. The risk has become too extreme for me. May I try one of your cigarettes?" He picked up the pack on the dashboard, his motions quick and jerky, reflecting the sudden tension in his voice.

"By all means. Please keep the pack. Do you think the British are finished?"

"With Churchill they will go on fighting, no matter what kind of offer Hitler makes, but whether they are finished or not I cannot say. Militarily the only maneuver they excel at is in retreating, and strategically they have managed to ignore every warning I have managed to send." He exhaled, sitting back with a sigh. "A pleasure to enjoy a real cigarette. Thank you." He took another puff, like a thirsty man taking a drink of water. "I'm sorry you've been injected into this situation. If all goes as planned, there should be no trouble, but once I've handed you the Führer's statement, you will be in danger until you are out of the Reich and even until you have delivered it."

The needle of fear in Sturm's eyes pricked him. He saw again the Iron Duke in *Truxton*'s wardroom and said, "You're risking your ass for us, Colonel. I guess I'll have to risk mine in return."

Sturm's eyes went wide with surprise. Then he gave forth a whinnying laugh. "I—I like the way you put it. But bear in mind, Berlin is not the place you knew as a boy. Because of the great victories, there is on the surface a more relaxed air. The public still finds it difficult to grasp, and there have been losses—well, I'm sure you know how to be on guard, and be careful what you say to anyone. As I said, with the police I will be effusive in my praise of you—an example of good American-German relations. I want the story to be spread, and there is no better chance of spreading it than by the police. It will add credibility to my offering you an invitation to the reception."

"Might someone not suspect that the whole thing is a setup?"

"Indeed, someone might, particularly the SD. And if they do, I'll be happy to admit that I arranged the accident. After all, I'm a military intelligence officer, and America and Americans are my area of operations. There's the police headquarters ahead. I'm sorry, Peter, this has been so brief and so unnatural."

13

When Pruck called him in and showed him the priority slip from Abwehrstelle Namur, Sturm was only momentarily surprised. "Heydrich," he said almost automatically.

"Ziege, indeed. An SD captain signed Reardon out. Do you suppose he could have been one of Golt's people?"

"Not likely. After all, his material came through Ribbentrop, not SD intelligence, and if he'd been one of Golt's, we'd never have seen any of it."

Pruck laughed. "You're right there, old boy. Well, small matter, I suppose. But you know, there's something that stuck in the back of my head about this. I had a distant cousin who I recall married an American named Reardon many years ago, and I believe he was in the Foreign Service. Odd coincidence." Indeed, it was, Sturm thought, because he, too, seemed to remember the name out of somewhere.

"There might be some connection," Pruck mused. "Run a check, Paul, and see what you find. Whatever Ziege is after will be of no benefit to us. When are you seeing him?"

"Tomorrow. Maybe he canceled our earlier date so he could question the American first."

Pruck grinned. "I like your suspicious nature. Maybe he's going to share this Reardon fellow with us."

Sturm could hear Pruck's mellow rejoinder as he walked along Prinz-Albrechtstrasse past the five-story monolithic *Geschwür* that housed the Gestapo and the party security apparatus. The only real difference in the building's ugliness from that of the Tirpitz-Ufer was its size. It ran the length of the block, and he was pleased that Heydrich had his headquarters in an unobtrusive town house around the corner on Wilhelmstrasse. There was irony in the thought that the Gestapo headquarters had once been an arts and crafts school. No matter. Before him were a concealment of shrubs and a walled courtyard, offering a feel of closed-in privacy. So here he was to play the cat-and-mouse game.

Actually he was feeling up to it. The successful contact with young Burke had improved his mood. Action always produced that effect. He had liked the quick perception and confident manner of the American—something of the father in the son. Resilience, adaptability, self-confidence. He knew within himself there was a stubbornness, a perversity, a daring that when stimulated by another—by risk—improved his capabilities and gave him the capacity to act with dispatch.

Passed by guards through a narrow iron-grille gateway, he was escorted into the house by an orderly, who ushered him into a windowless reception room watched over by a trimly uniformed *Mädchen* whose figure and sex appeal illuminated the Spartan setting. She was bright and brittle, knew who he was, and guided him through the routine of SD registry. She then led him down a stone corridor, the clicking castanets of her heels supplying cadence to the tight sway of her behind. Arriving before twin doors, she swung them open onto an unexpected scene.

He had assumed his meeting with Heydrich was to be private. Instead, he saw four other attendees standing in a conference room, none of whom was the RSHA chief. They were conversing among themselves and broke off their talking as he entered.

A moment of silence as they observed him. He knew them all, and then Werner Bekker said, "Paul Sturm!" and came forward to shake his hand. "A pleasure to see you. Where have you been keeping yourself?" The chief of the criminal police seemed genuinely glad to see him.

"Hello, Sturm," Ulrich Golt barked. The head of SD foreign intelligence loved to strut. He had, Paul knew, gained the deep-seated dislike of the admiral.

SS Sturmbannführer Klaus Kersten waved a perfunctory greeting and turned to continue speaking with Heinz Lissner, the director of SD *Inland,* the internal security service. Lissner, with his full features and smooth manner, was in civilian dress.

Of the quartet, only the tough, wily Kersten seemed out of place. In the early SA days he'd been a street fighter, then an SS hatchet man, a rumored assassin. Now he ran the SD technical department at Dellbrückstrasse. Sturm had never liked him. In fact, it was only Bekker with whom he had any rapport.

"Tell me what you've been doing," Bekker said, not because he really wanted to know, Sturm guessed, but because he wanted to fill time that was being wasted.

"Well, I suppose what I've been doing, Werner, is what you've been doing—waiting for the Führer to speak."

"Is that why you're here, so Heydrich can tell the Abwehr what he's going to say?"

"I'm not sure why I'm here." He dissembled somewhat.

"Nor am I." They both laughed, Bekker glancing at his watch. "Do you think the *Engländer* will call it a day? I don't. Too bloody stubborn, as they like to say. Is England your specialty, or is it America? America, isn't it?"

"North America—the United States and Canada."

"Yes, yes, that's right. I just saw some mention of that, didn't I? You and an American. Did you pick one up or something and make a police report?"

"No, no, he picked me up. Had a slight road accident. He was very helpful, a courier."

"Oh, yes, now I recall. They push everything across my desk. Tell me about it."

He had no chance to tell about it because the door at the rear of the room opened and Reinhard Heydrich made his entrance. Automatically with the *Gruppenführer*'s appearance, all had snapped to attention. He simply gestured for them to sit, and they took their places at the rectangular conference table with himself at the head, handsome leather folder before him.

In Paul Sturm's eye, Heydrich, in looks and manner, was an uncoiled whipcord of a man. Neck nearly as long as head gave him a knifelike aspect. His lengthy aquiline nose narrowly separated eyes of a peculiar coldness, the blue devoid of light. The fleshy mouth and tapering chin, the high forehead—all fitted into a tight mold of flesh, capped by a covering of straight blond hair. There was something feral and explicit in his nature, a cold magnetism.

"It is a pleasure to have you join us, Herr Oberstleutenant Sturm." He spoke in a clear, high voice. "We can always use the Abwehr's expertise in our planning. Is that not so, Ulrich?"

Golt, caught off-balance, responded automatically. "Yes, yes, of course, Herr General."

"I'm honored to be present." Sturm responded in kind. "Admiral Canaris asked me to convey his best regards."

"Always. Fine." He opened his folder, Sturm noting the length and suppleness of his fingers. Not only a gifted violinist but a champion swordsman, Heydrich had led the German fencing team at the '36 Olympics. "The Führer will speak in the Reichstag on Friday evening at seven. The formal announcement will be made Thursday. Until then no mention is to be made of the decision. I have received an order direct from the Führer to supply him with up-to-the-minute intelligence on peace attitudes amongst the English public as well as important figures in and out of the ruling circle. Also, the reaction of the Americans to peace offers suggested by Dr. Goebbels and Ribbentrop's people." He spoke swiftly, precisely, and there was nothing in his words that was intimidating or should have produced an air of tension amongst his subordinates, but Sturm detected it immediately.

"Golt, what can you tell us?"

The secret service chief was prepared to recite. In the early days Sturm had known him, a Munich lawyer, voluble, outspoken, brusque.

"Herr Gruppenführer, no one in the Churchill government is prepared to negotiate, and those outside it who might be more reasonable are not willing to risk being hanged for treason." He said nothing that was not generally known, and he had no intelligence to offer of any moment. He concluded, "The *Engländer* are preparing for invasion."

"We will not keep them waiting long." Heydrich smiled. "What can you tell us concerning American reaction?"

Again it was *pro forma.* What Golt knew about U.S. public opinion could be read in the American press, and Sturm listened, wondering whether the intelligence gathered by the American section of SD *Ausland* was indicative of the entire department's capability.

Heydrich had a single question: "Should we invade England, what are the chances of Roosevelt continuing as the American leader?"

"We believe there is a good chance he will be defeated. The Americans are soft. They do not want to go to war to save England."

"Put that in writing for me with an analysis." Heydrich raised his eyes. "Colonel Sturm, since the United States is your area of operation, I wonder if you would care to give us the benefit of your view."

The ploy did not surprise him. It was standard Heydrich, an attempt to embarrass or to antagonize his own people against Abwehr officers who spoke out. He opened his briefcase. "Yes, of course, Herr Gruppenführer. I brought with me a report received yesterday, that Admiral Canaris wished to share with you." He coated the word *share.* "I believe you will find it complements Colonel Golt's appraisal." He saw a flick of a smile crease Bekker's lips as he passed the report to Heydrich. The idea had been Pruck's.

Heydrich thumbed the pages. "Most helpful, I'm sure. Please thank the admiral. And the question of Roosevelt?"

"His election remains in doubt, we believe. A great deal will depend on his reaction to the Führer's offer of peace."

"The Führer does not ask for doubters, Herr Oberstleutnant Sturm. He asks for answers."

"I regret it is not an answer we can give at the moment, Herr Gruppenführer."

Heydrich did not reply, his eyes cast on the papers before him. His black uniform with its silver facings and epaulets was a pedestal for the chiseled cut of his head. He called on Heinz Lissner next.

Chief of SD *Inland,* the internal security information service, Lissner had matriculated from SA to SS with a smoothness reflected in his large, knowing eyes. *Cunning* was the word for Heinz. His organization kept its fingers fixed tightly to the pulse of the *Volk,* and while his having the reputation of a brilliant economist did not contribute all that much to the pulse taking, neither did it hurt.

He spoke with broad gestures, which added nothing to what he imparted. The German people were expectantly waiting for their leader's words. The general population was in a euphoric state. Like the fine summer weather, the *Volk* were basking in the sunlight of the Führer's genius and the Wehrmacht's invincibility. Morale had never been higher from farmstead to factory. *Mellifluous* was the word for Lissner, and Sturm knew his report was largely nonsense. He had read an Abwehr internal report indicating a sense of bewilderment and uncertainty, at least amongst Berliners. Informed only as Dr. Goebbels chose to inform, a broad section of the public at all levels found it difficult to accept that the victory was real. Rationing was no less. The food was no better. The restrictions were, if anything, tighter. The chimed propaganda announcements continued to blare. British bombers were attacking German cities. The war had not ended. Wait and see.

Until Heydrich spoke to Reichskriminaldirektor Bekker, Sturm assumed that the conference was being held because Hitler's order made it necessary or that such meetings were a matter of routine and he had been invited to sit in because Heydrich found it convenient to make it clear to some of his key subordinates that he had established an open liaison with the "opposites," as the SD termed the Abwehr. Either way or both, not a single word had been said that added new information to what was already known. He could not believe the exercise was to be that simple, and it struck him that the air of tension he had detected might result from the fact that no one else in the room thought so either.

"Herr Kriminaldirektor"—Heydrich addressed Bekker formally—"as you know, the Führer remains unsatisfied with the results of the Bürgerbräukeller investigation. He believes, as does SS Reichsführer Himmler and as I do myself, that although Elser constructed and planted the bomb, he did not act alone and that today, here in Berlin, the British SIS controls an active ring of traitorous spies who are not only managing to send intelligence to London but, more to the point, are planning another attempt on the Führer's life."

Sturm had watched the color rise in Bekker's cheeks, the nostrils of his nose expand with anger. He opened his mouth to respond, and

Heydrich raised his hand and voice. "Wait!" He paused and continued. "We have no time for recriminations or for past failures. When the Führer speaks Friday evening, he will be vulnerable to attack, even more so than he was in Munich. To kill him must be Churchill's most important wish. His first order. No doubt Roosevelt's also. It is all the *Engländer* have left. There are two questions. Has Kripo uncovered any leads that point to the British spy ring and what additional security precautions do you recommend for the Reichstag?"

Sturm immediately concluded that both these questions had been raised not so much to provide answers as to establish protection for Heydrich should another assassination attempt be made. They all were present to hear the answers that would incriminate the head of Kripo should anything untoward occur. And even if not, Heydrich's open criticism of Bekker and the criminal police had been heard by three interrelated SS-SD security heads and an Abwehr representative.

All waited for Werner Bekker's reply, their eyes on him. When it came, Sturm wanted to say, "*Bravo, Werner.*"

"Herr Gruppenführer"—he did not look at Heydrich, his voice guttural, his rather large soulful eyes on his hands resting on the table—"I will send you my answers in writing this afternoon. I have nothing further to say here."

There was a long silence. Heydrich stared at the criminal police chief. As Himmler's deputy, a lieutenant general, and the head of the RSHA, he was Bekker's overall superior in the security apparatus. Nonetheless, they all knew Bekker's party membership long antedated Ziege's, and the little man had strong support among Hitler's closest advisers—Göring, Goebbels, Bormann, and Hess.

Sturm waited, believing Heydrich was too adroit to push a confrontation here and now. He had made his point for the record.

"Very well," he said, closing his folder. "I think we can adjourn the meeting. Will you remain, Herr Oberstleutnant?"

Without a word, Bekker, Golt, and Lissner rose and departed. Kersten stayed seated and lit a cigarette.

Heydrich arranged some papers and looked up with a thin smile. "Well, Sturm, I must say I've found your reports worth reading."

"Thank you, Herr General. The material, of course, is what we depend on, and our sources are good and solid." As he spoke, he took the diary extracts from his case and handed them forward. "Admiral Canaris felt you would find these of particular interest. They deal principally with American politics and the Roosevelt question."

"It is an important question," Heydrich said, perusing the extracts. "He calls for fifty thousand aircraft, even though you point out the annual manufacturing capacity is less than five thousand."

"At the moment, but that will change quickly."

"Yes, but not that quickly. You have lived in the United States, have you not?" Heydrich did not look up.

"From 1929 to 1932, when I was recalled, Herr General. I lived in New York City and Chicago." Heydrich's signal was clear enough. *We know all about you. We have a dossier on you a foot thick.* Piffle!

"Do you feel the Americans look to Roosevelt as the German people look to our Führer?" And now Heydrich was giving him his full attention.

"I left the United States just at the time he was elected for the first time, so I have no firsthand knowledge. For him to seek election for a third time is, of course, unprecedented, and it is apparent to us in IH West that he is very popular with the working class, which is very large."

"But according to this, there are many who oppose him."

"It is a question, of course, of how many, but as the writer of the diary points out, they will not be prepared for war for another two years no matter who becomes their president."

"That is as it may be, but the Führer's concern is with Roosevelt, not that other fellow—Wilins or Willie or whatever his name is. In any case, please convey to Admiral Canaris my thanks for this intelligence. I'd appreciate receiving it regularly. Sharing and cooperation between our two services are what we need more of."

It might have been the expression that flitted across Kersten's saturnine face or the inflection of Heydrich's high-pitched voice; but suddenly Sturm believed he knew what was coming next, and he moved to get ahead of it.

"With regard to that, Herr General, Colonel Pruck wished me to raise a point. Is the American we were holding in Namur one of Colonel Golt's agents or in some way connected to RSHA?"

Heydrich's glacial eyes brushed him, swinging to Kersten.

"Major, you have something there?"

"Yes, Herr General." Kersten cleared his throat, bringing up from beside him a thick interrogation book.

"The admiral as well as Colonel Pruck is welcome to this transcript of Major Kersten's interview with the American Reardon," Heydrich said. "We could not help wondering why the Abwehr, having taken him into custody had not seen fit to question him. We took the opportunity to do so and have placed him under our control, at least temporarily."

"I'm sure the admiral and Colonel Pruck will be most interested," he said, not bothering to hide a smile. "What sort of fellow is he?" he said to Kersten.

Kersten looked to Heydrich, who gave a jerk of his head. The major rose and went to the door, opened it, and gave an order. He then stood to one side, and Sturm knew it had been his own failure to act that had given Heydrich the advantage in what was to come next.

The nail-thin newcomer strode through the door, leaving his guard behind. Luminous eyes, so deep-socketed the impression was skull-like, glittered. *Demonic* was the word that flitted through Sturm's mind. Classical features in a half-starved face, like a Grecian relic time-smudged beneath ancient seas. The blond hair, burnished, not unlike Heydrich's, recently trimmed, blended with sun-browned skin. Twin lines furrowed from nostrils to disdainful lips. He carried his head high, arrogance in the angular jaw.

"Sit down," Kersten ordered.

"This is the man from Namur," Heydrich said, sounding amused. "Herr Reardon, this is the chief of the American section of German military intelligence."

Reardon sat down, and Sturm absorbed the impact of those strange eyes. They were probably reflecting exhaustion, starvation, fear. But strange, nonetheless.

"Your intelligence was most useful," he said, smiling.

"It was totally wasted on you." His German was excellent, his tone rude.

"Hardly that," Heydrich said mildly.

"Yes, that!" He smacked his palm on the table. "Had you used the gold mine I sent, Roosevelt would have been finished. Now I'm told by Major Kersten that he is to be nominated for a third term. Well, I'll tell you this for nothing." He leaned forward on the table with his hands flat on the surface, looking like a piano player reaching for a crescendo. "You can bet he'll be elected, and he'll be at war with you in a year or sooner."

"How can you be sure of that?" Sturm said, interested in drawing him out, intrigued by his belligerence and his go-to-hell manner before Heydrich.

"Lieutenant Colonel Sturm," Heydrich interrupted, "Major Kersten will be glad to arrange a suitable time and place for you to interrogate our unappreciated friend. As you can see, he holds very strong opinions. They may be of benefit, they may not, but for now"—he nodded at Kersten—"you may be excused," he said to Reardon.

Kersten stood, but Reardon remained seated. "You're a pack of damn fools," he scoffed.

Heydrich put back his head and studied the impudent scarecrow. "Do not presume upon my good nature," he said. "Right now it's a question of sending you back to Namur or turning you over to the American Embassy as a gift. You go along with Major Kersten unless you'd like a decision now."

When the door had closed behind them, Heydrich looked at Sturm and, smiling thinly, said, "What do you make of him?"

"Difficult to say, Herr General. Certainly outspoken. Very American."

"After you've read Kersten's interrogation and talked to him yourself, I'll be interested in your appraisal."

"His personality aside, what he sent was definitely top drawer."

"And it was properly utilized." With his head cocked, his toed-in, close-set eyes, he had the momentary look of a mandarin. What he had just said was not put as a question, yet was not altogether a statement; it was more like a baited hook.

"I believe Admiral Canaris's recommendation in March was to take direct action with a comprehensive white paper to be distributed in conjunction with the *Weserübung* plan for Norway and Denmark. I know, Herr General, because I drafted the recommendation." Indeed, he had, and he had attempted without success to send a warning to Washington.

Heydrich nodded. "I regret I did not see it at the time, nor do I believe did the Führer, thanks to the OKW. Too late now, do you think?"

He felt the hair on the back of his neck rise. Heydrich was looking at him intently. Had he somehow found out that it was Paul Sturm who had managed to block his own recommended white paper—his single American success? "Certainly something could be put together," he said as though thinking about it, "although the impact would probably be less in view of the present situation."

"You don't think it might defeat Roosevelt? That's what this Reardon thinks."

He knew the correct answer should be: "*Why not let Reardon make a selection from the papers he sent us and try it? What is there to lose?*" Instead, he shrugged. "What did the Polish paper Ribbentrop put out gain us? There was plenty of good material in it. The American press paid little attention to it, and Roosevelt made it a joke. But—" He threw up his hands. "After I've talked to Reardon, I'll give you an opinion. Do you think he's unbalanced, Herr General?"

Heydrich threw back his head and laughed, and Sturm blinked at the unexpected sound. "I'll tell you this, he has a special talent. He plays the bassoon."

As they had talked, Heydrich's manner had changed. The formality and brittleness had been laid aside. He was speaking openly, man to man, relaxed, and Sturm sensed he was leading to the point Canaris had anticipated. "Why do you suppose I invited you to come here, Paul?" And there it was.

"I should imagine for something more than a drink and a cigar, Herr General," he said lightly, feeling the needlelike pain stab into his gut. Heydrich was totally without humor. His expression indicated that though he had relaxed, he did not appreciate Sturm's lack of deference.

"You're an intriguing fellow, Lieutenant Colonel Sturm. You joined the party very early on. You were Freikorps before that and helped put down the KPD, the Spartacist Revolt, as many of us did. It would seem you have an unblemished record of loyalty to the Führer and to the party." The accent was on the word *seem.* Heydrich paused and tapped his desk folder. "I have looked over your vitae with care." He glanced up. "Tell me, what was your purpose in meeting the American courier?"

Coming as it did, the unexpected question jolted, and the pain fanned out. He smiled. "Herr General, you undoubtedly know how long I've been an intelligence officer. I consider meeting any newly arrived American an opportunity."

Heydrich continued as though he had not asked the question. "There comes a time, Sturm, when one must make a choice. It happened in '34 with the SA, and you know it has happened in numerous ways since. What do you suppose the Führer intends when he has had his way with England?"

"I can only guess. I think the view is eastward, more than west."

"Perhaps with the Japanese both. But whichever, SD responsibilities will grow accordingly, and anyone within SD ranks will benefit. For an officer of your experience and intelligence, *Obersturmbannführer* is not recognition enough, nor is full colonel. There is no need to tell you the Abwehr does not reward its professionals as it should. You have a future, but you must grasp it now before it passes you by."

Sturm listened to the predicted offer, musing that Heydrich was no latter-day Brutus, emoting on the tide of human affairs, but a scheming, dangerous *Jagdhund* who was out to use him as a spy within the Tirpitz-Ufer. The irony was like the pain in his belly, deep and expansive. Did this offer promote him from double to triple agent or double double agent because whatever he passed to Heydrich would first be passed by Canaris? How many others in the Abwehr had been suborned, blackmailed, frightened into cooperation with Reinhard the Goat?

Heydrich was looking at him, waiting for an answer.

"There is truth in what you say, Herr General, and I admit I have grown, shall we say, restless, marching in place, so to speak. May I think over the possibility you raise?"

"By all means. Incidentally, after the Führer speaks on Friday, I will be hosting a private reception at the chancellery apart from the general reception. I would be honored if you and Frau Sturm could be free to attend. The Führer may stop in. You can give me your decision then."

When he returned to his office, he was surprised to learn that both Pruck and the admiral had left for Spain. There was no reason he should have been informed of their plans. Perhaps Franco was preparing to become a full Axis partner or a move was going forward to take Gibraltar. His disappointment was in not being able to report to them the details of his meeting and to receive approval from the admiral as to what his reply should be.

In reading Kersten's interrogation of Reardon, he found additional irony that sent his temporarily uplifted spirits into a nose dive. He and the American had certain abnormalities in common. Reardon, as a traitor to his country, claimed to be motivated by patriotism in attempting by his actions to prevent war between the United States and the Reich. For himself, as someone who had despised and hated Hitler for the past fifteen years, he had been betraying his countrymen for similar reasons. Reardon's usefulness to the Reich at least was now ended. His own usefulness, after he had passed to young Burke a copy of the Führer's speech, which would contain between the lines everything of value he could give to his old friend in Washington, would be ended also. His SIS contacts were gone. Using the railway union's method of smuggling intelligence by train personnel to Geneva was too dangerous, if still functioning. Now Heydrich wished to use his services to discredit Canaris and the Abwehr. Maybe Ziege would employ Reardon in a similar effort, and they could work together. Two of a kind. He snorted disgustedly. Reardon, of course, was a liar, like himself. It was apparent in the transcript that the American's underlying motivation for betrayal was not patriotism but was personal. Revenge, hate for some perceived injustice. Hate, like his own old hate for the SA thugs who had raped and murdered Leah. Sweet, gentle Jewish Leah of so long ago.

He brushed her hazy image from his mind, thinking: *Each of us follows his own course to an uncertain end, but mine will be certain, violent, and soon.*

There was one final note to the day, the most intriguing of all. Pruck had asked for background on Reardon's antecedents. What there was had come in a very thin folder. There were several faded new clips of U.S. Embassy Counsel Dwight Reardon's marriage to Hilma Pruck, eldest daughter of Baron Friedrich Gustav von Pruck of Koblenz, evidently no relation to Horst. The clips were followed by two official Abwehr reports. The one dated 1928 cited embassy posts held by Reardon during the days of the Weimar Republic and the suggestion that word be circulated in the right diplomatic quarters that Reardon, if appointed, would be acceptable as the American ambassador. The second was a counterintelligence memo, dated January 17, 1932, reporting that Reardon had secretly met on four occasions in the past three months with NSDAP SS Reichsführer Heinrich Himmler.

"My God!" he said aloud. "Like father, like son."

He turned the page, and the face in a faded photo, with tennis racket in hand, was staring up at him. "My God!" he said again. He knew the man, knew why the name had rung a distant bell. He had played tennis with him several times. Alfred Burke had introduced them.

14

Throughout most of the afternoon Burke had rediscovered Berlin—*Strasse, Stadt,* and *Platz.* It had been his first chance to do so, and much of his exploring became a long walk down the avenue of yesteryear. He found the memories intrusive because he knew he needed to keep his thoughts focused on the present.

Four days ago, when he had driven along Unter den Linden, beneath the Brandenburger Tor, turned past the Adlon Hotel and into the embassy courtyard, he'd been greeted like a pony express rider, bringing word that the 7th Cavalry was not far behind. He was met and welcomed by a group of the embassy staff led by Gary Donovan, the first secretary, and then ushered inward to be introduced to the headman, Andrew Amidon, the chargé d'affaires. Amidon shook his hand fiercely and said, "We're certainly glad to see you, Cannon. I'll want to talk to you about your trip before we pack you up and send you out of here tomorrow."

It was Ralph Picard, the third secretary, who spotted the Studebaker's dimpled fender and bent flagstaff, and jokingly asked if he'd run into a tank. His explanation brought a quick introduction to Horace Tobin, political officer, who said he'd like a written report with the details of the incident ASAP. The general plan was that with the dawn he'd be heading for the Swiss border with the outgoing pouch. For the night he would bunk with Sam Buttrick, chief cipher clerk, whose two-room palace was just across the hall from his workplace, the code room.

Sam, mustached, loquacious, wisecracking, made him feel at home at once. "Come in, come in, Pete. Don't trip on the mess, and have a Dortmunder to get the dust out of your tonsils."

He'd done that and had several more of the same, for it seemed what Sam lacked in space he made up for in cases of beer and congeniality. In short order, Sam informed him that the embassy staff was down to less than forty and that most of the married officers had sent wives and children home or to Switzerland. "There's a circle-the-wagons mentality around these here parts, pardner," he said, rolling his large, baggy eyes. "The krauts are playing snotty."

"But you must have some friends among them," Burke said, raising his bottle, settling back and really relaxing for the first time since Bordeaux.

"You know the saying *klein aber mein?*"

"A little but mine own," he translated.

"Hey, you know your German proverbs."

"Used to teach it before I got into this racket."

"Speaking of mine own, did you bring any real cigarettes? We've been reduced to choking on the local burnt rope. I'll swap you a carton of Aristones, Muratts, or Kemels for one Chesterfield."

"No need." He was reaching in his pocket when the phone rang.

Sam's conversation was brief, but his information said something about the accuracy of Colonel Sturm's information. "That was Evenrude, the Wicked Witch of the East, with a message for you," he said. "She's Amidon's secretary, and every evening after she bids him *auf Wiedersehen,* she reports to the Gestapo. She and her fellow snoopers pass the word on what we do here all day."

"And what message for me will she report?"

"Word just arrived from the Foreign Ministry that no embassy travel outside Berlin is to be permitted until after Friday midnight and then only with special permission. So put your feet up and have another. And since you're going to be here longer than you thought, I'd better fill you in because we're so shorthanded we don't even have a security officer."

And so Sam filled him in. The one artful countermeasure was that in the presence of German employees everyone who had mastered the technique as a child spoke in pidgin English, which befuddled the Nazi secretaries and custodial staff.

"When some knucklehead asks what language we're speaking, the answer is 'pure American.' "

"What's the head man like? He said he wanted to talk to me later."

"He acts like a stuffed shirt, dresses like one, too. But he's not. He's a real pro, a good guy. And he's always given me a square break, nothing phony about him at all, like some of the troops in this joint. A lot of them have cabin fever, go sneaking around, trying to prove anyone they don't like is a Nazi sympathizer. Like me." He let out a raucous bark. "Yeah, I've got some good kraut friends. They hate Hitler as much as anyone. Sometime I invite a few of them in, and we maybe get a little noisy. Then the sneakers and the watchers begin to bellyache, and then Donovan or Tobin or Picard comes and gives me hell. Going to have me sent home with a bad record and all that crap, but Andy Amidon knows what I'm doing. Anything my friends pass on to me that's worth repeating I pass on to him, like how people are feeling about things."

"And how are they feeling?"

"Berliners don't buy much of the Goebbels crap. They don't want to fight the Brits. They wish Hitler would make a deal with Churchill. Maybe he will, but that's why they're holding you up till Saturday. Can't have anybody leaking his BS until he leaks it himself."

"Now that I've got to stay here till Saturday, maybe I can get out and look around a little."

"Well, you want to be careful. The damn Gestapo now makes a practice of tailing us, trying to compromise us. But I'll make you a bet. We're so shorthanded someone will draft you, and you won't see the outside of this place till you hit the road again. Of course, if I can grab a couple of hours, I'll be glad to show you around."

He felt that part of Sam Buttrick's bet was in hope that he would be his guide, should time be found to go exploring. It was obvious that as the embassy's chief cipher clerk Sam was able to snatch only a few beers and a few minutes here and there in which to catch his gregarious and outspoken breath. He offered one other unexpected bit of information at the session. Looking at him—a short, rumpled, graying figure with wiry, thinning black hair, heavily lined forehead, and wolfhound eyes—Burke thought of the difference between him and Scott Reardon. Was it that Sam did not fit the picture of a State Department staff man or that Reardon did not fit into the picture of a State Department code clerk?

It was almost by reflex that he asked, "Did you ever know a fellow clerk named Scott Reardon?"

"That son of a bitch!" Sam said, and then laughed. "I hope he's not a friend of yours."

"No. No, I—someone I know told me Reardon owes him ten bucks and if I ran into him to try and collect."

"Fat chance. I knew him in Moscow back in '37, '38. He was a stuffed-shirt jerk. He knew more than anybody else. He spoke the language and had a Bolshy girl, and there was talk around that he was passing confidential stuff to her. Maybe confidence for tail, hey?" He laughed. "Anyway, he was weird."

"What happened to him?"

"Last I heard he was in Warsaw, but we're so cut off here it's hard to pick up what's going on outside."

Sam had been right. With a shorthanded staff, an extra, no matter how ill prepared, was not going to be left to while away the hours drinking warm beer and smoking god-awful German cigarettes.

Since the embassy included a British and French interests section, he was injected into that tangled web, which, for him, involved the filling out of forms and the sorting of correspondence in a kind of impossible paper chase. Interwoven were brief meetings with the embassy's key people. His single worry concerned his encounter with Sturm and what it could lead to. Ralph Picard and Tobin, the political officer, questioned him together and acted as though they didn't quite believe him. They insisted on a written report describing every detail. They could not accept the friendly manner of the German officer when they knew the word had gone out not to be friendly. They were extremely critical of his having permitted an unauthorized person, regardless of rank and nationality, to ride in U.S. property carrying confidential and classified information. They speculated that the accident might have been a trap, that an incident was being sought, and that possibly Burke's quick action had avoided it. He saw them both as nervous Nellies. That, or they were anxious there would be an incident which would give them something to be really nervous about. He was sure they would hit the fan when Sturm's invitation to attend the chancellery reception arrived.

By Thursday noon, deciding he'd been locked up long enough, he informed the security guard he was going out for lunch, his aim to try the Adlon bar.

And so he had spent the afternoon as a returned tourist, trying to measure memory against the new reality about him. He went down the Wilhelmstrasse, saw the overly ornate palaces of Ribbentrop and Goebbels, the yellowish brown, heavily glassed masonry of Hitler's chancellery with its huge bronze doors. He toured Leipziger, looking for Wertheim's department store, where the family had once shopped. He found it a block-long shell of itself, shoddy and run-down, and knew why. The Wertheims were Jews. They were gone. He found the Pschorr Haus and tried a stein of beer, sitting under the awning and watching the holiday crowds—for it was a holiday—scurrying in and out of the Bahnhof. Later he observed a parade, the victors goose-stepping with precise and concentrated rigidity along Unter den Linden. He noted that while the avenue was lined with spectators, few seemed overly enthusiastic. In the summer green of the Tiergarten and the zoo, he walked trails he and Rod had once known, and on the Kurfürstendamm he stopped in at the Café Kranzler on impulse because he remembered its name and recalled it as a favorite watering hole for the grown-ups. He had no sooner been seated than the sound of chimes sounded loudly. All laughter and conversation snapped off as though a switch had been thrown, and everyone in the place froze, turned to wax. A commanding voice sounded: "Attention! Attention! This is a special announcement."

"*Sondermeldung,*" he remembered Sam saying. "Every time they have something they want everyone to hear, they ring the gong, and everybody better give a listen."

The special announcement was that at seven o'clock sharp the Führer would speak from the Reichstag to the nation and to the world. All were invited to listen on their radios to the Führer's message. "Heil Hitler!" There was a scattering of heil Hitlers in response; but for the most part he noted the reaction was perfunctory, and as soon as the *Sondermeldung* was done, people in the café went back to what they had been talking about.

As Sam had warned, he was followed. His police dog was a short, square nonentity with brown bowler. He was tempted to invite him to have a beer but decided it was better not to play cute. The afternoon was warm and sunny. Why risk spoiling it? But his attempting to retrace the half-forgotten footsteps of boyhood with the ghost of his brother in a city whose closed-in atmosphere and Babylonian structures no longer had any real connection with the hazed-over past was spoiled.

By the time he returned to the embassy the urge to get on the road to Switzerland was foremost in his mind. He could feel his hand on the wobble pump, see the magnetos switched on, hear the fine hum of the energizer. For God's sake, he was an airplane driver, not a goddamned State Department errand boy playing I spy—thanks to a parent he'd like to strangle!

His mood was in no way improved by the reception awaiting him. The beribboned invitation to attend the Nazi party chancellery celebration as the special guest of Lieutenant Colonel Paulus Manfred Sturm of the Oberkommando der Wehrmacht had arrived, and the political section of the embassy was in a swivet. Fritz informed him he was to report to Herr Tobin's office at once.

Tobin, large of girth, round of face, florid of complexion, greeted him sarcastically, "Well, Cannon, it's nice of you to take the time from your busy sightseeing to stop by and chat with us."

Picard was sitting in the corner smoking, and a man he had not met was walking up and down the room as though deep in thought.

He made no response, not sure one was necessary.

Tobin lifted the handsomely engraved card from his desk by the corner and held it as though it were something unclean. "Perhaps you'd like to tell us about this." He read the formal wording, emphasizing "Honorable Peter B. Cannon" and the title "Adolf Hitler Reception."

"Somebody's got to be kidding!" He hoped he sounded sufficiently bowled over.

"The Führer's idea of a joke perhaps," Picard said.

"For God's sake, John, will you please stop wearing a hole in the rug and sit down?" Tobin snapped. John went and stood by the window instead.

"Sturm was the name of the German officer I told you about," Burke spoke to Picard.

"And why in the world do you suppose he'd want to see you again?"

"Ralph, would you please let me handle this?" Tobin said, annoyed.

"Cannon, the only person in this embassy who has been formally invited to hear Hitler speak tomorrow is our chargé d'affaires, the Honorable Andrew Amidon. No one in the embassy, including Chargé Amidon, has been invited to the after-speech reception but yourself. Do you have any idea why?"

"Hell, no! How would I know, sir? Why don't you call the colonel and ask him?"

"I'll thank you not to get flip with me, Cannon. If—"

"According to Major West"—John, a thin man with a soft voice and preoccupied look, turned from the window—"Lieutenant Colonel Sturm is an intelligence officer and a gold card party member. Did he indicate any interest in any person or activity of your own or anyone else?"

"No, sir. As I reported earlier, he was grateful I had managed not to do any more damage to his car, and our conversation until we reached the police station was largely on the merits of American automobiles and the car I was driving, in particular." To be a spy, he realized, was to be a liar. He wanted no part of it, but he had to play it out.

"It doesn't sound like OKW, not very Prussian," Picard commented. "I noted that earlier."

"West said Strum's an Austrian." John tugged at his chin. "Perhaps he's invited Cannon for some internal reason . . . to prove a point to someone."

"Or to rub our nose in it." Picard sighed.

"We're not dealing in possibilities; we're dealing in facts," Tobin pronounced, shaking the invitation. "The first is that this doesn't make sense. The second is we don't know what's behind it. The third is that the Honorable Mr. Cannon sends regrets, and the fourth is that Saturday at daybreak he leaves with the pouch for Geneva. Are there any objections?"

He knew it didn't matter whether he had any or not. He did feel a strong tug of regret for Sturm, a guy risking his ass for everyone present.

The phone rang, and Tobin raised his hand for quiet as Picard began to speak. The conversation was very brief. "Tobin here. . . . Yes, yes, he is, sir. . . . Right away." He looked up at Burke, gray patches of exhaustion magnified through his horn-rims. "The chargé wants you to report to him at once."

Andrew Amidon was dressed as though ready to participate as master of ceremonies at a Newport garden party: off-white cotton flannels, dark blue double-breasted blazer with pocket monogram, damask silk lapel kerchief, and matching floral cravat. Standing behind his desk, he appeared thinner, more rapierlike than when Burke had first been queried by him. He had a squarish face, a long, straight nose, black hair parted in the middle, grayed at the temples, a neatly trimmed pencil mustache. His features were nicely balanced; his eyes, large and steady, guarded.

"Well, congratulations, Cannon," he said in greeting. "You're well named. You've created a lot of noise around here, I understand. Do sit down." Unlike Tobin, his sarcasm was light, amused.

Because of Sam's appraisal of him, Burke remained relaxed. "I can assure you, sir, it came as a big surprise."

"I'm sure it did. You must have impressed the good colonel. Well, you get the best of it. Sure you wouldn't rather listen to the god with the mustache? I'd be happy to change places with you and drink their captured French champagne." He smiled. "My guiding rule, Cannon, is never to do anything abrupt, but I suppose your being invited to this grand *Feier* must be placed in that category. Still, I imagine at your age you are not unfamiliar with the abrupt."

"I suppose not, sir, but according to Mr. Tobin, regrets are to be sent."

"Would you like to attend?"

"Well, sir, it's certainly something a courier doesn't get a chance to do every day."

"A nice piece of understatement, Cannon. Keep it up, and you'll be a diplomat one day. Well, let's put it in practical terms. Will your attending this grandiose party circus benefit this embassy in any way? I can hardly see how. On the other hand, I can't see how it would hurt us. We don't know Colonel Sturm's motivation in inviting you, other than to show he's a fine gentleman. More likely you may be the bait in an internal pas de deux."

"So one of the people in Mr. Tobin's office thought."

"John Ericson. Yes, John would conclude that. On the other hand, this could be another way for Ribbentrop to thumb his nose at us. All other embassies will be represented by ambassadors and chief diplomatic officers, and you, who are an itinerant mail carrier, will represent the United States." He threw back his head and bayed at the possibility. "It's probably something more like that. I understand that a German Army staff car will be sent to pick you up. A bit like Cinderella, don't you think? No fun wandering around in the blackout. Buses with blue lights are frightening. Best you get back before midnight or who knows what you'll turn into?"

He'd been running on as though the entire affair were some kind of a practical joke. Now he stopped and went silent, and when he spoke again, his manner was serious. "You see that alcove in there? That's where I sleep when the urge takes me. When you return, I'll want you to report to me, whatever the hour. Keep your eyes and your ears open. Say as little as possible. Whatever their game, we don't want you making the headlines in Goebbels's *Das Reich.*"

Amidon had made Burke see the diplomatic enormity of the invitation, but it took Sam to explain the reason he was being permitted to accept. "Don't you get the pitch? The invitation is an insult."

"That's what the Honorable Mr. Amidon thinks."

"Sure, and having you go is his way of telling them to stuff it. To object or to request a ranking officer to attend in your place would indicate the USG takes the reception seriously. To permit you to go is Amidon's way of letting the bastards know how little he thinks of their hog wallow. Let's try another beer."

Knowing that they all were wrong did nothing for his sleep on the uncomfortable cot, nor did having to listen to the fulsome snores of the cipher clerk. *Maybe the joint will be so stacked with the high and mighty that I'll just be another face in the crowd,* he thought. *Maybe they won't give a damn what embassy I come from. But, my God, if they do—And suppose Sturm is under suspicion and is being watched . . . and he hands me the speech.* He could envision the scene, Nazi guards surrounding them. Caught! His father's presence rose like Banquo's ghost to put anger in his thoughts, and he finally fell asleep, wrestling with the central question: To go or not to go?

It was a military staff car, a Daimler-Benz, that called for him, its driver an army *Unteroffizier,* wheeling into the driveway at exactly eight-thirty. At the moment most embassy personnel were grouped around radios, listening to Hitler's peace offering. Earlier, before Amidon had driven off to the Kroll Opera House to attend the Reichstag event in the embassy Renault, he had given Burke a last chance to withdraw. He had replied that someday he might have some grandchildren who would enjoy the tale, and the chargé smiled and said, "I hope you won't have to wait that long to tell us about it. It may be a memorable event."

It was that. Through Sam he had made the loan of a tux. Looking at himself in a mirror, he thought he might be mistaken for a waiter. A cummerbund was the only item of apparel that lent a modicum of style to his dress. He knew Horace Tobin and his buddies were upset by Amidon's decision, but they did not come to see him off, no doubt glued to Schicklgruber's oratory. He himself did not rush off, letting his coachman wait for a half hour. The reception time on the invitation was nine o'clock, and he did not wish to attract undue attention by arriving sooner.

As soon as the *Unteroffizier* turned into the Wilhelmstrasse, Burke knew there was no fear of that. In what was left of the twilight he could see that the area was cordoned off, heavy with troops and one-way traffic, the latter barely inching forward. He was but one of many heading for the same destination. There was no turning back, and the sensation was not unlike the one he'd felt in climbing into FO Dunbar's Blenheim. He wondered what the Aussie would say if he could see him now, or better, Claire. Not "a piece a cake" by a damn shot. Sturm had better be on hand to guide him. He wanted to get in and out fast, no staying till midnight and turning into a pumpkin.

By the time their car reached the great bronze gates, now opened onto a long courtyard partially illuminated under pale blue lights, his identity had been checked and double-checked by SS troopers of Hitler's special palace guard. The staff car had a number. His invitation had a matching number. His driver announced him as the representative of the U.S. Embassy. With the window lowered, he had handed his credentials to the uniformed checker, who shone a flashlight in his face and then stepped back with extended arm and heiled Hitler.

"*Guten Tag,*" he responded with a half salute.

From within the courtyard the entrance to the chancellery was up a broad reach of marble stairs, and from the vehicles ahead, groups of invitees were drifting up them, looking indistinct and ethereal in the pale blue lighting. He wondered whether at ten thousand feet the lights would be visible. Apparently not. That, or these characters were confident the RAF could not reach Berlin.

It was a clear, warm evening, and he left the Daimler, hearing voices raised in greeting. He went up the steps amidst the chatter. The stylishly gowned good-looking women somehow reminded him of the garden party where he'd first met Claire. He did not think she'd like to be here with him now. Although most of those ascending with him were resplendently uniformed, he was pleased to see he was not the only one in civilian dress. But mostly his eyes sought sight of Sturm.

The entrance foyer led into what he took to be the reception room, but then he saw the tide of guests, now brilliantly illuminated, was flowing across it toward towering double doors, opening in turn onto a hall decorated in mosaic. My God, he thought, Hollywood couldn't beat this. The hall led to more steps, which carried the ambling throng into a domed rotunda. The sound of an orchestra playing a waltz supplied an echoing background as they all paraded across the red marble floor, which opened onto a gallery, stretching away into the great beyond. He had never seen a longer gallery, not even in the Hall of Mirrors at Versailles. Here, instead of mirrors, there were high, deeply draped windows on one side and huge, darkly hued oils on the other. The overall impression was not of a gallery of art but of overpowering ostentation.

And then he saw Sturm, and architectural impressions dissolved. The lieutenant colonel gestured in greeting. Standing beside him was a plumpish, overly begowned woman, looking tense and uncomfortable. No doubt Frau Sturm. In sharply tailored dress uniform, Sturm, despite baldness and bulk, fitted into the scene, in which the variety of different-shaded uniforms, greens, blues, blacks, and whites, provided a framework for the massive array of Iron Crosses, swastikas, sashes, ribbons, gold and silver decorations of their wearers. Booted, belted, and knived, they complemented the setting.

"Welcome to Valhalla," Sturm said in English, sotto voce, smiling and with a click of his heels as they shook hands, and then louder in German: "A great pleasure that you could come, Herr Cannon. May I present my wife, Frau Sturm?"

They went through the formalities. Her extended hand was clammy, her smile forced; her pale blue eyes were uneasy. He couldn't believe that Sturm would have told her what this was all about. More likely she felt out of place, overwhelmed. He tried to relax her by being the enthusiastic American.

"I can't tell you what a surprise your invitation was." He included her in it. "And this is a most unusual setting. I've never seen anything quite like it."

"As you know," Sturm said, "it's very new. Only completed last year. Let us show you its magnificence."

And so they slowly strolled the length of the great gallery, stopping to admire the wall paintings, lingering before conveniently located hors d'oeuvres tables. Waiters in light gray uniforms moved about with trays of champagne. The orchestra, pocketed off the main thoroughfare, had become somewhat martial in its sound.

By the time they had traversed the hall and reached a centered statuary bust of Bismarck, Frau Sturm had downed several glasses of champagne and was looking for more. She had lightened up and had begun to tell him about how much she missed Chicago, where she had once lived. The voice level in the gallery had risen as the attendance swelled, and it was possible for Sturm to speak to him and not be overheard. His acting was professional, for as he spoke, he gestured broadly, smiling as though enthusiastically describing their surroundings.

"Unfortunately Elsa and I must attend a special reception to be given in what is called the Führer's office—a room he never uses, I should add. I don't think it would be wise for me to invite you. When we turn around, you will see on the table behind the Bismarck statue the complimentary copies of Hitler's speech. We will move over there, and I will make a presentation. Then we will go back down the gallery, and I will see you to your car." He turned to his wife. "Elsa, dear, you wanted to powder your nose. Just follow where those other pretty ladies are going. I'll meet you here."

"I'm going to have something to eat," she said firmly, grinning at Burke. "Don't go away. I like Americans." She nearly slipped on the marble as she turned and waved at a waiter with a champagne tray.

Stationed behind the linen-covered table with its handsomely bound copies of the address was an SS junior officer, and Burke wondered how Sturm was going to select the doctored copy. Other guests were at the table, picking up their mementos—the German eagle engraved across the red and black cover with Hitler's name centered, a swastika set in a circle at the bottom.

Sturm moved inward. "Untersturmführer," he said, the tone of command in his voice, "the special copies for the United States Embassy, if you please."

The SS lieutenant complied by sidestepping to a separate stack, checking through it, and bringing forth two copies, a card attached to one reading "For the Embassy of the United States of America with the compliments of the Oberkommando der Wehrmacht."

Sturm took the copies, clicked his heels, and jerked his head in formal response, and Burke found himself letting out a great sigh as they turned and started back down the now crowded gallery.

Sturm resumed his concealed manner of speaking. "The copy with the card attached is for your chargé Amidon. It will prevent his asking for your copy and give him something to think about. After all, why should the OKW present such a token from an affair hosted by the party? Call it a diversion of sorts, but try to make sure your own copy stays out of anyone else's hands. Conceal it however you must. My sincere regrets for the briefness of this meeting. Tell your father I can no longer continue. There's no organized contact, no sources, no methods from his side. This kind of arrangement won't do, and the situation for me has become isolated and overly hazardous. All I have left is prayer." His voice cracked with anguish as he sought to laugh over the word *prayer.* Its sound came through, and Burke knew that behind Sturm's facade lay fear, that all the glitter and pomp were a stage setting to hide it.

Suddenly the noise level down the gallery rose, and he saw a surge of celebrants swirl about as though in a quadrille. The name filtered through the cacophony of voices: "Göring! Göring . . . made *Reichsmarschal.*" The throng had cleared an avenue, and down it he saw the short, overly fat Luftwaffe chief come striding, a coterie of aides and sycophants strewn out behind, forming a wake.

He was grinning with satisfaction and pride, sporting a multicolored ribbon around his neck with a jeweled ornament. The medals that decked his gold-braided white uniform hid chest and belly and were in such profusion that he clinked as he passed by, one pudgy hand fingering his neck ornament, the other resting on the haft of his ceremonial dagger. "A rolling hock shop," Burke muttered. "Who comes next—Hitler?"

"I doubt it. He has a private entrance. Goebbels, perhaps, but we must move along."

They did so, Sturm in a hurry to see him off.

"There's nothing more I can say, Peter. God willing, someday we'll meet again under different circumstances. Good luck to you. Get to Switzerland safely. Get to your father."

They reached the entrance through which guests were still arriving. Sturm handed him the copies. Daylight was gone, the courtyard limbo-like in its blue lighting. The line of vehicles had thinned out, but each moved slowly as it approached the stairs. A klaxon sounded. Not a siren, not a horn, but a strident, impatient, get-out-of-the-way sound. Two identical black Mercedeses came swinging past the other cars, cutting off the one approaching the stairs, causing the driver to jam on his brakes. Sturm's fingers gripped Burke's arm fiercely. "Peter, go on alone," he whispered. "Good-bye. Good luck."

He caught a glimpse of Sturm's distraught expression. Then he was standing alone at the top of the stairs. He started down, the tautness he had felt in the gallery moderating. All he had to do was to find his driver. He saw SS troopers jumping forward in the pale light to open car doors. He descended, moving off to one side to be clear of whatever important functionaries debarked. There were four in the group of the lead Mercedes, led by a tall, quick-moving officer decked out in black and silver, as were the three who swiftly followed behind. Obviously they all were in a hurry, and the grim thought struck him that maybe they were hunting Sturm. Others on the stairs cleared out of their way.

From the second Mercedes came an additional quartet. But they were not in a hurry, and in the dim light their uniforms seemed plain and unadorned, without identification or rank. Reaching the bottom of the steps, he was able to see that they were busying themselves with cases; from the shape of one these were musical instrument cases. Nothing very ominous. He moved to skirt the rear of their vehicle. It may have been in warning or an accident, but the cutoff car momentarily switched on its headlights, catching him and the musician closest to him in its glare. They stared at each other. In the instant of recognition he was stunned motionless. Then the light was gone, but he had seen the look on Scott Reardon's face and knew that he had been recognized as well. He strode across the courtyard, hurrying, his thoughts caught in an inverted spin.

15

He had not slept, worry and pain conspiring to prevent it. With Elsa flubbering beside him, tossing and moaning, sleep was impossible anyway. She had gotten drunk. Sick. Made a mess of herself, attendants having to cart her off to the ladies' salon. He couldn't blame her. Heydrich's private reception had been a wretched affair. He had gotten drunk himself.

His thoughts were like fingers busily pulling apart some rotten mess over and over. Scenes emerged out of the roiling sea of some two hundred boisterous party zealots and their women, a high-pitched background, a Walpurgis Night chorus tuned to the smashing of champagne glasses, punctuating interminable raucous toasts, the pealing shrieks of party Valkyries, the sound and fury a rising whirlwind on wings of conquest and glory.

His mind kept replaying the arrival of Heydrich and his entourage. He had rightly guessed who it was and had fled to the gallery as though by doing so he could erase any connection to young Burke. Then, too, there was the need to retrieve Elsa and prepare her.

She had met Heydrich only once, yet she had a visceral, intuitive fear of the man. "You know how frightened I am of devils." He could hear her choked voice, her hands actually trembling. "That man has the mark of Satan, of evil." A devout believer in astrology and all allied beliefs in the occult, she claimed to be possessed of clairvoyant powers. So much rot, but he did not belittle her Ouija board, her tarot cards, so long as her table-lifting exercises did not intrude on his activities or become known and talked about. "After all," she had pointed out, "if the Führer believes in astrology, so can I."

When he had told her they would be attending the chancellery affair, she had been pleased and excited, had rushed off to see if she could find an appropriate gown. It was not until they arrived at the chancellery that he had informed her of the Heydrich invitation. The look on her face resembled the Greek mask of tragedy. "Dear God! Why have you done this to me, Paul?"

He had done it because he felt that having her present would make it more apparent to Heydrich that he was willing to be more closely accepted into his party circle, socially as well as politically. An added touch. "There'll be such a crowd you'll hardly know he's there." As he had sought to calm her, he had spotted Burke, and there was no more chance, and by the time they were alone again, she was half drunk, and there was no point in trying. Instead, he had led her to a crowded buffet where he saw familiar OKW faces. They mingled, and he allowed her to stuff herself. Then, when he felt the time was right, taking her gently by the elbow, he guided her down the corridor. "I promise you we won't stay long."

"I don't believe your promises. As long as there's something to drink, I don't care how long we stay, but I'll tell you something." She stopped, the anger and bitchiness showing through the glaze in her dark eyes, and said, "I had a dream. He will kill you."

They entered the room. Beamed ceiling. Parquet floor, panoramic murals of Teutonic Knights along the rear wall. Perhaps fifty guests were already present, while Heydrich and several aides, the reception committee, were resplendent in dress uniforms and decorations.

He will kill you. Elsa, head high, the line of her jaw angling upward, looking beyond, arm and hand extended stiffly. Heydrich, blond hair hiding lowered face. *"Gnädige Frau . . ."* and then Ziege's narrowed gaze meeting his. "You did not bring your guest."

He should not have been surprised, but he was. The leak had not been from the Tirpitz-Ufer, so it had to have come from the U.S. Embassy.

"But naturally." He could hear his own nervous laugh. "He had his orders, Herr General. There was nothing I could do to change them. I was surprised he came at all."

"Were you really?" Tissue-paper words covering total disbelief.

Much later, the room filled with bodies and noise and Heydrich, the golden beast—as he was called by his own people—before the mural with a Rhine maiden on his arm, not Irma, his wife. She was home, no doubt, minding the children. Pity they had no children with whom Elsa could have stayed. She, lost somewhere within the panoply, her ripe giggle blanketed by the sound. And it was sound that drew him.

Snatches of music through the maze of noise. An orchestra playing in another room, tinkling notes seeping into their midst. He paid no real attention to it. Saw Colonel Erwin Lahousen, head of Section II, across the room, made his way toward him, only too aware that Heydrich's guests were mostly RSHA, very few of the military and the Luftwaffe present. The incongruity of the kind of music grew louder—violin, cello, other instruments. He saw the alcove and the quintet of musicians working away. My God! What were they playing? Mozart, Schubert. Their presence wasn't incongruous; it was bizarre. A classical group sawing and blowing away, trying to serenade a brawl.

He plays the bassoon. At the moment he recalled Heydrich's words he saw the American Reardon. Reardon's look of recognition. Shaking his head as he played . . . in greeting, warning, admonition? In what? Nothing threatening in the passing encounter, yet the moment would not leave. Reardon, head shaking, head shaking.

And at the end Heydrich.

He was planning to leave as soon as several ladies-in-waiting had revived Elsa to the point where he wouldn't have to carry her out of the chancellery. And then his host suddenly before him. No sign of drink, no sign of relaxation. "Please call my office in the morning and an appointment will be arranged." Before he could respond, Heydrich had turned away, and he was left with the cold impact of this order, for it was that, as was the expression of icy disdain.

He will kill you.

The phone rang. His body went rigid with its clang, breath choked in his throat. Elsa gave forth with a gibbering yelp, half rising in her stupor, falling back with a moan.

"Shut up!" he hissed in reaction, hand grasping for the receiver, and then, trying to clear his throat: "Sturm."

He heard a windy echoing in the earphone and a scratchy voice coming through the static. "Paul, only answer directly. Do you have a scrambler phone in your office?"

He was not sure he could recognize the voice, but he knew the caller was using a scrambler connection. "Yes."

"Go there at once. Call four-eight-four-seven on the second circuit."

The click cut off the sound in his ear.

"What is it?" Elsa burbled. "Is it Mother?"

"No. It's no one to worry about. I have to go out. Go back to sleep."

She rolled over and groaned, "Dear God!"

He reached the Tirpitz-Ufer as the first thin grayness was beginning to bleed away the dark. By then he believed he had identified the caller.

"Werner?" he said as he heard the receiver lifted.

"Yes." The static was much less. "Paul, why did you invite the American to the chancellery?"

He was prepared for the question no matter who asked it. "Orders from above," he said.

"I thought as much. Do you know what motivated the admiral?"

"I can give you an educated guess. After all, Himmler and the party hosted the affair. Pointedly no one from the American Embassy was invited. My invitation to the courier and his acceptance could be viewed as a psychological slap at Himmler, not only by the OKW through me but also by the Americans in permitting the courier to attend."

"He didn't stay long, did he?"

He forced a laugh. "Only long enough to pick up copies of the Führer's speech. Werner, is this why you got me out of bed with a terrible head? Heydrich invited us to one of his drunken parties." He tried to keep lightness in his aggrieved tone, fishing.

"Heydrich woke me first, Paul. He gave me orders to pick up the courier on charges of spying, espionage. I thought you'd appreciate knowing."

Bekker's matter-of-fact announcement cut off his breath, his ability to say anything for a moment. His thoughts raced in place, going nowhere. "I don't—I don't understand."

"Nor I. He says that the courier is using false papers, that he's a military agent."

"But that's nonsense. The Americans aren't that stupid."

"That may well be, Paul, and if it is, I suspect Heydrich is out to create an incident that reflects on myself and Kripo and possibly you and the Abwehr. Ordinarily this would be a matter for Müller and the Gestapo."

"Yes, I was just thinking about that." He wasn't thinking that all but was frantically fumbling to conceive of a way to get word to the American Embassy or to Burke.

"Where are you going to pick him up? Somewhere where no one will know about it until Heydrich has him ready to say anything he's told?"

"Oh, no. He wants everyone to know about it. We're going to pick him up at Herzberg. It will be daylight, plenty of people out. He wants the arrest to be as public as possible."

"So it's obvious he's out to cause embarrassment or worse."

"Worse for me, Paul. Is there any way you can delay this fellow's departure, at least until I can get in touch with Hess or Bormann or someone who can get to Hitler and stop this thing? What about Admiral Canaris?"

"The admiral is out of town. You know all lines in and out of the American Embassy are monitored." Even the distortion of the jumbling effect of the scrambler could not conceal the worry in Bekker's voice, and he wondered if his own alarm was apparent. "Listen, it's starting to grow light, and I imagine the courier will be leaving soon. We'd better stop talking. I'll do what I can to cause delay. I have one recommendation, Werner. Be taken suddenly ill. Go to the hospital. Let your deputy handle it."

"Maybe I just will, Paul."

He sat in the ear-ringing silence. The dawnlight from his single narrow window outlined the Spartan furnishings of his office. He felt an irrevocability in his surroundings, an overwhelming depression. The foul taste in his mouth, his stomach on fire, something Werner had said. Delay. Delay. How? How! Head it off. By God, head it off! He lifted the receiver and contacted the duty officer, prepared to give orders under the admiral's authority.

When he had completed giving the orders, knowing he was risking all, no matter how efficiently the instructions were carried out by the special Abwehr Kommando, his hands were trembling and his neck wet with sweat. The note he scrawled, addressed to the residence in Dahlem of Major Albert West, U.S. assistant military attaché, was barely legible: "Imperative your embassy inform FM that courier will not depart today even if he has already done so."

He put the message in a plain envelope with no marking and took it to the dispatcher, giving him orders to deliver it at once. Then he left the building and walked in the gray of the dawn beside the Landwehr Canal, knowing there was nowhere to hide and no way to get out.

At some point Burke had fallen asleep. It could not have been for long because when he awoke, the darkness through the parted curtain had not lessened and Sam's snores had not varied in rhythm or tone. It was three-forty. In twenty minutes he'd rise, report to Tobin, and make final plans to take off. But, oh, my God, was he in a flat spin, and sleeping had done nothing to pull him out of it.

Always expect the unexpected. What bright soul had preached that wise cliché? Mason? No, not that stoic. Boice? Lieutenant Leo Boice. They were standing beside the Peashooter, and he was going to take it up solo. Hell, there wasn't any other way to take it up. "Always expect the unexpected." *That's fine advice when you're up there winging along. Boice, old buddy. Throw a couple of rods, put her down somewhere. Lose a wing, bail out, and join the Caterpillar Club. Pick up ice, run into fog, bracket the beam, pray a little. Needle ball and airspeed will get you there. But this, this was something for the ground pounders. Whatever you did, you shot yourself in the ass.*

He could see the look on Amidon's face when he had knocked on his open door. "Good Lord, Cannon, what are you doing back so soon? Did they throw you out?"

"More or less, sir. Gave me a tour of the chancellery, gave me a copy of the speech"—he held it up—"thanked me for coming and saw me out."

Amidon threw back his head and laughed. "I hope you got at least one drink."

"Yes, sir, I managed that. My host was very cordial."

"I'll bet he was. So they played their little game. Have you read the Führer's speech?"

"No, sir, not yet."

"Oh, it was a grand performance. 'I see no reason for this war to continue.' " His imitation was droll. "Well, you'll be off at daybreak then. Perhaps none the wiser, but at least with a good story to tell. The Foreign Ministry sent the route you're permitted to travel. Tobin has it for you. Think you can make Switzerland before nightfall?"

"I plan to, sir."

"Well, Cannon, do you have any comments or observations on what you saw that might be edifying in a report to the department?"

He knew what he wanted to say that was edifying, but how could he? The unexpected was not an aeronautical problem in which only his tail was at risk. To reveal Reardon's whereabouts to Amidon would not only unravel his own identity but, worse, put Sturm in extreme danger. A cable would go out on Reardon, maybe several. Sam had mentioned in passing that he assumed the Nazis had broken all their codes. He recalled Uncle Bertie declaring the same. On top of that, his own neck was in one helluva sling. Whatever Reardon was doing with that goddamned venturi tube he blew on, he would tell somebody in authority that Second Lieutenant Peter Burke was on the scene. If he did, they'd be checking and hunting him. His only hope was that they would not connect his role as a courier, might think he was assigned to the MA's office, and by the time the Gestapo had figured it out, he'd have made a dead-stick landing in Switzerland. Wishful thinking, buddy.

All night he'd wrestled with it, had seriously considered confiding in Sam, not only because Sam knew Reardon but also because he was the savviest guy around. But he'd decided no, he couldn't. He had to go solo all the way.

Sam snapped off in mid-snore and awoke. "Hey, Pete," he gargled, "isn't it time for you to bust your butt?"

Horace Tobin was waiting for him in the parking area, actually pacing up and down beside the Studebaker. There was enough light to distinguish his bulk, if not the details of his face. "Cannon, have you studied the route carefully?" was his greeting, concern in his query.

"Yes, sir. It's pretty direct."

"You may be stopped. They may harass you. I want you to phone us at whatever intervals are convenient."

"I've got more than eight hundred kilometers to go, sir, and—"

"I know how far you have to travel. I'm just telling you. We want to hear from you. We want a progress report."

"Stopping to make calls can use up a lot of daylight, sir."

"Look, Cannon, don't argue with me. I'm giving you an order. You do as you're told. Try not to let your importance go to your head."

It was on the tip of his tongue to tell Horace he took his orders from Mr. Amidon. Instead, he did a preflight check on the Studebaker, looking under the hood, checking the tires, the windows.

"Here is your travel permit." Tobin tagged alongside him. "Don't deviate from the authorized route, or you'll be in serious trouble, and there will be little we can do for you." He handed him a manila envelope. Burke took it, opened the passenger side door, and loaded his personal gear, including a thermos. On the back seat were two bulging canvas pouches, padlocked and stamped with official seals.

He went around and climbed in, rested his hands on the wheel, looked through the windshield. He could make out the form of the gate and the bulk of buildings beyond. The light was growing. The dashboard clock read four-twenty. A good time to try a bit of blind flying. He started the engine, listened to its beat, letting it warm up. Then he put in the clutch and shifted into first. Tobin was at the window, his moonish face practically pressed against it. "You cannot leave before five!" He was almost shouting.

Burke lowered the window. "Mr. Amidon told me to leave as soon as I could see enough to drive. I can see enough. Good-bye, Mr. Tobin."

"But you can't! You'll be stopped! You—you haven't signed for the pouches!"

"Good-bye, Mr. Tobin," he repeated as the political officer jogged beside the car, protesting and declaiming all the way to the gate. They had routed him to Leipzig by way of Blankenfelde, Luckenwalde, Herzberg, and Torgau. The question was, Did he hold the course or did he take a wrong turn at Jüterbog and cross the Elbe at Wittenberg, skirting Leipzig by way of Bitterfeld, and head for Weissenfels? Sam had cautioned that the krauts were damned careful about who went where, and getting lost was one way to make sure it took longer to get where you wanted to go. But Sam didn't know the load he was carrying, and once Reardon had squawked— Forty-five kilometers to Jüterbog, he had that long to make up his mind.

With the approach of daybreak the sky had become translucent. He had the road almost to himself. He did not particularly like that, nor did he like what he suddenly saw ahead, the airman's peril—fog! Ground fog, a thick blanket carpeting the lowland he was coming down into. He had not figured on it. It was going to slow him to hell and gone! No ADF, no beam to guide him.

He slowed, and as the mist engulfed him, he switched on the headlights and windshield wipers. Neither would do much good. "The first unexpected," he said aloud. The fog was not patchy. It was solid. He detected a heavier coloration ahead and braked. Easing forward, he saw a signboard with an arrow pointing forty-five degrees to the right and the word *Fahrtrichtung,* "direction to be followed."

"Chalk up unexpected two." He turned as directed, felt the front wheels move off the road onto the shoulder, and then he was fighting for control as the Studebaker went slithering down an embankment and came to a bouncing landing where the terrain leveled off. Swearing, he brought the car to a stop. What had he done? Misread the sign and driven into a fine mess? He opened the door to get out, heard pounding feet, and saw figures materializing out of the fog on the run, sensed hostility in their movement. *Trap!*

He had the car in reverse, backing. Doors were locked. Men in army fatigues, they were running beside him, pounding on the car, shaking it. He slammed on the brake, shifted into first, and stamped the accelerator to the floor just as a rifle butt smashed in the window on the passenger side, spraying him with glass. His arm went up instinctively. The engine stalled. The passenger side door was yanked open. Hands reached for him. He had no way to avoid them, no way to resist or fight back. He was dragged, struggling out of the car, reaching for his assailant's throat. He landed on his knees in the grass and, breaking the hold, came up swinging. It was all reaction and rage. His fighting back took them by surprise, and he had the very momentary satisfaction of knocking the window breaker down. But he had no chance against what seemed a horde or to reflect on being prepared for the unexpected.

It ended with him flat on his face in the wet grass, unable to rise, his head knifed with pain, the muttering of voices, inconsequential, meaningless.

There was movement. There was darkness, yet the darkness was not complete. It was dawnlight. It was time to get up and fly. But he couldn't. Something was holding him down. The weight of himself? Yes, that. Better to sleep. Better to lie still against the pain. Sam would wake him in plenty of time.

And later he woke to the same movement and the same amount of light and realized the movement was that of a vehicle and the light was coming in through the van's small rear window. His head ached fiercely. His face was swollen; there was blood on it. His body was full of hurt. He sat up carefully and made a surprising discovery. The thermos jug had accompanied him. The coffee was tremendously restorative—at least to the extent that he now knew he should have confided in Andrew Amidon. He was a damn fool in any case. No doubt, these bastards were hauling him off to a concentration camp. God, what a mess he'd made of it. If he ever got out of this, he was going to get even with that flint-eyed pecker who had sired him!

It became an interminable journey, periods of which he slept fitfully on the van's wooden floor, periods of which he could not sleep, body too sore to accept sleep. The ceiling was low, and he could only stand in a crouch. The few times he did so, in order to look out the rear window, he saw unrecognizable countryside, getting soaked in a steady rain. There were several stops in which he heard voices but could not distinguish words. He knew it must end sometime, and it did as he took the final drag on his last cigarette.

There was no more light leaking through the window as the van came to a slow halt. This time the engine was switched off. He heard the cab doors open, and a moment later the hatch bar on the van door activated. The door swung open, and a flashlight blinded him.

"Come out" was the order.

He did so carefully, the pain making it difficult. He could not see his captors because they kept the light on him. What he did see was the setting. They were parked on a narrow road in woodland; he could smell the conifers. The rain had stopped. It was close to dark, but not so dark as to hide the bulk of a large military truck parked ahead of them. Its loading doors were being opened by its crew. Speaking quietly, they slid a ramp in place, and down it, to Burke's disbelief, the Studebaker was rolled.

"What the hell goes on?" he blurted.

"At the end of this road you turn right. You are three kilometers from the border control at Lustenau."

"I don't get this."

"Get in your car and go. There is no time."

"What do I do? Thank you for beating me up so you could save me a long drive?"

"There was no choice. You fight too hard."

By the time they reached the Studebaker the truck had pulled away, disappearing around a bend. Everything was in a big hurry, coming at him too fast to sort out. The pouches were where he'd last seen them. The shattered window had been removed.

"Go. Hurry." was the last that was said to him.

He heard the van start up. His guide turned and ran toward it. In a moment it had sped down the road, and he was alone. Whatever was going on, these guys were awfully anxious to be rid of him. Gingerly he climbed into his car, knowing the unexpected had been topped by the unexpected.

He drove with no lights very slowly, but once he had turned the corner as directed, the trees were gone, and there was enough illumination left in the sky to guide him to the border control. Earlier in the van he had used his handkerchief to wipe the blood off his face, but however he looked, he did not expect to be well received. His courier permit was in his pocket, the envelope Tobin had given him in hand as he came to a stop before the formidable blacked-out border station with its humped pillboxes.

"*Raus, mein Herr*" was the command.

Actually the sergeant in command was not a bad fellow. He'd been in the United States, had made lots of friends in Yonkers. He'd like to go again soon, and maybe he would. As for his bruised condition, Burke confessed he'd fallen in the blackout, and sympathy was extended. The inspecting team took no note of the Studebaker's having lost a window in passage.

It was not until he reached the fully lighted Swiss douane that the god-awful enormity of what else he had lost in passage struck home. His briefcase was gone! He pawed around on the floor, front and back, desperately seeking, realizing that when he had been dragged out of the car, it had been dragged out with him. God almighty, it was gone! And with it Colonel Sturm's secret intelligence report hidden within the copy of Adolf Hitler's ersatz bid for peace.

16

Reardon, lying on his back naked, right hand resting on the artistry of Sigurd's bottom. The chill of September morn had awakened him. If he moved to pull up the eiderdown, she would awake. Come after him. Never satisfied. Demanding. He was weary of her.

Lord knew she looked like Venus and performed like Aphrodite. Memory of Fanny paled in comparison, but Fanny had more than bed work to offer, and this Rhine maiden didn't have a brain. Today he'd kiss her good-bye, and then maybe in memory he might regret not having her under his hand. Such was life, and life in these past weeks of summer had been, if nothing else, stimulating, the flame holding steady.

Reinhard Tristan Eugen Heydrich, who had been his master, had become his mentor. Oddly, or ironically, the change in relationship had not been because of services he had provided the Reich but because of his musical talent. A quirk of fate that such an icebound son of a bitch could be such a dedicated musician, a really fine violinist, the precision of control in all things, murder or Beethoven.

He could pin the change in his own doubtful future to the night nearly two months ago when he had come face-to-face with Burke. God, what a fall that had been. The encounter actually was no more unreal than the asininity of being part of that quintet. No one could hear what they were playing, and no one wanted to but Heydrich. He had come over to them with Sigurd hanging on him like a cloak to listen to their Schubert. When they finished whatever it was they were playing, he told of meeting Burke, and a line had been crossed. The quintet had become a quartet because Heydrich had told Sigurd to go join her friends and had led him off into an anteroom, where he had questioned him at length about Burke.

Kersten had dragged him out of bed early the next morning, carted him to Heydrich's headquarters, and stuck him in a room where he could see and hear what was going on in an office where Heydrich was questioning old owl face Sturm, as he'd come to think of him, particularly after last night when he'd spotted him watching their playing. A blinking owl, if he'd ever seen one. Heydrich was questioning him about a U.S. Embassy courier named Cannon. Very shortly he realized Sturm was talking about Burke, but it was apparent Sturm had no idea of Burke's real identity and that he had invited him to the chancellery reception because he had been ordered to do so by Admiral Canaris.

Thanks to Surov, he'd known who Canaris was, but after Sturm had gone limping off, he'd sat in Heydrich's office and told him he had no doubt that Cannon and Burke were one and the same.

"I want a written report, telling me everything you know about this Burke—background, family, everything." It was not difficult to see that Reinhard was piss-eyed furious.

And so he had written everything he could, but when he had been brought to see Mr. High-and-Mighty again, it was not to talk report but to talk music. Heydrich was planning a musicale at his home, a lawn party. He was open to ideas regarding selections and the appropriate size of the ensemble. They had gotten into a long and interesting discussion on the importance of the horn as opposed to string instruments amongst German composers during the Romantic era. Nothing was said about Burke or his whereabouts. When he asked Kersten, he was told to mind his own business.

The lawn party at Augustastrasse, bordering on the Grunewald, had been a posh affair. Frau Erika Canaris, the admiral's wife, proved her musicianship, performing several Mozart sonatas with her host. Heydrich's brother, Heinz, had played the cello, and Ernst Hoffman the viola. The guests pretended great appreciation, although it was obvious they were more interested in discussing news of Luftwaffe victories over the RAF and the successful bombing of British shipping in the Channel. The betting was on invasion, Operation Seelöwe, by the end of August or, at the latest, mid-September.

Well, they were close to the date right now. What had intrigued him most at the affair was the obviously friendly relationship between Heydrich, his good-looking blond wife, Lina, and Frau Canaris. The admiral was not present, but Erika Canaris treated the host and Lina almost as family, and he wondered if the same relationship existed between Heydrich and Canaris, If so, Surov had been wrong in maintaining that a major weakness between the Abwehr and RSHA was the dislike and distrust its chiefs had for each other.

Following the lawn party, he had been assigned to SD *Ausland* as an analyst, reporting on the U.S. presidential campaign. Shortly after he'd written an appraisal of the far-reaching meaning of Roosevelt's agreement between the United States and Canada on a joint defense plan—a neutral country joining an active belligerent of the Reich, plus the blatantly unneutral act by Roosevelt of handing over fifty destroyers to the British—Heydrich had summoned him.

Without preamble he said, "Do you know anything about the techniques used in concealing coded messages in seemingly innocent documents? Have you had any experience in cryptanalysis, the encoding or decoding of such intelligence?"

"I know something about what to look for. I don't think I'd be very adept at breaking a code."

Heydrich held up a bound document with Hitler's name engraved on it. "This is a copy of an important address made by the Führer in July. Look through the text, and see if you find anything suspicious."

"But don't you have experts who—"

"Do as I say," Heydrich said shrilly. "Show this to no one. Speak to no one about it."

Actually he knew precious little about cryptology, but he had not been about to reject any offer of opportunity to impress Reinhard, the iceman. And so he'd gone ahead and discovered nothing out of line, nothing suspicious in Adolf's words: "In this hour I feel it my duty before my own conscience to appeal once more to reason and common sense. I can see no reason why this war must go on. . . ."

The offer, as he saw it, was as clear as the typeface. There was nothing, absolutely nothing he could detect in the lettering or the juxtaposition of the words on each page that gave any indication of tampering, and neither magnifying glass nor microscope gave the slightest clue to a hidden script. Steam, milk, lemon, the usual surfacers surfaced nothing. A whole day and half the night, and zero. And yet he knew there must be something fishy about the document or Heydrich never would have given it to him. A test? he thought. A test for what?

In a half dream, going over enlarged letters, clue hunting and a voice lecturing, not Surov but Fallin, not on decoding but on selecting dead drops. "Often the best location adjoins the most obvious one. A book. You open it, and you find the interior cut out. An obvious location, but it's empty, so it is cast aside when the place of concealment—" Fully awake and out of bed in a bound. Under the lamp and under the glass, he operated on the handsome cover of the speech with a razor blade. What a delicate operation was that! Not the front section but the rear, the lovely rear, almost as nice as Sigurd's. Horns sounding, tympani pounding, strings soaring on the flame.

The tissue paper was a single sheet, numbered in five sections, each filled with closely packed numbers in blocks of five. He was no code breaker, but by God, he was one hell of a code finder.

Heydrich had thought so, too, addressing him for the first time by his first name. "Herr Scott, you are to be commended. Excellent work." And then, with a glint of suspicion: "Have you shown this to anyone?"

"Haven't had time, Herr General," he said, grinning.

"You are an impertinent fellow," Heydrich remarked without rancor, studying the coded numbers. "Are your fingerprints all over this?"

"Possibly a few around the page but not on the coded part."

"I want you to make a copy, and then I want you to deliver it to the Forshungsamt, the research office at the Hotel am Knie in Charlottenburg. Herr Prinz Christoph is the director. I'll send word and give you a note for him. Leave the copy with the prince and no one else."

About a week later Heydrich had brought him in for a repeat. Again he was placed in the cubicle, and again Reinhard's visitor was the owlish Sturm. It was obvious he was cooperating with Heydrich, giving him Abwehr estimates of British military capabilities against Operation Sea Lion. Puffy as he looked, he appeared relaxed and in good humor, sharp-minded. That was until Heydrich brought up from beside his desk a muddied attaché case. "I think the admiral will be interested in this. Have you ever seen it before?" He flipped it open, facing the interior toward Sturm.

He watched Sturm react, stiffen a bit as he sat up straight, one hand going to his stomach as he glanced at the papers.

"May I?"

"Of course."

There was no change of expression as he adjusted his glasses. Then, after a moment, he looked up at Heydrich, who was watching him closely. "My word, where did you find this, Herr General? These are U.S. State Department documents, are they not?"

"It would certainly appear so. And if you look closer, you'll find they belong to the American courier who was your guest so briefly at the chancellery reception. You'll note the copy of the Führer's speech."

"Why, yes, it is." He picked it up. "We gave it to him to pass on to his embassy. Apparently he kept it."

"Apparently."

Sturm stubbed out his cigarette. It seemed an agitated action, but he sat back and shook his head. "Where in the world, Herr General, did you find this case? I thought the courier had left long, long ago."

"He did. Only through some error he left his case behind. Isn't that odd?"

"I should certainly say so." He leaned forward again to shuffle through the papers. "Is there anything here of significant interest? Where on earth did he leave it?"

"Some workers found it in a field beside the road near Trebbin.

Kripo is looking into it. Other vehicles might have been involved." Heydrich did not raise his voice.

"I'm sure Admiral Canaris will be interested in seeing this and learning the details. May I borrow it?"

"Will you tell the admiral I'll be calling him?"

"Yes, of course."

After Sturm had left, Heydrich called him in. "What was your impression of Lieutenant Colonel Sturm's reaction?"

"He had a pain in his stomach. He hid it well, but I think you shocked him."

"Indeed."

And that was that, swept away the very next day by a written order from Heydrich: "Meet me at Tempelhof noon tomorrow. Bring a change of clothes." He had known they were going to fly somewhere, but he had been impressed to find that Heydrich was the pilot. There were two other passengers, Sigurd and Kersten. The aircraft was a small Messerschmitt monoplane. He had not enjoyed the flight at all. It was best forgotten, dips and falls and the awful struggle to keep from throwing up. The only satisfaction was that Kersten was green as a pea.

Heydrich had brought them here to Fehmarn Island on the Baltic coast. They had landed at Lübeck, where they boarded the ferry. The crossing had been fine. Rough seas had never been a problem. Water was not the wretched air.

This was a grand place, the thatched roof chalet overlooking the sea. Lina and the children had departed, and Reinhard had brought Sigurd in her place. He recalled being awakened the first night by her "Ride of the Valkyrie" yelps. Indeed, he'd found out soon enough what she meant.

But far more to the point, he'd learned what Heydrich meant. They had gone sailing that first morning, and if there was a war going on, it was very far away until Heydrich brought it up.

"Colonel Schellenberg was speaking to me about you. He raised a question that I have in mind also. We'll come to that in a moment. You can handle the jib sheet. And the question is, What are we going to do with you? Ready about."

The change in course made smoothly, he waited for what was to come next.

What had come next had come simply with Heydrich leading him over past actions, long-held political beliefs and confessing, "The British will fight and fight hard, and defeating them will be costly, and even more so should you be correct about Roosevelt's bringing America in against us. And that is the point."

Point! What point? he had wondered, and then Heydrich told him, "Schellenberg and I had similar thoughts, but I did not tell him mine, which means that only you and I are to know of this plan. Others will be called on to participate, but no one, no one—" he emphasized the words—"will know. There will be nothing in writing at any time."

The sun was scattering gold across the water, whitecaps curling smartly, main and jib taut, hull canted nicely, feet braced on gunnel. His thoughts were racing as they were racing. He would never forget the moment, Heydrich head up, knifelike profile to the wind, divulging his plan.

It wasn't that he hadn't considered the option often enough. But it had not been with any degree of resolve because there was no way to accomplish it without support and a workable plan. There had been no freedom of action. Now, as Heydrich revealed it, there was. Oh, yes, there was. Now it would be his turn!

When they came in from the sail at sunset, his mind was in a daze. Heydrich had not asked his opinion, whether he approved or rejected; but he knew he was watching him closely, and after they'd all had too much to drink that night, when he wasn't watching Sigurd, he was watching him.

In the morning a call had summoned Heydrich back to Berlin, Kersten went with him, but before they left, he'd taken Reardon aside.

"I'll not be back for at least two days. Write a critique of the plan. Include ideas, suggestions, improvements," and then, cocking an eye at him, he added, "Don't let Sigurd distract you too much."

Oh, but she had, she had, and had the plan been anything other than what it was, he would have given up concentrating on it and spent his time joyously allowing her to drain the marrow from his bones.

As the thought passed through his mind, she raised her sleep-filled face from the pillow. One very blue eye opened. She grinned wickedly and rolled onto her side, reaching for him, giggling. "I know what I need to wake me up."

There were seven steps to the plan, and all but the last one had been rehearsed as realistically as possible. This morning he would be practicing with the bassoon in preparation for tonight's performance. Sigurd pouted and said he did not love her when he disentangled from her, and she then threw the pillow and swore at him as he grabbed his clothes and hop-stepped from the room.

There were troops on the island, and through Heydrich's orders he had been assigned an isolated spot well away from the shore and habitation. He had to hand it to Dr. Richter. It was less than a month ago that Kersten had taken him to the Technical Department on the Dellbrückstrasse. Once the SD training center, it was a vast building with laboratories on the top floor. And in one was Richter, his polished bald dome glistening in the overhead light.

"So what is it you have for me, sir?" he asked, eyes on the bassoon case. "Something to play with, I bet, hey?" He was as heavy as his humor.

While Kersten explained, he had knelt and extracted the bassoon's sections.

"Do you want me to assemble it?" He looked up at the two of them.

"Of course, of course. Ernst," Richter called, "come here if you will."

They had gone into Richter's cluttered office and discussed the requirements. It was agreed they would return in a week to have a look at the results.

"One thing you must take into consideration, Herr Doktor," he had told Richter. "As a musical instrument I don't mind the weight. There's a shoulder strap here and a seat strap, but for my purpose, I need something lighter, easy to carry and easy to assemble."

"Young man, don't tell me my business. I won't ask yours."

He smiled as he recalled the remark, moving up into the gorse, carrying the case, the weight of which was indeed lighter. He spent an hour practicing. This was his fourth day at it, and he was pleased with how well he had mastered the score. Richter had created a stunning instrument. And now tonight for the grand performance, the culmination of all his training.

Just as he had mastered the technique of landing by rubber dinghy at night, he had practiced the art of covert travel. Lübeck, Hamburg—he'd been caught by two air raids there—Schwerin, not unlike Manchester, Wittenberge, Neuruppin, and Berlin. Of course, none of them duplicated the actual itinerary, and the situation in each was different from what he could anticipate. But the practice had been good, if for no other reason than to match wits with the locals, always knowing that if he got into real trouble, Heydrich would be there to intercede. More, the doing helped perfect the plan, to know who would be where at each stage and particularly the last stage of all. Heydrich, he was sure, would leave him dangling in the wind if it suited him, and it probably would. But Reinhard, for all his supposed expertise in Soviet affairs, did not know the role he had played, did not know that he, too, had a trick or two up his bassoon.

He arrived back at the chalet to find Lina Heydrich waiting with a message from her husband. He was to meet him in Oldenburg. So that was where the coming-out party was to take place. It surprised him. The RAF had been hitting Kiel regularly. An attack tonight could interfere with the program.

He did not say good-bye to Sigurd, leaving her to believe he'd be back the next day. It was a quick ride across the channel and then the train to Oldenburg. During the ride he thought about how Heydrich had recruited the players.

"Sachsenhausen is full of actors, bad actors. Afterward they will not talk. We can be sure of that. They have been told they are to be used in a film, and if they perform their parts well, their sentences will be shortened. Totally shortened!" His shrill laughter was an unpleasant sound.

He was pleased that Oldenburg turned out to be a pickup point, and from there they journeyed southward with Heydrich behind the wheel. A great many aircraft were in the sky, and he asked, "When is the invasion to begin?"

"Göring's Day of the Eagle has turned out to be longer than expected, but soon, soon," Heydrich said, sounding impatient. "I'm more interested in Richter's additions to your bassoon. You don't seem very impressed."

"I won't know really until I try it out; but it's something that will have to be attached to the instrument, and that will take time, and there may not be that much time."

"Well, you'll have an opportunity to find that out. I assume otherwise you're satisfied."

"It could be lighter, but it's easy to assemble. I've gotten used to it. It's got good range, and it's quiet."

"When we arrive at the camp, you can demonstrate for me. What is your feeling about the Jews?"

It was odd, he'd been looking at Heydrich's profile, vaguely noting that the structure of his nose gave him a Jewish look. "Jews," he snorted, knowing exactly the answer desired. "Look at the Jews around Roosevelt—Frankfurter, Morgenthau, Baruch. Where they are, there's always trouble. Don't you think I know what they did to Germany before Hitler? I know what they're trying to do to my country. Need you ask, Herr General?"

"Do you recall the Abwehr officer Sturm?"

"Of course. Is he a Jew? I didn't know you allowed them in your army."

"You're a silly fool!" The remark had brought swift annoyance. "No, we do not allow such vermin in our Army, not even in the Abwehr." He snorted sarcastically. "Sturm is not his real name. He's a filthy spy. Reach in the back and fetch my case. Take out the top papers. Read them."

There were three pages, divided into five sections, and immediately he knew this was the code he had taken to the Forshungsamt. The first section was a listing of names, ranks, titles, giving the structure of the RSHA and the Abwehr. Section two offered a list of SD agents, code names, and addresses in the United States. Section three was a longer list of Abwehr agents in the United States, Canada, and the Panama Canal Zone. Section four was a single-paragraph description of Admiral Canaris's plan to take Gibraltar with Franco's support. The final section was an appraisal of SS Gruppenführer Reinhard Heydrich, his position, his power, and his authorship of the plan to exterminate all Jews within the boundaries of the Third Reich. The writer recommended an operation be mounted to assassinate him.

"Sturm?" he said, half question, half statement. "And Burke was carrying this message."

"You are a clever fellow." Heydrich had been driving at 120 km. Now he advanced the speed to 140. "And what would you do about Sturm were you in command?"

"Old owl face?" he said, enjoying Heydrich's confidence. "First, I'd pluck his feathers. Then I'd escort him to the place all caught spies are escorted. How did you find him out, if I may ask?"

"Patience, digging. The record is always there if you know where and how to find it. His name was not always Sturm. His mother was a Jewess from Brno. His uncle Fronc was deputy to Moravec, the Czech intelligence chief. Through his uncle he changed his identity, joined the party early, was a lickspittle for both the British and the Americans. As a rotten spy he was very lucky, hiding inside the Abwehr. Now we have him."

"As one spy to another, *ave atque vale.* What are you going to do, eat him?"

Heydrich glanced at him. "Sometimes I find your smartness more than I am prepared to tolerate. You, too, are nothing but a failed spy. Just remember that."

He busied himself, putting the paper back in the case, thinking, *Humorless troglodyte.*

They rode in silence for some time, Heydrich concentrating on passing a truck convoy packed with troops, leaning on the horn, missing a head-on collision by what seemed inches.

He had closed his eyes, his body braced, sure they were going to be obliterated. "Jee-sus! You do make life interesting, General." He sighed.

Heydrich looked at him and let go with a whinnying laugh. "You've enjoyed this game of pretending, haven't you?"

"You mean preparing, don't you?"

"It's made you feel very self-important, special, hasn't it?"

"Why not? Who's doing it? Preparing, I mean." He wasn't going to let the bastard belittle what he himself had originated. "It's your idea, isn't it?"

"Of course. But the playacting is yours."

"Yes, Herr General, but when the playacting is done, I'm the one who will be running the risk."

"Yes, you will, and that is why the playacting concerns me."

"Why so, sir?" He didn't like the direction of Heydrich's line. He was trolling for something.

"Up to now it's been easy for you, too easy."

"Too easy! Hell, I've been bombed at—"

"Be still! Whatever you've been, it's, as I say, playacting. This climax tonight will be more of the same, and while you may be very adept in carrying out your part, the charade lacks the reality required and leaves me wondering whether, in fact, you have the dedication and loyalty, the true spirit to carry out the mission."

It was a wet towel in the face. A rush of anger swept him.

"I want proof that you have the resolve to carry out—"

"Well, you damn well won't get that, General, until I've done it!" he snapped.

Heydrich braked hard, swung off the autobahn into a rest *Platz,* and brought the car to a jarring stop. He turned to Reardon, an erlking in gray and braid. "Yes, I will," he said, his voice piercing. "The actors in tonight's performance are all Jews. You will shoot the selected one, and you will shoot to kill. There will be no more playacting!"

Sturm's thoughts were on Else when Büller greeted him, stepping out of his cubicle beside the Tirpitz-Ufer entrance. "Good morning, Herr Oberstleutnant," he gargled. "May I inform you that you are being watched over by a pair of Gestapo thugs?"

"Thank you, Corporal. They've been at it for three days now."

"Four, sir, I believe. Soon they'll be pissing on the gatepost."

"Just so long as they stay outside."

"I'll see to that, sir."

"Good. If they remain, you might call out the guard and have them picked up for loitering."

"Yes, sir!" Büller clicked his heels and saluted smartly.

What neither of them remarked on, Sturm reflected as he took the lift, was the open blatancy of the surveillance, the pair making no attempt to conceal their movements. It was this signal as much as the discovery that his personal files had been tampered with that had forced the decision to try to get out. If Elsa behaved he could at least assure her safety.

"But, Paul, I can't leave Mama!" Her bleating was in his ears, matching her puffy face, the tearful myopic eyes.

"They don't want your mother. They won't bother her," he lied. "We'll try to get her out later."

"She'll never leave, never!"

"Well, that's her decision to make, but if you do not do as I say, you will find yourself in a work camp or worse."

"Oh, why have you done this to me?" she had moaned, shaking her head weeping. "Why? Why?"

He gripped her wrists, trying to hold his anger in check, knowing he could never explain, not wanting to, wanting only to penetrate the thickness of her mind, knowing the only way was through fear, and yet realizing that her fear could give away the plan.

"Elsa, listen! Listen!" And he had told her once again what she must do. There was no problem with her taking the noon train to Leipzig. It was a frequent enough weekend routine to arouse no suspicion. The train to Geneva would arrive in Leipzig an hour later, and he would be on it with the necessary travel documents to get them across the border. All she had to do was fill in the time between, making herself inconspicuous, and, with the ticket he would give her, pass through the checkpoint and board the Geneva express. The one thing she must not do was to contact her mother, and that he knew would be most difficult.

As for himself, his most difficult task was to board the train unobserved and unsuspected. The travel orders he had drafted were in the name of OKW Generalmajor Hans von Kampf, whom he resembled. He would be traveling to Geneva on special orders from the high command.

He had no illusions. The attempt was both thin and desperate, and if he managed to save his own life, he would be in a position to save another more important that his own. He had learned how Heydrich was planning to use the American, Reardon.

The pain in his stomach had become more intense, spreading to his flank. He reached his office breathing hard. He had always known it would come to this, so why should he be surprised that it had? Surprise really had nothing to do with it. It was fear of Heydrich that now possessed him.

In the darkness he lay on the edge of the pine grove, waiting. No longer relaxed, but tense, troubled. He could hear Heydrich scoffing, "*They're all Jews.*" And they all were Jews. Stricken wraiths in shapeless clothing, half dead, half ghosts, moving about under the direction of one of their own on a set that was supposed to be the village square. He had arrived near dusk, parked in the square, and become a part of the dress rehearsal. Heydrich had been right about that. It was all make-believe in which the area was guarded by Waffen SS troops to make sure none of the performers attempted to slip away. All of them assumed their roles—burgomaster, parade leader, café owner, townspeople, men, women, children—as though it were real. Professionals, performing in the vain hope that their expertise would ease their lot. They all were going to be shot, and he was to shoot first to prove to

Heydrich he had what it took when the actual time came. He knew he had that. There was no doubt he had that for good and sufficient reason, but this—this was sickening! He didn't give a damn about Jews one way or the other. He'd humored Fanny with her hate, but hell, Surov was a Jew. What would he say about this? *"My friend, you are a damn fool. I warn you. You do not think things through. Learn, or your smartness will catch up with you."* Well, it had caught up.

When he left the set, he had told the SS major in command, there might be a change in plans. He might join the parade at the castle, but in any case, wait for final orders.

He knew better than to try to talk Heydrich out of the grand finale. At the SS chalet the bastard strode about restlessly, like a man with the hots waiting for his new mistress. He was carrying a quirt, smacking it against his leg, asking questions, truly keyed up. "I'll be watching the performance with interest"—his head tilted back—"particularly your performance, Herr Reardon."

He had not gone back to the set where the parade was to assemble although that had been the original plan. Instead, he drove to the escape point, having to move with great care in the dark. There he assembled the bassoon and, with the same degree of care, slipped through the SS guard line to the pine grove.

It was true that the preparation, the training, the outsmarting of all who questioned his movements had been great sport. For obvious reasons the actual effort should be less dangerous until this point. But this, this was not it! This was not even close. Its purpose to test him was really to satisfy a sadistic son of a bitch. If he failed, refused, purposely missed, he risked being another Jew in Heydrich's book.

He lay with his cheek pressing against the pine needles, their smell sharp, sharp like the agitated flame within. There was a chill in the still air, and on it he caught the sounds of the marching band in which he was to have paraded, the band leading half a hundred make-believe villagers. It was time to move.

The point selected was in the unplanted bed in the rose garden a hundred yards from the castle portico with its overhead lights. There were two guards there, but he saw no others as he began snake-crawling across the open uncut lawn. By the time he was in position, the parade was coming up the drive. Mixed with its *umpah umpah—boom,* the crowd was cheering, making its own enthusiastic music.

He brought the telescopic sight from his pocket and attached it to the bassoon barrel.

The gates of the portico swung open, The celebrants, family and guests, sallied out on cue, playing their parts with élan.

Jesus, God, what kind of dream was this!

The paraders were cheering as he raised his instrument, cocked Dr. Richter's button trigger, and put his eye to the sight.

Between the castle occupants they brought him forth in a wheelchair. He could no longer stand, so they had him in a wheelchair, an aide on either side to lift him.

They lifted him up, and the crowd's cheers rose with him. HIM! HIM! HIM! HIM!

They were calling his name. Not the right name! But HIM! Face barely recognizable. *Pluck his feathers.* STURM! STURM! STURM!

Head raised higher, trying to understand, looking out over the crowd, looking for something.

Crosshairs fixed between owlish eyes. He pressed the trigger, the flame gone dead within. GONE!

PART III **WASHINGTON**

17

U-47 surfaced in shallow water, two hundred yards off Nimrod Beach at 0300 hours. In ten minutes the tide would turn, and the boat's captain, Lieutenant Prien, wanted to be submerged and heading out of the area before then.

Reardon came on deck through the forward hatch, lugging his equipment. He was followed by two crewmen. One carried the rubber dinghy and inflated it with a pressure pump; the other carried the coiled line and made it fast to the dinghy. No words were spoken. The offshore breeze was gusty, with a bite. He could detect the smudge of the beach, the waves breaking on it. Aside from the rotating beacon to the south, he saw no other shore lights. He turned and waved at Prien's figure on the conning tower, wondering how far the sound of the U-boat's idling engines would carry. Then, with the two crewmen aiding him, he stepped off deck into the dinghy. They handed him the paddle, his knapsack, and the instrument case and eased him away from the side, playing out the line as tide and breeze took him.

He paddled swiftly, finding the approach not unlike the practice session at Fehmarn. He hoped landing would be no more difficult, that he would ride in on the backside of a wave. Once he was ashore, the dinghy would be hauled back aboard *U-47,* and there would be no trace of his arrival or any need to worry about hiding the rubber doughnut. He was feeling good, excited. He was returning, coming home from "wandering on a foreign strand." Coming home to make a name for himself, a name no one would ever forget. He was in familiar waters.

Yes, we've sailed here on many a yare day, father mine. He could hear the laughter of welcome on the breeze. No fire on the shore to guide him home but a fire within to guide him home and beyond.

His eager musing was suddenly dumped in a shower of icy spray. He was not making way. Something was holding the dinghy! It spun around and was on the verge of broaching. He backpaddled furiously, water sloshing over the rubber gunnel. The line was taut! The damn thing was too short! No time to paddle back to the sub. Tide against him. And before it turned, Prien would go, submerge. No choice. With an angry slash of his knife he cut the line. The dinghy was released, swerved around, and once more he was headed shoreward.

The landing was anticlimax. He caught a rising wave neatly and rode it right into the shallows, was on the shore, dragging the dinghy clear of the backsliding undertow, hardly getting his feet wet. He sat down in the sand, wanting to shout obscenities at the U-boat navigator, who had misjudged the distance from ship to shore. He no longer heard its diesels. The only sound was the surf and the huffy breeze. In it he could hear Heydrich's scoffing snort. He'd arrived with an unnecessary burden. Well, no real problem so long as he could get his bearings and find the cottage where he'd last seen it six years ago. It had been left to them both, and he knew from Karen that she and Tom, her fat-assed husband, made good use of it during the summer. Now it was his turn to make good use of it.

He knifed the dinghy, an angry reflex over an unnecessary problem, folded its remains compactly, and, with knapsack on back and dunnage in hand, made his way carefully up the dunes to the headland. Almost immediately, and in spite of the dark, he recognized the terrain, and his good humor was restored. Prien might have sold him short on his navigator's gauging distance to the shore, but he'd practically landed him in the family backyard. The road sign loomed out of the dark, pointing to Harbor View, and although he could not see the cluster of cottages that made up the summer settlement, he knew exactly where they were. There was a scattering of lights sprinkling the late watches of the night, but he needed no lights as he walked the well-remembered road.

Always they kept the extra key under the rock by the right corner post; but the rock was no longer there, and feeling about the post, he could discover nothing but broken seashells. The cottage, like the others to either side and down the lane, was tightly boarded up for the winter. He sat on the porch step, breathing the damp, salt-spiced air, blaming Karen's husband for removing the key because he felt the need to blame someone. Then he rose, knowing he had to find a way in, and soon. Presently he was cursing Tom again for having done such a good job of blocking illegal entry. After circling the house, he chose the side kitchen window and with the knife went to work, prying away at its clapboard cover. It took time, and by the time he'd pried the covering up far enough to get his fingers under its edge, he'd lost patience. With all his strength he levered it upward, the nails giving, making a screeching sound, one of the boards snapping loudly. He stopped, listening, wondering if anyone could have heard. But who? Hell, no one was here now, and if there were any people, they were sound asleep.

With the haft of the knife he broke the pane of glass by the catch and raised the window. It, too, made a racket.

Standing in the kitchen, in the cold silence, the opaque darkness a ghostly blanketing, he was immediately haunted by voices lost in time.

"*Scotto! Hey, Scotto! Come on, Scotto, bring the oars! . . .*"

"*Who wants to lick the dasher? . . .*"

"*Karen, come help in the kitchen. . . .*"

"*You stop teasing me. Mother, make him stop, stop, stop.*"

Yes, for God's sake, stop. He shook his head, disturbed by a distraction he could ill afford. Get in tune. He opened the door to the storeroom, the light from the uncovered window giving him an assist. At least the rowboat was stored, bottom up, where he recalled, and he slipped the deflated dinghy in under it, knowing it would not be found until summer, and by then it wouldn't matter. Using the pencil flash, he located his old bike, and as anticipated, the tires were flat. The storeroom was a clutter of all the artifacts and knickknacks of summer, but he could not find the tire pump. It had to be somewhere here. Sure as hell the battle wasn't going to be lost for the lack of a tire pump. He went hunting, using the flash sparingly, deciding if he had no luck he would adjust his schedule, remain here until tomorrow night and walk instead of biking to Cokee Bend. But again his luck reassured him. He found the pump in the hall closet and returned to the storeroom.

He had just finished inflating the tires when the sound of a key turning in the kitchen door hit him like a punch in the head. He spun around, banging into the wall.

The kitchen door squeaked open. "Who's in there?" a voice queried loudly, the bright beam of a flashlight probing. "I know you're in there. You come out!" It was a shaky voice, unsure, frightened.

Gripping the metal haft of the pump, he pressed himself against the wall, holding his breath, thoughts swirling, remembering. Dugan, no, Dunlop. Took care of all the cottages in Harbor View.

"I—I'm armed. I have a gun, a pistol. You come out now. I know you're here."

He could see the beam of light fluttering, seeking vainly, heard Dunlop move farther into the kitchen. The storeroom door was wide open, and the light played over the wicker chairs, the flower pots, the rowboat. Unless Dunlop entered the room, he was out of its swath. But he saw that the beam had picked up the dripping of water on the floor from the dinghy, and Dunlop, for some stupid reason, was following the trail.

When he stuck his head through the doorway, saying something unintelligible, Reardon struck a furious downstroke. Dunlop went down with a hoarse cry, hands gripping his head, his light flung across the floor, the beam extinguished.

He had the pump raised to strike again, but the caretaker lay flat and motionless, moaning faintly.

"Why the hell couldn't you stay in bed?" he hissed irrationally. Dazed by this horrendous intrusion, he wheeled the bicycle into the kitchen and out the back door, his actions automatic. Bassoon case and knapsack followed. The pump went down the well. Dunlop did not move. He did not touch him or his flashlight. He could see no gun. He closed and locked the kitchen door, its wooden slab making the cottage look tightly shuttered. There was no time to reshutter the window carefully, but he concealed his point of entry as best he could.

It was ten minutes to four. If the information supplied by Golt's research section was accurate, he had just twelve minutes to reach Cokee Bend, where the railroad track skirted the pond. His original plan had been flexible. Either delay twenty-four hours and catch the rattler to Taunton tomorrow, giving him plenty of time to reach the bend and lie in wait for the early-morning freight, or catch the train upon arrival, time permitting. Now there was no question. The only question was how to get there.

One good thing, even in the dark, he had not forgotten the way.

Long ago he and his friends of summer had made great sport of hopping the afternoon freight, riding the boxcar to Wellfleet to call on their dates. There would be no sport in this ride—if-if-if he got there in time, if the damn train were running, if he missed it—if. The sound of his pedaling matched the rhythm of his worry.

It was exactly four-ten when he reached the bend. The track lay on the far side of the pond. He wheeled the bike around its rim, listening for the sound of the train, hearing nothing but the breeze shushing in the jack pines, the bicycle wheels turning. Beside the tracks he lay down and put his ear to the rail. Nothing. This had not been a beginning; it had been a disaster. All the planning, the training and this. If there was no train, he was going to have to find a place of concealment until, and when it was light and—

It sounded like a fire bell clanging, distant but imperative. My God, they were on his trail already! He had to get out of here. Where? Where? Get to Provincetown. Catch a bus, but—

Then he heard it, and there was no need for a bus. The clanging must have been at the crossing. Get rid of the bike. Good-bye, old bike. He lifted it with both hands and flung it as hard as he could. It made a solid splash. He didn't think it would be found any sooner than the pump. But here came the wondrous 402, slowing, slowing to round the bend. He crouched low, closing his eyes against the glare of the engine's headlight. And now, his daimon was with him. Between two boxcars was a flatbed, bulked with canvas-covered freight. Great! He trotted alongside it, got the bassoon case aboard, and, with a hop-step, joined it.

Boston's South Street Station had not changed since he'd last passed through it. His looks had changed, though. He was dark-haired. He wore rimless glasses, and aboard *U-47,* he'd grown a mustache. Yesterday's morning bus ride from Taunton had been uneventful, if tense. His overnight at the Blackman had been less tense; it was not the kind of hotel where questions were asked, catering to undergraduates and their weekend wives. He had gone shopping and outfitted himself accordingly, and now, ready to move on, he was in complete control, watchful but no longer tense.

In the phone booth he inserted his nickel and made his first call. He let the number ring five times and hung up. He stopped next at a passenger window and bought a round-trip ticket to New York. Psychologically, round-trip was less suspicious than one-way. As he headed for the cafeteria, he became aware that the concourse and waiting room seemed overly watched by police. He had not bothered with a newspaper, had not really wanted to, hoping that the story of the caretaker's bruised skull was not all that big a news item. Sitting down with coffee and sandwich, he realized a cop he'd noticed when buying his ticket was approaching. He concentrated on his coffee, real coffee.

"Hey, fella, mind tellin' me where you're goin'?" The Boston *a* was mixed with Irish stew.

"I'm going to New York," he said, and bit into his ham and cheese.

"Mind tellin' me watcha got in that case, fella?"

"Not at all. I'm a musician. It's the instrument I play."

"Yuh don't say. What kinda instrument?"

He forced himself to remain calm, looking up at the beefy, ripe face. "I play the bassoon."

"The what! The baagoon! Don't try to kid me, fella. Let's have a look."

This was so unnecessary, but he could not risk telling the mick to go chase himself. He took another bite of his sandwich, aware that other diners were now interested and watching. He lifted the case up onto the table and opened it. "This is a bassoon, Officer. Like I said, I play it."

"Is that so?" He leaned over, looking at the parts. "Well, put it together, me boy, and give us all a tune." He was being jocular, covering his ignorance, bullying.

"Why don't you come to my next concert, and I'll play it for you? Right now I've got to catch a train." He closed the lid of the case.

"Oh, is that so?"

Behind the cop he saw another approaching, and tension dug back in.

"What's the problem, Leary?" There were stripes on the questioner's sleeve. Leary turned, and Reardon rose, picking up bag and bassoon case.

"No problem, Sergeant," he said loudly. "Officer Leary and I were discussing the merits of the bassoon as opposed to the contrabassoon. Sorry, I have to run." His response brought a titter of laughter from the diners who had been listening.

He left them, striding away, forcing himself not to run, In training, Lübeck had been substituted for Taunton and Hamburg for Boston. Now he had found the police in Boston were no less a danger than the police in Hamburg. And then he found out why.

As he passed a newsstand, the black headlines stopped him cold: CAPE COD KILLING NAZI SPY HUNTED. Officer Leary had been more than an Irish bully.

The sensation of buying the paper and walking to the passenger gate and along the ramp beside the train brought a vivid recall. Victoria Station all over again. He wanted no return to Dunkirk.

He did not look at the *Herald* until the "All aboard!" had sounded and the train, with a lurch, began its slide out of its berth. The coach was only half full, and he had the entire seat to himself. He lit a cigarette, inhaled, and spread open the paper. There it all was, the words running chillingly through him. James Dunlop, dead of a fractured skull. Police searching for the weapon. The rubber dinghy found, the markings of Blum & Voss revealing its place of manufacture. And then the knifing blow. The G-men had been called in to investigate. The *Herald* speculated that a Nazi spy or spies had been landed on Cape Cod and for reasons known to themselves had broken into a summer cottage. The caretaker had heard them break in and had gone to investigate. The police were receiving a steady stream of calls, reporting suspicious-looking strangers and mysterious lights at sea.

The more of them, the better, he thought, but he could not deny he was shaken by actions he had taken in haste and the results attending. Had he used patience, employed the training taken under Heydrich's direction to avoid such a mess, he wouldn't be sitting here sweating. From the outset there had been one major weakness in his making use of the family cottage. If someone looked deeper into the ownership than Tom and Karen Stokes, they'd find his name. Had he been in less of a hurry to get into the place, foolishly prodded by fond memories, Dunlop would never have interfered. "*Fool!*" Heydrich's voice shrilled in the train's whistle. *Ho-ho-ho,* Surov echoed.

Entering the vast marble lobby of Grand Central Station was restorative. It was swarming with evening commuters, crisscrossing its rectangular expanse. He was an unnoticed face in the crowd. Safety in numbers. This was better, much better, nothing unfamiliar even after so long an absence. He checked the bassoon case in a wall locker and walked through the heavily peopled passageway, exiting on Lexington Avenue, where the sidewalk was even more crowded, the traffic thick and noisy, the air pungent with exhaust fumes.

In the lobby of the Lexington Hotel he waited his turn at the reservation desk. This would be the first real test of support. "You have a reservation for Christopher Todd," he said.

The clerk repeated, "Todd," and checked his file. "Yes, we do, Mr. Todd. Would you fill out the card, please?" No request for identification. This wasn't Berlin or even London. He was Christopher Todd of 14 Eagle Street, Albany, New York. Yes, he would be staying the one night. Room 514.

The bellhop was garrulous. A two-bit tip pleased him. "Anything you'd like, let me know. I can get it for you wholesale." He winked.

It was just seven o'clock when he left the hotel strolled north and then over to Third Avenue. He had forgotten the racket the el made. He climbed the steps and boarded the local, getting off at Forty-second Street. He was sure he had not been followed. Amid the cacophony of the street he felt secure but cautious. No more damnfool moves.

He reentered Grand Central at the Vanderbilt Avenue entrance, went to the line of phone booths and dialed the number. When the receiver was lifted, he said, "Five-one-four," and hung up.

He bought the late edition of the *World-Telegraph* and proceeded to Janssen's, the ever-busy hofbrau. The front page dealt not with Nazi spies but with the Nazis BLASTING LONDON for the twenty-ninth consecutive overnight assault. An AP bulletin from Berlin reported that waves of bombers flying toward England would soon be followed by hundreds of thousands of troops. At home the U.S. Navy reserves were being called up, and Navy Secretary Knox was shooting off his fat face, warning the Axis of the fleet's strength, defying "brigand Nations." Three newspapers in California, Kansas, and Ohio indicated that Wendell Willkie was doing well in the polls.

On page five he found a half column on the Cape Cod Murder. It added nothing to what he already knew. Even if they recovered the pump and the bike, they'd find no fingerprints. There was no mention of who owned the cottage where the crime took place. If Karen was contacted, he knew she would never implicate him unless faced with the evidence that she was his sister. It was that meatball husband of hers. He'd wet his pants if someone said boo. He hoped the G-men would go Nazi hunting and not house hunting.

He was back in his room before eight. At eight-fifteen came the gentle knock on the door.

Her name, she said, was Angie. She wore a pert hat, a coat with a fake fur collar, and her accent was pure Bronx. In spite of the makeup, she was not bad-looking, and when she took off her coat, he saw she was shapely and dressed to advertise her trade. She was also all business. She opened her purse, and "You got a name, sweetie?"

"Gordon Stein. What do I call you?"

She took the proffered cigarette. "All my friends call me Angie. Are you a friend, Gordon?" She handed him the envelope.

He put it on the table and handed her a ten-dollar bill in return. "A good friend, Angie." He knew she had already been paid. She eyed him speculatively and then held the bill up to the light.

"Oh, it's okay. I made it this morning." He grinned at her.

"Yeah? Well, thanks. Nice of you." She stuffed it in her purse.

"Are you in a hurry, Angie?" He laid his hand on her shoulder.

"Go on, sweetie, for you I'm in no hurry. I'll give you ten bucks' worth of the best."

He told himself having her leave so quickly might be noticed by one of the bellhops. Authenticity must be observed.

After she had left, he lay on the bed and opened the envelope, thinking that using a prostitute as a message bearer was an efficient way of doing business, provided the lady of the night had absolutely no knowledge of the circumstances surrounding her extracurricular activities or could care less.

Angie, he was sure, was strictly cash and carry. He opened the envelope. Written on the single slip of paper was a date, October 13, and time, 4:15 P.M. He rose, went into the bathroom, tore up the note, and flushed it, saying to the swirling water in the bowl, "Your support system is working well."

18

It was George Wheeler's custom to type up Secretary Stark's daily handwritten notes after the staff had left for the evening. He had been performing this service of trust for more than three years, and for the last year he had been betraying that trust. He tried not to think of it, but like a pinched sciatic nerve, the pain was always there. And today it had become acute because combined with his constant remorse lay the fear of discovery. And that fear had been agonizingly sharpened by the unexpected arrival in the office of Special Agent Lee Fleming of the Federal Bureau of Investigation. It had been unexpected because as the secretary's special assistant he was usually fully aware of Stark's appointments. Even though Miss Kubek kept the appointment book, it was his responsibility to know who was expected next. In this instance he had had no prior knowledge. Worse, he had been asked to leave the secretary's office when the FBI agent arrived. Most unusual. Terribly disturbing. After all, he had been privy to the president's request, along with that of Secretary Hull, for Stark to meet with the Dies Committee investigator Robert Stripling. He had been present at that meeting when Stripling informed the secretary of improper actions by German Embassy personnel in connection with Manfred Zapp of Trans Ocean News and Ernst Schmitz of the German Railroads Information Service. Not only had he been present, but he'd typed the details of the meeting, the money coming from Mexico to the German Consulate in New York and then handed to Zapp. More, although not asked to sit in on the October 4 meeting, which the secretary had called as a result of Stripling's information, a meeting which included Mr. Hoover of the FBI, General Sherman Miles of MID, and Admiral Richardson of the ONI, he had as usual recorded the secretary's notes and had been planning to include them in the package for Noel. Not now. Not now!

He opened the file and read the entry once again.

It was a clear enough warning. But worse, not only had the secretary failed to pass on to him notes of his private meeting with SA Fleming, and that was extraordinary, but his manner after the FBI man departed had been strangely reserved, abrupt as well. With his pencil he underlined on the carbon copy the sentence "The FBI already has a considerable list which it has been working on for some years and has kept current with the Army and Navy files."

From the beginning he had known that in order to protect himself, he must cover every move with methodical precision. Being methodical and precise was part of his nature. He only regretted it was not all of it, for had it been, he would never have become attracted to Noel Pasek. That part was the dark part, the awful black part that he could not control, and Noel could. It was a curse, a cruel curse, his only satisfaction being that over the years he had learned how to conceal it from all those around him, particularly the secretary, whom he truly revered. Noel was Satan. Vile, vile! And yet he could not free himself from the awful magnetism of a man who delighted in abusing him.

If somehow the FBI had discovered their relationship, he did not believe it could have been through his actions. His technique had been simple but safe: carbon copies of selected information, the carbons personally put in the burn basket, the originals in the secretary's safe; the selections carried from the building between the pages of his newspaper to the flower shop and left with Noel.

Once, when Noel had been drinking, he bragged that Hitler was reading the secretary's diary. He didn't believe him, but he was sure that someone high up in the German government was. That made George Wheeler a traitor to his country and a betrayer of the man to whom he owed everything. He made a dry, choking sound. Often in the cold, sleepless hours of the night he had thoughts of suicide, but he lacked the courage. Perhaps he'd find it now.

For sure, this time he would bring Noel Pasek a different kind of message, one he could not sell. He would present him with the account of the October 4 meeting. It would show him that the intelligence services were determined to root out Nazi and Communist agents and sympathizers. This dangerous and despicable routine must cease, or they both were going to end up in jail, or worse. Maybe if they were not already exposed, the threat was a blessing in disguise. Whatever it turned out to be, there would be no more carbon copies of the secretary's confidential diary leaving this office. He looked at his watch. He'd delayed long enough. It was time to face Noel.

He left the building, bidding the security guard at the front desk good evening, a copy of the *New York Times* jutting from his topcoat pocket. He knew the guard never checked anything in or out, but when he had crossed the street at Pennsylvania and Seventeenth, walking toward Farragut Square, he wondered how he would know whether he was being watched or followed. It was well past official closing time, and there were few pedestrians in the block. He heard the clang and grumble of the trolley, the subdued hum of traffic; the streetlights were dull, but the Army and Navy Club was aglitter. There was a chill breeze against his cheek that complemented the chill in his mind.

He had once heard Gifford Taylor remark to the secretary, "My God, Bert, that assistant of yours isn't a person; he's a shadow," and they both had laughed. But he hadn't been offended because that was exactly what he sought to be, a shadow, unnoticed, doing his work for the secretary unobserved, concealing his mortal sin. His smallness had helped. He'd never gotten in the way, not as a thirteen-year-old dishwasher and busboy at Harvey's, his first job in Washington; not as a student going to school on his day off, learning typing and shorthand, picking up Italian and French argot from his fellow waiters, first at the Willard and then the Mayflower, where the night porter had been Noel Pasek. That had been the way of it.

He reached the square, hurrying through it. Was the man behind him following? No, he was going toward K Street. Would to God he were going to K Street or to any street but the one he was heading toward now.

The wretched irony was that he owed his position in the department to Noel. It was Noel, knowing of his secretarial abilities, who had thrust him at Secretary Stark, who in those days lived at the hotel during the week.

"Georgie, get your pad and pencil and run to room four-o-four. Honorable Secretary Stark has a crisis at hand. He needs someone who can take shorthand and type right now. That's you, Georgie. I'll take twenty percent of what he pays you for your hidden talents. Run along, and don't say I never did anything for you."

The door he had long sought opened that night, opened beyond anything he'd ever dreamed . . . until Noel Pasek turned it all into a nightmare.

On the Connecticut Avenue side of K Street, he thought of stopping at Stohls for coffee but decided nothing was to be served by delaying longer. If anyone was following him, stopping anywhere was not going to help. He quickened his pace, going up Connecticut, crossing L Street, approaching the Mayflower.

That first night he had met Jay Bertram Stark, the diplomat had just given up his law practice to return to the department. His being summoned by the secretary had become a routine. At least once a week he would be called to suite 404 for several hours of dictation and transcribing. He would never forget the evening Stark had suddenly stopped in mid-sentence and said, "Look here, George, what's a bright young fellow like you doing wasting his talents in a place like this?"

That was eleven years ago, 1929. Two months later he had been accepted in the department on a year's probation as a supply clerk at eight hundred dollars per annum.

Then one fine day he'd been told to report to Secretary Stark's office suite. And that was where he had been ever since, first as a clerk typist, then as office manager. The secretary had taken him to Buenos Aires as an assistant at the embassy, and since the return in '36 he'd been his special assistant. And Noel had never let him forget to whom he was beholden. When he, too, had left the hotel and opened his flower shop, he'd insisted they live together at the Bay State. "You come live with me, Georgie. It will be better that way." There had been no escape. And then this, held in the vise of blackmail: "You'll do as I say, Georgie, or they'll find out what a naughty boy you are."

He could feel his nails digging into his palms as he passed the Mayflower with its dominant marquee. Up the street three blocks, just short of Dupont Circle, was the Ever Fresh florist shop. Noel had chosen his location well. The shop had a rear-entrance second-story apartment which he rented out. There was no denying Noel had a shrewd, tough business sense. His flowers were always fresh; his stock in any season was broad. He knew how to deliver, to convey both authority and dependability to his customers, exuding an air of bonhomie, ingratiating, the full-toothed smile, the deep-throated repartee, never obsequious, always simpatico. At this hour most shops were closed. Not Ever Fresh. Noel's clientele along Embassy Row was always in need of last-minute floral touches.

Through the glass window front he saw Pasek in animated conversation with a customer while wrapping a bouquet of mums. He did not believe the man, a tall, elderly gentleman, was the special caller. He did know that the regular caller, the one with whom Noel had dealt for so long, had suddenly been replaced by someone who apparently visited the city from Boston. Noel was most taken with him. He paid more, very handsome, suave, wonderfully appealing, he'd remarked.

Now, peering through the glass as though window-shopping, trying to see if anyone was noticing him, he was disturbingly aware of his nemesis. The way he stood, feet spread, accentuated his square-set muscular body, the chest broad, hips narrow. In profile, with his thick mop of curly black hair and proprietary chin, he resembled a prizefighter, that or a circus acrobat. Yet, face to, the startling green eyes beneath heavy brows, curling full lips conveyed an entirely different impression. He could have been an actor, a magician, a Gypsy, the devil! "You'll do as I say, Georgie boy."

He entered the shop. Noel glanced at him. "Oh, good evening, sir." He smiled in greeting. "I'll be with you presently. Have a look around." He returned to chatting with the customer, explaining the late planting of dahlias.

When the customer departed, he moved to the counter. Behind it, smile fixed, he said, "You little bastard, you're an hour late."

"I nearly didn't come at all, Noel." He cleared his throat, knowing how reedy his voice sounded.

"Good thing you did, love." He returned to the bin with the glass doors. "Just leave your newspaper on the counter," he said lightly, opening the doors and taking out a mixed bouquet. "Here are your flowers. Take them home and put them in a pot, and put some dinner in the pot. I'll be along soon." The smile had not faded.

"I'm not leaving the newspaper. I may have been followed. The FBI is suspicious."

The smile fell off, the eyes hardening with the voice, "Don't play games with me, Georgie."

"This is no game, Noel." For once the tone of his response had force. "I'll explain at the apartment. This may be very serious for both of us." He emphasized *both,* and surprising himself, he picked up the flowers and walked out of the shop.

As he did so, a taxi pulled up, and when the occupant got out, he heard him say with a slight accent, "Please to wait."

Something in the tone and accent caught his ear, and he turned and got a good look at the man in the illumination of the streetlight.

He was startled. He knew him, had seen him somewhere. Distinguished, handsome, obviously Noel's special caller. Where? Where? The secretary's office! He'd been a caller there, too. He scrambled through his memory, searching for name, identity.

Not until he'd reached Massachusetts Avenue did he dig out the answer. Dr. Franz Hentig had been counselor at the German Embassy. He'd called on the secretary way back—sometime in early 1939. He was being reassigned as his government's consul in Boston. And then he heard the secretary saying, "George, that debonair, charming fellow is suspected by the FBI to be the head of a Nazi spy network."

His legs felt weak. Thank God he'd left nothing with Noel. If the FBI thought Hentig was a spy, certainly it was watching him.

He had dinner ready and growing cold when he heard Noel come in. He had prepared himself as best he could for what he feared, positioning himself by the kitchen table, a barrier to physical intent.

"So, my little chickenhearted bastard, you just cost me five hundred bucks." The fixed grin was in place. He'd had a drink, and all it took was one, and he was coming at him.

"Noel, wait! Read that paper!" He was nearly shouting, his hand thrusting him the October 4 entry from the secretary's diary, which he had placed on the table.

The page halted Pasek's advance. He snatched it up and perused it quickly.

"So what's a list of pinko labor leaders got to do with it, you frightened little mouse?"

"It's not just labor leaders. The man who came to see you tonight is on that list. I know who he is. He's a Nazi diplomat. The FBI thinks he's a spy." His voice had risen shrilly.

The grin left Pasek's face. "How do you know him?"

He explained and then told him of Fleming's visit and the secretary's cold manner afterward. "We've got to stop this, Noel . . . at least for now." He tried to temper the statement.

"You must have blabbed to someone."

"You know better than that. The FBI is naturally suspicious of all German diplomats. And from that paper you can see how seriously the Army and Navy take the threat."

Pasek turned away, heading for the liquor cabinet. "Did anyone follow you?"

"Not that I could tell."

"If anyone suspected the arrangement, they would have come to the shop."

"How do you know they haven't?"

"No one has come around while this new man—what's his name?—Hentig has come to pick up his roses. If they had anything on him, they'd have picked him up." He turned, bottle in hand, pleased with his reasoning. "If they don't have anything on him, they don't have anything on us."

"And I don't think we should give them any more reason to have anything on us."

"Georgie, you're a pussycat. I'll decide how we'll play it, and you'll do as you're told." The grin was back.

19

The order did not come by mail or over the teletype. It came over the phone. "Lieutenant Burke, this is Captain Clay, Headquarters, Mitchell Field. Are you closer to Boston or Albany?"

"Albany, sir."

"I want you to be at the Albany County Airport tonight by twenty hundred. Can you make that?"

"Both our AT-7s are out on long-range training missions, sir. I'll have to try to scrounge up something nonmilitary."

"Just so long as it will get you there, Lieutenant. When you arrive, a Mr. Lee will be looking for you."

"Mr. Lee," he repeated, waiting for a fill-in. There was none.

"How's your weather up there? Any skiing yet?"

"Not during Indian summer, sir."

He hung up disappointed. He'd hoped the forlorn hope: recall. No such luck. They still had the purple shaft in him. And who the hell was Mr. Lee?

He left the operations shack and walked the length of the tarmac, the late-afternoon light of the October day gossamer in its soft radiance, the hard beat of the biplane's engine an intrusion on his state of mind. A Stearman, PT-13, did not have the look, sound, or purpose of a pursuit ship, any more than did Harold Pugh's Stinson SM8A, dubbed the Barn Door. It was perched in front of the hangar, looking like an overlarge crow with a red nose. FLI-RITE SCHOOL OF AVIATION was emblazoned on its fabric fuselage.

Certified by the CAA to give flight instruction in the government's civilian pilot training program, Pugh found the lean years of trying to make a go on private instruction and charter work behind him. With his seamed face, bulbous nose, and jug-handle ears, he bore the apt nickname Moose. Hangar fliers claimed Moose had taught the Wright brothers to fly. He never denied it, but one thing was for sure: He had taught Peter Burke to fly, back in his undergraduate days at UVM, and the only good thing about being assigned to duty in this nonmilitary outback was the welcome extended by Moose and Gracie Pugh.

From his chair by the hangar he called, "Hey, army boy, you lose your aeroplane?"

"Yeah, Moose, it flew off when I wasn't looking, and I'd like to borrow your Barn Door to go find it."

"Well, come on over to the house, and Gracie will fix you a cup of coffee."

He took off into the setting sun, turned quickly southward, heading down the long rim of the lake. Climbing, he raised the sun off the mountains, and its light limned the rusty fields in amethyst. Even flying the Barn Door, he was aware of the majesty of the scene. The airspeed was such that at three thousand feet he had the impression he was walking to Albany. The circular block of the Jacob radial engine packed all of 245 hp, only about 800 less than a P-40, but what the hell, as Moose said, if it flew, what more could you ask?

He adjusted his earphones and cranked the overheard frequency knob to 365, faintly raising the north leg of the Albany beam. He had filed a visual clearance, but he'd do a little beam bracketing as the sun resumed its descent and darkness extinguished the woodland fires of autumn. His course was direct enough, his ETA 1945 hours. As long as the fan kept turning, he'd be on time to meet Mr. Lee, whoever the hell he was.

One thing for sure, he was getting used to living in an unpredictable world, not just the politics of it but the outside spinning effect the politics were having on the life and times of the Air Corps in general and First Lieutenant Peter Burke in particular. The promotion was the one big plus. It followed close on his battered return from Europe, and that had been as unpredictable as all the rest. He hadn't changed the brass bars for silver for services beyond the call of duty but because rapid expansion of the corps was making promotion almost automatic. Responsibility rose with rank, and here he was stuck away in the north of nowhere, being very responsible and totally po'd. The 41st hadn't waited for his return. It was now enlarging itself at March Field, rumored to be headed for the Philippines. No, he'd reported back to Bolling, looking for old buddies, and found Major Carlucci instead.

"Sit down, sit down, Lieutenant. Smoke if you wish." He was busy pawing over the dear old 201 file. "Well, you've had some interesting TDY, haven't you?" He glanced up, large brown eyes probing.

"And now if possible, sir, I'd like to rejoin my squadron."

"First things first, Burke." The major did not wear wings. He wore a smudge of a ribbon. "I see you've had some G-2 experience, intelligence."

"Not really. I'm just a pursuit pilot, sir." He knew his temperature was rising.

"I'm thoroughly aware of your aeronautical qualifications, Lieutenant, also of your recent experience. You have the advantage of having been on the war front."

"I left before the bombing began."

"But you've been there." He accented *been.* "You can appreciate what the British are facing."

He could appreciate what Claire was facing, and not having received any letters from her had him really worried. He simply nodded.

"As you know, we are putting at the disposal of British and Canadian pilots bombers which they fly to England."

Suddenly he was interested. "Yes, sir, I've heard about it. We fly them to the border, and they come get them."

"Exactly. Well, a new situation has arisen. Neither the British nor the Canadians have the pilots to spare for ferrying, and our government is making it possible for qualified Americans to volunteer to take on the ferrying."

As the major explained, he had seen a new ray of sunlight. "You mean, sir, you want me to go to Canada and—"

"No, no, no, no." Carlucci threw up his bony hands in protest. "These are civilian pilots. As an Army officer you, of course, cannot fly aircraft for another nation, particularly one at war, even though you may have done so inadvertently." He had large teeth. "But—you certainly can aid in the operation."

The overcast had thickened again. "We do not have an overabundance of qualified civilian pilots to take on the job, but there are a number of pilots, mostly with single-engine time, who are anxious and willing. It's a matter of giving them the necessary transitional flight and navigational training. General Arnold has quietly passed the word that the Air Corps will supply the necessary personnel and equipment to do so. For reasons you can well understand, the less said about this program, the better."

He couldn't have agreed more. In fact, he'd wished he'd never heard of it.

"Three sites have been selected for the training. The eastern base will be the airfield in Burlington, Vermont, where I believe you attended the university."

"Yes, sir, I did. I majored in languages, not twin-engine training.

I've had no air training in the latter." He did nothing to hide his rising annoyance.

"You'll be running the school, Lieutenant, not teaching flight training. The CAA is providing two qualified instructors for that. You'll have two AT-7s and a Link trainer at your disposal. The program will start with ten students, the syllabus provided courtesy of Northeast Airlines. Each program is scheduled for sixty days, the first to begin on September third." He smiled knowingly. "An auspicious occasion, don't you think?"

He thought the whole thing was a crock, and while Major Carlucci could have put him down hard over his protests, he didn't bother, knowing the orders had been cut and there were important details to cover.

And so, by God, here he was six weeks later, winging toward Albany to meet Mr. Lee, some CAA type who didn't want to bother coming up to Burlington to make life more complicated when he could do it just as well 123 miles to the south.

Seated in the darkened cockpit, the instrument panel greenly aglow, breathing the warm smell of flight, engine fumes, and greased metal, the beam signal bleating loudly as he approached its source, he prepared to call the tower and ask for landing instructions. The old Barn Door didn't fly fast, but it did get you there if you were patient. The tower's rotating beacon was waving him inward as he descended. He had landed at Albany often enough to know its layout. He taxied along the flight line to the operations wing of the Administration Building, swung around, leaned out the mixture, and switched off.

"How's the Moose?" the attendant greeted him, recognizing the plane.

"In full cry. Better top me off, I'll be going back tonight."

Only the dispatcher was in the operations room. He was reading the weather sheet on the teletype. "You're Lieutenant Burke," he said, tearing off the sheet.

"That's right."

"Your party's in the coffee shop." He tacked up the weather information. "You closing your flight plan?"

"This end of it. I'll be filing a return later." It was on the tip of his tongue to ask the dispatcher if he knew Lee, but the guy's perfunctory manner stopped him.

He had no trouble singling out his man. He was the only customer in the little restaurant. He stood up, tall, going bald, a melon-shaped face, pleasant smile of greeting. "Lieutenant Burke?" The accent was Deep South.

"Mr. Lee, I presume."

A crinkling grin. "Lee is my first name, Lieutenant. Fleming is my surname."

"I beg your pardon."

"No need. Would you like a cup of coffee? It's not bad."

"Sounds fine, thanks. We'll make it Dutch."

"I insist, sir. You've come a long way. Was it a good flight?"

"Just fine. CAVU all the way."

"CAVU?"

"Clear and visibility unlimited. Aren't you with the CAA, Mr. Fleming?"

"No." He waved to the waitress. "No, I'm with the Federal Bureau of Investigation, the FBI." As he spoke, he produced his official identification from an inner pocket. "I see you're surprised. I assumed you had been informed."

" 'Fraid not. They just gave me the wrong name and no identification. SOP in the army."

The waitress came and poured the coffee. When she left, Burke brought out his cigarettes, offering one to Fleming, who declined.

"So what is it you want to question me about?" he said, wondering if it could have something to do with one of his students.

Fleming looked at his watch. "I'm catching the nine o'clock flight to Boston, but I would like to be able to talk to you in total privacy. Suppose we take a walk when we've finished here."

"We could go sit in my plane, and that would be as private as you can get."

"An excellent idea, I do declare. Meantime, tell me about your progress in Burlington, if you would."

By the time they were ensconced in the Barn Door, he had gotten the impression from Fleming's questions that the FBI's interest centered on aircraft sabotage. Not just Nazi or Communist sabotage on the production line, but more directly, possible sabotage of aircraft already on the flight line ready either to fly to England or to go by ship. He was wondering how his present duty fitted in when Fleming, remarking this was indeed an excellent place to talk, flipped him. "I'd like you to tell me all you can about Scott Reardon."

He was silent for a moment, having hoped to distance himself from the unsavory end of the affair. "I believe I covered everything in the report I wrote on my return from Germany."

"I read your report," Fleming said. "Secretary Stark provided the director with a copy, as did MID."

"Well, then, what else can I tell you?"

"If you'd indulge me, I'd like to go over your relationship and impression of him again. Did he ever mention his tour in Soviet Russia?"

And so they sat in the darkened cockpit, the breeze making the old Barn Door's wing struts creak and fuselage mutter, and he went through it all again. He was mildly annoyed at having been summoned from Burlington to recite verbally what he had already labored to put down on paper, but at the same time his curiosity was piqued. Fleming made notes, writing in the dark, using a pad on his knee, and during a pause he asked him, "Can you tell me why the interest in Reardon? It can't be routine."

"No, it's not, sir. He may be here in the U.S., and I'll tell you what I can; but now I'd like to turn to another matter. As you might guess, we sometimes exchange information on certain mutually sensitive matters with the British. Would you be available to talk to one of their people concerning Lieutenant Colonel Sturm, the Abwehr officer you met? They're very anxious to question you about him."

"The way the colonel put it, Mr. Fleming, the Brits left him out to dry, just as MID did."

"From your report you believe he had something to do with the unusual way in which you got out of Germany."

"Yes. I think he had me grabbed by his people so I wouldn't be grabbed by the Gestapo. Secretary Stark must have told you the embassy learned they were going to pick me up."

"Evidently this officer used a very daring and imaginative way to save you."

"Yeah, and surely risked his butt doing it, for all the help he got from our side." Fleming had come across as a competent low-key guy, and he was somewhat sorry to sound a sour note.

"The bureau does not engage in foreign intelligence" was all the FBI man said in defense. "Would you be willing to speak with a British representative?"

"If they have a copy of my report, I'm sure I don't have anything more to tell them they don't already know."

"I have no idea whether the information was shared or not."

He said nothing, and as the silence drew out and the plane creaked and shivered, he realized the wind was picking up. The weather report had indicated a low-pressure system was due in by morning. Maybe it was coming sooner, and suddenly he was impatient to head for home.

"Where does this British guy hang out? I've got a job, and I just can't pick up and leave."

"I understand, Lieutenant, and I appreciate your meeting me here. If you're agreeable, I'll pass the word that they'll have to make the arrangements with you."

"Okay"—he sighed—"but if you people could send him my report, maybe there wouldn't be any need."

As he flew north, the Barn Door bounced and shrugged in the turbulence. The roughness suited his roiled mood. Two points jabbed at him. Fleming had never mentioned the first, the bitter disappointment of having failed Sturm, and the second he had tried to blank out altogether.

Now on the rushing wake of the slipstream, the scene overtook and invaded the privacy of the cockpit. Powerless, his eye registering the distant blinking glow of the airway beacon, his ear tuned to the surging sounds of night flight, he relived the encounter, again felt the rage and tasted cold ashes of remorse.

"You realize, of course, your carelessness has probably cost Paul Sturm his life. I put my trust in you, Peter. I wanted to test you. Paul put his trust in you because of me, and in failing him, you have made me a heavy part of your failure. I made a grave error, a terrible mistake. I committed a cardinal sin in letting parental pride interfere with my better judgment, my duty to Paul." The heavy monotone, the melancholy, devastating accusation, the lean, faded sadness, stressing *self* before all else.

He exploded. He was not sure of the words, only in the need to speak them, to get them out before he came across the desk and strangled the son of a bitch. "You miserable prick! God damn you to hell!" he was shouting. "You stay out of my life! You ever give me another order, I'll kick your teeth in."

He wasn't sure of what he'd said or even if he'd said the words, shouting in the slipstream. "Stop it!" he ordered himself aloud. "Turn it off!" He pulled the earphones into place and began fiddling with the overhead frequency knob, cutting away the memory, trying to erase the stricken look of shock on his father's face, an expression he'd never seen before. High in the darkness he busied himself with the mechanics of flight and cursed the day he'd ever heard of Scott Reardon.

20

He had done some reconnaissance, and the Westchester Towers apartment complex—with its neatly shrubbed inner court, its Gothic arches and commanding front—did not impress him as a place to make a key contact. It was too imposing; the neighborhood too private and well-off. It meant that a close watch was kept by the police, that strangers were more readily noticed by shopkeepers. This would be particularly true of the porter, whom he would have to get past. Throughout his training the point had been stressed: Anything that attracted notice was dangerous. A pity the same caution had not been stressed at this end.

Of course, this was Washington, not Berlin, and nobody much gave a damn who he was or where he went. He had found no further mention of Cape Cod in the *Post, Times-Herald,* or *Star.* Still, the key could have been left in a far less conspicuous drop. Like Angie, this person was to have no knowledge of anything other than the mention of a name. *"I am Robert,"* he would say. *"I am Ann,"* she would reply, hand him the envelope, and he would be gone. She was someone's maid or servant, and the mistress would be purposefully out.

The method of approach now occupied him. There was to be a car available at the safe house. He would delay checking out of the Commodore until tomorrow, when he could come back and pick up his bag. The question was, Did he leave the bassoon in the room? The answer was, He did not, even though carrying the case might attract attention. He would arrive at the Westchester Towers in a taxi.

And so he did, having first traveled by trolley, by bus, and on foot. The driver, a garrulous black man, regaled him with stories of how the town was being overrun "with folks comin' in from everywhere. Must be they all figurin' on gettin' in duh war. Lotsa money to be made in duh war. Yes, sir, hey?"

He asked him to wait.

The doorman, wearing a pale green uniform, was lean and grizzled, his eyes small and watchful, the type who remembered. "Who is it you wish to see, sir?"

"Miss Lindstrom. I'm Mr. Carter. She's expecting me."

The doorman made the necessary call, his eyes never leaving Reardon. "You may go up," he said as though giving an order. "Suite eight-oh-four. If that cab is waiting for you, he'll have to park in the parking area."

"I'll only be a moment," he said, moving toward the elevator.

It was not a maid who opened the door but a smartly coiffed, sportily dressed bundle of blond joy. "Come in, come in." She greeted him, hands outstretched. "I've been waiting for you."

He entered immediately disturbed and on guard by the unexpectedness of her Scandinavian accent.

"Well, Richard," she said, the door shut behind them, "I'm Greta."

At that he knew it was wrong, all wrong!

"And here is what you came for." She took the key off the hall table and handed it to him, still smiling, her mouth too large, her eyes too winsome, her perfume signaling "Come hither."

He took the key. "I've got a cab waiting."

"I sent him away. Henry, the doorman, paid him. I'll show you where the key fits best." She giggled. "Come in and have a drink, and do put down that heavy case. It looks as if you've come to tune the piano. Yes."

The train was off the track. Whoever she was, she didn't fit. The SD could be infiltrated here better than in Germany, and he'd walked right into it. He had two choices: Get out now, or stay and play along.

"My, you're a talkative one," she said, leading him into a large, smartly furnished living room.

"I didn't plan a social call," he said. "Also, I have an appointment . . . to tune a piano."

"How droll. Well, since you can't stay and be polite, let me give you a ride to where you wish to go."

He wasn't about to refuse the offer. It was an opportunity to check out just how much she did know. Heydrich had said the location of the safe house was known only to the resident SD chief, Dr. Franz Hentig. If this dame knew its location, then it was not a safe house at all, and he'd have to clear out of Washington. "All right, fine," he said, looking at his watch. "Let's go."

"Such a man in a hurry. All you Americans are in a hurry. I'll have my car brought around."

"Where are you from, Ann, where there's no hurry?"

"My home used to be Copenhagen, Richard. And my name is Greta," she corrected. "I'm the Countess Lindstrom."

She drove a maroon Nash convertible with the top down, and she gave herself away almost immediately. "Now tell me, Richard, where I'm to drive you."

"You mean where the key fits?" He grinned at her.

"But, of course." She returned his grin.

"It fits at the Music Conservatory on Wisconsin Avenue. It's for a locker where I keep my piano tuner."

She laughed. "You know, I don't believe you."

"And we've only known each other for such a short time."

"Perhaps we could do something about that. Why don't you call me sometime when you're not busy with your instrument, or whatever you call it?" She had a throaty, sexy voice, and with the accent her appeal was too much—the kind of woman you could enjoy strangling as you screwed her, he thought, pleased that whoever or whatever she was, he wasn't going to be seeing her again.

The safe house was on Norton Place in Cleveland Park. It belonged to Dr. Aaron and Esther Deiches, Austrian Jews, chemists. They were being blackmailed through Hentig, their daughter and son-in-law in the hands of the Gestapo, their survival depending on complete cooperation. The safe house was a basement apartment, below stairs and isolated from the rest of the house. With it there was a car, a Pontiac coupe registered in Deiches's name. It was a very secure arrangement, Heydrich had assured him. The couple was never to approach the apartment or its occupant. He was to make it his headquarters.

He arrived on foot well after dark and once inside felt as though he'd entered a burrow, a hidden place, a place in which to make quiet plans. But he could not deny he had picked up a new worry. Had this Greta creature outsmarted him? Did she know this location? If she did, she'd report it to whomever she was working for, and every time he moved he'd be under surveillance. He believed that if he were being watched, he'd know soon enough. Already he knew the system of support promised by Heydrich was not as secure as promised, and there was damned little he could do about it but stay alert.

When Secretary Stark summoned him, George Wheeler could feel the perspiration rise above his upper lip. The secretary's voice had been noncommittal. "George, will you please come in?"

Come to what? He gave a single rap on the door and entered. Stark, standing at the window, back to him, turned at the sound of his entry. He was immediately struck by the worn look on his face, which only heightened his own fears.

"Sit down, George," the secretary said, gesturing, not looking directly at him, his head lowered in thought. "George, I haven't had an opportunity to give you my notes for the past several days, particularly my recommendations as director of security for the department. I have them here for you now." He waved toward his desk, and Wheeler felt as though the gesture was one of benediction. The awful weight that had been pressing him down suddenly dissolved. He wanted to cry out his thanks but made a coughing sound instead.

"Did you ever know Scott Reardon, I mean, here in the department?" The secretary's head was up. He was looking at him, frowning.

"I may have seen him once or twice, but no, sir, I never knew him."

"It seems to me that Mr. Amidon sent back a report on him when he was in Russia. We must have filed it somewhere. I'd like you to see if you can locate it. Also, I'd like you to dig out everything the department has on Reardon. I'm not interested in the FBI report of some months ago. What *we* have, George, what *we* have," he emphasized.

He left the secretary's office feeling like a new man, full of bounce and surety, eager to carry out his assignment. Noel was not going to learn of it. The days of betrayal were ended.

He spent the entire morning in the file room and was not surprised at how little he unearthed. He did find the memorandum from Andrew Amidon to Jay Stark, really a confidential letter, commenting on Reardon's undiplomatic behavior, his unauthorized mixing with Russian nationals, some of whom it was believed might be connected with Soviet military intelligence. Amidon's recommendation was that Reardon be recalled.

Secretary Stark's letter in response was somewhat puzzling. It was an apologia for Reardon, stressing the tragedy of his father's death and the suspect manner "in which the lad's appointment as a Foreign Service officer had been rejected." Wheeler was surprised that he found no record of the examination hearing or decision.

It was late in the afternoon when the secretary summoned him again, but this time Stark was not alone, and the shock of seeing who the visitor was hit him like a blast of winter wind. It was the FBI man Fleming again, and as before, he had not been apprised of the caller's name by Miss Kubek.

"George, this is Mr. Fleming from Mr. Hoover's office. I have told him that you have been looking into the files, and he'd like to see what you dug up; but first he has a few questions."

"I'm afraid there's not very much that you don't already have." He was speaking to both of them, not liking the way the FBI agent's eyes were fixed on him. "I haven't made copies as yet."

"Well, never mind that for now." Stark was impatient. "Mr. Fleming?"

"Yes. In your material, Mr. Wheeler, did you come across the name Thomas Stokes?"

"Stokes?" Inwardly he sighed with relief. "No, sir, not that I recall, but I can check that again."

"Karen Stokes?"

"Mr. Reardon has a sister named Karen, I believe."

"I'd like to see what you have on her."

"It really isn't anything more than her name listed in her brother's application form, father, mother, sister, and so forth."

"What about photographs of him?"

"There's only a passport photo taken some years ago."

"I'd like to borrow that and the application form."

Fleming took all the items away with him, smiling as if he'd struck gold, and Secretary Stark sat behind his desk, wearing a deep look of concern, his hands tightly joined. "George," he said, "we may be facing a crisis. You recall the story about two weeks ago concerning the suspected landing of Nazis, the killing? Well, the FBI strongly suspects that Scott Reardon was one of them, or perhaps the only one. The summer house that was broken into is owned by a family named Stokes. The wife may be Reardon's sister. If it is Reardon, he couldn't have arrived without German aid, and there will be German agents here to hide him. If the FBI's assumption is correct, do you have any idea what this could mean?"

For the moment he did not. The information had him scrambling.

Stark continued. "Reardon will undoubtedly seek to make contact with leading isolationists, particularly in Congress. He may be carrying the very documents that he stole and sent to Berlin. They are bound to embarrass and even compromise the president. They could ruin his chances for reelection. The Republicans will have a field day."

"But, sir, if it is him, isn't the FBI hunting him? Is—isn't he wanted for murder?" He was trying to say something helpful.

"With the help he'll get, that won't prevent him from putting terribly sensitive information into the wrong hands. This is terribly, terribly serious." The secretary shook his head, his hands fumbling with opening a fresh pack of cigarettes. "There's also Ambassador Kennedy, who wants to come home right now. The other day when Welles and I met with the president, Sumner had just spoken to Kennedy on the telephone. Kennedy told him he'd rather have orders to come home, but if he didn't get them, he was coming anyway to resign. The president sees him as a troublemaker out of hand. Sumner is going to write and tell him not to come before the end of the month and not to make any public statements until he meets with the president. The president believes Kennedy might come out for Willkie and tell the public the British are about to collapse."

He was used to the secretary's confiding in him, using him as a sounding board to get things off his mind, but seldom had he gone so far. It only indicated how upset he really was.

"Now all we need added to Kennedy, John L. Lewis, Lindbergh, and Al Smith is Scott Reardon, spreading secret communications between ourselves and Great Britain and the election could be in grave jeopardy. I've a mind, George," he said, cocking an eye at him as he raised his cigarette lighter, "to get in touch with Edgar Hoover and explain why, if Reardon is apprehended, he should be held incomunicado until after the election, that the public not learn of his identity until after November fifth."

The momentary flame of the lighter raised to the secretary's cigarette became a blowtorch in George Wheeler's mind. *Documents!* If Reardon were carrying documents, some could be extracts from the secretary's diary! *Could they not? Could they not! Theycouldtheycouldtheycould! Oh, my God!*

"George? . . . George, are you all right?" Stark was looking at him intently.

"Oh. Oh, yes. Yes, sir. Excuse me, sir. I was—I was just thinking that—if—if it is really Reardon and he brought the documents you spoke of, wouldn't they have already appeared in the press?"

"That's a good point, George. But he must know the police are looking for him. He must be in hiding. More likely he and his protectors are waiting until, say, a week before the election to release their bombshell." The thought had him on his feet, starting to pace.

"Do—do you think it wise, sir, to inform the FBI? I mean, the possibility that he might have embarrassing information about the president—might that itself get into the newspapers and cause damage?"

The secretary stopped still, assimilating the thought. "I hadn't considered that. I've always trusted Mr. Hoover. Of course, there may be people working for him who are not in favor of a third term." He strode back to his desk. "This is devilish. The whole thing is devlish."

To Burke the sound of her voice took away his own. It was not so much a matter of disbelief as it was a forlorn hope, suddenly taking flight.

"Peter, are you there?"

"Oh, woman! Where are you? Where are you?"

Her laughter even over a telephone line made him want to shout her name. "Are you really you!"

"Yes, Peter, I know it's really me because I can hear you." She laughed again. "That doesn't make much sense, does it?"

"It makes marvelous sense, but tell me where you are before I pull this telephone by its roots."

"I'm at the Vermont Hotel on Main Street, and I need to talk to you."

And then he laughed. "Indeed, you do! I don't believe this, but tell me your room number so I can memorize it before I wake up and go insane. Claire, Claire, you're really here, aren't you?"

"Yes, Peter, I'm really here . . . on business."

"You know," he said, stretching and yawning. "I never knew the date I'd get married before."

"You didn't?" She raised her head from his chest, her dark hair nicely tousled. "How do you know now?"

"Because it takes three days to go through all the hoopla to get a license, and three days from now will be our wedding day."

She kissed his nose and said, "Dear man, you've forgotten I said I was here on business."

"Business," he repeated, stroking her back.

"And it might be a good idea if we got down to it."

He laughed, putting his other arm around her. "I agree."

"That's not what I'm talking about, Peter, and we do have to talk. So let's be serious and talk."

"Today's Sunday. Sunday in this country is a day of rest. We'll talk on Monday." He yawned again, wanting to extend every second of being with her, knowing how short their time was to be.

"Why don't we get up and have breakfast and go for a walk by the lakeside? It looks like a lovely day, and we can talk as we walk."

"I had forgotten how efficient a lady you are." He swung around, easing her onto her back, and kissed her. "A lady as lovely as you so very full of efficiency."

He began kissing her, and she sighed and raised her hands to his shoulders. "Oh, Peter, you—you overwhelm me."

They sat on a ledge by the lakeshore, a mild breeze coming off the water, the dark mountains on the far side, humping highly in the October haze. She talked, and at first he only half listened, her voice melody to the swirling memory of their night when the only business had been to mind each other's . . . She spoke quietly and quickly, looking not at him but out at the water. "You know I'm here on what we call special operations. I'm assigned to the British Purchasing Agency on Bond Street in New York City and have been for all of a week. Actually I report to something known as BBS. What I'm telling you is for you alone, and I'm telling you so whatever relationship we have, it will have to be secondary to my assignment here. I trust you and love you, Peter, or I wouldn't tell you anything at all, and I wouldn't be here now and you wouldn't know I was in America if by our great good fortune, possibly a miracle"—she glanced at him and smiled—"you weren't discovered to be important to a line of inquiry my superior at BBS is pursuing."

Her telling him he was second fiddle to her work was jarring. It reminded him of how her capacity to turn from being wonderfully alluring to a stone maiden had annoyed him in London. Now he held his annoyance in check and lay on his back, eyes closed against the sun.

"You knew Lieutenant Colonel Paul Sturm. He was of tremendous value to our people in Germany."

And now he did speak. "That isn't what he told me."

"I know. Mr. Fleming was good enough to show us your report. Nonetheless, he was."

"Evidently you didn't have any way of letting him know it."

"Do you have any idea how he knew Scott Reardon?

"No. He never mentioned his name. Where is Sturm now?"

"We know he was caught trying to escape."

"I'm damned sorry to hear it. Are you going to tell me it was my fault?"

"No, of course not. How can you think that?" She was silent for a moment and then continued. "In Germany we do have certain methods and sources. One is the use of the railroads. There are those in the system who hate Hitler enough to risk their lives to aid us. Colonel Sturm and his wife were on a train to Zurich when he was arrested by the Gestapo. Somehow he managed to leave a message in a drop slot on the car in which they were traveling. It reached us. My superior thought you might be able to shed some light on its meaning."

He sat up, ready to interupt again, to protest.

"The message was scribbled on a part of his ticket." She looked at him, reciting slowly. "Burke-slash-Cannon, Reardon *toten,* and what looked like the letter *P* or *R.* It was written so hurriedly and was so illegible that even under magnification it could be either. Our people, of course, have reached a conclusion on its meaning. But since you were with Colonel Sturm, however briefly, and he made a point at a desperate moment to include your name, we wondered if you might add any clarification?"

Her explanation had removed his automatic defensiveness. "If he didn't know that I loused up on getting his intelligence to MID, his message must have been for MID. Otherwise, why use my name, real and invented?"

"That's very good, Peter."

"It's very obvious, Claire," he shot back.

"And the rest?"

"I haven't a clue. He thinks Reardon is going to kill P or R, or PR. Your guess is as good as mine."

"Do you remember when you searched Reardon's flat with Inspector Goddard of the Special Branch and you discovered some personal papers and one had a short list of names, three names?"

"Two names and an initial."

"Exactly. And what was the initial?"

"R, I think. So who is R? I have no idea."

"Could it be President Roosevelt?"

"Reardon may be nutty, but I don't think he's that nutty."

"Was Colonel Sturm, as you say, nutty? He was trying to warn us."

"Us? Us? How do you mean us? What's G-2, MID, the FBI got to say about us?" He knew there was a bullying tone in his voice.

"Like you, they seem to resent the suggestion. I understand your Mr. Hoover scoffs at it. He believes that if indeed Reardon is here in America, he's here to set up a sabotage operation." She was no longer the quietly contained British agent. There was color in her cheeks and anger in her eye.

"And MID, what does General Burke have to say? I suppose he sent you up here to pump me?"

"Why do you have to act so bloody beastly?" she snapped.

"Because a man in love is apt to be bloody beastly, particularly if the woman he loves is only out to use him."

"Oh, Peter, that's not fair." She looked away.

"No, it's not," he agreed, and moved over to put his arm around her, "but you can't come in and out of my life like a tide and expect me to be reasonable. I don't know what Reardon is up to. How could I? If our people don't think he's out to kill the president, why should yours be so concerned?"

"Because, my dear, angry man, your president's safety is more important to us than anything else we can think of."

21

He was being watched, followed, and while he prided himself on his capability to detect the danger, its threat was basic to all else. He had first noticed him at the Amphitheater of the Unknown Soldier. He had gone to Arlington Cemetery to familiarize himself with the lay of the land. Others were there, tourists for the most part. The watcher was in such a group, and while snapping pictures, he'd spotted him. Two clues: The man was not listening to the tour guide, and he quickly turned away when the camera had inadvertently been pointed in his direction.

Although Reardon did not consider the pristine beauty of the amphitheater, with its white marble and pines, a primary point of contact (escape would be impossible from such a place), he felt it necessary to check out numerous areas of possibility. As Heydrich had said, it was good practice and a way to gather additional information before approaching the selected locale. Roosevelt would come here on Armistice Day whether or not he won the election. It was best to have a look, and in so doing he began to suspect that someone was looking at him. On the twenty-third at the Philadelphia Convention Hall, he found that his suspicion was correct. He was one of a huge throng, listening to the lying cripple brag that "He must think not only of keeping us out of war today but also of keeping us out of war in generations to come."

He was not there to puke over the oratory. His purpose was to study the bastard's protection. Naturally the setting was no place to employ the bassoon, but it was good for observing the sharpness of the Secret Service watchdogs. When the speech making ceased and the cheers of the assembled filled the hall, like many in the crowd, he joined the surge forward, the idea to get as close to the great man as possible. It was then that he again saw the watcher. Recognition shook him because he had not been sure at Arlington and now there could be no doubt.

That night he sat in his hotel room in the dark with a bottle of Three Feathers and contemplated the problem. From press accounts he had a fairly concise itinerary of Roosevelt's movements. On Sunday night he would go by his special train up to Newark, New Jersey, where he would be greeted in the early morning by a mob of voters and political hacks. By motorcade he'd be making stops at federal shipbuilding yards in Kearny, then on to Jersey City and Staten Island, with a speech stop planned at the site for a Brooklyn-Battery tunnel. Lunch at Hunter College with a second speech planned before an ROTC unit at Fordham U. Dinner aboard his train, arriving at Madison Square Garden for his ten o'clock bull sling.

Previously he had debated going to the Garden. Now he knew he would, not to hear the mellifluous charlatan spout his lies but to flush out the watcher. About him there were two questions. Who was he? How had he picked up the trail of Scott Reardon?

No one had known he was going to visit the amphitheater at Arlington. The same was true of being here in Philadelphia. And now his yet undecided plan to dog the campaign trail through the boroughs of New York, up through Connecticut to Boston—who could know about that? He saw only one answer. He was being surveilled by one of Heydrich's SD butterflies. It meant the safe house was being watched and every time he moved, he was being watched. It was either that or he was under the eye of the FBI, army CID, or some other government agency. And that just didn't make sense. If they knew he was here, then he was wanted for killing that poor sap, and they wouldn't play games, waiting to find out what he was up to. They'd pick him up fast. No, it was Heydrich, trying to keep his tentacles on him to see if he was really going to carry out the plan. And if he didn't? Get rid of him. And if he did? Maybe he'd get the answer to that at Madison Square Garden. He wouldn't carry a bassoon, but he had an instrument that would make for singing. And after that he'd head north.

The evening was cloudy and cool, and he was one of thousands—later he read twenty-two thousand—who packed the Garden. He tried not to listen to the man's attack on Wendell Willkie's accusation that the Democrats had ignored national defense and the blatant nonsense about upholding the Neutrality Act. God, if he could only let these cheering morons see the cables he had collected. They whooped it up inanely when Roosevelt ridiculed the names of Republican Congressmen Martin, Barton, and Fish. And when he repeated their names, the crowd joyfully roared them back at him. What the hell, Hitler was right. Democracy was a bull pit full of idiots, cheering a cripple to lead them to war. While suffering through the rhetoric, he tried to locate the watcher. In the veil of cigarette smoke, the packed mass, the poor light, he did not find him.

When it was finally over, he drifted with the cackling throng out onto the avenue. He crossed the street, heading east and circuitously made his way to Penn Station. Before boarding the train, he picked up the next morning's first edition of the *Herald Tribune.*

After the train had pulled out and the conductor had collected his ticket, he got up and walked through the cars. When he returned to his seat, he was sure the watcher—if there really was a watcher—was not on the train.

He sat down and opened his newspaper. Polls were giving Willkie the lead in key states. The Democratic National Committee had released a half hour of radio time on CBS tomorrow night for the great Irish fruitcake Kennedy to speak his piece. Speculation as to whether he would come out for Willkie was rife. Well, if any hypocrite could upstage Franklin, it was that shanty Irish crook. And beyond beyond, Mussolini's Roman legions had bravely attacked Greece. The Luftwaffe was pounding nightly hell out of London. The RAF was bashing Berlin, and Whitehall felt the invasion danger was past for the year. Well, bully. Stiff upper lip, lads. And oh, tomorrow and tomorrow was lucky number day. The great peace lovers were about to draft a million of the innocent. A "muster" Roosevelt had termed it, a typical coating of the poison pill. Well, maybe they could call his execution a departure. Sixteen million plus had registered for the draft, but they'd have to get along without Christopher Todd or even Scott Reardon. He turned to the editorial page, and there was Walter Lippmann regurgitating. Under the terms of the newly announced Axis pact between Germany, Italy, and Japan, "the U.S. must either abandon Great Britain and China or it will be attacked by all three totalitarian powers. . . ." How cute. Declare war at once, or else. Damn ass.

He glanced at the lead editorial: "The Senate has taken at least one step in the right direction by passage of a bill, compelling such organizations notably the Communist Party and the German American Bund, to disclose their membership and the source of their finances. . . ." Fat chance. He folded the paper, put back his head, and closed his eyes. He drifted off, mulling the Nazi-Soviet alliance. Ribbentrop going to Moscow and Molotov to Berlin. The guessing was that Stalin would join the pact. If Heydrich was any measure of what Hitler was up to, Stalin and his comrades might be in for a bloody surprise. But on the other hand. . . .

He awoke as the train eased into its berth. He took his time walking down the ramp to the station building. He was looking for a tall, hefty man with cropped salt-and-pepper hair, a twisted nose, thick lips and a gray top coat with collar turned up. By the time he passed through the waiting room he had not spotted him and was relieved. Wherever the bastard was, he wasn't here.

He existed, turned right, heading along the pillared station front toward the trolley stop. The lighting was poor, obscuring detail. He did not see or hear the watcher come from behind the pillar. The point of a knife pricking his back made him gasp with pain and shock, instinctively arching away from the source. "Just keep walking slowly." The voice was full of rust. "Turn around, and I'll mark you good. General Surov is very disappointed with you. You'll be receiving instructions from—"

The flame within soared out of control. His hand had been in his pocket, holding the knife. He leaped forward, spinning in the air to land en garde, the released blade extended. He took two rapid steps forward, feinted, and lunged, aiming at his oncoming assailant's throat.

His attacker managed to get his arm in the way, and Reardon felt the blade sink into flesh and strike bone. The harsh cry of pain caught the attention of exiting passengers. They paused and watched in the dimness as the attacker, grabbing his wounded arm, turned and ran back between the pillars.

Reardon moved quickly in the opposite direction, raising his hand and calling, "Taxi!" He had the knife back in his coat pocket, hoping no policeman had seen any of it. He was breathing deeply, exhilarated by the feel of the blade striking home. Heydrich couldn't have done it any better. But in the taxi the excitement evaporated, and he knew he'd come within an inch of ruining everything.

He sat in the dark by the window, looking out on Norton Place, knowing his safe house was no longer safe. Surov's people had penetrated the SD. Long ago the general had said as much. Someone here in Heydrich's apparatus was reporting not to Berlin but to Moscow. Even though only he and Heydrich knew what his mission was, the Fourth Bureau, having penetrated the backup apparatus, had learned that he was here. He had been correct in assuming the house was under watch. Now he knew by whom, and he had to get out of here. Not in a frantic rush but coolly and carefully. The undecided plan to track the Roosevelt cavalcade up through Connecticut to Springfield and then head either to Boston or Albany was out. He did not like canceling. The scheduled stops in Connecticut would offer an ongoing opportunity to observe Secret Service protection, not a static situation or inside a convention hall.

At Fehmarn, Heydrich had supplied him with considerable background on the White House Secret Service detail. It was surprisingly small, numbering only eleven. It was under the direction of that Jew Morgenthau at Treasury. Chief of the detail was a gumshoe named Frank J. Wilson. There had been a stack of photos of the unit members, most of the photos taken of motorcades with the agents riding on the running boards of the president's limo. An important point was that it was not an armored car, and not even the windows were bulletproof. There was no two-way communication. The bodyguards used hand signals. A motorcade had one car in front filled with Secret Service and local police, and another behind the limo equally staffed with Secret Service on the running boards or alongside the vehicle. Rooftops and windows were kept under close watch, and wherever the great man traveled, the local police were on hand to support the Secret Service agents. "Not on as high a level as our SS." Heydrich had sniffed. "After all, the main occupation of these fellows is not protection but looking for counterfeiters. Ha!" Much had been made of the assassination attempt in '33, and Heydrich insisted that it be studied carefully. The attempt had taken place in Miami at Bay Front Park. Roosevelt had come in from a fishing trip on Vincent Astor's yacht to make a speech. If Zangara hadn't been such a rotten shot and hit the mayor of Chicago instead of Roosevelt, he wouldn't be sitting here making plans. Heydrich had insisted the Miami attempt was important because it illustrated not only the vulnerability of a motionless target in the open but also the ineptness of the protection.

He wasn't willing to take comfort in it. That was a major reason for wanting to study the Secret Service operating on the move. The only comfort in canceling was that it would give him more time to reconnoiter the point of contact, if he chose to do so. The risk was in arriving too soon and attracting attention. For now he must decide when to depart here and get clear of Surov's hammer and sickle. He purposely slept late, and after coffee, toast, and a cigarette, he loaded the Pontiac, planning to depart at noon. With the coupe concealed in the adjoining garage and the occupants above long gone, he wished to give the impression that his departure was not forced, was local and routine. When the phone rang, its sound startled him almost as much as the feel of the knife point nicking his back. He stood rooted, counting the rings. Five meant get out. At the seventh he lifted the receiver and listened.

"Hello, Richard, is that you?"

He said nothing.

"This is Countess Greta Lindstrom. Greta to you, darling. Our friend asked me to reach you. Please come at four."

Her voice infuriated him. "No."

"But you must, you know. It's a request from H, darling." She giggled and hung up.

The unexpectedness of it, the utter damned foolishness of it! Hentig was the chief arranger, but there was to be no meeting, no contact. Never! Worse, no one else was to know. No one! How did that silly bitch get into it? Was H Heydrich or Hentig?

His immediate reaction was to get away as planned, but the more he weighed it, the more he knew he was in a bind. If, indeed, H was Heydrich, then something had happened, the whole effort possibly compromised. The way outsiders were becoming involved pointed in that direction. If it was Hentig, then he either should be avoided or the risk taken to meet him and to tell him to stay the hell out of it. Heydrich had praised Hentig's intelligence and sharpness, much more astute than Westrick, the SD resident courting isolationists, he'd said. Perhaps Hentig, using that woman, was not so stupid. These wires could be tapped. In the end he knew he would have to stop at the Westchester Towers, but this coming on top of last night was bad. He departed Norton Place at three o'clock and drove at a leisurely pace down into Georgetown, where he pulled into a service station and filled up with gas. He spotted no following car, even after driving the long length of Pennsylvania Avenue to the Washington Star Building on Eleventh Street. There he parked and went into the lobby to inspect the *Star*'s new classical record opera appreciations series, featuring Verdi's *Rigoletto.* He was genuinely interested, having read the newspapers ads; this was the fifth offering in a series of seven operas. However, he was more interested in seeing if anyone was interested in him. No one appeared to be, either inside or out. On the drive to the Westchester Towers, he kept an eye on the rearview mirror while he adjusted his mood to what might lie ahead.

He entered a lobby festooned with balloons and a noisy gathering, displaying WIN WITH WILLKIE placards. He was accosted by a bear of a man, his coat decked with Willkie buttons, "Here, young fellah, say no to a third term." He thrust out an overlarge one.

"No, thanks. I'm too young to vote." He smiled, brushing past him, heading for the elevator. Some of the enthusiasts, mostly female, crowded in with him.

"Floor, please," requested the operator.

They all shouted, "Eight!" and continued their well-oiled chatter as the car ascended. He got off last and watched them rush down the corridor toward the sound of beckoning merriment. Good cover, he thought as the sound rose and then was tamped way down by the closing of a door. If celebrating victory a week before the election could elect Wendell Willkie, he'd win in a breeze. Idiots.

As he approached suite 804, it became apparent the party was going on close by, and suddenly he knew how close by. Automatically he spun around to get away as around the corner and down the hall came the bear man and his fired-up entourage. "There you are! There you are!" he shouted. "Knew you were one of us. Open up, Greta! Open up!"

He tried to get around them but couldn't. The door behind him opened, and he was carried on in by the press, backpedaling furiously to keep his feet. And there was Greta, out of the way in the entrance alcove, grinning and laughing.

"Oh, Richard, darling, how good of you to come." She reached out her hand to him, but he was swept into the heavily crowded living room, where in the shallows of the flood the occupants were closely joined in communion for their candidate, anxious to toast him well and frequently.

Immediately, through the sound he heard German-accented English. Heydrich had shown him a photo of Franz Hentig, and he recognized him at once. He also recognized the oh, so elegant lady he was talking to, and the sight of her stunned him. Claire Hollier's eyes met his before he could turn and move away. He had to get out! But first—

Greta had just let in a new quartet of celebrants. He maneuvered around them to her and took her wrist. The big China blue eyes opened wider, the smiling teasing. He had noted the powder room in the entry hall, and he hauled her into it, opening and shutting the door in one swift motion, slamming her against the door, his hands around her throat, ready to kill her.

She had had no chance to cry out. Her eyes were bulging with terror, her overripe mouth open, her hands tight around his wrists.

"How did you get my telephone number? Tell me quick or you're dead!" His words came out in a whispered growl. "Tell me!" He released the pressure, and she gulped in air, sobbing. "Tell me, quick!" He banged the back of her head against the door.

"Fr-from Franz" she wheezed. "P-please!"

"Did he give it to you?"

"No—no-no. I found it in his little book. He—he didn't know. I thought it might be you. I was only playing, please! Plea—"

He tightened his grip, and she struggled frantically, thrusting her body at him, trying to escape.

"You stupid damn fool!"

He relaxed his grip, and choking, she began whimpering. "Please . . . please, don't hurt me. I only wanted—"

"Shut up! If you ever mention I was here, I'll come back and kill you. Tell that damn fool with the little black book, the lady he's busy impressing happens to be a British agent." He swung her away from the door and gave her a push, and she sat down on the toilet, her hands massaging her throat, her breath coming in sobs.

He opened the door and went down the hall and out of the place just as a group of new arrivals swept past him, chanting, "Win with Willkie! Win with Willkie! No third term!"

Urgency rode with him as he drove north. The twin shocks of exposure, completely different in character but equally dangerous, had forced his hand. He had not wanted to arrive on the killing ground so soon. As it was, he did not stop until he reached New York City. It was after midnight when he checked into the Belmont, satisfied at least that he had not been followed. He fell asleep, knowing General Surov's troops might be around, but they were obviously few in number. In fact, maybe he'd wounded all there were. It was Hentig who worried him most. What in the hell was he doing with Claire Hollier? Had she recognized him?

And that crazy bug-eyed bitch he was using as a bedpan. The hell with it. He was out of there. The question was: Was the plan still in place regardless of the change in timing?

The next morning he made the call from an Automat on Forty-second Street. He let it ring six times, hung up, waited five minutes while he finished his coffee, and called again.

The receiver was lifted on the first ring, and his question was answered.

"This is Richard," he said.

"You're expected at Keeler's at eight o'clock, table forty-eight, ask for the New Orleans crabs."

Heading north again on 9W, he felt he'd gotten over a barrier. Whatever Hentig was up to with the ladies, he had been able to make the correct arrangements, and unless something went seriously wrong, there would be no further need to use him again.

It was after dark when he reached Rensselaer and crossed the bridge into Albany. He did not know the city, but he had no trouble finding the Hampton Hotel on the corner of State Street, having studied a map of the area while training at Fehmarn. Within, the flame lay banked and steady, but it was hot. Oh, it was hot.

Keeler's restaurant was only a few steps from the hotel, not far enough to get wet in the light rain. From without, the eatery did not seem all that large or imposing, but once he was inside, his impression was of a maze of oak-paneled dining rooms, its clientele being served by fast-moving tray-laden waiters, wearing black jackets and long white aprons. The table he was escorted to was not in the main dining room decked with wall mirrors and glittering chandeliers but in an upstairs smaller room, where he was seated in a corner alcove, an excellent choice for private dining.

He was no sooner seated than Fritz appeared; at least the medallion nameplate on his jacket so named him. Bald, short, gray-mustached, very erect.

"Zur. Good evening." He placed a large, handsomely rendered menu on the table. "Zomzing to drink, *ja?*"

"*Ja, mein Herr.* It is a good evening," he replied in German.

"Ah, you speak *deutsch.*"

"Yes, and you're right. I would like a Beafeater martini." He flipped open the menu. "I understand your New Orleans crabs are a specialty."

"Everything is a specialty here, sir, but yes, they are the best."

"Well, I'll study this while you instruct your bartender."

"*Ja.*" Fritz left-faced and marched out. No one in the room was paying the least attention. The exchange had been correct so far.

The martini was served with a dividend. He said he would enjoy it before he ordered, but having studied the menu, he informed Fritz he was having a difficult time making a choice—what with crabs, shrimp, and lobster from which to choose.

"Where do you get your shrimp?" he asked.

"Our shrimp comes from Georgia, sir."

"And you have venison, I see. I suppose it comes from the Catskills."

"Sir, the deer think it an honor to be served here."

Once all the right things had been said, he settled for the lobster. When the check was presented on its silver tray, he placed a twenty-dollar bill on it, looking forward to receiving more than change in return. Fritz marched away, and he sipped the last of the Chardonnay, waiting, knowing he was tense as he observed those around him occupied with each other and their food.

When the waiter returned, he placed the tray on the table with his back to the room. Reardon pocketed what looked like a folded receipt, leaving a five-dollar tip on the tray.

"*Danke,* zur. Do please come again." Fritz reverted to English.

"Most enjoyable," he replied.

In his hotel room he opened the receipt and gave a sigh of satisfaction. It was a map, as he knew it should be, and while the success of receiving it had been accomplished so smoothly, it was the one step in the final stage of the plan that had concerned him most. He could hear himself raising doubts to Heydrich. "Whoever he is, he can draw only one conclusion from what I need, which means he will know, and that could be very dangerous to me after the job is done."

"No. First, he will be informed that you are a special courier and must have a secure place to remain for as long as necessary. Second, once you have carried out the plan, he will know that his life depends on absolute silence."

"Who is he, anyway?"

"A very dedicated German-American bundsman."

He wasn't pleased by the need for the contact or the geography of it, but Heydrich's arbitrary insistence, backed by the argument that success depended in part on his being able to avoid involvement with strangers in whom he might arouse suspicion, gained his acceptance. As dangerous as the preparation, his life depended on his being able to lie low after it. This had been the major reason for wishing to delay arrival in the area until Sunday. Roosevelt would not be arriving at Hyde Park until election eve, Monday. What his early arrival meant was being in the danger zone three days early. Conversely, of course, it meant more time to prepare.

He burned the map in the wastebasket, opened the window, and let the night breeze scatter the ashes.

The turnoff lay between the hamlet of Staatsburg and Hyde Park. He came to it from Rhinebeck and nearly missed it because of the smallness of the entrance and the old stone marker blending in the dusk with the brush.

It was a dirt and gravel track, more a wagon path than a road. It led toward the railroad tracks and the river beyond. He was to follow it seven-tenths of a mile and look for the No Trespassing sign on his left, where he was to turn again. The meadows on either side gave way to heavy timber growth. He did not want to use his lights or meet anyone on the road which paralleled the adjoining estate, but the light was fading fast. He slowed to a crawl, saw the sign nailed to an oak, and first thought there was no turnoff, then saw that brush was concealing the entrance. He drove through it slowly and was on an even narrower track, a onetime logging road or a bridle path. He stopped the car and went back to restore the brush as best he could to conceal his entry.

It took fifteen minutes of careful maneuvering in fast-settling darkness to reach the vacant caretaker's cottage in an overgrown field rimmed by woodland. Immediately, he saw the falling-down barn was an excellent place to conceal the Pontiac, but living in the joint, he could tell, was going to be like camping in a cave. Still, as a safe house it had appeal. How far he was from the Hyde Park boundary was the big question.

He lay in the pine grove close to the dirt road which bordered the flank of the grassy promontory, curling sharply up to the rear lawn of the estate. He found himself thinking of that other pine grove. Then it had been dark, and he had been facing the target. Now in the chill gray light of autumn he was studying the landscape. But the parallel was there because of Sturm. The irony was special. He could thank his being here to the man Heydrich had forced him to kill.

When he had first examined the collection of aerial photos of the Hyde Park estate, he'd been truly impressed. The photos were in color, which was unusual, and their clarity and coverage were such that they encompassed not just the Roosevelt holdings but the adjacent land as well, running all the way from the river's edge and the New York Central railroad tracks beside it, easterly to the Post Road, fronting the estate.

"How in hell did you manage to get hold of these?"

Heydrich had smiled smugly. "A gift from the Abwehr, courtesy of our friend Sturm."

"But how? You just can't fly over the president's house and take pictures."

"In this case you could. I asked Sturm the same question. The photographs were taken by the director of the Army Air Corps Photographic Laboratory to be presented to Roosevelt as a gift. A set of them was obtained by Bötticher, our military attaché in Washington, and he passed them on to Sturm."

Poor old owl face. He'd been a clever fellow. Well, you take your chance. Looking through the binoculars, searching for movement, he could see Sturm's ghostly face in the flickering torchlight, bloodied, dazed, looking out at what? Death. And he its bringer. He began playing through his mind the "Winter" part of Vivaldi's *The Seasons.*

From the photographs he had memorized the terrain—woodlands, orchards, buildings, and, most important, the trails, the twin dirt roads that ran down from the north side of the promontory to the river. He believed he knew every salient detail, and for the past hour he had lain on the pine needles, watching and surveying, the binoculars bridging distance. He did not believe the Secret Service contingent had arrived yet in any strength. It was busy with the Monarch, protecting his ass as he swung midwestward, denying Willkie's claim that he was leading the country straight to war.

They would come in full strength soon enough. Meantime, he was preparing. The land lay open before him, rising to the lawn, but to the right bordering it, there was a grove of tall trees marching up the side of the promontory, curving gently in close to the front lawn. As the aerial photos had shown, there was a path accompanying the trees. There was a scattering of workmen about, busy with daily chores, and in daylight he could not risk crossing the open ground to reach the path.

He would return when it was dark. Now it was time to work his way off the estate. It was good practice, reconnaissance in reverse. Mostly it was a matter of orientation and care in movement. He timed himself. He made note of checkpoints, the pond, the stream where it turned sharply, the marsh ground, best of all, the U-turning dirt road with its snaking northerly fork that led him across the boundary no more than a mile from his hiding place. He stayed clear of the road, keeping to the trees.

When he had set out at daybreak, his first point of reference had been the railroad tracks. Heading west toward the river, he came on them no more than a quarter of a mile away. In the night the traffic on them made them seem even closer. Following the tracks to where they crossed the Hyde Park boundary was easy enough so long as he avoided the marshland inlets over which they ran. It was all very well to reconnoiter by daylight; but in the dark it would be another matter, and he knew in the time left he must work out a route over which he could move swiftly.

As he worked his way back toward the safe house, Sturm lingered in his thoughts, thoughts entwined with phrases from Roosevelt's speech last night, picked up through the crackling static of the old radio he'd unearthed in the damp and musty Bleak House, phrases and concerns about Surov's intentions. Roosevelt with that damned twanging voice. "*We must remember what the collaborative understanding between Communism and Nazism has done to the process of democracy abroad.*" And Surov, lighting his pipe: "*There is not a place anywhere where we are not at work.*" Was it too outlandish to think that Sturm could have been reporting to Surov? And what difference did it make if he had, since he apparently was reporting to everyone else? Then the difference came to him. Heydrich's request for the photos would have alerted Sturm to their possible use. That was as good a reason as any for killing him, but suppose he'd gotten the word out beforehand? That would mean Surov's GRU trolls wouldn't have to follow him here. They'd be here already, waiting. The possibility, however remote, was not comforting. The only comforting thought was that if Sturm had been able to alert people on this side, the place would be swarming with troops, and there was no sign of anyone.

That night he made his first approach in the dark. Except for one dim center light the three-story stone and stucco manse with its blocky wings appeared empty, at least of any activity. From his earlier-found vantage point he crossed the lower reach of the meadow to the trees which lined the steeply rising slope. He reached the path and, in following it, made what he considered a major discovery, a piece of luck that would greatly aid him in his escape.

The path led in amongst the trees to a gully, a small funnel-shaped ravine ascending sharply and ending at the edge of the lawn beside a towering pine. The tree was the largest in a scattered grove. Through the trees he had an excellent view of the white-faced front portico with its pillars, its expansive porch with low railing. It would be an angle shot of no more than 150 feet. The setup was far better than he had anticipated from the photos. Equally the gully was going to make for a much swifter departure. All he had to do was make sure he had a clear track and didn't break his neck when he jumped down it. He lay on the lawn beside the pine, studying angles of fire. On two previous election nights the townspeople of Hyde Park had marched to the drummer's beat and the trumpeter's horn to the home of their leader, celebrating his victory. And he had come forth to thank them. On Tuesday they would march again, and he, Scott Reardon, would march with them, his bassoon adding a different note. Arrival should be no problem. He was glad now that he had bought extra time to prepare for departure.

It was nine-thirty when he parked the Pontiac on Elm Street. The day was pure Indian summer, mild and mellow, rusted oak leaves still clinging to the bow. There were cars parked along the Post Road and all along Main Street. He could see news photographers and radio men scurrying about, getting their equipment set up in front of the town hall. He joined the swelling throng in its festive mood, townspeople and out-of-townspeople bubbling along, anxious to glimpse their dictator cast his vote. State police were out in numbers, and he recognized two of the Secret Service agents he had seen at Madison Square Garden. They had not been out last night, when he had made his final test penetration of the property and the escape route down the gully. The place had been brightly lit up. Much coming, if not going. He had lain in the brush, companion to a log with a patrolling watchman standing by the big pine, no more than a spit away. He had not seen the master of the house because he did not wish to risk it, but he heard the cavalcade, voices of greeting and welcome, even the barking of the dog.

Later, when things quieted down, he had made his careful exit, knowing the next time the exit would be like no other. What was the Latin? *Crede quod habes, et habes.* "Believe that you have and you have."

Standing in the waiting crowd across the street from the town hall, he believed. He noted that the small white clapboard building looked like the joining of a church with a farmhouse kitchen, boasting cupolo and brick chimney. The church part had a marquee entrance with half-moon side windows, the abutting kitchen staired entrances front and side. The scherzo from the Mozart C Minor was bouncing along on the point of the flame. Who amongst these good and loyal burghers, anxious to knuckle the forehead to their liege lord, could guess his purpose?

On the Post Road a siren announced the coming. A motorcycle policeman rounded the corner, followed by the usual Secret Service vanguard vehicle. Behind it came the royal chariot, open for all to see, the high gray fedora, a crown, worn at a jaunty angle, the familiar pince-nez firmly secured to lengthy nose. The man looked beefy, dapper, and he smiled and waved to the well-wishers who had given forth with a ragged cheer. His crone of a queen mother beside him and the good, toothsome Eleanor joined the waving and the grinning.

"Good morning. How is everybody?" The greeting stirred more cheers and jabber.

"We'll celebrate with you tonight, Mr. President."

'Deed, you will, you stupid bastards.

The Secret Service unit was on the watch in all directions, backup car unloaded, news photographers and cameramen hopping about, snapping shutters. A couple, wearing large campaign ribbons declaring, "We stand with Roosevelt," had come to the side of the limousine to chat with its occupants and then backed off as the car door was opened, and the man, using his ivory cane walking stick and the arm of his aide, came forth. He was now bareheaded. Again, the crowd sounded with cheers and whistles as he smiled broadly, paused for the photographers and cameramen, and, then followed by his women, walked up the path where the town hall doors stood open to receive him.

He stood with the others, waiting for the trio to appear, enjoying it all, letting the music in his head dance around the secret thought that here amongst these awed fools he knew something none of them knew. It was not that arrogant patroon in there who was in command. He,

Scott Reardon, was in command. *Oh, father mine, if you could but join me here now—or better, tonight.*

All watched the hallowed procession return to the car, heard His Greatness tell the photographers, "Go climb a tree," when they asked for more picture opportunities, and then observed the well-protected departure.

When the gathering dispersed, he went back to the car and got the bassoon from the locked trunk and went looking for Hyde Park's bandleader. In discussing with Dr. Richter the conversion of the bassoon to a rifle, he had insisted that the instrument must retain some musical capability, and the German, mechanical genius that he was, had engineered the construction of the weapon in such a way that it was possible to play a few simple scales.

Bandleader Mike Wappinger had never been up close to a bassoon before, had never heard one play, and when he asked Reardon to give him a tune, he said it sounded like a duck, but "Sure, sure, come along and join the parade. We'll meet here at eleven o'clock sharp. What's your name anyway?"

"Stone. Dan Stone."

"Where you from, Dan?"

"Albany right now. I'm taking special classes at the Albany Conservatory. I thought this would be a great chance to show what all I've learned," he said jokingly.

"Oh, yeah, yeah." Mike nodded knowingly, not knowing. "Well, you bring your duck quacker along, and we'll whoop it up for old FDR. Gonna be a big night. Where you stayin'?"

"With my aunt in Rhinebeck. I might talk her into coming, too."

"More the merrier, Dan."

And it was merry, oh, so merry. He had left the Pontiac in the barn and walked all the way out to the Post Road, where he waited for the Poughkeepsie bus to Hyde Park. The bus was packed with celebrants, and already road traffic was heavy. When he got off with most of those on board, he saw the area around the town hall was well lit up and filled with a boisterous gathering. A radio had been hooked up to a PA system, the election returns being broadcast to shouts and cheers. To him, there was absolutely nothing about the scene and its genuine excitement that duplicated the staged dress rehearsal he had been a part of in Germany. How could it be? Then he had refused to march in the danse macabre. Here everything depended on it.

There had been one detail of concern: the instrument case. He did not want to leave it behind, giving his hunters an important clue. Out of a piece of canvas he had fashioned a cloth casing to hold the main components, packing the smaller parts in his jacket pockets. Should he be asked what he was carrying, he could always joke and say it was a fishing rod built for shark catching. But no one on the bus asked, and once he was amongst the revelers, no one noticed.

He moved about, smoked several cigarettes, chatted with strangers, and was pleased to learn the parade would have torchlight bearers to guide it. At exactly eleven o'clock he joined the group starting to limber up on instruments in front of the town hall. He saw Wappinger standing on the kitchen porch part of the building, checking off names.

"Don't forget me, Mr. Wappinger," he called.

The bandleader, looking resplendent in parade uniform, shielded his eyes against the dark, "Right you are. The duck quacker. Where shall we put you?"

"Why not next to the bass drum? Then you won't hear me too much."

"Good idea, good idea. In the rear rank next to Rob."

In the sharp chill of election night band and marchers set forth on the mile-long hike down the Post Road to the Roosevelt turn-in. Cars were parked along both sides of the road; traffic was at a halt. The band raggedly blared a Sousa march. Torches flared. Paraders already knew their champion had been victorious and were making the welkin ring. SAFE ON THIRD, proclaimed one banner. KEEP THE FIRESIDE CHATS COMING, read another.

He was marching in a triumphal mob scene. He couldn't have asked for better cover; Heydrich should see him now. Rob and his big bass drum drowned out the weak squeaks he was sending forth so vigorously. *Perfect tah-tah-tah-tah. Perfect tah-tah.*

When they turned into the estate grounds and started up the drive, the flow of the procession moved around and ahead of the band, spreading out over the long, wide carpeting of lawn with its majestic scattering of maple, pine, and tulip. News photographers were bobbing about, taking flash pictures. The sound was such that when he said to Rob,

"Hey, I've got to take a leak," he had to raise his voice, as did Rob in responding, "Hurry back."

In the past three days he had choreographed in his mind the moves he must take in separating himself from the band. He had assumed the parade would follow the long, straight drive to the front of the house and not spill onto the lawn. But it had flowed onto the lawn. It was both a help and a hindrance, a help because he would not be seen as a single figure crossing the area, a hindrance because his fellow travelers might take note of his movements. Step one was to reach a center grouping of heavily bowed pines. He did so. Stood a moment amongst them, making sure no one followed or approached. Second move was to cover the remaining open space to the fringe of trees bordering it. Everyone was moving forward to the sound of drums, bugles, and voices raised on high. He detected no sign of watchers. Down on his belly, using elbows, hips, legs, he snaked his way to the trees. Before rising and taking the final step, he lay still, feeling the pound of his heart against the grass. Wild exhilaration gripped him. *Don't rush it. Don't rush it.* The herd had yet to reach the portico, now aglow with lights, as was the entire house.

He rose and, using the trees as a screen and a guide, eased his way to the gully's edge and sank down in it. On his back, he completed the assembly of the weapon, adjusting the long joint, fitting the crook to form the stock, and snugging the telescopic sight to the boot. He pressed the nickel-plated breech key, and the chamber clicked open. The lean bullet fitted the chamber like a cock come home. He smiled at his metaphor, closed the breech, rolled onto his stomach, and was ready to move into position. It was a matter of crawling ten feet to the pine, then snaking into the shallow depression a few feet from the trunk. He did so and carefully raised his head.

Beyond the flares of the torches, the backs of the massed callers, the bandsmen, whose playing trailed off to the sound of five hundred voices raised in a cheer, he saw the portico door open, and through it, on the arm of his son, came the man who was about to die. He was no Paul Sturm being hauled up out of a wheelchair. He was a man in his glory, ready to betray his country into war, just as seven years ago he'd betrayed a true patriot and sent him to his death. Well, now it was reckoning time.

Out onto the porch with him had come family and friends. He lifted his hand, and the crowd grew silent. His voice rang out. "My friends, we face difficult days in this country, but I think you will find me in the future just exactly the same Franklin Roosevelt that you have known for a great many years."

The reaction was thunderous, just what he wanted. It would cover the sound of the shot. He breathed evenly, brought the weapon up, and through the sight saw the smiling chimera. Saw Sturm. Saw the look. A voice was speaking again. It was not Roosevelt's. He paused, finger on trigger key, waiting for the crowd to cheer again. "You have heard of Washington, Jefferson, Jackson, and Wilson; but here is the greatest American of them all, and if you won't believe me, ask John L. Lewis or Wendell Willkie!" The covering roar of approval was on key, but with it a portion of the celebrants surged forward and others were pushed to the side. Instead of his target in the sight, he was looking at a barrier of heads. *Get the hell out of the way!* he shrieked inwardly. But they did not get out of the way, and lying where he was, he no longer had a target. Rage swept him. He could not let him get away! He could not! He would not! *You bastard! You bastard!*

In fury he made the one move he had known could be fatal. He rose on one knee, saw he could not bring the target to bear, and stood upright. He was in time to see father and son turning to enter the house and, out of the corner of his eye, a figure rushing toward him, revolver in hand. He swung and fired all in one reactive motion. His attacker went down on his face, skidding along the lawn. The whomp of the bassoon gun was absorbed by the noise of the crowd, by Rob's drum starting to thump again.

Reardon moved by reflex, reaching the edge of the gully, leaping down into it in darkness and rage. He landed hard, went to his knees, was up and running, stumbling, the ravine widening, leading to his escape route. He stopped to vomit, his fury so all-consuming, his failure so stunning that he staggered along in a daze, his thinking disoriented, unwilling to accept the reality of defeat.

22

For George Wheeler Sunday afternoon was his weekly period of relaxation and of privacy. Noel opened his shop at one and remained open until eight, and Wheeler used those hours as he chose, to attend concerts, to visit the art galleries, to go to the movies, or just to stroll in Rock Creek Park. He was about to leave, planning to see the film musical *No, No Nanette,* featuring Anna Neagle, when the phone rang.

"Georgie, shake a leg and come by, will you? I'll meet you in the apartment upstairs." The usual intimidating undercurrent was missing in Pasek's voice. He knew better than to ask if anything was wrong. For more than a month he had successfully held off Noel's demand that he return to supplying him with extracts from the secretary's diary. He took satisfaction in using the threat of exposure, which he knew was real enough although he felt he had the secretary's continuing trust. By insisting to Noel the trust was no longer there, he had managed to hold him off. He feared his unexpected order to come indicated trouble.

There was a Closed sign in the window of Ever Fresh, and he went through the alley to the rear and up the outside steps to the second-story apartment. It was a single-room affair with Murphy wall bed, kitchenette, and bath, none of it new or particularly attractive. He knocked and entered. Noel was in the kitchenette, cleaning up the mess in the sink. The place stank of cigarette smoke and garbage.

"Ah. What took you so long?" Pasek greeted him, stepping away from the sink, flinging the suds off his hands, reaching for a filthy dish towel, and then deciding against it. "I got rid of him, but look what he left." He gestured, shaking his head. "Georgie, I've got to open the shop. I can't get anyone to come in today and do the cleaning. Would you be a good fella and help me out?"

"Noel, couldn't you have told me on the phone? I'm wearing my good clothes."

"When I called, I had no idea Parini had left the place like this."

"Well, then, what made you call?"

"You are being a bit stuffy, aren't you?"

"I was going to the movies."

"Well, you can still go. Just make it a later show. You can help me out, Georgie, can't you? You haven't done that for a long time."

Victor Mature and Roland Young were in the movie with Anna Neagle, but he could not relax and enjoy the singing and the action. He was sick and tired of being used by Noel Pasek. He was going to do something about it.

When the movie ended, he walked down G Street to the sound of the jingle bell of the uniformed Salvation Army lady, ringing for nickels and dimes. The stores were decked with Christmas decorations, the papers reporting a surge of gift buying with the holiday only three weeks away. Several political columnists had claimed that what underlay increased shopping was the belief by the man in the street that this would be the nation's last peaceful Christmas and that Roosevelt's election to a third term was a harbinger of war to come. He did not know. What he did know and could not shake from his thoughts were the comments Ambassador Kennedy had made to the secretary the day after the election.

Only he and the secretary had been in the office when the ambassador had come sweeping in, warmly welcomed by Stark. He had not been privy to their long session, which included Hull and Welles, only to the secretary's notes following it. Their impact remained. Kennedy believed England was finished, that Lloyd George would replace Churchill, that the United States would have to assume a fascist form of government to get along with Hitler and that democracy could not continue.

The secretary had made no comment in his notes other than to ask the ambassador not to voice his opinions publicly because they might scare the American people, who needed educating in foreign policy, that for Kennedy to speak out too suddenly could be disastrous.

The ambassador had agreed not to speak out. Yet, less than a week later, on Armistice Day, he had spoken out, voicing essentially the same opinions while the president was declaring democracy would be saved in the world at war and that America was proud of maintaining it.

The *News of the World* film short had shown footage of the German nightly blitz on London and the cleaning up still going on in Coventry nearly three weeks after the Luftwaffe's devastating attack. He thought of all the confidential material he had put in Noel's hands and wondered if any of it could have benefited the Nazis in their terrible killing of helpless civilians. He took cold comfort in the belief that there was no connection. The real world was so cruel, and one could escape for only such a short time into the frothy make-believe of *No, No Nanette.*

He was surprised to hear voices when he let himself into the apartment.

"Is that you, George?" Noel called.

"Yes" was all he could think of to say, wondering, as he took off his coat, who else Noel could think it was.

He entered the living room on guard. Noel was standing by the mantel, glass in hand. His visitor, seated in the beige lounge chair, rose as he came in. He was tall, youthful, dark-haired, wearing horn-rimmed glasses, sporting a neatly trimmed mustache.

"George, meet my nephew Stanley Ruark. Stan has just arrived from Des Moines."

"How do you do." He felt the strength of the nephew's grasp.

"Pleased to meet you." There was something that seemed slightly out of place in Ruark's looks. Maybe it was the mustache.

"We were just having a drink. Fix yourself one and join us."

Noel was playing some kind of part, trying to impress, he supposed.

"No, thank you. Have you eaten, Mr. Ruark? I can wrestle up something."

"Oh, no need, no need, thanks. I ate on the train." The deep timbre of Ruark's voice was attractive. Noel had never mentioned a nephew.

"If you'll excuse me, I think I'll put on the coffeepot. It's getting colder out."

When he returned, they were talking football, something about Tom Harmon of Michigan receiving some kind of trophy. It was a sport in which he had no interest, although he recalled reading that the Army-Navy game had been played in Philadelphia on the thirtieth and that Navy had won 14 to 0. He said so. Noel shifted the conversation to the movie, asking how he had liked it, and the nephew joined in: Had they seen Jimmy Stewart and Rosalind Russell in *No Time for Comedy"?* From the movies the talk switched to the weather and Roosevelt's having moved Thanksgiving a week back and then the reaction in Des Moines to FDR's election. All of it was small talk, and none of it was really relaxed, Noel attempting to convey good humor, the nephew calm on the surface, eyes and hands in motion. No doubt, his arrival had come as a surprise, and Wheeler suspected there might be underlying family problems.

"Uncle Noel tells me you work for someone important in the State Department."

He didn't know why the question disturbed him except that in view of all else, he was very sensitive to anyone talking about his position, as Noel certainly knew. "Yes" was all he wished to say.

"Do you think we're going to get in this war?" Ruark was smiling, attentive.

"I know no one where I come from thinks we should."

"I'm sure no one wants to."

"I say again, and again and again your boys are not going to be sent into any foreign wars." The imitation was quite good.

Noel overdid the laughter. "Stan, you should go on the stage."

"Well, I hope he meant it. Do you think Hitler will invade England next year?"

"Really, Stanley, I don't know any more than what we all read in the newspapers and hear on the radio." He tried not to sound impatient.

"Stan tells me he's very interested in foreign affairs," Noel added.

"Well, it's a subject anyone my age should be concerned about even though I am classified four-F. I think the Japs are as much a problem as the Nazis. I don't envy the president." He finished his drink with a gulp and stood. "Well, I don't want to wear out my welcome, Uncle Noel, but I did want to stop by and bring greetings."

"Sure you wouldn't like another, Stan? Not often I get to see family." He was already moving toward the hall.

"No, thanks. A pleasure to meet you, Mr. Wheeler, hope to see you again soon."

Once more the handclasp stirred him. The long face was really quite classic, the eyes unusual in their birdlike quickness. Only the mustache was incongruous. What was there in his look that struck a distant chord?

"Well, Georgie, what do you think of him?" Noel had put away the playacting and reverted to self, grin in place.

"Seems like a nice enough young fellow. What does he do? You never told me about him."

"Lots of things I don't tell you about, hey. My sister Donna's boy. I want you to do me a favor and get him a job."

"Me!"

"Yes, you, Georgie boy. With your contacts you should be able to get him some kind of pencil pusher's spot. It doesn't have to be anything much, but like he said, he's four-F, and he's interested in your line."

"He'd have to take a civil service examination and get on a waiting list first. I just read where the Post Office is going to hire three thousand temporaries on the sixteenth for Christmas. Why—"

"Nah, nah, nah. You don't get it. He wants a job, any job with the State Department, and—"

"Well, there's nothing I can do about it." There was a churning in his stomach.

"Oh, yes, there is something you can do about it." Noel had come over and was standing in front of him, hands on hips. "And, Georgie, you're going to do something about it as a favor to me. You haven't done me a favor in a long time, and there's no risk in it. You just talk to the right people. He doesn't need much, like I said; but he wants to work in the State Department, and for my sister's sake I want to see that he does. Do you understand, Georgie?" Now he leaned forward, his face close, his teeth white and ugly, his hands on the arms of the chair, trapping him.

He shook his head, pressing it against the back of the chair.

"You—you—you don't understand! I don't—I don't have that kind of influence."

"Oh, yes, you do. You're a clever fellow. Clever enough not to risk your ass in refusing to do a favor for a dear friend."

"But—but I know nothing about him!" His voice cracked.

"Oh, you will, you will. He's coming in to see you first thing in the morning."

It was all déjà vu. "Would you please inform Major Cutter that Lieutenant Burke is here?" He had to speak loudly to the operator, the foyer of the War Department Temporary being crowded with a mix of askers, movers, and brass. Once more he climbed makeshift stairs to navigate wallboard halls. The only difference was the acrid smell of water-soaked burnt wood. There had been a hell of a fire awhile back that had gutted part of the fourth-floor wing where they kept the codes. Well, thank God, he was out of that business—or was he? Cutter's summons had been just as perfunctory as the first time. He found him where he'd last seen him. The only change was that his desk was more cluttered and he had two filled ashtrays instead of one.

"Well, Lieutenant, I see you made first," was his greeting.

"Yes, sir, and congratulations on your promotion, too." He had noticed Cutter had exchanged gold oak leaves for silver.

"You might say we both have gone up in the world even if we haven't gotten off the ground. It's not the internal-combustion engine that will cause you to rise but expansion. Sit down and tell me about life in the far north."

"Snow is expected, sir. And I hope I'm here to learn I'm going south to Langley, where I've heard the P-40s do fly."

"Hope, that paints the future fair," Cutter quoted, leaning back and stretching his arms. "The only direction I can give you is much closer to home. Two blocks down to Seventeenth and one long block up. The secretary has asked to see you again. Don't look so shot down, Lieutenant. Maybe he wants to wish you a Merry Christmas."

"Look, sir, damn it all, am I in the Air Corps or what?"

"I assure you, you are, but evidently you're also in demand at the State Department."

"This is a crock, sir."

"Whatever it is, Burke, you don't have much choice, do you?" Cutter had dropped the levity. "You're expected at fourteen hundred. And if possible, we'd like to know what the secretary has in mind for you this time. But in the meantime, suppose you let us planners in on how your training program is going. Are any of your students capable of reaching England?" Cutter's two colleagues were now giving him their full attention.

He had met with Uncle Bertie very briefly on his return from Europe; but he had not seen his aide then, and when the little man came out to usher him in, it took him a moment to recognize him.

"I'm George Wheeler, Lieutenant," he said with a deprecating smile.

"Yes, of course. How are you?"

"Fine, thanks. We'll go right in. The secretary is looking forward to seeing you."

"Well, Peter!" Stark came striding forward. "So good of you to come." He shook his hand, clasping it with both of his. "I think you've met Mr. Fleming."

He had half wondered if Reardon could be the reason for Stark's having him ordered to Washington, hoping it wasn't. Sight of Fleming with his diffident expression gave the unwelcome answer.

"How you-all, Lieutenant."

They shook hands, and Stark said. "We're waiting for another party, but come sit down and perhaps we can fill you in, Peter." He led the way to the couch with its facing Moroccan leather chairs, glass-topped coffee table between. "George, suppose you wait for our missing guest. Sit down, sit down." He gestured. "I know it's not necessary to repeat it, but it's *sine qua non,* Peter. What we say here is not to be mentioned beyond this room, ever. Mr. Fleming, suppose you fill in the lieutenant, regarding November fifth."

Fleming did not need to read from his notepad. "On election night at the president's home at Hyde Park, there was an attempt made to assassinate him. One of his Secret Service agents was shot and seriously wounded. The would-be assassin escaped and is still at large."

"The president, Mr. Hoover, military and naval counterintelligence have agreed that the attempt be kept secret," Stark interjected.

Fleming continued. "The individual in question was able to conceal himself in the large crowd. His weapon evidently had a silencer because no one heard the shot. The agent, badly wounded as he was, tried to go after him. He fell down into a gully or ditch close to the mansion. No one else knew the attempt had been made until everyone had left and the agent turned up missing. It was more than an hour before he was found and a week before he was able to give an explanation of what had happened."

"Peter, we believe it was Scott Reardon," Stark said.

"I didn't think he was that wacky." His response was automatic because he could perceive where Fleming's recitation was leading, and he recalled he had made the same comment to Claire.

"We have a fairly good description of him," the FBI agent said. "He evidently joined the band that led the parade to Hyde Park."

"With his bassoon, of all things," Stark added. "Very clever."

"The bassoon may be a rifle. The caliber of the bullet that wounded the agent would not fit any weapon we manufacture."

For some reason he was pleased that Claire and the Brits had been right in their fear of Reardon's intention. "I thought you people had decided that Reardon was working in some Nazi sabotage operation," he said to Fleming.

The FBI man shook his head and cleared his throat. "Well, yes, you-all may recall that was one consideration we were looking into."

"And a very valid one," Stark said in support. "It's no secret. The papers have been full of it. Nazi sympathizers and Communists engaged in disrupting essential industries, particularly aircraft. The Vultee strike is a good example."

"It was just one line—" Fleming began when the secretary interrupted again.

"Believe me, we had other concerns. Before the election we were worried that Reardon might have brought back from Germany compromising information that he planned to turn over to the president's enemies. So you can see"—he spread out his hands—"we had more than one line of inquiry over Reardon's return."

"Where do I fit into it, sir?" It was the one answer he wanted.

"Identification is a—"

The knock on the door cut off the secretary. He rose automatically as Wheeler opened the door and Claire Hollier walked past him. Stark strode across the room, hand outstretched. "Miss Hollier, how kind of you to come!" Burke's stomach gave a pleasant bounce as he and Fleming stood.

"I'm sorry to be so late," she said, glancing toward him. She looked terrific, and he wanted to tell Uncle Bertie and the FBI to go chase Reardon someplace else.

"Not at all," Stark said. "I believe you've met both these gentlemen." He led her toward them.

"Yes, I have had the pleasure." She gave away nothing, looking coolly at him.

"Nice to see you again," he said, putting out his hand so she would have to shake it.

And when she did, she pacified him with a gentle squeeze. "Hello, Lieutenant."

He supposed if he kissed her, Uncle Bertie would do an outside loop. They got resettled, and sitting across from her, he refused to take his eyes from her. She seemed not to notice, and he admired her sangfroid although he wanted to wring her damned lovely neck.

Uncle Bertie was filling her in, and when he said, "I wanted Lieutenant Burke to hear your account," Burke came down to earth. "So why don't you just go ahead, Miss Hollier?" Stark gave her the floor.

"Yes. Well, some weeks ago I made the acquaintance of a popular socialite, Mary Holcomb. She's in the press a good bit. She introduced me to her friend Countess Lindstrom, a Danish expatriate who invited me to a party. It was a political affair in support of Mr. Willkie. While there, I believe I caught sight of Scott Reardon. It was very brief. He recognized me and left. His looks were quite different. That was a week before the election."

"I'm sorry, I don't quite get it," he said. "If he was out to assassinate the president, what would he be doing attending a Willkie rally?"

And now she looked at him. "I have no idea. At the party there were several important German Embassy people."

"Two of whom we suspect may be Nazi intelligence officers," Stark added quickly.

"If you-all don't mind," Fleming stepped in. "Miss Holcomb is well known to the bureau, as is the lady who calls herself Countess Lindstrom. Both are wined and dined regularly by German Embassy officials."

"What are they, a couple of Mata Haris?" he said, looking at Claire.

"Needless to say, Peter, they are both exceedingly pro-German." Stark sounded prim.

"We've questioned Miss Lindstrom," Fleming said. "Her story is that the party was a large affair and she had no idea who all was there."

"But the point is, that like you, Peter, Miss Hollier has known Reardon and believes she saw him." The secretary was anxious to keep the point in focus. "We have her description, and we have a composite description put together by the FBI through interviews conducted at Hyde Park. We'd like you to look at them."

Fleming brought forth a carefully rendered pencil sketch, full face and profile, and laid it on the table. "Take your time," he said. "His hair, as you see, is dark, not blond."

He studied the drawings. "You realize I never did spend a great deal of time with him. I suppose you could say there is a resemblance, but whether I'd recognize him or not, I don't know."

"Here are two photographs that were taken of the crowd that was present when the president arrived to vote. See if you can pick Reardon out." Fleming passed him the photos.

"Kinda blurry. It looks to me like I'd just be guessing. This guy back here has glasses."

"Well, here's a sketch without the glasses and the mustache."

"Yeah, that does look more like him, particularly around the eyes and the mouth. What about your sketch, Miss Hollier? Does he look like this?"

"Very similar. It was his eyes that caught my attention, but I don't believe our artist got what I saw." She took the drawing from a manila envelope and placed it beside the FBI renderings. "You may have this if you like," she said to Stark.

"Look," Burke said, "you've got drawings and descriptions from two sources that look like they might be the same person. What difference does it make whether I recognize him or not?"

"Peter"—the secretary was irritated—"I shouldn't need to tell you that anything that adds to apprehending Reardon is most important. We're thinking of running these drawings in the press. The president is scheduled to appear in public on Christmas Eve to light the ceremonial tree on the Ellipse. There will be thousands present. Mr. Hoover is very concerned Reardon may take the opportunity to try again. He has recommended that the president catch cold and allow Vice President Garner to do the honors. The President has said no. He personally wants to deliver a message to the nation. He wants to throw the switch that will light the tree . . . a symbol of hope, you understand."

"I understand, sir," he said by way of apology. But what he understood more clearly was something quite different. If the president's life was in danger, so was Uncle Bertie's.

"Whether these drawings will be released or not will be decided at the White House," Stark continued. "The president is very sensitive about the matter. Is there anything else you can add, Peter?"

"No, sir. I'm sorry I can't add more, but if you have an extra moment, I'd like to talk to you privately."

He saw the blink of surprise. "Why, yes, yes, of course . . . Well, then—" They all stood. "I certainly want to thank you for coming." Stark smiled at Claire, prepared to escort her across the room. "We'll be in touch, and although I know I can't wish you and yours a very Merry Christmas, I can wish you a safe one."

"I wonder if I might have the privilege of doing the same." He was not going to let her get away that easily.

She turned with a smile. "Yes, of course, Lieutenant."

"Is there anywhere I can reach you? Do you plan to be in Washington for the holidays?"

"Try me at the embassy," she said, extending her hand and again giving his hand her mollifying squeeze.

When he and Uncle Bertie were alone, the secretary tramped back to his desk. "A very charming girl," he said, "involved in risky business."

"Well, at least she's among friends here, sir."

"Not everyone here is a friend, my boy. You know it's interesting your wanting to see me. I was going to ask you to remain."

Oh, Lord, no! he thought. *He's going to come out of the sun with some wild-assed game.*

"Sit down. I hope you really perceive the importance of our having your opinion of Reardon's description. For six weeks we've been trying to locate him. He's obviously deranged but very clever and, no doubt, has lots of help."

"Sir, I don't think the president is the only person he's after. I think he might plan to kill you, too."

"Me!" The secretary straightened up so stiffly his ears had a pointed look. "What do you mean?"

"I didn't put this information in my report because I didn't think it had anything to do with Reardon's swiping cables and hopping it to Berlin. I thought probably the Brits had told you anyway. It was my error—stupid of me, but—"

"Tell me what you're talking about, Peter."

He told him in detail, able to recall some of the lines from Dwight Reardon's undelivered *J'accuse.* He concluded with a description of the piece of paper with the two names and the letter *R.* "Carlton Forbes, the officer you told me about who was murdered in Moscow, had a red line through his name. Your name was next, and under it the letter *R,* which undoubtedly stood for Roosevelt."

Stark had not said a word. Twice red splotches had appeared on his cheekbones. By the time the recitation was completed, he'd swung his chair around so that he was facing the window. "Obviously, I never received the letter," he said, his chair still turned away. "You don't know how sad a story you've just told me. I suppose it supplies some part of the motivation for the son's behavior." He swung his chair back and brought out his cigarette case. "I appreciate your telling me this, Peter. Had you put it in your report, I don't think it would have made much difference at the time. Somewhere fate takes a hand, and there's little you can do to stay its course." He concentrated on getting his cigarette lit, and for the first time Burke was aware that Uncle Bertie had aged. The job must be a pressure cooker. Diplomacy, security, refugees, embassy personnel, he had one hell of a full drill, and now this.

"Well, Peter"—he looked up—"what you've told me ties into what I have to tell you. Dwight Reardon was my roommate at Princeton, a delightful person, brilliant, great wit, gifted. His career in the department was assured, at least until he became consul general in Munich.

He had a mercurial streak which became more pronounced as he grew older. He drank too much, had several mistresses, and was also inclined to talk too freely. As you must be aware, these are not rare traits in the diplomatic world. However, they are not traits one looks for in the field of intelligence. Sometime in the twenties Dwight became very much interested in the Nazi party. Early on he saw the Nazis were going to come to power and would present a danger to Europe. It was Dwight who learned of the secret military pact between the German General Staff and the Red Army and reported to the department the establishment of German training bases in Soviet Russia. The more Nazis he cultivated, including Himmler and Rudolf Hess, the more he believed he could outsmart them by seeming to become one of them. He'd always had a flare for the theater, and he told me that once he actually played different roles—would disguise himself as a journalist, attend SA rallies, or at party meetings pose as a professor spouting Nietzsche. I believe he often posed as an Austrian military officer. He thought it was great sport, and I suppose for him it was. He gathered voluminous information on the Nazi leadership, Hitler, Röhm, the whole SA. He sent back reports that were quickly filed or passed on to MID, G-2, for the same treatment. Whether you know it or not, Peter, the intelligence services in the War Department and the navy, not to mention this department, are not held in high regard, particularly when it comes to career advancement. They are looked upon as a catchall of the incompetent."

He wanted to interrupt and say he knew something about that.

"That is the case except amongst a very few—your father being one." Stark gave him a long stare and continued. "When Hitler became chancellor, Dwight Reardon proposed that he become an agent within the Nazi party, that he be transferred to Berlin and, assuming one of his roles, go underground. The proposal was referred to your father, who rejected it out of hand. Your father felt Dwight was too irresponsible and lacked the discipline to take on such a sensitive job. Our policy then, and even now, is that we don't send Americans to spy on our enemies. We do recruit from amongst them, and this was exactly what your father had been engaged in doing. You met the man he considered the most valuable to us. He did not wish to have Dwight involved in any capacity.

"Dwight would not take no for an answer. He thought the rejection had come from the department. He asked for my aid and went so far as to approach the secretary, whom he knew. It's possible the secretary raised the question with the president. In any case, I was asked to write Dwight and say the president thanked him for his diligence but would rather he did not continue the effort. I don't know exactly what happened after that because, as you may recall, I was assigned to Argentina. He got into some kind of nasty set-to with Forbes—they'd been hostile to each other for years—and a very messy scandal over the wife of an important German financier and party member. I had several letters from Hilma, worried about his drinking and decline. Finally, I heard he was being dismissed, dropped. I was asked to sit in on the review board, said I couldn't although my name was listed as a member." He exhaled a cloud of smoke and stubbed out his cigarette. "Perhaps I should have come back and sat on the board. I've thought of it many times. Did I abandon him? I did not want to vote for his dismissal although I knew the evidence was damning. I took the easy way." He sighed, eyes lowered, staring at his hands laid flat on the desk, not seeing them.

The silence was drawn out. It was a sad story, but who had caused it? Whom did it all come back to? "I guess the moral is," he said sarcastically, "if you want someone shot down, just contact General Burke."

The secretary's head shot up, eyes narrowed, angry. "Young man, I never took you for being stupid." His voice trembled. "Your father is one in a million. The Army has too few like him. He is the reason I wanted to speak to you. I brought you here as much for him as I did to have you identify Scott Reardon. Your father is a very sick man; he has cancer; he's dying."

23

He brought the freight elevator to a stop, opened the gate, and eased the supply dolly into the hallway. He was humming the theme from the fifth movement of the Brahms Serenade for Orchestra in D to his own unsung lyrics: *One more day—one more day—one more day—and what a day that will be.* He checked his list of room numbers and began the daily routine of delivery, an unnoticed working stiff, tunneling like a mole through this vast imperial labyrinth with its two miles of corridors, the checkered black-and-white marquetry of its floors an endless chessboard. Who could ask for more? Was there not something marvelously inspired in reaching his goal under the cover of this vast rabbit warren, the hutch of his former employer? He was willing to admit that the germ of the idea had come from a Surov axiom: *"If you are being hunted, the best place to hide is in your hunter's home."* Indeed, indeed.

From Hyde Park to Boston had been a long way; from Boston to reemployment in the State Department even longer. Despair. Fear. Frustration. It seemed for a time the flame had gone out or had sunk so low in the darkness of defeat that he could not detect its glow. His daimon had fled. Coward in the clutch.

He did not like to dwell on what had happened that night. He had gotten lost, trying to find his way off the estate, and then, instead of following the well-conceived steps of the escape plan, he had fled, nonstop, to Boston. For nearly two weeks afterward he had walked around in a kind of daze. His money would not last forever. To get a job required identification papers, a new name and legend, a draft classification. But he had no number to call, no contact; he was without a signal. And then the signal appeared. It restored his balance and put an end to the infernal ringing in his skull.

There had been a contingency plan against the unexpected. He had not wanted to consider it because he had not expected to fail. "Really, do you think that's necessary? I don't need to try twice what I intend to do once." He could see Heydrich's eyes glittering with anger, the shrill voice threatening to have him boiled in oil or some such, and so the contingency was added.

The *Boston Herald* was the paper of choice. Daily he read it, looking and finding nothing, until the morning he found everything. He was sitting on a park bench in Copley Square, smoking a cigarette, thumbing the pages when he saw the headline: DR. FRANZ HENTIG—GERMAN CONSUL FOR NEW ENGLAND INTERVIEWED BY HERALD. He skimmed the piece quickly. Hentig was defending his activities in trying to assist the German Trans Ocean News Service, declaring the service was "merely an article of commerce, another salesman interested in marketing his product." He did not like to be referred to as an agent for any individual but, like American consuls in Germany, wanted to be known as a servant of his government. "So it is my duty to help a businessman of my country by answering his inquiries."

It was the sweetest piece of news he had ever read. He had fled to Boston out of desperation, for had he succeeded at Hyde Park, it was here that his journey to Mexico was to be arranged. With no signal appearing, he'd come to believe that he had been cut adrift. Heydrich had ended the connection. And now coming off the page at him was Hentig, sending a message—his duty to help.

That had not been all the gold he had mined from the *Herald* that day. On the very same page was a critical analysis of Roosevelt's decree, dating Thanksgiving back to November 21 in order to give retail businesses a longer Christmas shopping season. What caught and held his eye like a shaft of light was the additional information that on Christmas Eve the president would address a large public gathering on the south lawn of the White House, commemorating the annual lighting of the ceremonial Christmas tree.

There would be the Georgetown University Chorus to sing carols; the Marine Band would be on hand to accompany the public. He read the account several times, excitement coursing through him. The flame within was restored. His daimon was sitting on the bench beside him, chortling with glee.

The next day he ran the contingency ad: "Business opportunity. Capital wanted. Excellent business offer. Partnership, active investor. Box 872."

The response resulted in a new telephone number. Everything followed from it. He had met not Hentig but a used-car salesman in a bar. Through him the Pontiac was exchanged for a Ford with registration and license in the name of Stanley F. Ruark. The salesman also cited time and place, and on a rainy evening Reardon walked up the narrow street from the Old North Church to Copp's Hill Burying Ground and located under a fallen tombstone the dead drop containing his new legend. With the material was Noel Pasek's name and address. It was obvious Heydrich had not given him up.

Smooth as was the structure of the contingency plan, he did not know, until he arrived back in Washington and met Noel Pasek, exactly how he would carry it out. He did not like Pasek with his phony grin. The bastard had demanded five hundred dollars for the stable over his flower shop. What was beautiful, what made the price worth it, what made him realize that he was on a course laid down by destiny was George Wheeler, a little butterfly of a man with downcast, troubled eyes. The lines in his brow were faintly drawn but deep. He had the look of a man carrying a heavy burden, particularly that first morning.

He had come unannounced to the State Department, and Wheeler, instead of having him sent up to his office, had come down to the lobby and taken him aside, fluttering. "Really, Stanley, your uncle told me you were looking for a job, but unless you have a civil service rating—"

"Oh, I can get that. I'll take the exam."

"I'm sure you can, but there is a long waiting list. And to be a clerk, you must also have typing and secretarial skills."

"I think I can satisfy those requirements also, sir. But really, I'd as soon work at something more basic, you know, start from the bottom."

"Do you have some record of employment, recommendations, something I can look at?"

"Yes, of course. But, Mr. Wheeler, if I could just be taken on over the holidays while you check me out—"

It had ended up with his being sent to personnel and a chat with Mr. Perkins, who told him how lucky he was to have the recommendation of George Wheeler and to be 4-F. "You know the Congress cut out seven hundred thousand dollars from our budget this year. We couldn't hire a cricket until September. Now the dam is about to burst. It'll take time to process your application, but I think we can find something temporary for you to do.

And so he had come back to work at the State Department, the largest building in town, the east side of the great gray eminence looking over the White House and its grounds.

Yes, of course, he repeated to himself, moving the dolly along the corridor.

There were sixteen evenly spaced ceiling lights running the length of the corridor, and beneath the fifteenth was the entrance to his third stop, the office of the Division of Commercial Affairs. The second door down from it was for delivery people, like himself. He off-loaded the bulky package, knocked, and entered.

Marian was peering over her horn-rims at him. "Oh, there you are. It's about time. I thought you'd gone off to do your Christmas shopping."

"And miss a chance to say hello to you. Not on your life." He plopped the supply package down on the counter. "Here's a Christmas present for you, and you sign right there." He patted the requisition sheet.

"Oh, what a love you are." As she went about signing, he looked past her to the tall, curtained window and through it to the back lawn and south entrance to the White House. There were workmen there, setting up for tomorrow. Of all the offices on the corridor, this was the one he had selected. Visibility and angle of fire were better than from offices above or below and point of departure down the circular staircase, close by.

"Are you in a trance, Stanley?" Marian was speaking to him, and Joan and Flossie, sitting at their desks, were giggling at him.

"Oh. Oh, I'm sorry. I was just thinking this will be the first time I'll be away from home for Christmas."

"It's a hard life, as they say, sweetie." Marian patted his hand. "I'm surprised you don't have a girl to invite you home."

"But I do. She's going to bake me a pie. If I don't see you before I eat it, I wish you all a merry one."

They thanked him, wished him the same, and he left knowing that the image he had created in the three weeks he had been on the job of a friendly, not too bright dolly pusher had been well established. There were people in this building of nearly two thousand employees who had known him before his posting to Moscow. None would recognize him now; he knew that. He knew, too, he could have gone after Jay Stark directly, but there was no point in going after a fox when hunting a lion. *One more day—one more day,* he hummed, wheeling the dolly to his next stop.

Wheeler was glad tomorrow had been proclaimed by the president to be a holiday for government workers because he was going to use it to move. He was breaking free of Noel. Noel's threats of blackmail could work both ways. He would leave a note, warning that if anything were done to expose him, he in turn would act. Why he had not reached this decision sooner, he realized, was a matter of fear and weakness. The fear, he was sure, would remain, but for Christmas he was giving himself the present of moving out of the Bay State, taking up new residence at Macomb Gardens. The arrangements had been made. He'd be gone before Noel, tied up in the Christmas rush, had any idea of it.

Now he could sit down and concentrate on the secretary's notes of last week. He had had to set them aside because of the urgent request by Secretary Hull and the White House over the three members of the Paris embassy staff. They had been declared *persona non grata* by the German government for aiding an escaped British prisoner of war, an alleged agent, actually hiding him in the embassy. The secretary was very angry over the breach of diplomatic behavior, and the trio was being brought home for a hearing and probable dismissal.

He began reading over the notes of the Friday meeting, which he had not been invited to sit in on. Miss Hollier, he realized, must have a position with the British Embassy although he was sure he'd seen something about her being connected with the Purchasing Mission. Her telephone number had been scribbled in the margin. The subject he knew was Scott Reardon. The secretary had written, "We discussed the Hyde Park events," but offered no further explanation of the events, which was not like him. Miss Hollier's account of the Willkie party and the belief that Reardon was there was intriguing, as was the Danish hostess. Lieutenant Burke had evidently had little to say. At the bottom of the page the secretary had added a comment and date: "We are still waiting approval from the White House to distribute the FBI composite to the press." What composite? He turned the page and found he was looking not at handwritten notes but a sketch titled "Miss Hollier's drawing."

He studied Miss Hollier's drawing, thinking it resembled someone he knew, someone, someone. There was a photograph beneath it, a shot of a crowd of bystanders along a sidewalk, looking off camera. One individual's face had been circled with red ink. Above it along the margin the secretary had written "Scott Reardon" and after the name a question mark.

He had no question mark. His hands began to tremble. She had written a facial description, but he did not need to read it. The enormity of recognition, and of what he had done, made him incapable of movement, of ongoing thought. The silence was like a breath held too long. His breath. He made a choking sound, and the air rushed out of him.

"Oh, God! Oh, God! How could this be?" he whispered aloud,

fumbling with the pages to see what else there was. He sat down limply. Noel! Noel, working for the Nazis, had done this to him. Damn him! Damn him! Something like rage suffused him. He reached for the phone.

It was not Noel but his helper who answered. "Ever Fresh. Can we serve you?"

"This is Mr. Wheeler. Tell Noel I must speak to him." His voice sounded unfamiliar.

"He's tied up right now. Can I—"

"Tell him! Tell him! It's very important!"

"Okay, okay."

He waited, gripping the receiver.

The helper came back on. "He says he'll see you later. We've got a flock of customers."

He swallowed, unable to respond.

"Hello?"

"Tell him I'm coming there now!"

He slammed down the receiver. He could feel his heart beating very fast, and he knew he must gain control of himself, must try to think calmly. He must reach the secretary. What on earth would he think when he told him that Scott Reardon was here working in the department and that George Wheeler had seen to his hiring!

There was no answer at the Dupont number, and when he reached the Oxon Hill residence, the maid informed him the Starks were out for the evening. He left his name and told her it was urgent. He would call in the morning. Taking that step calmed him a bit, and he decided to try to reach the English girl. If he could talk to her, she could clarify doubts, the remote possibility that he'd made a mistake, was seeing too much in a sketch and an indistinct photograph.

He used the secretary's name to the operator at the embassy, and she was immediately ready to locate Miss Hollier if it meant going to London to fetch her. After a long wait, fetch her she did.

"Miss Hollier, this is Secretary Stark's aide, George Wheeler, and I apologize for troubling you at this hour."

"Not at all, Mr. Wheeler."

"This—this is rather difficult to explain. I—I have been looking at your sketch. You know the one I mean?"

"Yes, of course."

"I suppose—I—I—would it be inconvenient to ask you to meet me for a drink or, ah, dinner?"

"That's very kind of you, Mr. Wheeler, but I'm attending a reception right now with dinner to follow, and I'm afraid—do you suppose you could tell me on the phone what the problem is?"

"I guess you'd call it a problem of identity if you know what I mean. Your drawing, your sketch—it—it appears to resemble someone a friend of mine may have seen, and since you're the only person who has actually—"

"Wouldn't it be a good idea to call Mr. Fleming?"

"Yes, yes, of course, but we—I—I'd like to be a bit more certain, surer. A sketch after all—"

"Yes, I understand. Perhaps I could meet your friend tomorrow."

"All right, yes, fine. That's a good idea. He runs a florist shop, Ever Fresh. You may have heard of it. It's on Connecticut Avenue near Dupont Circle. His name is Pasek—Noel Pasek. The name is on the window. He has an apartment in the rear where we might talk."

"Would ten o'clock be convenient?"

After he hung up, he wondered if he had made a mistake. What good would it do to take her to see Noel? He couldn't expect her to fight his battles. She was right. Fleming was the person to call. But he couldn't bring himself to do that yet. As for tomorrow, he wasn't going to wait. He was going to face Noel right now. He picked up the drawing, the photograph, and the secretary's notes.

There were four customers in the shop, fewer than he'd expected. Noel, he saw, had noted his entrance but was tied up attending a loquacious woman. The helper was free first. He handed him the note. "Give this to Mr. Pasek. Tell him I'll be in the apartment above."

He felt Noel's eyes on him as he left. He knew his way through the darkened alley to the apartment backstairs. He had a key because when Noel had asked him to clean up the place, he'd forgotten to return it and quite by accident had appended it to his key chain.

Noel had said the apartment was going to be rented, but he didn't know it had been until he entered and switched on the lamp. There was an occupant, sure enough and apparently as messy as the last. The unmade Murphy bed was pulled down, clothes strewn on it. Well, he couldn't wait here. He would go home and wait at the Bay State.

He was turning to leave when his eye caught the green and white application form on the table beside the door. It had an ink blot and had been discarded. The name Stanley F. Ruark was clear enough. Surprisingly the proof of his suspicions gave him a solid feeling of accomplishment. He'd been right! Right! He walked across the room. A suitcase lay half packed on a chair, a package of unopened laundry on the floor beside it. The unlit kitchenette had the usual unwashed smell. There was a closet in the far corner, and his eye took in the rectangular case on the floor. He was drawn to it, knowing what it was before he knelt. Scott Reardon played the bassoon, and here it was, disassembled in three pieces with a crooklike metal mouthpiece. There were two pockets on the side of the case. The first held something that did not look like a part of a musical instrument. It was cigar-shaped with a glass at each end. He held it up to the light, saw magnification, crosshairs. His breath caught. He set it down gingerly and opened the other pocket. He counted four pencil-shaped objects. "Bullets!" he said aloud, picking one up. He heard the squeak of the door opening behind him, and over his shoulder he said excitedly, "Noel, come here and see what I found."

The light went out, and he was in darkness. He rose frightened and sensed something black and monstrous was hurtling at him.

"The poor little bastard," he kept repeating as he drove. He hadn't meant to kill him any more than he had meant to kill that fool caretaker. What in the hell was he doing there in the first place? How had he gotten in? Had Pasek sent him to snoop? He had had to clear out fast. Had he left behind anything by which he could be traced? There was no telling how long it would be before Wheeler was found—unless and until the bed was pulled down. If Pasek came looking, it could be very soon. If not, Wheeler would not be missed until the day after Christmas, and by tomorrow this time it wouldn't matter anyway. His resolve was being tested in the flame. He was not off-balance. He was moving precisely. The traffic was heavy, Christmas shopping heading toward its climax. He would give it a climax no one would ever forget.

He parked in the lot on North Capitol Street, tipping the attendant two dollars, telling him he'd be picking up the car in the morning.

At Union Station he caught a train for New York, and he got off at Baltimore. By nine o'clock he had checked into the Hotel Royal, was lying on a bed, smoking a cigarette, reading the *Star*'s forecast of tomorrow's Christmas Eve festivities in the capital. "The bright lights of Christmas will go on officially in the United States at dusk tomorrow when President Roosevelt touches the silver switch that will bring life to 10,000 watts of brilliance on a stately living red cedar on the Ellipse. The President is to appear about 5 PM to light the nation's community tree and to deliver by radio a Christmas message to the American people who he said are acting this year as trustees of the Yule tradition. . . ." The miserable phony! "The business of Christmas Eve will be virtually the only task faced by the Government tomorrow as Government workers have a holiday and, no doubt, they and thousands of Washingtonians will fill the stores for last minute shopping. . . ."

He got up and went into the bathroom and looked at himself in the mirror. He needed a haircut. If Wheeler's body was found tonight, it was possible that tomorrow's papers would include a description of his suspected killer or even the photograph submitted with his application. It was time to get his hair cut, to change color, to revert to true self. To become Scott Reardon.

24

He was in the Officers' Club having a noontime beer with Sam Ryan when he was paged. "Lieutenant Burke, you're wanted on the telephone."

"Do you suppose someone wants to give me an unexpected Christmas present, like get your butt back to Burlington for the carol sing?"

"That's no way to look at it. Maybe some good-looking chick wants to celebrate with you. I won't order you a refill just in case."

He found Sam wasn't far off. "Peter, I hate to disturb you, but—"

"You disturb the hell out of me, woman! I've been going through the old infuriating routine of trying to reach you—"

"And you have, and it's important."

"You're damn right it is. If—"

"Hush. And listen. Can you meet me in say an hour?"

"If you're inviting me to lunch, no. I'm taking you. Where?"

"Somewhere convenient to Connecticut Avenue. And this is business, not lunch."

"The coffee room at the Mayflower. You can 'ave tea."

The coffee room was filled to overflowing. The streets were crowded with shoppers. The spirit was in the air, the tinsel and bright decoration lending background to snatches of recorded caroling, bells ringing.

"Could we sit down somewhere for a moment, Peter?" He knew her mind was not on Christmas joy. She had that removed look.

"Sure, we'll find a spot." He took her hand and led her down the long avenuelike corridor that extended all the way to Sixteenth Street. There were scattered lounge chairs and couches along its rim, and he located a couple of empties.

"What is it?" He was not going to play games. He was thinking of the present he was going to buy her.

"It's Mr. Wheeler, the nice little man who serves Secretary Stark. He called me last evening. He was very upset."

He listened to her account, obvious questions coming to mind.

"This morning I went to the florist shop, and he did not come. I went in and asked the proprietor, Mr. Pasek, if he expected him. He told me Mr. Wheeler had gone to spend the holiday with his mother in Philadelphia. I didn't believe him, Peter. He was quite abrupt, nervous, I believe."

"And Wheeler told you that this guy may have seen Reardon. Seems odd, doesn't it?"

"Yes. I tried to reach Mr. Fleming, but I was told he's out of the city and not expected back till later this afternoon."

"Well, I have a suggestion. Why don't we go back and see this guy Paycheck, or whatever his name is? Maybe I can be a bit more direct. Do you have a drawing of Reardon?"

"Yes. We made copies."

"Good. You know I haven't had the chance to tell you that your guys were right about Reardon and J. Edgar had it wrong."

She smiled. "Yes, I don't believe they were very happy to admit that; but of course, they have no doubts now, and I should imagine the president will be well protected at the ceremony this afternoon."

He stood up, extending his hand. "Let's go see if we can dive-bomb the flower boy."

Ever Fresh was crowded, and while they waited, he studied the proprietor: smooth apple; behind the grin toughness. How would Wheeler know this guy? Their turn came, and he saw the look of recognition in Pasek's eye as he took in Claire.

"Mr. Pasek," he said. "I'm Lieutenant Burke." He flashed his

WDAGO card, hoping it would be mistaken for police identification.

"Nice to meet you, Lieutenant. How about a dozen American Beauties for the lady? Have you located, Mr. Wheeler?" He spoke to Claire.

Burke laid the sketch on the counter. "Mr. Wheeler informed us that you might know this individual."

Pasek picked up the drawing and studied it. "Well, an awful lot of people come in here, Lieutenant, as you can see. I don't know if this man has been in. He's not one of my regular customers, I can tell you that much. What's he wanted for, shoplifting?"

"Murder." He said it loud enough so that other customers heard it.

The expression on Pasek's face became fixed. "Murder?"

"Yes, and anyone giving him aid would be in deep trouble."

"Yeah. Well, I'll, ah, keep my eyes open. What precinct are you with, Lieutenant?"

"Why do you suppose Mr. Wheeler told me you know this man?" Claire interjected.

"I haven't the foggiest, miss." The niceness had hardened. "And now, if you're not interested in a Christmas bouquet," he said to Burke, "I have people who are."

"We'll be in touch," he said, knowing they had gotten nowhere.

"Anytime, Lieutenant, and Merry Christmas." The grin had no Christmas in it.

They walked down the street in silence until she said, "He's lying, Peter, I know that."

"Yes, but I couldn't push it any farther."

"You were splendid." She squeezed his arm. "You really startled him."

"But not enough. I'm wondering if we shouldn't go to the police and fill them in."

"I think there's something else we might try first. Mr. Wheeler must have an address. Let's look it up and call him. He may be home ill, or someone will be there who can tell us where he is."

"Not likely, but let's give it a spin. We need a phone book."

As he expected, no one answered the phone. "Why don't we go there?" she said. "There must be a concierge, a porter."

He agreed, anxious to keep her with him whether they located George Wheeler or not.

Andrew, a beaming round-faced attendant, did have information.

"Mr. Wheeler, suh, he told me he was leavin' us. Going to move away. Sorry to see him go."

"Do you know where he moved to?"

"Yes, suh, but I don't think he moved yet 'cause he said he was movin' today, and I ain't seen him or the movin' truck. You family maybe?"

"No, just friends. We wanted to wish him a Merry Christmas."

"You know Mr. Pasek? Mr. Wheeler and Mr. Pasek, they share quarters here. Maybe he can tell you where Mr. Wheeler's at."

They stood on the corner, and he said, "Claire, I think we should skip the police and go directly to the FBI. Whether Fleming is there or not, someone should know what we're talking about. If we can't find a cab, we'll grab a trolley or a bus."

When they entered the bureau headquarters at Ninth and Pennsylvania and saw one lone attendant on duty, he suddenly realized the reason. "For the loveamike, this is a holiday. Maybe nobody's home."

Somebody was, and after their inquiry had been sent upward, they were informed that Special Agent Fleming was expected in an hour.

"What shall we do?" Claire asked.

"There's only one thing to do," he said, taking her arm. "We're going to have some long-overdue lunch."

He knew the escape would be difficult, more difficult than carrying out the act itself. The hue and cry would be enormous, nothing ever like it. They'd tear the place apart, hunting him.

Although only he and Heydrich had known what he would be escaping from, methods of escape had been discussed at length with Kersten and his experts. He had attempted several dry runs with one success and two failures, and although duplication of time, place, and circumstances was impossible, the plan devised was applicable to either Hyde Park or Washington. It was agreed that to travel any distance directly after the killing presented the greatest danger. He must reach a secure hiding place and go to earth for no less than a month before moving on. With the proper disguise, he could then reach safety.

That had been the plan at Hyde Park, and in retrospect he had come to believe it had not been all that good. Isolated as the caretaker's shack was, he now felt that the bad luck that had prevented him from killing Roosevelt might have been good luck, that the hunters would have found the cottage. The difference here was that to find him, they would have to tear the entire city apart. All he needed was time to reach the safe house on N Street. In the immediate confusion and uproar that would ensue, he knew he had it.

He looked at himself in the mirror. The rinse had done the job. His blond hair was neatly cropped. He was glad to be rid of the mustache and glasses. A month from now he would appear as an elderly arthritic cripple on his way to Mexico to find treatment in the warm sun. "Scott, my boy," he said to his reflection, "you're ready to go."

After they'd eaten, they returned to the FBI Building. The lobby receptionist was a different person. Whoever she called above responded with the same information: SA Fleming was expected within the hour.

"Look, do you mind if I speak to Mr. Fleming's secretary?" Burke asked.

"I'm speaking with Mr. Gwyer, the officer on duty," the receptionist explained, not wanting to turn over the phone.

"Would you tell Mr. Gwyer that Lieutenant Burke of the Army Air Corps and Miss Hollier of the British Embassy are here on a matter of urgency and that we would like to speak to him."

"Yes, sir." She repeated in essence what he'd said and handed him the receiver.

"Mr. Gwyer, Lieutenant Burke. We need to talk to you right now."

"Take the elevator to the fifth floor. I'll meet you there."

It was just four o'clock when he parked the car on F Street, a half block from Seventeenth. He got out, carrying the long Christmas-wrapped package. He crossed Seventeenth and walked toward Constitution Avenue. There were no shops here and, as he had assumed, few pedestrians.

He had not made a duplicate of the key to the below-sidewalk entrance at the south end of the building. He'd simply swiped it off the keyboard in the head janitor's office. He knew there would be no inside light burning when he opened the door because yesterday he had loosened the bulb. The key fitted. The lock tumbled. He went in quickly. There would be a skeleton force on duty. He was sure that for the most part they'd be at the front on the ground floor. Duty officers were supposed to be keeping watch over the principal secretaries' offices, like shepherds he supposed, watching over their flocks; but he wouldn't bet on it, and it didn't matter to him anyway. He knew also the Secret Service might be on the prowl, but the agents would be on the roof, watching the crowd, not exploring locked office suites. He would keep the wrapping on the present. If he met anyone, he'd bluff it. Merry Christmas. He'd left the present in his office to hide it from his wife. He looked at his watch. Four-ten. Time to climb those circular stairs.

They had just finished explaining their concern to SA Gwyer for the third time, he, writing notes, asking quick questions, when the office door opened and Fleming strode in, full of apologies.

Burke filled him in fast.

"Joe, I'm taking Miss Hollier and Lieutenant Burke with me. You've got the address of Ever Fresh. I'll report from there if necessary."

Previously he had timed himself both walking up and rapidly descending the circular stairs. The descent would be more important, but he ascended with great caution, his sneakers making no sound on the granite steps. He paused frequently to listen, to hold his breath. Even at this fashionable hour the old building was full of ghosts, particularly because it was so empty of the living. He would stir them as never before. Twice he froze in mid-step, once thinking he heard footsteps and once the soft mutter of voices. Possibly guards were being stationed on the roof or on the crowning East Pavilion. Good place for them. When he reached his floor level, he checked the long, empty corridor. Then, key in hand, he walked quickly down it to the room and entered.

His movements were exact. The light, though fading, was such that he could move without fear of making noise. A glance out the window and the sound of music thinly filtering through the glass showed that the festivities were under way, the south lawn heavily peopled.

He removed the books and folders from the mahogany table, its top level with the windowsill. He lifted one end of the table and jockeyed it around so that its width faced the window. He lay down on it, testing to see if its height would afford the prone position he sought and just how high he would need to raise the window. He had decided that if it did not provide the base he needed, he would shoot from a kneeling position.

"Perfect," he whispered. "Oh, come all ye faithful."

He had the bassoon to assemble, the window to raise, and when the Monarch stepped forth, he'd play him a carol and light him a tree the like of which would ne'er be forgot. Oh, the flame, the flame, the flame.

Ever Fresh was not as crowded as they had found it earlier. Fleming led the way. "Excuse me," he said, looking at Pasek but speaking to the customers. "I'm Special Agent Fleming of the Federal Bureau of Investigation"—he had his identification in hand—"and if you folks don't mind, I'd like to speak to this gentleman privately."

It took a moment for the startled shoppers to begin filing out. "You want me to stay?" the startled helper asked.

"Do you work here regularly?"

"No—no, just during this week."

"Wait outside if you don't mind." Fleming turned to Pasek. "You have an apartment upstairs. I'd like you to give me the key for it."

"It's not for rent," Pasek snapped. He was white-faced, eyes skittery with anger and apprehension.

"I don't have time to chat with you, Mr. Pasek. You could be in serious trouble. I suggest you cooperate. Right now."

"The guy who rented the place is gone. He cleared out last night."

"Is this the guy?" Fleming placed the drawing on the counter.

"Like I told them, he might be. I don't know. How can I tell from that?"

"The key to the apartment, if you please." He held out his hand.

"There's nothing there." Pasek angrily divested a key from his chain, "You don't have a warrant; you've got no right."

"Lieutenant, would you have a quick look?"

"How do I get to it?" Burke said, taking the key.

"I think I saw a walk-through earlier," Claire said.

Although there was still enough daylight to see by, he found a wall switch, and they stood in the doorway, looking at the place.

"I'd say he was right. Reardon cleared out in a hurry."

"We should look around," she said. "He may have left something."

"Hardly a forwarding address." His eyes registered that the fold-up bed had not folded up properly, the upper part projecting.

"Peter, look what I found." She had picked up the uncompleted application form. "He uses the name Stanley Ruark."

"That's a government form." He took it from her hand. "Holy

smokes, he was trying to get a job in his old place of business."

"Maybe he did get a job. It's dated nearly a month ago, and Mr. Wheeler saw the sketches and may have recognized him."

They heard footsteps, and Fleming entered. Claire handed him the form as Burke told him what she had found. "Fingerprints," Fleming said, folding it carefully. "We'll have the room properly looked over." He paused, his eye catching the protruding bedstead. He cleared his throat, moving closer to it. "I wonder, Miss Hollier, if you would mind stepping outside for a second or two."

Burke looked at Claire. She had seen what Fleming was staring at. She said nothing but walked out the door onto the landing. Fleming nodded at him, and together they pulled the bed down. George Wheeler's body lay half bent in the fetal position; he looked asleep. His hands were tightly curled. The light reflected off something bright clenched in the right one.

He felt shock and sadness as Fleming laid his hand on Wheeler's bloodless cheek, observed him hunt for a pulse, then work loose the object in his hand. He held it up, the thin metal object expertly machined, sharply pointed. "Holy Mother of God!" he breathed. "The Christmas tree ceremonies."

He had opened the window just enough, hugely pleased that the lifting had been almost soundless. A final preparation, before taking the prone position on the tabletop, was to turn the doorknob and leave it unlatched. He considered it a small but necessary refinement of time-saving and sound removal. He wanted to depart as soundlessly as he had arrived and with the speed of light. . . . Oh, glorious light on high.

Extending himself on the table, he raised the weapon and looked through the telescopic sight. What he saw and heard was just what he had anticipated. The lawn was packed with celebrants, perhaps a thousand, and more thousands around the Ellipse. They would not get in his way this time. Trees and shrubs blocked much of the view, but the line of fire was perfect. A temporary platform with canopy had been erected, extending out from the White House portico. The lectern was festooned with the microphones of the national networks. The presidential address was scheduled to begin at five, the Marine Band was playing "The First Noel," and the crowd was joining in. The weather was cool and clouding up. Rain for Christmas. Oh, how he would make it rain for Christmas. The music ended. The university glee club began humming "Silent Night," and he saw activity at the portico. They were starting to come out. He knew from the press reports there were to be the usual prayers. The district commissioner would get his oar in with a five-minute introduction. Then the man with one of his sons holding him up, wife and coterie clustered behind, would light up the tree with a zillion flashing bulbs and begin his last babble.

He would wait for the moment of conclusion when the crowd was giving voice, when the sound of the bassoon would not be heard . . . only the effect. He was tremendously excited. He knew he must contain himself. He had come a long way to this.

The traffic was tied up, moving at a crawl and Fleming's horn was not moving it any faster. Before they piled into his car, he had called Gwyer, telling him to alert Reilly at the White House. Reardon could be in the crowd. Now he looked at Burke with an expression of shocked comprehension. "I got it wrong! He got a job in the State Department. He's not in the crowd. He's in that building, sure as hell he is!"

Burke saw the motorcycle cop ticketing a car parked by the curb. He stuck his head out the window, cupping his hands and began shouting, "Mayday! Mayday! Officer!"

"FBI!" Fleming roared, waving his arm.

The cop revved up his engine and beeped his siren, weaving through the traffic.

"State Department, east entrance, emergency!" Fleming called.

The cop wheeled his Harley-Davidson in front of them, hit his siren for real, and cars skittered out of the way.

In spite of speed and siren, the avenue seemed interminably long. Claire was very silent, holding on in the back, and he was wondering how the hell anyone could find Reardon in that granite palace, if indeed that was where he was. He braced himself as Fleming skidded into Pennsylvania Avenue, just missing a trolley, its operator jangling his bell angrily.

Through the telescopic sight he watched the president being aided by his son and then heard the voice sounding through the crisp dark of eventide.

A clear view, a perfect view. The illuminating of the tree had improved it. The crowd shouting "Merry Christmas!" The band bursting forth with "Joy to the World," all the voices raised in song, all were joining in to aid his cause. The only cause. The death of one man to save the lives of millions. *I am the true patriot, not that yapping traitor down there!* A vision of Sturm's last moment intruded. He blinked it away. From Sturm to this. He would wait no longer. The moment was too swift. Bring the music in. He steadied himself, centered the cross-hairs on the jowly face, fedora shading it, glasses glistening, and placed his finger on the trigger button.

The sudden light flooding in from the hall was paralyzing. Not believable! As he tried to swing around, he glimpsed bulk.

A voice hissed like steam, "From Comrade General Surov."

Within, the flame exploded . . . and then went out.

They did not find him. Later, when an organized search of the east wing was made, they discovered the open window and the table and knew he'd been there. But when Burke and Fleming and the motorcycle cop had charged up the stairs, leaving Claire to explain to the lone security guard, they saw no one except a pair of workmen at the freight elevator, off-loading from their shoulders a bulky Persian rug.

"Have you seen anyone up here?" Fleming called.

The pair looked at each other. "Ain't no one here but us. We're movin' the secretary for Christmas."

They ran on down the empty corridor, really not knowing where to look for Scott Reardon.

Christmas 1940—Arrival

It was not a white Christmas. When he picked her up at the British Embassy, courtesy of Sam Ryan's rasping, unheated flivver, the sky was treacly, midafternoon light blotted out. After he told her how wonderful she looked, he apologized for the lack of snow and for not showing up in a sleigh.

"It's quite enough of a sleigh for me, thank you," she said, huddling deeper in her coat. "Where, may I ask, are you taking me?"

"Since there was no chance yesterday to buy you a gift, I'm giving you away as one. We're going to my folks for Christmas dinner."

"Oh, what a lovely surprise." She hooked her arm through his. "You're lucky to have family."

"I know, but there's something you should know. My father, the Iron Duke as we call him, is not very well. He may be critically ill. He and I have been on very rotten terms for a very long time. I think I may have mentioned that to you once. Well, I called my mother the other day to see how she thought it would work. She broke up. We decided not to tell him, to make it a surprise, a real Christmas present. I don't know how it will fly, how he'll take it, but there it is."

She leaned over and kissed his cheek. "It'll fly fine, my love."

"Well, you don't know him. He's a stubborn, mean-tempered, hard-nosed army curmudgeon with a mind like an eight-point slow roll."

"You mean, he's like you."

"No, he's way ahead of me, and although there's no reason to go into it now, he's been more mixed up in all that's been going on over Scott Reardon than the both of us put together."

"Really?" She became serious. "Does he know where Reardon is?"

"No, I'm sure he doesn't know that, at least not yet. I spoke to Uncle Bertie, Secretary Stark this morning, and he said no one had come up with anything, except that the police had ticketed a car with Massachusetts tags in a no parking zone on F Street. It disappeared, and they're looking for it; but that's pretty small potatoes."

"Potatoes?"

"Yes, you're going to have some sweet ones for dinner."

She was silent a moment, and then she said, "I always knew there was something—something dark about him. He had a look. I don't know how you'd describe it."

"Yeah, he had that all right. I remember once telling him I had him in my sights. Hell, nobody had him in his sights for very long. He was way out ahead . . . heading in the wrong direction. Would have made one hell of a pursuit pilot."

"He was a killer. Look at poor Mr. Wheeler."

He took her hand. "Whatever he was, and wherever he might be, we aren't going to talk about him anymore today. We're going to talk about the old port town of Alexandria, which we are now approaching."

His mother answered the door. She smiled at them, holding out her hands, conspiratorially. "Come in, come in." Her eyes were on Claire. He made the introductions, keeping his voice low, feeling a tenseness in his stomach.

"Who is it, Ann?" He heard the familiar voice with its underlying whiff of annoyance, and then he came around the stairs into view.

The Harris tweed jacket hung on him as if he were a rack, making the Scotch plaid bow tie appear overlarge. The crease in the gray flannels was knife sharp. In the pale light it seemed his cheeks had caved in, his lips were blue, the patches under his eyes dark brown. But as Burke went toward him, he saw the eyes were as firm and steady and as unyielding as ever. He would carry it off no matter what was devouring him inside.

He did not know from the look whether his hand would be taken when he extended it and said, "Merry Christmas, Dad." It hung there in the void for a very long instant before it was gripped and the Iron Duke, muttered something in return. "Dad, this is Claire," he said, reaching out for her to bring her closer. "She's going to be your daughter-in-law."

"Well . . . I'm pleased to see you have some talent." He smiled faintly, breaking the ice. He put out his hand and took hers. "You take her coat, and Claire and I will go sit in the corner and get acquainted."

She laughed. "Now I know where he gets it from."

He went into the kitchen with his mother. "Oh, I think she's grand, Peter," she said. "How did you ever find her?"

"With a bit of Burke luck. How is he?"

"Well"—she sighed, her face more lined and careworn than he had remembered, her shoulder feeling thin under his hand—"the doctor says he's holding his own. He goes to Walter Reed for treatment. Oh, Peter, I'm so glad you did this."

"We'll work it out," he said, kissing her forehead. "Your cooking would solve anyone's problems."

"Peter!" The Iron Duke's voice cracked in its ordered call. "Are you going to make us a drink, or shall we die of thirst?"

"Mother, I want to talk to Dad privately. Can you show Claire what you're fixing or something."

"Of course." She stuck her head out the door. "Claire, would you like to come see my new oven?"

He carried two glasses and in a paper bag a bottle of Jack Daniel's. "I brought you a Christmas present," he said. "Why don't we go in the den and open it?"

His father rose, looking at him, not saying anything, and followed him into the small book-filled room and sat down.

He put the glasses on the circular table, brought forth the sourmash, opened the bottle, and poured two powerful drinks. He handed one to the silent man before him, looking into eyes grown filmy with pain and illness, all the years, and the iron being chipped away.

"Dad, Father, Iron Duke," he addressed him, "you and I have been at war long enough. I'm your son, your only living son. I don't know if we're going to be in a real war soon, but I do know everything in life is too goddamn short for us to waste our time battling each other. What do you say we become allies and fight on the same side?"

He watched his father's protruding Adam's apple work up and

down, watched him lower his head and look at the glasses. Then, without raising it, he jerked his head in a nod and replied in more of a choked whisper than a voice, "Sounds reasonable, son."

"We'll drink to it, sir."

His father straightened with glass in hand. "Yes, we will." And they did.

It took several moments for the power of straight whiskey to settle down so he could do more than gasp. His eyes were wet; so were the Iron Duke's. They looked at each other and laughed.

"Powerful, hey? Well, I've got one more to offer. Then you can have your turn. Dad, I want you to be my best man."

His father stared at him, and his eyes dropped again to his glass. "You do come hard at a fellow, don't you?" he said softly. Then he looked up, snapping into form. "Of course, I'll be your best man, proud to be. But make it soon, son . . . not just for me, but for all of us."